GRACE

THILO WYDRA

GRACE

A BIOGRAPHY

Translated by Rachel Hildebrandt

Skyhorse Publishing

Copyright © 2014 by Thilo Wydra

Thilo Wydra: GRACE. Die Biographie © Aufbau Verlag GmbH & Co. KG, Berlin 2012

Skyhorse Publishing books may be purchased in bulk at special discounts for sales promotion, corporate gifts, fund-raising, or educational purposes. Special editions can also be created to specifications. For details, contact the Special Sales Department, Skyhorse Publishing, 307 West 36th Street, 11th Floor, New York, NY 10018 or info@skyhorsepublishing.com.

Skyhorse® and Skyhorse Publishing® are registered trademarks of Skyhorse Publishing, Inc.®, a Delaware corporation.

Visit our website at www.skyhorsepublishing.com.

10 9 8 7 6 5 4 3 2 1

Library of Congress Cataloging-in-Publication Data is available on file.

Cover design by Laura Shaw
Cover photo credit AP Images

Print ISBN: 978-1-62914-541-9

Ebook ISBN: 978-1-62914-967-7

Printed in the United States of America

To my parents—in memoriam
Ursel Wydra & Siegfried Wydra

TABLE OF CONTENTS

— II. THE LATER YEARS

— APPENDIX

Fairy tales tell imaginary stories.
Me, I'm a living person. I exist.
If the story of my life as a real woman were
to be told one day, people would at last discover
the real being that I am.
—Grace Kelly[1]

Only Grace Kelly could have created Grace Kelly.
It must have been a concept in her head.
—John Foreman[2]

Her very name—Grace—could not have been
more fitting.
—Louis Jourdan[3]

— FOREWORD

Reflections:
The Two Lives of Grace Kelly

> *Grace Kelly's apparent frigidity was like a mountain*
> *covered with snow, but that mountain was a volcano.*
> *—Alfred Hitchcock*[4]

The last thing that she may have ever seen was the view from her car of Monaco. Of her principality. Of the azure sea. Of its shimmering, bright light.

Then all must have suddenly gone dark around her.

It is the morning of September 13, 1982, shortly after 9:30 a.m. It is a Monday, a glorious late summer day on the French Riviera. The sun beams. A new week is beginning.

As he follows behind the brown Rover 3500 on the small serpentine road that leads from La Turbie, high in the French highlands, down to Monaco, the truck driver Yves Raimondo notices at some point that he can no longer see the brake lights of the car in front of him.[5] At this speed and incline, the red brake lights should have been burning for a while already. Suddenly the car begins to skid and skirts along the rock wall. Observing all of this, Raimondo honks repeatedly. For a moment, the car seems to right itself. It accelerates down the hill, and the next sharp, hairpin turn is already in sight. There is still no indication that the driver of the Rover 3500 is slowing down to brake. Then, Yves Raimondo witnesses how the Rover, at full speed, races out over the curve. The car plunges off the steep, 130-foot cliff and comes to rest in a clump of trees and bushes in a private garden. A pile of steel. A wreck. Grace Kelly is in this brown Rover.

Alongside her sits her 17-year-old daughter, Princess Stéphanie, who survives the fall, crawls out of the left side of the car, and implores the passing motorists for help: *Maman*, her mother, lays in the car. *Maman*—the Princess of Monaco.

First, cars stop above. People scurry around. One farmer calls for two rescue vehicles, which soon arrive at the scene. Grace Kelly lies across the interior of the car, her head toward the rear, her legs near the front. One of them seems twisted. Her eyes are glassy, she is nonresponsive and clearly unconscious. On her forehead is a gaping wound. The emergency personnel must pull her through the bushes, and she is immediately placed into one of the ambulances and transported to her namesake hospital, Hôpital Princesse Grace. Her daughter lies in the other ambulance. At the hospital, Grace Kelly is examined and undergoes a four-hour emergency surgery. She urgently needs a CT scan of her head. However, the only CT machine in the principality is not located in this hospital, high on a craggy hill, but is instead in the office of Dr. Mourou, at the Winter Palace on the central boulevard of Moulins 4, at the opposite end of the district. Thus, the gravely injured woman is transported there. However, when the stretcher does not fit horizontally into the narrow elevator, it is carried up the stairs to the third floor. Valuable time is lost. At this point, thirteen hours have lapsed since the accident.

The night between September 13 and 14 is a night of uncertainty, a night of trepidation and hope for one husband, Prince Rainier III, and his two children, son Albert and daughter Caroline. The third and youngest child, Stéphanie, is completely unaware of this. She is in the hospital, suffering from a serious vertebrae injury and concussion, and Rainier wishes to spare her the shock. It is several days later when she first learns the full measure of the tragedy. Only after the burial, in the company of her family, will she be taken to the grave of her mother in St. Nicholas Cathedral.

On the next day, neither the Monegasque people, nor the world at large, know exactly what has happened to the princess.

Now the doctors finally share with Prince Rainier how things truly stand with his wife. They had operated on her the day before, opening her chest cavity as well as the abdominal wall. The bleeding from her head wound is very heavy. Her brain damage is serious and permanent. She lies in a coma from which she will never awake. Since 6:00 a.m., she has been, for all intents and purposes, clinically dead. There is no hope.

The family comes to bid farewell. After son Albert and daughter Caroline have said their good-byes, Rainier stays behind, alone with his wife. They had spent 26 years together. At noon, Rainier gives the doctors permission to turn off the life support machines, which have until now kept his wife's body functioning. It is a difficult decision in a lonely hour.

On September 14, 1982, at 10:35 p.m., the actress Grace Kelly, the Princess of Monaco, Gracia Patricia, dies. At the age of 52, she is much too young.

Only at this point does the world learn of what has occurred.

A legend is born.

In the chapel of the Prince's Palace, high on a rocky point, Gracia Patricia's open coffin is visited by countless people who wish to have one last look at her. They have come to say farewell to their princess, the mother of their country. It is also a farewell to a legendary actress and beauty icon. Three days later, she is buried. On September 18, the coffin is ceremoniously carried several hundred yards to the Notre-Dame-Immaculée Cathedral, Saint Nicholas, and at regular intervals, a bell sounds a single tone. This solemn sound echoes through the streets, landing heavily upon the slow, advancing funeral procession.

About 100 million people worldwide sit in front of their televisions. In terms of viewers, this media coverage is unparalleled.

Among the 800 funeral guests are dignitaries from around the world, old friends, and relatives from Philadelphia. Princess Gracia Patricia of Monaco is finally laid to rest in the choir of the cathedral. It is the same cathedral in which Grace Kelly and Prince Rainier III had married 26 years ago on April 19, 1956.

The Monegasque people are in a state of shock, and the small principality sinks into mourning. The world reacts in empathy, a phenomenal wave of mourning, comparable only to that which followed the death of John F. Kennedy in November 1963 or the tragic car accident in Paris that killed Lady Diana in August 1997. And just as Kennedy and Diana were icons of the modern age, so were James Dean and Elvis Presley, Marilyn Monroe and Romy Schneider, and later: Michael Jackson, Amy Winehouse, and Whitney Houston. For them, death came all too soon. Their legendary status, their iconization, is solely due to the fact that they never grew old, that they were in the prime of life when it abruptly ended. A singularity distinguishes all of them, separating them from others of their generation; their lives are exceptions. Such is the case with Grace Kelly.

For the millions of sympathetic people, Grace Kelly was, like few others, "a perfect canvas for everyone to paint a dream on," as noted by her old friend Don Richardson.[6]

The world press outlets tried to outdo each other in their coverage of her death, reporting facts both actual and unsubstantiated. How could the princess lose her life in a simple car accident? This seemingly banal, dark end did not adequately fit her ostensibly bright, glamorous life—not to mention the irony that she had been killed on that same serpentine route she had once taken, at the age of 24, with Cary Grant in Alfred Hitchcock's *To Catch a Thief* (1955). Even then she had driven that road at an excessive speed.

Before the actual cause of death emerged, there was much speculation over the details of the crash. One rumor claimed that 17-year-old Stéphanie had sat at the wheel. Other rumors presumed that Grace and her rebellious daughter had been arguing heatedly with one another, a typical occurrence at the time, during the drive. Even following the royal family's release of the official cause of death—a stroke (a nonlife-threatening stroke that under other circumstances would have only caused dizziness but, in this case, had caused her to lose control of the car)—speculation swirled to suggest suicide, an intentional swerve around the hairpin curve. Additional rumors attributed her death to political intrigue—an assassination attempt, perhaps. Others whispered that, from the very beginning, the doctors had not treated her properly, and that with the right medical care she could have survived. Regardless of all these sensational theories, the only person who can actually speak to their truth or falsehood is Princess Stéphanie herself.

A myth was born with the death of Grace Kelly, the myth of a woman who held various roles and who lived various lives. Her life, which can be divided into two halves, each exactly 26 years long, was dominated by an involuntary discrepancy between appearance and reality—a dualism that caused her great suffering.

Despite being surrounded by the facade of beauty, she strove for an authentic reality. Within herself, she carried a core that ultimately did not correspond with the artificiality and pretension of Hollywood.

Above all, Grace Kelly was a woman whose complex personality was colored by a pronounced ambivalence. The characteristics that Grace Kelly embodied—an unwavering pose and a flawless, almost cold facade on one hand, and a tender emotionality and warmth on the other—function, even today, as a surface against which millions of people create identities. It is not inconsequential that contemporary luxury brands continue to use her image to advertise their watches, jewelry, and high-end fountain pens.

The so-called *Kelly Bag* is among the most famous of these accessories. Its name originated on a day in 1956, when Grace used *"le petit sac haut á courrouies"* (the little bag with straps)—a leather handbag by Hermés, one of her favorite designers—to conceal her first pregnancy from the paparazzi. The photograph that captured this moment was widely publicized in *Life* magazine, and with the permission of the royal family, the *Kelly Bag* from *Hermés* has borne her name ever since. The *Kelly Bag* combines elements of simplicity and nobility, just like its namesake.

Grace Kelly—the fragile girl from Philadelphia who worshiped her all-powerful father, the ethereal actress from Hollywood, the classic fashion and style icon from New York and Paris, the benevolent Princess of Monaco—spent her entire life preserving her legendary poise, both inside and out. She did this to keep from losing herself, and to keep from burdening others. Perhaps also, to sometimes be someone else.

After her death, her image became timeless—a stylish woman who functioned as a role model for others. A woman who was shaped by inner and outer class. Despite her inner fractures.

She had that inner strength, that ability to stand on her own and to stand by her convictions, but yet she was incredibly sensitive to the world around her, to other people, to other people's unhappiness or stress. She tried to help other people in a very genuine way. But also to other friends of hers, if they had problems in their lives. She had that great sensibility, this loving nature.
—*Prince Albert II of Monaco on his mother* [7]

— LIFE AND WORK

1870
A German-Irish (Pre-)History

We were German girls.
—Peggy, Grace Kelly's older sister[8]

The ancestral history of the woman, who became one of the most admired actresses of the 1950s and 1960s and who was ultimately named the Princess of Monaco, reaches far back into the past. It is not only the story of the seemingly fragile, blonde girl from Philadelphia who came to marry the Prince of Monaco. Neither is it merely a realization of the American Dream. In its origins, it is also a German-Irish story.

In the second half of the seventeenth century, the surname Berg was first chronicled in the Oden Forest of southern Hesse. The first Berg seems to have been Johann Berg, who was born in the 1650s and who died in 1731. Descending from him, numerous Bergs lived in this area through to the turn of the twentieth century. Among these were two women named Margaretha, one born in 1688 and the other born in 1742, and two men named Johann Georg, who, from time to time, were called Johann Georg I and Johann Georg II. This family line can be traced from the 1650s to the late 1800s, the time in which the roots of this particular story begin.[9]

The Bergs lived in the small villages in the vicinity of the Oden Forest—in Heppenheim, Sonderbach, Wald-Erlenbach, and Erbach. One half of Grace Kelly's German ancestry is directly tied to the Hessian village Heppenheim, located on the Bergstrasse.

At the time that Grace Kelly's German grandmother, Margaretha Berg, lived there, Heppenheim was a small, perhaps somewhat dreary locale. The village was primarily shaped by agriculture and manufacturing. Additional industries included a stone quarry, a clay manufacturer, and several cigar factories supplied by the local tobacco farmers. However, above all, Heppenheim's most valuable asset was its mountainside location. Though a lovely site, it was never possible for the town to become wealthy from farming. Residents mainly pursued careers in old industries that had been established in the 1800s, as opposed to the newer, more modern ones which were coming of age in the 1900s. In and around Heppenheim, no smoking chimneys could be seen; however, the town did try to attract the attention of those with wealth.

Even though Heppenheim has 25,000 residents today, and is the last town and county seat on the border of the states of Hesse and Baden-Wuerttemberg, back in the early 1900s, the town was little more than a kind of southern Hessian annex to the grand duchy. Shaped by Catholicism, this area primarily belonged to the greater Mainz region. With the influx of Protestants of higher social standing, the natives felt "occupied," a sentiment that remained in place for a relatively long time.[10]

For this reason, a tension existed between the established local residents and the newcomers of higher status, who largely settled in the villa neighborhoods on Maiberg Hill. These people were neighbors, but they did not mingle with each other. Most of the native townspeople were Catholic, and were predominantly employed in the long-established local professions and industries. Meanwhile, the Protestants (many of whom came from the Protestant city of Darmstadt, which was then ten times bigger than Heppenheim) were engaged in the administrative offices for the local schools and other institutions. A stratified social system emerged from this reality, and the members of the upper classes gathered regularly in the most prominent building on the market square, named "Zum Halben Mond" ("At the Half Moon"). Those residents who had carried out their small livelihoods in this town for many generations were not welcome there.[11]

This situation is somewhat similar to that in Philadelphia, where the Majer-Kelly family later lived and where again the emigrant Catholics of German-Irish heritage belonged to the minority. True acceptance was hard to come by. The Catholic element, rooted in her German and Irish backgrounds, and refreshed through her association with Monaco's devoutly Catholic, Vatican-oriented culture, accompanied Grace Kelly her entire life. It was both her mainstay and her burden, her blessing and her curse. However, that story begins much later.

Grace Kelly's maternal grandmother, Margaretha Berg, first entered the world on a Sunday, "in the year of our Lord 1870, on July 10 around 9:30 a.m.," in Heppenheim.[12] According to the baptismal register: "On this Sunday, the Heppenheim 'Liderzweig' choral society and the 'Instrumental Society' gave a major concert to benefit the local beautification society in the restaurant 'Zum Halben Mond.'"[13] On July 15, only five days after Margaretha's birth, war with neighboring France broke out. According to the "Excerpts from the Baptism Register for 1870 of the Roman Catholic Parish of Heppenheim," the child was baptized only ten days after her birth, on July 20.[14]

Margaretha's birthplace still stands today, House Number 8 on the Great Market (as clearly marked on the house) in the historic center of this quaint village. In 1869, Georg Berg II and his wife Elisabetha purchased this two-storied house, which had been built in the first half of the eighteenth century, and attached a barn. The Great Market, with its well dedicated to the Virgin Mary, is ringed with restored Hessian, timbered houses, all painted white and decorated with red or brown timbers. One of these is the Berg house, while one of the others is the town hall with its bell tower. The Great Market rests on a hill that rises a little above the town. From behind the Berg house, one can see the ruins of the medieval Starkenburg Castle, built around 1065. The scene is as perfect as a postcard.

Margaretha was the daughter of the prospective master saddler, seller of architectural moldings, and wallpaper hanger Georg Berg II. He was born on October 17, 1841, in Erbach, near Heppenheim, and his wife Elisabetha Roehrig was born in Sonderbach, also near Heppenheim, on January 23, 1843. (Today Erbach and Sonderbach, as well as other neighboring villages, are incorporated into Heppenheim.) They were married on July 28, 1868, in Heppenheim, and two days later, Georg Berg opened "a saddle business. He also registered a grocery shop, a brandy tap over the street, an unparalleled wallpaper business, and a salt shop."[15]

During the 1870s and 1880s, the Catholic-baptized and educated Margaretha grew up in the house on the Great Market along with her thirteen siblings. She completed her schooling in 1884, when she turned fourteen. Following her oldest brother Georg Nikolaus, Margaretha was the second-born child, and in such a large crowd of fourteen children, individuality was sacrificed in order to remain part of this confined, familial group, where no exclusive place or space existed.

However, the young unmarried Margaretha did not choose to stay in this town of 5,000, where her personal development would have been suffocated, her horizon forever ending at the hilltop ruins of Starkenburg Castle. She broke out of this narrow life in 1890, leaving her Hessian homeland and abandoning her historic roots. At this point, Margaretha was twenty, and she immigrated to America, vast and unimaginably far away.

Two of her thirteen siblings, her brothers Franz and Philipp, decided to follow in her footsteps.[16] It is unclear if the three of them made the long trip together or if Margaretha undertook the voyage separate from her brothers. Often, at this time, families changed location or actually emigrated as groups. However, in 1890, Franz was only eleven years old, having been born in February 1879, and Philipp, born in May 1881, had only just turned nine. Therefore, it is likely that Margaretha attached herself to a larger group of emigrants and then left her homeland with the aid of an emigrant agent.

Beginning in the 1870s, emigration from the region was a common occurrence.[17] Even in sleepy Heppenheim, there was an emigration agent, who could, in emergencies, aid in the booking of ship passage and the arrangement of arrival details. These agents and ship lines advertised their services publicly in the local newspapers, frequently including a small image of a ship in their logos. Thus, there was a regular tide of legal emigrants who sold off their property and goods to collect enough money to cover the costs of provisions and passage across the Atlantic.

Only several decades later, at the start of the 1930s, did it become customary to leave one's homeland illegally, vanishing in a proverbial swirl of darkness and fog. This way one could easily leave behind a catastrophic financial situation or personal debts.

A journey in this period—especially from the Old World to the new promised land of America—meant undertaking a trip that lasted several weeks, accompanied only by the most essential goods and the uncertainty of what waited at the end of the voyage. This trip first entailed making one's way from south Hessian Heppenheim to one of the port cities, traveling up the Rhine River to either the Netherlands or Belgium. Ultimately, one needed to reach a port, such as Rotterdam, in order to catch the transatlantic ships. The large steamers that traveled westward across the ocean usually docked in New York, and from here, the immigrants who did not wish to remain in New York could reach their destinations by train.

In 1890, Margaretha Berg's destination was Philadelphia, Pennsylvania. Besides the Italians, the Germans made up the largest immigrant group to this city, and from this ethnic reality, the Philadelphia neighborhood Germantown drew its name. The neighborhood of East Falls is located south of Germantown, and it, too, was a haven for newly arrived immigrants. In the 1920s and later, the Kelly family made its home here, at 3901 Henry Avenue, a road that directly bordered the University of Pennsylvania.

Margaretha's parents remained in Heppenheim. They never left, staying there until their deaths. Her mother, Elisabetha Roehrig, died in March 1886 at the age of forty-three. Her father Georg Berg lived into the twentieth century and passed away in August 1908 at the age of sixty-six.

When Grace Kelly married Prince Rainier III of Monaco in April 1956, the small birthplace of her grandmother wanted to give a suitable, personalized wedding gift to the couple. The current politically independent mayor, Wilhelm Metzendorf, prepared the present and sent it through the protocol chief of the German foreign office, Dr. Mohr. The gift comprised a heavy book about Heppenheim's 1,200-year history, illustrated with black-and-white photographs, and an original engraving by Matthaeus Merian from 1645, bound in red leather, decorated with gold leaf, and nestled in a silk slipcase. Today, one can see an accurate reproduction of the book in the municipal archives of the South Hessian county seat on the Bergstrasse.

After presenting the gift to the royal palace on May 2, 1956, Dr. Mohr delivered a written account to the mayor, in which he wrote: "Miss Kelly was delighted by the personalized present. As I found out in a subsequent conversation with Miss Kelly's parents, she had originally planned to visit Germany and also Heppenheim with her family. Because of the wedding between Miss Grace and Prince Rainier, these plans did not come to pass. She hopes to resume her travel plans next year."[18]

Almost exactly two years after the wedding, Margaret Majer-Kelly visited Heppenheim during the last week of February 1958 without her husband. Before her marriage, she had been here once before, in 1914, in the company of her mother, Margaretha Berg. At that time, the visit was brief, with the outbreak of World War I already at hand. For this reason, their visit ended abruptly, since both mother and daughter had to immediately leave Germany and return to America.

What must it have been like for Margaretha Berg, at the age of forty-four, to be back in her German homeland, almost twenty-five years after her emigration? What did she feel standing in front of her birthplace at Great Market 8? This time, in February 1958, there was more time. Grace Kelly's mother landed at the Frankfurt Rhein-Main airport, where she was greeted by a Heppenheim delegation and "surprised with several bottles of fine wine."[19]

"In Heppenheim, Mrs. Kelly walked around, tracing her ancestor's footsteps and looking extraordinarily fresh and youthful."[20] She carefully explored her family's hometown and the outlying areas. From the great hall on the second floor of the town hall, she gazed up at the market square and could see, to the right, the birthplace of her mother Margaretha: the house at the intersection of Muehlgasse and the square. Accompanied at all times by Madame Cornet, the spouse of the then Monegasque press chief, she visited the open-air theater on Kappel Hill and took an excursion up to the ruins of Starkenburg Castle. She dined at the Winzerkeller restaurant and strolled through the old city district. From the old black-and-white photographs, one can see her standing in front of her mother's birthplace, visiting the town hall, and receiving a bouquet of flowers, often in the company of the Mayor Metzendorf as well.

One resourceful, local journalist found out that during her Germany tour, Margaret Majer-Kelly wore a golden charm bracelet. Each of the eight charms was decorated with jewels, and one of the charms was in the shape of a crown. The charms represented Margaret Kelly's grandchildren, whose names and birth dates were engraved on the backs. The one with the crown was for Grace Kelly's firstborn child, her daughter Caroline, born on January 23, 1957. Already by this time, a ninth charm had been ordered, again with a tiny crown. In March, the birth of another grandchild was anticipated. This would be Grace Kelly's second child, Prince Albert, who was born in Monaco on March 14, 1958.[21]

In departure, Mrs. Kelly spoke in fluent German, which she modestly and unnecessarily described as 'housewife German': "During this visit, it seemed to me as if time stood still, because here one can encounter the Germany which might have existed for my mother in the 'good, old days.' I will tell the royal couple that it is worth coming to Germany, specifically here."[22]

After a thorough tour of her mother's birthplace and several additional days in Germany, Margaret Majer-Kelly traveled on to Constance and Immenstaad, to the birthplace of her father, Carl Majer.

On May 26, 1999, twenty-one years later, Prince Albert visited Heppenheim and toured the familial home of his great-grandmother.

Almost seven years before Margaretha Berg's birth, another young life began. Carl Majer was born on December 11, 1863, in Immenstaad on Lake Constance, and was baptized into the

Lutheran church. His parents were Johann Christian Karl Majer and Luise Wilhelmine Mathilde Adam who originally came from Tuebingen, where they were both born in 1837, and married in 1860. The young Majer family lived in Helmsdorf Castle on Lake Constance, which Joahnn Christian Karl Majer had acquired in May 1860 for 25,000 guilders. A wine merchant in Immenstaad and Constance, Johann remained the estate owner of Helmsdorf Castle until 1872, when he was compelled to sell the estate to cover his debts.

Along with his two older siblings, Emil (born in 1861) and Frieda (born in 1862), Carl Majer, grew up here, directly on the lake, several hundred miles southwest of Heppenheim, where his future wife, Margaretha, was born six and a half years later.

Carl also emigrated to America from Germany. In his case, he traveled with his mother Luise. And he, too, stayed permanently in his new country. Carl and his mother followed his father Johann Karl Majer, who had emigrated before them. According to family lore, Father Majer died in Fredericksburg, Virginia, on April 27, 1888. Carl's mother Luisa died sixteen years later in New York on December 26, 1904.

They eventually met in Philadelphia, the young Margaretha from Heppenheim and the young Carl from Immenstaad. Philadelphia was where more than a few Germans found a new home, albeit a home in which respect for the immigrants from the Old World was not very great. On January 22, 1896, Margaretha and Carl were married in a traditional Lutheran ceremony in St. Paul Lutheran Church in Philadelphia. From this point on, the Majers lived in the northern part of the city in a solidly middle-class neighborhood.

They had three children over the years. The firstborn was son Carl Titus, whose birth on January 24, 1897, almost coincided with the Majers' wedding anniversary. Two years later, another winter child was born, this time Grace Kelly's mother, Margaret Katherine Majer. She was born in Philadelphia on December 13, 1898 (in some publications, her birth year is listed as 1899, but this is inaccurate[23]). The last child, son Bruno Majer, was born at the turn of the century.

Grace Kelly never knew her grandfather, since Carl Majer died in 1922. However, she did know her German grandmother, Margaretha from Heppenheim, well. She was described as "a round, laughing, bouncy little woman,"[24] and was always addressed by her Kelly grandchildren as "Grossmutter." In 1949, Margaretha Berg died at the age of ninety-seven in Philadelphia. Her granddaughter Grace was only twenty years old at the time.

Grace Kelly's father, John Brendan Kelly, was born on October 4, 1889, in Philadelphia. (His birth date is often given as April 10, 1889, but October 4 is the actual date.[25]) John was the last and youngest of ten children—six boys and four girls—born to Irish immigrant parents, John Henry Kelly and Mary Ann Costello.

John B. Kelly's parents both came from County Mayo, Ireland, but they first met each other in America, in Rutland, Vermont. In 1869, one year after both had arrived in the United States, they married in this small New England town. She was only seventeen years old; he was five years older. In order to find work, the Kellys had to move multiple times, and at one point, they lived in Mineville, New York. With the help of one of Mary Ann's cousins, they finally settled in Philadelphia, Pennsylvania. The cornerstone for this family's future was laid when they moved here.

John B. Kelly's father, John Henry Kelly, grew up in County Mayo, in northwestern Ireland, during the 1850s and 1860s. As part of the Connaught Province, County Mayo is located several miles from the western Atlantic coast. This landscape is dotted with numerous lakes. In this area, close to Newport, John Henry Kelly was born in 1847. The Kellys worked as farmers, and their farm could be found in Drumilra. Their lives were hard and shaped by extreme poverty. On their struggling farm in Drumilra, they possessed only a house and two outbuildings.

Besides rivalries with, and uprisings against, the British authorities, the 1850s and 1860s were dominated by poor harvests, a dearth of potatoes, and hunger, especially among the Irish farming class. Within a few decades, the population of County Mayo had dropped to one-third of its original size. Above all, these two reasons are what motivated John H. Kelly, the third of four Kelly brothers, to undertake the trip to America in 1868.

John Henry Kelly ultimately sought work in the textile factory owned by the Dobson family, who had emigrated from England. This must have seemed to him an ironic trick of fate. After all, it was because of English authority and persecution that his family had emigrated from Ireland. Here, in Dobson's factory, Carl Titus and Bruno Majer also worked. They were Margaret's brothers, and they would eventually become the maternal uncles of young Grace. For the first time, the lives of the German Majers and the Irish Kellys crossed paths.

Margaret Majer and John Kelly initially met in the Philadelphia Athletic and Social Club, a kind of sports club and society located at the intersection of Columbus Avenue and Broad Street. They were both swimmers. She was fourteen. He was twenty-three. They were separated by almost a decade.

Margaret was a lovely girl: blonde with blue eyes and an athletic figure. In the coming years, the energetic, young woman with the expressive face, the wide cheekbones, and the healthy, athletic nature would be featured on the cover of various American periodicals, including *The Country Gentleman*. After two years of study at Temple University, she received her degree as a sport and swimming instructor and became the first woman to ever be hired at the University of Pennsylvania as a physical education lecturer. Ten years later, she married the successful Olympic athlete, swimmer, and building contractor, John Kelly, and they had four children, which she raised strictly and sternly. Considering her education and her employment as a teacher, this was an unusual life course for a woman during this period, especially for the daughter of an immigrant family.

Margaret Majer was a strong-willed and attractive young woman who knew what she wanted; and she got what she wanted, professionally as well as privately. It was an attitude she passed on to her children, including her daughter, Grace.

Grace Kelly's son, Prince Albert II of Monaco, recalled his German grandmother: "[I remember her] very well. In fact, I was

24

one of the last of the family to have seen her. She was in a nursing home. So I went there once, before she passed away. But she was an incredible lady, too. Very strong, very sort of no-nonsense with us kids. We visited her mostly in the summer time. She would always welcome us and cook for us, and be there for us, but she'd discipline us, too, so…"[26]

In describing the essential character of her background, Margaret Kelly wrote: "I had a good stiff German background. My parents believed in discipline and so do I—no tyranny or anything like that, but a certain firmness."[27]

Similarly, Robert Dornhelm, director and longtime friend of Grace Kelly, described her mother as "a good, typically stern German, orderly, strict, Prussian."[28] And furthermore: "When I met Grace Kelly's mother, she looked at me and said, 'Why do you look like that?' I asked, 'What do you mean?' 'You cannot run around with your hair being so long,' she said, and then she was gone. Grace's father was stern as well, in his own way. It would seem she inherited her straight-laced nature from both sides."[29]

Peggy, Grace's older sister, described the discipline of their family life as follows: "We were never allowed to sit with our hands empty. We just knew we were expected to knit. We had to knit and crochet from the time we were three or four years old. We had to because we were German girls… it was expected of us, and we had to do it."[30]

At first it was very important to Margaret Kelly that she share her heritage with her children, specifically the German language, which had been spoken in the Majer home. She spoke German for the first six years of her life, until she began to learn English. Margaret Majer hoped to pass her beloved mother tongue on to her four children. In the end, she failed in this goal, lacking support from her husband, from society at large, and not insignificantly, from her own protesting children. As the youngest, Lizanne, explained: "We gave her such grief when she tried to teach us German; we'd hide the grammar books. This was around the time of World War II and we'd complain how unpatriotic it was."[31]

"Most of the people in Philadelphia, as well as I, had no idea that Grace Kelly's mother was German. I had friends of the same age who, before they entered school, were told by their parents: 'Do not speak a single word of German, only English. You cannot speak German here!'" recalled Mary Louise Murray-Johnson, a contemporary of Grace Kelly who was born and raised in Philadelphia, until she moved away in 1958.[32] "Once, when a friend of mine spoke something in German, the other children began to throw rocks at her. I can understand well why the Kelly family did not want the children to speak German outside. It was forbidden."[33]

The German and the Irish, the mother and the father. The duality upon which Grace Kelly's complex personality was based undoubtedly had its roots in the strongly shaped characters of her parents, as well as their very different ethnic and sociocultural backgrounds. The German element stood for discipline, self-control, and perseverance, for willpower and industriousness, for modesty and frugality, and also for reliability and commitment. The Irish element emphasized drama and humor, romanticism and love of nature, wildness, and dreams. Two polar opposites. Margaret Majer and John B. Kelly could not have represented these any better.

These two equally weighted and contrary—as well as complimentary—forces tugged Grace in opposite directions her entire life. On the one hand, one could argue that this dichotomy was the root, in part, of her intrinsic inner strife. From this struggle sprang her two faces: the private and the public, the open and the closed, the accessible and the shy, the romantic and the disciplined, the dreamy and the ordered.

On the other hand, these two forces complemented each other almost perfectly. They instilled in Grace qualities of gentleness, tenderness, softness, and yearning. These were never expressed externally; however, they were well hidden behind a facade of composure. When she appeared in the public realm, whether as the actress or as the princess, she did not expose her true self. This tendency toward privacy distinguished her from others.

Prince Albert described how his mother also spoke some German with him and his two sisters: "Yes, a little bit. You know, I think

26

she explained it, of course my grandmother tried to teach them German. I think there was a lot of resistance to the war at that time. So, especially in the war years, it was a different attitude. But I think that's why she encouraged us, her kids—Stéphanie not so much, although she understands a bit, but Caroline and myself can speak more. She encouraged us to speak German also because she probably felt she gave it up too soon. So I wound up saying a few words, every so often, in German, to my grandmother but she didn't want to speak it; she didn't want to have one conversation. I guess she had fallen out of practice over the years, although she sort of humored us once in awhile."[34]

Even today, the fact that the actress Grace Kelly, later Princess Gracia Patricia of Monaco, had a German mother is often forgotten. This has been the case for decades, and the majority of American and English biographies of Kelly circulated partially false information, handed down simplified stories, or negated the facts altogether.

Even the first Grace Kelly biography, which was published in the United States in 1957 on the occasion of her marriage, only mentions her mother's heritage in a single, short sentence: "Mrs. Kelly, born Margaret Majer, of Philadelphia, of German parents (themselves talented and strongly individualistic) is a woman whose beauty equals that of her three daughters, and who has achieved success in many ways."[35]

In the subsequent, more comprehensive American biography by Gwen Robyns, which was published in 1976 when Grace Kelly was still alive, the author describes in detail John B. Kelly's Irish heritage over several pages but handles her mother's heritage briefly and offhandedly: "Princess Grace has inherited her mother's clear-cut bone structure, which comes from the Majers' Teutonic background."[36]

Only first in 2007 did an American biography appear that was more explicitly and critically focused: "Back in the early fifties, however, just half a decade after the end of World War II, with the majority of Americans still viewing the Germans as the enemy, it was crucial to Grace's success that the studio publicists promote her as an all-American girl of Irish extraction—completely suppressing the fact that her heritage was as German as it was Irish."[37]

Just as Margaret Majer's German heritage was marginalized to a very few sentences, it is not surprising that through a lack of substantiated sources, the claim has been made occasionally that her family supposedly came from Düsseldorf.[38]

Because Grace and her three siblings grew up in Philadelphia during the 1930s and early 1940s, it seems as if world events had caused a situation in which it was not opportune or advisable to be German, to speak German, or to declare oneself to be of German heritage.

In the summer of the fateful year of 1933—the year of the so-called Nazi takeover through the appointment of Adolf Hitler to the position of chancellor by President Paul von Hindenburg on January 30—the fourth and final Kelly child was born: Lizanne. And thus, Margaret Majer-Kelly's repeated attempts to raise her children bilingually came to nothing. In these difficult times, it was better not to be heard speaking German out in society. It was as though she needed to disavow or give up her German identity, here in a place far from her distant, restless homeland. Thus, Margaret implemented a policy through which everything German was not only systematically marginalized out of the story of the Kelly family, and especially that of her prominent daughter, but it was literally cut out and completely negated.

This is ultimately how the historically inaccurate picture was established, which claimed that Grace Kelly had purely Irish roots.

This also explains why Grace Kelly filled out her application to the New York American Academy of Dramatic Arts the way that she did. In October 1947, she completed the form, noting various characteristics, such as age, height, weight and figure, and hair color, and she included under the line for "Nationality" the following information: "American of Irish heritage."[39]

The Kelly clan still functions as an Irish group. Few words are ever spent on the familial culture of the mother. Considering the existing intersections that run through Monaco's royal family, including Prince Albert's South African wife Princess Charlène and her family roots (in 1861, her great-grandfather

Gottlief Wittstock and his entire family emigrated from Zerrenthin, in the modern state of Mecklenburg-Vorpommern, to South Africa via Hamburg), this decades-long development is quite astonishing.

Years passed before Margaret and John got to know each other better. John had to do much to woo his future bride. A challenge, since Margaret Majer initially did not want to have anything to do with John Brendan Kelly. This was an unexpected experience for this self-assured charmer.

An entire decade lies between the first meeting and the marriage of these two strong-willed personalities. On January 30, 1924, Margaret and John married in their home city of Philadelphia, in St. Bridget Roman Catholic Church, located in the East Falls neighborhood on the Schuylkill River. Margaret had to first convert to Catholicism. (Although her Hessian mother, Margaretha Berg, was Catholic, her Wuerttemberg father Carl Majer was Lutheran, and she was raised in his denomination.) The family moved to the East Falls neighborhood, to the now legendary house at 3901 Henry Avenue.

During their first nine years of marriage, the couple was blessed with four children, born at approximately two-year intervals. The oldest of the Kelly children was Peggy (all three girls were called by nicknames that end in a "-y" sound), whose full name was Margaret Katherine for her mother. She was born on June 13, 1925. The only boy, John Brendan, Jr., named after his father, was always called "Kell," and he was born on May 24, 1927. On November 12, 1929, Grace ("Gracie") followed him into the world. For three and a half years, she was the youngest in the family with all the benefits that typically come with this status. Finally, on June 25, 1933, the nestling, Elizabeth Anne, always called "Lizanne" or "Lizzie" within her family, arrived. With Lizanne, now the spoiled youngest child, the six-member Kelly clan was complete.

Not all the Kellys reached old age. However, excepting father Jack Kelly, all of them outlived their daughter and sister Grace. Margaret Kelly lived the longest. She survived her world famous daughter in a very tragic way.

On January 6, 1990, Margaret Majer-Kelly died at the age of ninety-one in Linwood, New Jersey, in a senior citizens' home not far from the family's home in Ocean City. This occurred after she had suffered a stroke and spent many years in increasing senility. At the end, she could no longer register reality, and she even forgot the early death of her daughter, Grace.

Ma Kelly, as she was called by her husband and two of her children (Peggy and Kell), was buried in the Holy Sepulchre Cemetery in Cheltenham Township, Montgomery County, Pennsylvania, located north of Philadelphia.[40]

John B. "Jack" Kelly died at the age of seventy of cancer on June 20, 1960, in Philadelphia. Only reaching fifty-seven years of age, John B. "Kell" Kelly, Jr. died on March 2, 1985, in Philadelphia. The oldest of the Kelly children, Margaret K. "Peggy" Kelly Conlan, was sixty-five years old when she died on November 23, 1991.

Only Lizanne Kelly LeVine, the youngest of the six-member family, survived to see the beginning of the twenty-first century. Until recently, she took part in the documentaries made about the life of her famous older sister Grace. She provided information and talked about her memories during various television interviews. Even as a young child, she often accompanied her sister Grace, and in later years, she kept her company on the film sets. "I can remember Lizanne Kelly quite well. She was relatively well-known because she liked to accompany her sister Grace everywhere. Thus, we began to follow Lizanne around Philadelphia but only because she was the sister," recalled Mary Louise Murray-Johnson.[41]

At the age of seventy-seven, Lizanne Kelly LeVine died of cancer on November 24, 2009, in Haverford, Pennsylvania. She too was buried in Holy Sepulchre Cemetery, separately in the grave of her husband, Donald Caldwell LeVine.

The only member of the family who does not rest in the hometown of Philadelphia is Grace Kelly.

Little Flower, you're a lucky one
you soak in all the lovely sun
you stand and watch it all go by
and never once do bat an eye
while others have to fight and strain
against the world and its every pain of living.

But you must, too, have wars to fight
the cold bleak darkness of every night
of a bigger vine who seeks to grow
and is able to stand the rain and snow
and yet you never let it show
on your pretty face.

Poem by eleven- or twelve-year-old Grace Kelly, circa 1940.[42]

—I. THE EARLY YEARS

1929–1947
The Years at Home:
Childhood and Youth in Philadelphia

> *Grace was overly sensitive, as far as her own family*
> *was concerned. It [her family] meant a great deal more*
> *to Grace, more—so it seemed to me—than Grace was*
> *important to them . . . Even if there was a strong solidarity*
> *in the Kelly family, it wasn't necessarily affectionate.*
> *—Prince Rainier III of Monaco[43]*

> *A German mother and an Irish father. There was the*
> *dreaminess, the poeticism, and there was also the very*
> *structured, intellectual, punctual, perfectionist German.*
> *She was the most punctual woman that I have ever known.*
> *The most dependable. When she said, "it will be this way,"*
> *then that is the way it was. Nothing could prevent it. At*
> *the same time, she could stand at the window and gaze up*
> *into the clouds, or she could sit in front of the fire and stare*
> *into it for hours on end, dreamy, her head somehow in the*
> *clouds. That was the contradiction.*
> *—Robert Dornhelm[44]*

November 12, 1929 fell on a Tuesday. In Philadelphia, Pennsylvania, the baby, Grace Patricia Kelly, was born in the Hahnemann Medical College Hospital. The hospital was located at the corner of Broad Street and Vine Street in the center of the city, in the City West district, not far from City Hall. At this time, Hahnemann was one of the largest private clinics in America.

Two weeks later, on December 1, Margaret and John B. "Jack" Kelly had their daughter baptized in St. Bridget Roman Catholic Church in the East Falls neighborhood. The baby's namesake was one of Jack Kelly's four sisters, one who died at the age of twenty-two of a heart attack that struck while she was ice skating. Interestingly, at the time of her death, this sister Grace had stood at the beginning of a potentially promising career as an actress.

By this point, the Kellys no longer lived in their small East Falls apartment at the corner of Ridge Avenue and Midvale Avenue, which had been their first home after their marriage. Before the birth of their son Kell, they moved in the spring of 1925 into a house that John B. Kelly built. It was a large, Classical Revival, two-storied home with seventeen rooms and a slate roof. The house was constructed in red Kelly bricks, delivered by John's company, *Kelly for Brickworks*. The facade of the house at 3901 Henry Avenue was ornamented with a columned porch. Located at the intersection of Henry Avenue and Coulter Street, the house sits on a northward rising hill, and behind it is a small green space. According to Robert Dornhelm, "they did not live very richly."[45] From their old apartment, which was situated only a stone's throw from the Schuylkill River, Midvale Avenue went uphill from the river bank, past St. Bridget Catholic Church (founded in 1853), and up to Henry Avenue. Stretching several miles to the upper rises and elevations of Philadelphia's Wissahickon Valley Park, Henry Avenue seems, in character, to fit more into the East Falls neighborhood than into the more prominent neighborhood of Germantown to the northeast, to which it is often ascribed. Germantown was founded in 1683 by Francis Pastorius to accommodate newly arrived German and Dutch settlers and immigrants. It is the oldest suburb in Philadelphia, and over time, with the integration of other neighborhoods, this area became a tightly knit district. Germantown is the area in which the schools that Grace attended in the 1930s and 1940s were located.

"Philadelphia is not pretty. It is an industrial city—many medical schools, much research, much art, much music; but the infrastructure is not good. The Kellys lived in East Falls, in a lovely mansion. It was very pretty where they lived, but it was not the Main Line, which was considered the best neighborhood and was home to the upper class."[46]

Nonetheless, Philadelphia's lengthy Henry Avenue was one of the streets along which the city's wealthier residents built their homes. Numerous villas and mansions lined the avenue, complete with spacious front yards and driveways that led straight to the front doors. If one lived here, one was well-to-do at the very least. However, despite his greatest efforts, Jack Kelly and his family never succeeded in becoming fully accepted and integrated members of the city's high society, a clique dominated by long-established, Anglo-Saxon Philadelphians. These were the families that lived along the Main Line. Long-established heritage and wealth were the prerequisites for the highest social status, and the Kellys only met the latter standard. Acceptance into this exclusive, Anglo-Saxon society was impossible to attain by the Nouveau Riche and the immigrants, including the Irish, the Germans, and the Jews. Members of these groups never received invitations to important city events and festivities, such as the exclusive Piccadilly Ball.

The Kellys remained outcasts, even if they did reach an elevated status because of their wealth. People did, indeed, know the Kelly name in the city, in part due to the untiring efforts by Jack to gain recognition. He sought political offices, athletic success, and financial influence. Later, the gossip centered on the continuously neglected young daughter and her ongoing, self-motivated attempts to find success as an actress. The Kellys were always the talk of the town.[47]

Throughout his life, John B. "Jack" Kelly impressively exemplified the American Dream, the dream of going from dishwasher to millionaire. He pursued this in Philadelphia, in the melting pot of greatly varied ethnic groups that sought new beginnings in this industrial and manufacturing city. Many older factory buildings still stand today along Scott's Lane, near the bank of the Schuylkill River. One of these buildings once housed the Dobson textile factory, where John Brendan's father, John Henry Kelly, once worked alongside several of his six sons, including Patrick, Walter, and John, all of whom were sent to work there around the age of ten.

Outside of school hours, Jack began to work here at the age of nine, first as furniture mover, in order to earn a little pocket money, and then as an apprentice mason. Young Jack later worked in the construction business owned by his brother Patrick, who was eighteen years older than him. Patrick started the business around 1900, and it went by the name *P.H. Kelly & Co.*

During World War I, Jack Kelly was unable to fly as a pilot due his nearsightedness, so he served as a volunteer for a medical unit in France. In 1921, he established his own company. He borrowed money from two of his older brothers, George and Walter, and personally took over the management of his new construction company, *Kelly for Brickworks*. In turn, his brother Charles left his job at Patrick's *P.H. Kelly & Co.* and took a position with Jack's *Kelly for Brickworks*. Charles's decision, along with the fact that the two firms were now in competition against each other, resulted in a tense situation among the Kelly brothers. Jack Kelly's construction company, which he later led as its president, grew over the years to become one of the largest of its kind in the United States. This obviously brought great satisfaction to the son of poor Irish immigrants. By the time he married Margaret Majer on January 20, 1924, in St. Bridget's in East Falls, the church where the Kelly family celebrated Mass every Sunday morning, Jack Kelly was well on his way to becoming a millionaire.

Prince Albert offered this account of the stories his mother told about his grandparents: "I hardly knew my grandfather, John B. Kelly. He died when I was two years old, unfortunately. And I always regretted not knowing him better and not being able to have some conversations with him. He's a legendary figure, not only in our family, but throughout the United States. But he was also a very generous man, and also had that spirit of entrepreneurship. On his own, in a country where he hadn't been born, he built his career pretty quickly. And I think also that that side, the Irish side of the family, is also very important. We are all very proud of that heritage, as we are of the German side, too. But I think that also adds to the character of, you know, being generous, and Irish people are usually very generous in spirit and heart and so on, so that's an added dimension to it."[48]

In 1935, Jack Kelly ran on the Democratic Party ticket for the office of Mayor of Philadelphia. His opponent was Republican S. Davis Wilson, who ended up winning by a small margin after a long and heated election. As an Irish Catholic, Kelly was defeated in the then predominantly Protestant Philadelphia, but this was not the only painful loss that he gritted his teeth and bore with composure.

Despite Jack's political failure, many years later the city of Philadelphia paid tribute to its popular resident by renaming the long road that runs along the eastern bank of the Schuylkill River, "John B. Kelly Drive." Since father and son bore the same name, it has often been claimed that Kell, the son, was also honored in this naming. Furthermore, in East Fairmount Park, which is bordered by the Schuylkill River and John B. Kelly Drive, a bronze statue stands. It was created in 1965 by Harry Rosin, and its base bears the following inscription: "John B. Kelly, Olympic Champion, Singles 1920, Doubles 1920, Doubles 1924." His like-named son, who ultimately won the Henley Regatta from which his father had been excluded, is not mentioned.

Only a quarter of a century after Kelly's mayoral defeat, the Democrat John F. Kennedy (1917–1963), an Irish Catholic from yet another legendary clan, took the presidential oath on January 2, 1961, as the second-youngest president to ever be elected. Even today, he remains the only Catholic who has held this office. Interestingly, John B. "Jack" Kelly and Joseph P. "Joe" Kennedy were personal acquaintances. Two patriarchs. Two businessmen. Two multimillionaires. The Kellys and the Kennedys shared many similarities. The same world views dominated these two dynasties: discipline, perseverance, ambition, social mobility, desire for victory. The one family sought athletic championship, while the other sought political power.

Besides the aforementioned mayoral election, yet another difficult defeat occured upon Jack Kelly's application to the renowned Henley Royal Regatta in England. One of Jack's greatest passions was sculling, a specialized rowing sport, which he viewed as a truly masculine activity. In 1919, he applied to compete as a rower in this coveted event, an honor considered almost as prestigious as the Olympic Games. John B. Kelly, Sr., trained rigorously, almost obsessively, with his newly purchased scull, day after day. He dreamed of winning the Diamond Challenge Sculls, the competition's main event. What happened next was bitterly disappointing. Only three days before the Competition, he received a telegram from England. The British Henley Committee had decided to exclude him from the contest. For John Brendan "Jack" Kelly, his entire world must have collapsed at that very moment.

Grace, who admired her father her entire life, was always quick to defend him, especially for this devastating disappointment. Although the official justification for his expulsion was that Kelly's rowing club and an Irish sponsor were unacceptable, the most likely reason was his undesirable status as a professional, working man. Jack Kelly was not an English gentleman, but rather an Irish immigrant and a simple mason. For the English organizers of the Regatta, this was enough cause to reject his application. An Irishman among gentlemen was considered distasteful. They ignored the fact that Jack Kelly belonged to the 1920 US Olympic team, for which he went on to win gold in both the single scull event and the double scull event along with his cousin Paul Costello, at the summer games held in Antwerp. In the 1924 Summer Olympics in Paris, Jack Kelly again won the double scull event with his cousin. In addition, he won multiple US National Championships in rowing, which increased his international fame.

Under massive pressure to win this coveted trophy, which had been denied to his father, son Kell entered the Henley Regatta in 1947. Since his father's time, the regulations had been updated and changed. Jack and Margaret Kelly, along with daughters Grace and Lizanne, traveled to England during the third week of June to support Kell in the competition. The Kelly family stayed in the Red Lion Hotel in Henley for the duration of the competition. At the age of twenty, Kell was expected to avenge his father's defeat, and avenge he did: Kell won the race, receiving the Henley trophy cup engraved with the words, "Diamond Sculls," on July 5, 1947. The Kellys celebrated the victorious son and heir, who had rowed wearing the colors of the University of Pennsylvania.

What a burden it is for a son, an only son, to hold his own among his three competitive sisters. And so it was for Kell—the only son and heir, his father's favorite child. He was pressured to fulfill everything that was expected of a Kelly: always stand on the winning side, never lose, and never show or admit weakness. This burden could hardly be carried.

It was as if Kell had no autonomy over his own life. He was no more than seven when his father first plunked him into a homemade boat and shoved it out onto the choppy ocean waters at Ocean City. This was how the seven-year-old was supposed to learn to row.

In March 1954, Kell married at the age of twenty-six. He had six children with his wife Mary Gray Freeman, and in later years, he turned completely away from his family. In the mid-1970s, he became romantically involved with a well-known transsexual Philadelphian by the name of Rachel Harlow, the former Richard Finnochio, who was an attractive, blonde night club and restaurant owner. Harlow had gained some fame as an actress in Frank Simon's film, *The Queen* (1968). Kell's liaison represented the greatest possible rejection of his family's Irish Catholicism. It seemed as if the son wished to catch up on everything that had been denied to him for so many years due to his father's rigid upbringing. In May 1981, he remarried, this time to the banker Sandra Worley. Increasingly, John B. "Kell" Kelly turned to alcohol, and he died on March 2, 1985, at the age of fifty-seven, two and a half years after his famous sister's death. He died of a heart attack while jogging to the athletic club after having taken his daily morning row on the Schuylkill River.

It is yet another tragedy that seems to astonishingly resemble those of the Kennedys in Boston, the other famous Irish clan.

At the time of Grace's birth, America was just entering the Great Depression, catapulted by the New York Stock Market crash on October 24, 1929, so-called "Black Thursday". The financial world was shaken to its very core. Miraculously, the Kellys were almost completely untouched by the collapse. Jack Kelly had never invested his money in the stock market, instead favoring government securities. This, combined with his rigorous management style, allowed his company, *Kelly for Brickworks*, to survive the stock market crash relatively unscathed.

From her earliest years, Grace's constitution was a cause for concern. She was the one of the four Kelly children who caused the greatest worry for her strict parents. Little Gracie, as she was called by everyone, was fragile, delicate, and often sickly. She was the first one to catch colds and the last one to recover. As the second of the three sisters, Grace received the least amount of attention after the birth of Lizanne. Already as a young child, she was susceptible to sinus and middle ear infections, as well as serious colds. She continued to be affected by these, as well as migraines, years later in Monaco. As a child in the Henry Avenue house, she often laid upstairs in her bed, because she was once again sick or about to come down with something. "What's Grace sniveling about now?" was frequently Jack Kelly's annoyed reaction to his wife Margaret, whenever something was wrong with his middle daughter.[49]

Once, when Grace was irritating her two sisters, they locked her in a closet where she remained for a long time, forgotten and unmissed by her family. Meanwhile, Grace sat on the floor and played with her dolls, some of her favorite playthings. She gave them all names and came up with various voices for them. This was her own personal dream world. When Ma Kelly eventually found her, Grace was engrossed in her doll games. The child seemed well-accustomed to not being missed.

Because of Grace's physical vulnerability, which is often pointed to as one of the sources of her uncertain, timid demeanor, she was the least athletic of all the Kellys. She took little interest in athletic activity, in any particular sport, or in competition in general. She did play hockey and basketball in school, and she swam and played tennis during the summer breaks, which the Kellys always spent on the New Jersey coast, in Ocean City near Atlantic City, in their whitewashed, clapboard vacation home at 2539 Wesley Avenue. However, in contrast to her athletic, competitive family,

Grace saw sports as leisure activities, something that she enjoyed but did not actually take seriously.

For father Jack, this child, his third, was somehow different. He did not connect well with Gracie nor did he try to be close to her. It may be that, from his side, there was no actual emotional connection. John B. Kelly could not develop an affinity for his ethereal daughter, who, already at a young age, seemed to most closely resemble her Uncle George through her preference for the arts and music. Between father and daughter existed an unbridgeable chasm. This remained unchanged through to Jack Kelly's death in 1960. Grace struggled her entire life with this discord, and she constantly sought to compensate for it. At the same time, her strong desire for her father's approval functioned as a driving force behind so much of what she tried to achieve in the coming years. For Jack Kelly, his daughter's ongoing poor health and her disinterest in sports was a double thorn in his side. He could not understand Grace's disposition, and besides, his main interest was in Kell to whom he not only gave his full name but whom he strove to raise as a younger version of himself.

"Grace and all the family—we were a competitive family. I think we got that from—I *know* we got that from our mother and father...They instilled into us a deep sense of competition and the love of sports, the thrill of winning...[and] also taught us how to lose gracefully," according to Grace's younger sister, Lizanne Kelly LeVine.[50]

In the summer of 1937, something happened to the young, seven-year-old Gracie for which she had long yearned and for which she would yearn for years to come, mostly in vain. The family was on the beach at Ocean City for an event, and for publicity reasons, the Kellys were asked to pose for a photographer who wanted to capture their family on film. At this moment, father Jack suddenly picked up his daughter Grace and whirled her through the air. He held her by her feet and twirled on his heels. Little Gracie stretched her arms wide into the air, as her strong father, in his 1930s striped bathing shirt, spun. There is only one sepia-toned photograph of this moment between father and daughter, which is kept at the archives of the royal family of

Monaco. In the photo, Grace's hair is tousled in the wind, and a delighted smile is on her face. There, for a moment, was the intimacy she had longed for all her life. Even if it was only a stunt for the photographer's camera, it must have been an unimaginably precious moment for her.

Young Grace's first experience on the stage came at the age of twelve. It was the stage of the East Falls amateur acting group, Old Academy Players, located on Indian Queen Lane. Under the direction of Ruth Emmert, the troop, along with Grace, performed the play, *Don't Feed the Animals*. Another, more significant performance by the players was *The Torch Bearers* (1922), a play written by Grace's favorite uncle George about Philadelphia. The original production had opened to critical acclaim on Broadway years earlier.

Grace's first acting teacher noticed right away that she was never late to rehearsals and she always knew her lines. Just as Ruth Emmert was impressed with these qualities in Grace in 1941, so were Grace's colleagues and teammates on film sets in Hollywood and New York in the 1950s. "She was the most punctual and the most reliable,"[51] said Robert Dornhelm, and she had at her disposal an amazing ability to memorize lines perfectly. Both of these characteristics were anything but a given in the acting world. The other major Hollywood blonde of this era, Marilyn Monroe, regularly arrived hours late on the set and could often not remember her dialogue.

George Edward Kelly (1887–1974), one of John B. Kelly's younger brothers as well as Grace's godfather, was an important person in her life. Although brother Walter C. Kelly (1873–1939) had been a vaudeville actor and had toured the United States and England to great acclaim in the musical *Virginia Judge*—which was also filmed in 1935 with him in the title role—it was mainly George who, like Walter, remained unmarried, who was acknowledged as the member of the Kelly clan with the greatest ties and commitment to the world of art, literature, and theater. For this reason, he was viewed as an outsider. Like his niece Grace, George Kelly was a visionary, a dreamer, a book lover. He refused to drink tea brewed from tea bags. Furthermore, in contrast to his actor brother Walter, this strong-willed, cranky man with the slightly snobbish yet stylish demeanor was homosexual. George Kelly lived his entire adult life with his partner William Weagly, a former bookkeeper, who also worked for George as a kind of personal valet. When George Kelly died and his funeral was held in St. Bridget's Church on Midvale Avenue, Weagly sat in the last row of the church and wept bitterly. He had been George's committed partner for fifty-five years, but the Kellys had only ever treated him as George's valet. He was not invited to George's funeral and, when he attended anyway, was not acknowledged by the Kellys.

For his brother Jack Kelly and the other Kelly brothers, Patrick, Walter, and Charles, George's homosexuality was a compromising situation that had to be rigorously and strictly denied and hidden. It was to stay a family secret. George was a homosexual in a clan that prided itself on its Catholic Irish provenance, to which the preservation of carefully crafted social roles and the pursuit of sports were of utmost importance.

Like Grace, George Kelly knew only too well what it felt like to be different and to not belong. Thus, it is no surprise that he was her favorite uncle, as well as the inspiration for her career. George Kelly's name played a pivotal part in Grace's acceptance to the American Academy of Dramatic Arts in New York, a process which was plagued by complications. George Kelly despised sports and loved Shakespeare. After his success with *The Show-Off* (1924), he won the renowned Pulitzer Prize in 1926 for his play *Craig's Wife* (1925). Uncle George was the only Kelly who fully understood Grace, who showed her empathy and understanding, who supported and inspired her. Even after Grace had long become a celebrity, she would frequently meet her favorite uncle for a meal, and this continued until his death in June 1974.

Uncle George showed Grace the very thing that father Jack always withheld from her: pride for his niece. "On Sundays many times we used to go to church. And then Uncle George, who lived in Southern California, would come and pick us up and take us for a ride around and take us to lunch. And she enjoyed those rides with George so much, that the two would talk. I would sit in the back seat, and maybe take a little nap. But the two of them would talk theatre and books and poetry," recalled sister, Lizanne Kelly LeVine.[52]

Only a few weeks before his death, George Kelly wrote the following lines in a letter: "I am so proud of my niece, Grace. She was not only a very fine actress but is a human being with considerable qualities. Had she stayed on the stage and continued her career, I think we would have seen some very fine performances from her."[53]

Grace received her first local newspaper review for the play *The Torch Bearers*. Her portrayal was praised, and in a play on the play's title, the review emphasized her status as a young, inexperienced amateur actress, emerging from the Kelly family to be a torch bearer on the stage. Even at this young age, Grace took every one of her roles seriously.

Beginning in the fall of 1935, at the age of six, Grace attended the Catholic Convent of the Assumption on School House Lane, commonly known as Ravenhill Academy. She went to "an excellent school, and she was well educated."[54] During this time, it was an annual tradition to act out the Nativity story, and Grace played the Virgin Mary, which in a way foreshadowed her later cultivated persona of virginal aloofness. Interestingly, after her marriage to Prince Rainier III, she was twice offered the role of Mary for two film projects.

"She was quite devoted to prayer and the community of saints. For this reason, we always prayed for each other," recalled Abbess Frances, teacher at Ravenhill, about her student Grace. "Even as a child, she had something spiritual about her. I remember well a specific Christmas pageant. She played the Virgin Mary, and she did this quite piously."[55]

It was customary at Ravenhill for the girls, as instructed by the nuns, to wear white gloves coming to and from school. Grace already knew this tradition because of the strict practices of Ma Kelly, who also periodically insisted that her three daughters wear hats. Grace carried on this habit, and later the wearing of white gloves became one of her unmistakable stylistic hallmarks.

Grace entered high school at the Stevens School in September 1943. At this time, she met Harper Davis, a classmate of her brother Kell from the William Penn Charter School. These two schools were located close to each other in Germantown. By this point, the small, thin, sickly, seemingly fragile girl had turned into a lovely teenager: tall with fine, blonde hair, striking blue eyes, and long legs. Trim and neat, she was often compared to a gazelle. The young Grace had developed into a natural beauty. The only feature she was self-conscious about was her backside, which tended to be curvy. Later, when on a film set, this physical characteristic was a sensitive issue for her, and she tried as much as possible to camouflage it.

Grace began to be noticed and to attract people to her. This radiance and allure accompanied her for the rest of her life.

Grace had just turned fourteen, and Harper was sixteen. Surprisingly, Ma Kelly allowed Grace to accompany Harper to a school dance. When Harper arrived to introduce himself and to pick up Grace, he presented her with an orchid at the door. Her mother stayed up until her daughter returned from this exciting experience. This was her first love affair; Grace and Harper were teenagers in love. Together they went dancing, to the movies, to other events. In 1945, Harper joined the Marines at the age of eighteen. They wrote letters back and forth. Whenever he was in Philadelphia on furlow, they joyfully reunited.

In her scrapbook, which, along with everything else ever collected by Grace, is housed in the archives of the royal family in Monaco, Grace pasted various souvenirs from this time, such as admission tickets; postcards; theater programs; Christmas cards from 1943, 1944, and 1945; dried flowers (thirty years later, in the 1970s, the Princess of Monaco spent many hours drying flowers during her leisure time); imprinted napkins; and even a green Wrigley's gum wrapper.

She collected, hoarded, reused, and archived everything—habits she may have learned from her German mother, Margaret. Both of Grace's daughters, the princesses Caroline and Stéphanie, wore clothing from Grace's own childhood. It was very hard for her to throw anything away. Even today, the closets of the royal palace in Monaco are full of preserved personal artifacts from her life, such as books, clothes, costumes, and bags. In the palace archives, there are numerous letters and cards, personal documents and photographs.

Underneath all the items glued into her scrapbook are captions written cleanly and neatly by Grace in blue ink. Several of the captions from this time simply read, "Harper." Under the green Wrigley's wrapper, Grace wrote, "Chewing Gum Harper gave me on New Year's Eve." Another item in the scrapbook is a small white envelope to which a white card is loosely glued. The following words are written in black ink: "To Grace with Love, Harper." In her neat, carefully formed schoolgirl writing, which bears a clear resemblance to her later handwriting, Grace inscribed: "This is the card that came with the parfume [sic] Harper gave me for Christmas."[56]

Harper was not the only boy Grace dated. There are also clues that point to other boys, boys with whom she went dancing and to the theater, and perhaps those with whom she took her first tentative steps into the realm of sexual experience. There is a white envelope from Bill D'Arcy, which Grace captioned with "Christmas dance—Dec. 16th 1944."[57] Bill, the seventeen-year-old son of a wealthy Philadelphia plasterer, was a lifeguard with the Ocean City Beach Patrol. Because Ocean City, New Jersey, was just across the water from the Kelly's vacation home in Margate City, New Jersey, Grace got to spend many summer months with him on the shore.

In 1946, one year after he joined the Marines, Harper was diagnosed with multiple sclerosis. In the early stages, Grace visited him at home, and then later, she went to see him in the hospital. Harper battled the disease for seven years, but in 1953, he died in his mid-twenties. Although she was in the middle of her first film project and was already being called a star, Grace traveled to Philadelphia for his funeral. It was one of the first times that she dealt with the death of someone close to her. (In 1949, her maternal grandmother, Margaretha Berg, had died at the age of seventy-nine.) As she once commented later in life, Harper was her first boyfriend. And she had loved him.

In May 1947, the same year as Kell's fateful winning of the Henley Regatta, Grace graduated from the Stevens School on Walnut Lane in Germantown. She was seventeen years old. Grace had hoped to go to Bennington College in Vermont after her graduation. Although Bennington did offer a four-year degree in dance, this hope was motivated less by personal preference than by a desire to please her parents and to follow in the footsteps of other girls of her age. However, Grace's application was not accepted because of her poor grades in math. Grace also did not excel in the natural sciences, especially chemistry and physics. Bennington's decision not to accept Grace greatly upset Ma Kelly, who took such things very seriously and had helped her daughter apply to various other colleges. However, Grace's life path would have been very different if she had decided to go to college after graduation. "The change came when she did not go to Bennington College. That was what changed everything in her life," recalled Mary Louise Murray-Johnson.[58]

"She was eager to go to New York and do her drama school... eager to work and to get on," said Grace's husband, Prince Rainier III of Monaco, about Grace as a young woman.[59] At this time, Grace could only think about one thing: taking her first serious step into the acting world by gaining a coveted spot at the American Academy of Dramatic Arts in New York. This was what she, and she alone, wanted for herself.

Later, Grace would tell stories to her children about her decision to become an actress. Albert, who was always very close to her, was usually the one who was most interested in these stories and would ask for them to be told: "She would start by saying that it was because of her interest in the theatre. And at first it was—as it is for a lot of actors—that wonderful thrill of performing in front of live audiences, so she really enjoyed that part, the theatre acting, her theatre years. And, of course, she went to the American Academy of Dramatic Arts. During that full time she was exposed to a lot of different roles, a lot of different, great theatre experiences...I think she really enjoyed studying plays, learning lines, and acting, and both the other actors and directors wanted her to continue. But it's true that at first... well, I was told when I asked my grandmother, that no one in the family seriously believed that she would become an actress."[60]

Once, while still a relatively young woman, Grace commented: "When I really want to achieve something, I do more often than not. I don't know what's responsible—my will, my lucky star, or my Kelly pride. Probably it's all of them together."[61]

This self-assessment remained accurate in terms of her decisions and her actions throughout her entire life.

1947–1951
New York—Freedom:
Theater, Television, and Fashion

*She was a normal girl. But she just had a terrible need to
have someone put his arms around her. What she needed,
constantly, was reassurance that she existed. She was
starved for affection because of her family. She was afflicted
with a great sense of emptiness...*
—*Don Richardson*[62]

*Grace was a very simple and unassuming woman, who
always searched for happiness.*
—*Robert Dornhelm*[63]

"Let her go. She'll be back in a week."[64] This was John B. "Jack"
Kelly's disdainful, unsupportive commentary on Grace's pursuit
of acting.

At the age of seventeen, Grace left her hometown of
Philadelphia. This was a giant step, not only for Grace herself, but
also for her entire family. The second youngest daughter moved
on her own to New York, to Manhattan, a two-hour drive away.
"She got away from home early...none of the rest of us managed
to do that," explained Grace's brother Kell.[65] One can hear the bitter undertones in this statement by the only Kelly son. How much
would he have loved to do what his sister Grace did in leaving
home? However, she is the only one who succeeded in doing this.

"He [father Jack Kelly] did not know either New York or the
theater life. He imagined the most terrible scenarios and was
afraid that his little daughter would veer off the straight and narrow there," described Grace's sister Lizanne, attempting to ratio-
nalize her father's attitude.[66]

Grace's decision to leave her hometown was a rebellious step,
which reflected a strong-willed, unyielding personality despite
her shyness and reserve. By this time, Grace was no longer timid
and shy, fragile and delicate, demure and quiet. She had finally

become the decisive and certain, the disciplined and patient, the ambitious and upwardly mobile Grace that people would come to embrace.

Thus, Grace entered into a brand new world in 1947. Over the next eight and half years—October 1947 to April 1956—she lived in the world of the theater, movies, and television. This is probably the period in Grace Kelly's fifty-two-year life in which she was truly happy.

August 20 was the day of Grace's audition for acceptance into the American Academy of Dramatic Arts. The audition took place in the afternoon, and it had been rescheduled from an earlier date by Dr. Emile Diestel, the secretary for the Academy's board of trustees. Marie Magee, an actress and a good friend of Margaret Kelly, lived only a few streets over from the Academy. Grace called this friend of her mother's "Aunt Marie," and she helped Grace by interceding on the young woman's behalf with Dr. Diestel. The Academy was actually no longer accepting applicants for that year, and Grace's application was initially denied. After receiving word of this decision, Marie Magee approached Mr. Diestel directly, outspokenly informing him that Grace was the Pulitzer Prize–winning playwright George Kelly's niece. Ultimately, Dr. Diestel opened the door for the aspiring actress's admission to the Academy. Grace soon won Diestel's approval. Her performances in George Kelly's *The Torch Bearers* and in Shakespeare's *The Merchant of Venice* immediately resulted in Diestel's recognition of Grace's talent. Her famous name combined with her intrinsic talent helped her to enter that world of which she had once dreamed as she played alone with her dolls in her upstairs room on Henry Avenue.

On Grace's 1947 application form, Emile Diestel made the following notations: "Voice: Improperly placed; Temperament: Sensitive; Spontaneity: Youthful; Dramatic Instinct: Expressive; Intelligence: Good; General Remarks: Good, full of potential and freshness."[67]

In October 1947, one month before her eighteenth birthday, Grace Kelly began her acting studies in the junior class at the

American Academy of Dramatic Arts. This renowned academy was founded in 1884, and often labeled "the Cradle of the Stars." Its graduates included such famous actors and actresses as Katherine Hepburn, Spencer Tracy, Lauren Bacall, and Kirk Douglas. At the time, the Academy was located in New York's Carnegie Hall. The Academy students fell under the guidance of Charles Jehlinger, who had belonged to the Academy's first graduating class. He had taken over as director when the Academy's founder, Franklin Haven Sargent, died in 1923, and he was the Academy's vice president until his own death in 1952. The Academy students were required to honor strict rules regarding decorum and behavior, as well as regulations pertaining to neat, decorous clothing. They had to address each other as Mister or Miss. Jehlinger was the feared master of the Academy, inciting fear in most of the acting students. Already at their young ages, the pupils were expected to behave as ladies and gentlemen. This was probably not easy for some of these eighteen-year-olds, who now found themselves in the middle of Manhattan for the first time.

The initial period of study lasted for one year. However, because of her discipline and diligence, Grace was selected in April 1948 to stay for a second year of study. This began in September 1948 and ended in April 1949.

In New York, Grace lived in the legendary Barbizon Hotel for Women, located on 63rd Street at the corner of Lexington Avenue. The redbrick building had been constructed in 1927, and it reflected a combination of Renaissance and Gothic Revival elements. Since 1928, the twenty-seven-storied Barbizon offered young women safe lodgings, particularly for new arrivals to this East Coast city. The doors were locked at 10:00 p.m. Male guests were not allowed to proceed beyond the lobby area. A fortress for the weaker sex. How countless admirers, as well as the Barbizon residents themselves, must have puzzled over ways and possibilities to attain evening and night access! Other prominent Barbizon residents included Barbara Bel Geddes, Liza Minnelli, and Gene Tierney (who later married and then divorced the fashion designer Oleg Cassini with whom Grace was seriously involved in the mid-1950s).

Grace attended courses, practices, and auditions daily at the American Academy at the corner of 57th Street and 7th Avenue (today, Madison Avenue). She enrolled in as many courses as were allowed. She was full of intellectual curiosity, anxious to be as engaged as possible in the Academy's offerings. She worked hard to diminish her Philadelphia accent and her high, nasal voice. Later, in her Hollywood movies, as well as her years as Princess of Monaco, she pronounced her words very carefully in a way that seemed almost snobbish in tone. Her soft, almost silky inflection seemed at times to be warm and then cool at a turn. Besides their training, the Academy students received reduced tickets to productions on Broadway, which was only five minutes away by foot. During this period, Grace saw plays such as Tennessee Williams's *A Streetcar Named Desire* (1947), Arthur Miller's *All My Sons* (1947), and Ruth and Augustus Goetz's *The Heiress* (1947).

Although she received a monthly check from her father, Grace decided, as much as possible, to make her way in New York without financial support from Philadelphia. Thus, she had to find a job to go along with her studies. She had to find some way to pay for her room at the Barbizon and her new life in Manhattan. Between 1947 and 1949, Grace worked as a model for the New York branch office of the John Robert Powers Agency. This agency was founded in Philadelphia in 1923, and many years previously, it had been the agency of Grace's mother Margaret, who also had her daughters photographed there. Posing for the camera had never been hard for Grace, even when she had been in Philadelphia and had been asked to pose for one event or the other. However, this was her first serious engagement as a photographic model, a job that eventually led to her appearance in television advertisements. Grace was featured in advertisements for shampoo, lotions, soaps, toothpaste, insect sprays, household appliances, beer, and cigarettes.

On one billboard for the Old Gold brand, Grace could be seen carrying a vender's tray full of various cigarette packages. She smiled at the viewer and wore long, glossy black gloves that reached her elbows. In several black-and-white television ads, she modeled clothing and hats, at times narrated from off-camera by a voice actor: "Grace wrapped in a lace veil;" "Grace presents herself in yellow;" or "Here is a particularly attractive summer hat. The price is quite high, but who wants to talk about money when Papa will be paying? True, Miss Kelly?!"[68]

The image of the demure young woman who knew how to dress well and behave herself was in demand and was well-received in the prudish America of the 1940s and 1950s. For this reason, this modeling period is highly relevant. These years set the foundation for the creation of Grace Kelly as a style and fashion icon. Even today, the fascination with this image has not waned. This is the icon that became world famous in the 1960s through, among other things, the naming of the *Kelly Bag* by the Paris luxury fashion house Hermés.

Sister Francis, abbess of Ravenhill Academy, remembered Grace's years as a model. "She came one Sunday morning—she was an exquisite girl and at the time, a model for hats and gloves. She said: 'Mother Abbess, I need your advice. I have had an offer to model underwear. Should I do this?' I answered: 'Grace, that is a decision that only you can make. Try to imagine what you feel when you think about this. You must have doubts about it, or you would not be asking me about it.' Later I learned that she did not do this. She must have been convinced that she should pass up this opportunity."[69]

Financially, Grace now stood on her own two feet.

Thanks to her lucrative advertising contracts, she received $400 a week (which corresponds to about ten times as much today). This was yet one more step away from the ties to her family in Philadelphia.

According to Robert Dornhelm, "She was always anxious not to disappoint her family. She wanted to prove to her father that she did not need her family's assistance. She could find jobs on her own and pay her own way. However, the ongoing fear that the next job would not materialize, this never left her. As a freelance artist and filmmaker, you constantly rely on the next job. And the fear that this would not appear was deep in her bones."[70]

Already in her early New York days, Grace was seen as an outsider—a loner. The reasons for this lay in her demeanor and in her clothing style. Both of these aspects separated her from her peers. Because of this, she found success as one of the highest paid fashion and commercial models in New York. This gave rise, time and time again, to jealousy and envy among the other Barbizon residents and Academy students. Of course, Grace did form friendships during these years, important ones that lasted her whole lifetime. For example, there was Rita Gam, a fellow actress with whom she decided to share an apartment in Hollywood during the early 1950s. (She stayed here during the longer film projects, and the apartment was located on Sweetzer Street near Sunset Boulevard.) Grace also became friends with Maree Frisby Rambo and Judith Balaban Quine, both of whom were later bridesmaids at her wedding. (The other bridesmaids were Carolyn Reybold, Bettina Thompson Gray, and Sally Parrish Richardson.) At this time, Grace also met Prudence "Prudy" Wise, who joined the other two in the apartment on Sweetzer Street and who later moved to the royal palace in Monaco as Grace's personal secretary. Regardless of these relationships, in general, Grace was again the one who did not really belong, who was not really assimilated into the larger group. She stood out and attracted attention.

This is also the period in which Grace Kelly met the acting teacher Don Richardson (1918–1996). He taught at the Academy. When they first met, Grace was eighteen, and Don Richardson had just reached thirty. He was tall and slim, a charmer, perhaps even something of a playboy—a cultivated cosmopolitan. And, although he was separated, he was still married. Furthermore, he was Jewish. Grace went into raptures whenever she talked about Richardson, whether when with her friends or when catching up with her mother. At home in Philadelphia, her parents were less than thrilled about this new relationship with a man from the theater world. Margaret and Jack Kelly imagined a very different kind of man at Gracie's side. They were certain that Grace should marry a decent, respectable, proper man from a good family, far removed from the world of art and other questionable things.

When Grace finally took Don Richardson to Henry Avenue to introduce him to her parents, and to perhaps earn approval for this relationship, disaster struck. The family received Richardson frostily, hardly speaking to the acting teacher. Besides that, Grace's brother Kell, as instructed by his parents, had invited over two buddies, two athletes, who had been asked to make Richardson's visit particularly unpleasant. The three young men cracked Jewish jokes at Richardson's expense, making crude imitations of Jewish mannerisms. The sensitive theater man was offended. An affront, a tactless embarrassment. Stuck in a corner of the room with her younger sister Lizanne, Grace was completely ignored by everyone.

And then, a proposal was made to take a drive in father Jack's car through the city. This gave Jack Kelly the opportunity to point out which buildings had been constructed with Kelly bricks and which public projects he had helped fund. Afterward, at supper in Jack Kelly's Country Club, Don Richardson was seated next to Margaret Kelly. Grace and Lizanne sat at the lower end of the table, while the upper end was taken by father Jack, his son Kelly, and his two teammates. As the men talked excitedly about athletes, discipline, and competitions, complete silence reigned at the other end of the table. Grace sat at the table with her head lowered. It was as if she was not even there. This was her family.

What Don Richardson unpleasantly experienced in 1948 on Henry Avenue and at the country club supper was very similar to what Oleg Cassini encountered six years later in 1954 at the family summer home in Ocean City. Grace's own family refused to make it easy for Grace to find a partner whom she could stand by and care for. The Kellys did not seem to realize, or to even really care about, what she actually wanted. Either way, the end result was hard for the daughter to bear. Once again, she found herself in conflict. As Richardson noted, "She seemed to be in a state of denial where they were concerned."[71]

Don Richardson eventually recommended Grace to the legendary agent Edith Van Cleve at the MCA Agency. Edith unhesitatingly agreed to represent her. One of Van Cleve's new male clients at this time was a certain Marlon Brando.

Grace Kelly's relationship with Don Richardson was one of the most important and formative ones prior to her marriage with Prince Rainier. Grace and Richardson—who died of a heart attack in 1996 at the age of seventy-seven—remained friends after their separation and even after the royal wedding in Monaco. This friendship did not end until Grace's death in 1982. "Don Richardson seems to have been a most significant friend. She spoke of him often," explained director and friend Robert Dornhelm, who spent much time with Grace during her last years.[72]

Once, in the late 1970s, Grace wrote to Richardson, explaining that she wanted to introduce him to a young director she had met when she provided the commentary for the dance documentary film, *The Children of Theatre Street* (1977): "a dear boy who reminds me a bit of you. He could almost be our son."[73] Having grown up in Romania and Vienna, Robert Dornhelm divided his adult life between Los Angeles and Mougins, near Cannes. He was a close friend of Grace during the last six years of her life (1976–1982) and worked with her on two film projects.

However, Richardson refused to meet Dornhelm. It seemed that twenty-five years after his relationship with Grace, Richardson was jealous of the young Dornhelm: "I didn't want to sit with him, on either side of Grace like bookends—you know, before and after."[74] And as Dornhelm himself explained: "I once called Don Richardson on the telephone. Grace wanted me to meet him at all costs. And he was quite strange on the phone and did not want to talk to me. I did not understand that. The whole thing was quite absurd. They had had a relationship, long before her marriage, and yes, it was very intense. She had told me a lot about him."[75]

The relationship between Grace and Richardson could be best compared to the young romance between Grace and Harper Davis, but it was, to a certain extent, formative for Grace's later love affairs. Although Don Richardson was "only" eleven and a half years older than Grace, this age difference may have been quite significant, considering Grace's youth at the time. Also, there were other differences between the young Catholic acting student and the socially mature, Jewish acting teacher. "We were like yin and yang—we were total opposites. And I guess I was *La Bohème* to her. When you're raised with money, Bohemia can have its attractions."[76] And just as Richardson described the two of them as yin and yang, he saw in Grace a deeply rooted dualism: "Her public persona was so completely different from her private self that it was phenomenal. She was so proper—people thought of her as a nun. But when we were alone together, she used to dance naked for me to Hawaiian music. And if you don't think that was an incredible sight, you're crazy. She was a *very* sexy girl."[77]

In Spring 1949, Grace completed her acting studies at the Academy. She was now nineteen years old. After her graduation in April, her parents pressured her to move out of the Barbizon. They also strictly forbade her to continue her relationship with Don Richardson. For a while, Grace lived in the family's vacation home in Ocean City, but then in the fall of 1949, Ma and Jack Kelly gave their blessing for her to return to New York. Of course, the assumption was that she would move back into the supposedly secure Barbizon. While in Ocean City, Grace and Richardson had called each other on the telephone and had secretly met each other whenever they could manage it. With Grace now back in New York, they immediately resumed their intimate relationship. Grace had no intention of following her parents' orders here in New York. She and Richardson met at his apartment regularly, until one day, when father Kelly unexpectedly rang the bell at Richardson's door on 44th Street West. Standing with his coat and hat in hand, he demanded that Richardson finally break off all contact with his daughter and offered, in exchange, to give him a Jaguar automobile. Richardson could pick the color himself. Clearly, the father placed great value on ending the relationship between his daughter and this very undesirable man. In outrage, Richardson refused the offer and was again offended. Father Kelly left. Despite the refusal of the Kelly Clan's offer, Grace and Richardson only remained together for a short time more.

According to Don Richardson, the relationship between him and Grace crumbled when she supposedly began to see other men, such as the manager of the renowned New York Waldorf Astoria Hotel, whose restaurant and bar she often patronized in the evening. The hotel's international flair stood in stark contrast to the rigid atmosphere at the Barbizon. Another love interest was the Shah of Persia: "The Shah also wanted to marry her."[78] Ali Khan, the Prince of Pakistan, was a great admirer. He gave her a large gold bracelet studded with several sapphires, which she proudly showed to Richardson. Hurt and jealous, Richardson angrily threw the bracelet into an aquarium and left.

That was the end of their relationship.

At the small yet renowned Buck's County Playhouse in New Hope, Pennsylvania, Grace made her true stage debut on July 25, 1949. Again, she appeared in her Uncle George's *The Torch Bearers*. She acted alongside Carl White and Haila Stoddard in this production, which was subtitled *A Satirical Comedy in Three Acts*. This was Grace's first stage appearance since she had received her acting certificate.

Just as the mention of George Kelly's name opened the door to the Academy, so did it now open the door to the acting world. In his play, which was already so familiar to her, she was cast as the part of a young, inexperienced actress. Grace also acted in the Buck's County Playhouse's staging of *The Heiress*, which was based on Henry James's novel *Washington Square*. Grace had seen this play on Broadway during her time at the Academy.

On November 16, 1949, only four days before her twentieth birthday, Grace made her New York Broadway debut in August Strindberg's play, *The Father* (1887). The play ran in the Cort Theatre, which has been an active theater since its founding in 1912. This was her first Broadway performance. In Strindberg's three-act play, Grace played the role of Bertha, the daughter of a riding master. Raymond Massey costarred as the riding master, and Mady Christians took the role of his wife Laura. *The Father* ran for sixty-nine performances and closed on January 14, 1950, only two months after its opening. Strindberg's play no longer drew large crowds into the 1,100-seat Broadway theater. During this New York period, both before and after her two performances in *The Torch Bearers* and *The Father*, Grace continued to apply for work. She went to several dozen stage auditions and was turned down time and time again. Often she was told that her legs were too long or that she was too tall. (Grace was 5'7".)

She was significantly more successful in a much newer medium; during the early 1950s, television was becoming increasingly popular. And Grace was one of the first and most widely employed television actresses not engaged in a weekly series. This work was almost groundbreaking in nature. The significance of Grace's television work is hardly known today, as it has been overshadowed by her Hollywood films and her fame as princess. Another reason for the loss of this knowledge can be attributed to the fact that many of the live broadcasts from this period were not fully archived because of the film technique related to the Kinescope recordings. (At that time, television programs were usually recorded via the Kinescope process, which involved directly filming from a screen. The Kinescope process was made obsolete by the introduction of the first analog videotape in 1956, the Beta system, and other techniques.)

Grace Kelly appeared in her first live television program on November 3, 1948, one year after her Broadway debut. Alongside Ethel Owen, Grace starred in the sixty-minute NBC production of *Kraft Television Theatre* in the episode "Old Lady Robbins," written by Albert G. Miller. This was Grace's only television appearance in 1948.

Although Grace did no television work in 1949, she followed "Old Lady Robbins" with additional live television roles between 1950 and 1954. All told, she appeared in forty-two live television productions.[79] In other sources, the total number of appearances ranges from more than sixty to one hundred. However, these claims cannot be proven, since there are no sources that substantiate these higher estimates.[80]

Director and producer Fred Coe, who was in charge of the direction or production for several of the television productions in which Grace appeared, once described her as follows: "[she] had talent and attractiveness, but so do a lot of other young people in the theater who never become stars. The thing that made her stand out was something we call 'style.' She wasn't just another beautiful girl, she was the essence of freshness—the kind of girl every man dreams of marrying." Coe further expressed a sentiment that was repeated over and over again during her film career by those who worked with her on set: "All of us who worked with her just loved her. You couldn't work with Grace Kelly without falling a little in love with her."[81]

On January 8, 1950, Grace played the title role in Sinclair Lewis's work *Bethel Merriday* (1940), which was filmed by NBC for the *Philco Television Playhouse* series. This was also the final week of Strindberg's *The Father*. With sixteen television programs, 1950 was Grace's busiest year in terms of television productions. For an actor on the stage, these live performances were enormously demanding when it came to concentration and dialogue memorization. If you botched a line, a prop fell over, or a technical malfunction occurred, millions of television viewers would be watching it happen live.

Director and friend Robert Dornhelm recalled this time: "Grace told me some about this period, about the live television performances. There were many directors whom I respected greatly—Sidney Lumet, John Frankenheimer—an array of famous American directors who were directing these live television programs. They were aired weekly and were half an hour in length, and because of this they were making many of these programs. Actors had to remember the entire text. If you made a mistake, it was on live television. Naturally, there was an element of discipline tied to this. They did not have much time to memorize the dialogue."[82]

Besides the handful of live television performances in 1951— five in all—Grace worked on fifteen additional half- or one-hour programs in 1952 for NBC and CBS. These included the CBS series *Television Workshop*, in which she acted in the first episode of Season 1, which was aired on January 13, 1952. This episode was a thirty-minute rendition of Miguel de Cervantes's *Don Quixote* as directed by Sidney Lumet. In this episode, Boris Karloff, the star of Frankenstein, played Don Quixote, while Grace Kelly was Dulcinea and Jimmy Savo was Sancho Panza.

For NBC's *Philco Television Playhouse*, Grace acted in the one-hour performance of *The Rich Boy*, based on a short story of the

60

same name by F. Scott Fitzgerald. On stage in front of the cameras, Grace Kelly and the Irish actor Gene Lyons (with whom she was later romantically involved) played the main roles of Paula Legendre and Anson Hunter. The performance aired live on February 10, 1952. Once before, they had acted together in another live television program, an adaptation of Ferenc Molnár's *The Swan* for the CBS series *The Play's the Thing*. Grace played Princess Alexandra in this short television version of Molnár's historic costume drama, which she again interpreted five years later in the almost prophetic MGM film, *The Swan* (1956). However, at the time of the CBS broadcast of *The Swan*, the two actors did not foresee their impending romance. Their time together was yet to come.

Until the filming on John Ford's *Mogambo* began on November 17, 1952, which was continuously filmed through the early months of 1953, Grace irregularly appeared most months in various live television programs. The last one of 1952 was the half-hour production *A Message for Janice* for CBS's *Lux Video Theatre*. This aired on September 29, 1952. Grace acted in four additional television programs in 1953.

Early in 1954, she performed one more time in front of a television camera for a live program in New York. (This was the year that she transitioned to making film after film and had to travel from one film location to the next; after the filming of Alfred Hitchcock's *To Catch a Thief*, she was completely drained and exhausted.) Her final televised performance was in the NBC series *Kraft Television Theatre* (1947–1958). It aired on January 6, 1954, and was a sixty-minute piece titled *The Thankful Heart*, written by Herbert A. Francis as episode 19 of season 7.

This was the conclusion of Grace's television career. By this point, another career had already long begun.

1951–1956
Hitchcock and Hollywood:
The Eleven Films of Grace Kelly

I was never happy in Hollywood. There, everything is
distorted by the importance people give to money.
—*Grace Kelly*[83]

She was sort of shy, and very talented, but really did not
have the typical characteristics of an actress. I think being
an actress actually helped her overcome her shyness.
—*Prince Albert II of Monaco*[84]

Grace Kelly's relationship with Hollywood was, from the very beginning, an ambivalent one. She never truly felt at home on the West Coast. She was not comfortable with the elements of artificiality, nor did she care for the fact that power and greed called the shots in the mecca of the West Coast film industry. In Hollywood, as had already been the case in Philadelphia, Grace had trouble feeling like she fit in. She never felt fully settled there.

Exiled from Europe to the California coast in the summer of 1941, Bertolt Brecht titled one of his poems, "On Thinking About Hell" ("*Nachdenkend ueber die Hoelle*"). In this poem, he mused that Hell must resemble Los Angeles: "I who live in Los Angeles and not in London find, on thinking about Hell, that it must be still more like Los Angeles."[85]

However, the German exile Brecht was not the only one who did not feel at ease here. Many others experienced the same things he did. This was the case for some of the numerous intellectuals exiled from Europe, who again found their lives to be difficult during the McCarthy Era of the late 1940s and early 1950s. And this was also the case for Grace Kelly.

It is telling that Grace never stayed very long in Los Angeles, Hollywood, or Beverly Hills. She never settled down here, rented long term, or bought a house or an apartment. Once she was finished with a film, she usually took the earliest possible flight back to New York or Philadelphia. She preferred the foggy rain or the snow flurries of New York to the ever-burning California sun, which shone brightly regardless of bad moods or dissatisfaction. LA was almost the opposite of New York. LA seemed to be a network of towns without its own cityscape; everywhere there were highways, suburbs and slums, expensive addresses and mansion neighborhoods. New York, on the other hand, was a culturally pulsating metropolis oriented toward Europe. "She did not like Los Angeles," recalled Robert Dornhelm.[86]

This ambivalence, this conflict in terms of feeling at home somewhere, exemplifies the life, the behavior, the thought process, and especially the sensibility of Grace Kelly.

"She was full of contradictions. That is where her fascination lay. Even if you knew her well, suddenly an entirely different aspect of her character would emerge," maintained Judith Balabin Quine, a long-time friend of Grace.[87] Quine went on to claim that "I think the thing that most people forget is that when all of this was happening to Grace, this extraordinary excitement about her career being generated and roles with the world's most famous leading men and the world's most respected directors, she was just a girl in her early twenties."[88] With these words, Quine tried to explain Grace's distaste for Hollywood and the subsequent public frenzy over it.

Furthermore, Grace's complex personality expressed itself in her thoroughly self-critical attitude toward her own films, as well as toward films documenting or portraying her career and life. Director and friend Robert Dornhelm accompanied Grace between 1976 and 1982 to numerous honorary events in various cities and countries: "When I was with her at any of the films either about her or in which she starred, she would always say before the performance, 'I am already bored.'" In addition, "she did not like to talk about her films. She felt they were over before they even started."[89]

According to Grace Kelly's son, Prince Albert:

I think she was very pleased with her performance in *The Country Girl*, but I don't think it was her favorite movie. I am not sure, which one was. [...] I think she liked herself in different scenes in different movies. I think she liked (and that's my personal favorite) *Rear Window* the best. That's not why it's my favorite movie—because I like them all—but it's a study of, you know, voyeurism and social behavior and psychological intensity. And it is still powerful so many years later.[90]

Regardless of her own self-criticism and her distance, Hollywood did bring some good things to Grace Kelly: eleven films, which even today are the basis for her fame and which contributed to her iconization. An Academy Award—an Oscar—for her most unusual and demanding role, filmed in black and white. Hollywood also gave her three opportunities to work and form a lasting friendship with the "Master of Suspense," Sir Alfred Hitchcock.

Fourteen Hours
(1951)

You make it sound dirty.
—Grace Kelly as Louise Ann Fuller

It was on July 26, 1938, that John William Warde climbed out of his room on the seventeenth floor of the New York Gotham Hotel and onto the ledge that ran along the front facade of the building. Friends and family, police and psychologists, all tried to keep him from committing suicide. Then evening came. After eleven hours, in front of everyone's eyes, Warde leapt to his death.

Twelve years later, Hollywood turned this real event into movie magic. The screenplay, written by John Paxton, was based on a story by Joel Sayre for *The New Yorker*, published under the title "The Man on the Ledge." *Fourteen Hours* (1951) was adapted from "The Man on the Ledge," changing the actual eleven hours into the fictional fourteen hours. Sol C. Siegel produced *Fourteen Hours* for Twentieth Century-Fox. Henry Hathaway (1898–1985) was the director. Two years later, he went on to direct *Niagara* (1953), one of Marilyn Monroe's most famous films.

It is Friday, March 17. Robert Cosick (Richard Basehart) is the young man who is standing fifteen floors up on the ledge of the New York Rodney Hotel. From the street, Charlie Dunnigan (Paul Douglas), a traffic cop, sees the young man standing up on the high-rise building. He hurries into the hotel and tries to help. Passersby start to collect below. Cars come to a standstill in the streets around the hotel. Emergency workers from the police and fire departments arrive and attempt to set a rescue plan in motion. Cosick's relatives and friends are eventually reached, and they all gather together without exchanging a single word. His domineering mother (Agnes Moorehead) does not speak to his shy, despondent father (Robert Keith); Robert's ex-girlfriend Virginia (Barbara Bel Geddes) does not speak to either of his parents. As

Dunnigan tries to get out on the ledge to join Robert, in order to talk him down—by talking to him about his life and bringing him water, coffee, and cigarettes—it is quickly made clear that the family life of this despairing young man is fraught with suffering. A state of rapidly shifting emotions is set off, and Robert seems about to jump but then he hesitates.

Already long before this point, radio and television crews have set up cameras and microphones everywhere to report the spectacle live. The salacious relish for sensationalism among the press, as well as the individuals, must have been astonishing, if not actually terrifying, considering the production year for this movie, 1950.

At the end, dusk has fallen, and it has grown late. Blinded by a sudden harsh, flaring spotlight that was set up in front of the hotel, Robert abruptly, involuntarily falls from the ledge and lands in a net one floor below, which had been spread out by the police. This ending was chosen in 1951 by the test viewers for the movie. Two endings had been made for the sample audience, one in which the young man dies, as had happened in reality, and one in which he was rescued. Reality lost the toss.

Edith Van Cleve paved the way for Grace to appear in her first silver screen role. Van Cleve was a theater agent as well as an agent for the large and influential Music Corporation of America (MCA), which was in business from 1924 to 1997. Another MCA agent, Lew Wasserman, represented Alfred Hitchcock for a while, and after the merger of MCA and Universal, as studio boss at Universal, Wasserman co-produced Hitchcock's later films, from *The Birds* (1963) through *Family Plot* (1976). After Don Richardson had recommended Grace Kelly to Edith Van Cleve, Van Cleve sent her new young actress to one of many casting calls and auditions, one of which was for *Fourteen Hours*. In addition to Edith Van Cleve's endorsement, producer Sol C. Siegel, who had previously seen Grace perform in Strindberg's *The Father*, recommended the young actress for the film. After a subsequent costume audition, director Henry Hathaway decided to cast her in a small minor role, in what would be her very first film project.

The filming took place between early June and early August of 1950, and the film sites were the Twentieth Century-Fox studios and various locations in Manhattan, along Broadway and Wall Street, for the exterior shots.

During the filming, Gary Cooper dropped by the set of *Fourteen Hours* to visit director Henry Hathaway. Here, during the summer of 1950, Cooper and Grace met for the first time.

Cooper was instantly taken with the twenty-year-old theater actress. She seemed to embody an anti-type, like the more androgynous-seeming Audrey Hepburn, who had also been born in 1929. Cooper immediately began to rave about Grace, about her well-bred manners, her charm, her beauty, which was so very different from that of the properly appointed, explicitly provocative silver screen goddesses, which were in vogue at this time. "I thought she looked pretty and different, and that maybe she'd be somebody. She looked educated, and as if she came from a nice family. She was certainly a refreshing change from all those bombshells we'd been seeing so much of."[91]

This was the first time Grace had met a Hollywood star of this magnitude. In the fall months of September and October of the following year, 1951, the two of them would stand together in front of the camera for the filming of Fred Zinnemann's black-and-white classic western, *High Noon*. However, Grace had no inkling of this at this time.

As Mrs. Fuller, Grace had only two or three scenes. One of them was outdoors, down on the street in the middle of New York traffic, through which she would walk to an attorney's office to sign her divorce papers. In another scene, she is in the attorney's office and from there she observes everything that is taking place across the way.

Grace's work on *Fourteen Hours* required two days of filming. On her first day, the street scene was filmed on the studio lot of Twentieth Century-Fox, on Stage 8. The scene went like this: Grace sits in a taxi that is stuck behind the blockade in front of the hotel. She rolls the window down and calls to the traffic cop (Dunnigan): "Officer, are we going to be able to get through?

I have an important appointment, and I'm late now."[92] He advises her to get out and walk the rest of the way. Grace exits the car and has to climb over the bumpers of two rows of cars. To be helpful, Paul Douglas takes her hand. "Take it easy," he tells her. "Thank you," she replies, as he gallantly helps her get around the bumpers. She shakes his hand. "It's alright," Douglas responds and smiles. Grace turns around and leaves the scene.

Grace's first appearance in the film occurs in the fourteenth minute, and it only lasts thirty seconds. She is wearing a fur coat, black gloves, and a black handbag. On her head is perched a hat that looks like a blend of a pillbox hat and a black circlet, and it is covered by a veil that reaches her eyes. A double strand of pearls and a pair of white earrings complete the ensemble. The lipstick is dark red, a color that she later wore quite often. This outfit makes it clear that this is a lady, a woman with style and class, with taste and manners. Although only twenty, with her stylish, elegant appearance, she seems to be much older and more mature than the majority of her peers. Already in this early screen appearance, Grace Kelly's trademark style is introduced. It is the same personal and inherent sense of timeless elegance that she cultivated through her work on Broadway, her live television programs, her commercial work, and her modeling.

Her second appearance in the film takes place in a large room at the lawyer's office, lined with books and furnished with heavy pieces of furniture. She is standing at the window, looking at the building across the way. This is the Rodney Hotel, where a man stands on the ledge and a group of people have gathered to observe what is happening above. The lawyer's office is located slightly higher than the floor on which Robert Cosick is perched on the ledge. Thus, Mrs. Fuller can watch what is happening from a relatively close vantage point. As the attorney turns to her to discuss the conditions of the prepared divorce papers and the support for her children, she turns in his direction and responds absentmindedly, "Yes?" It is almost as if the events across the way, the life and death decisions of this unknown man are, at the very least, just as important as her own decision to end her marriage. The plotline pertaining to Mrs. Fuller's thoughts shortly before

70

making her divorce final has no direct connection with the main storyline. Rather, this is set up as an independent parallel story, which reflects, on a different level, the consequences of the decisions that are made in life.

In the fifty-ninth minute, the husband, Mr. Fuller (James Warren), arrives. He had also been delayed. The lawyer reads aloud the clauses pertaining to the children, and the husband simply nods. The attorney asks, "Do you have any comment?" She finally responds: "Yes. I don't understand it. It's too complicated. Issue. One issue. Both issues. You make it sound dirty! They're children. Why don't you say 'children'? I don't want to do it anymore." Grace's voice shakes. At this, her husband almost jumps up from the armchair, on the edge of which he has sat, nervously smoking. He asks her if she really means it, if she really does not want the divorce. And she agrees, saying that she no longer wants to think about it. It is more complicated than being married. "Let's try again," Mr. Fuller says to Mrs. Fuller. They hug each other and stand at the window with their arms around each other. Grace turns to watch the events unfold outside the room. Then the camera cuts from inside the room to showing the embracing couple from outside the room. Grace and her costar stand in the left side of the frame, while in the right side, through a reflection in the windowpane, the viewer can see what is taking place on the facade across the way. A policeman is rappelling down the face of the hotel, and the man continues to stand on the ledge. To a certain extent, the drama at the hotel concerning the fate of the man is reflected in Grace's face. Both of them are standing—she inside, he outside—between the fifteenth and seventeenth floors of two Manhattan high rises, asking themselves if or how they will go on with their lives. Should she file for divorce and fight over the children, or not? Should the man on the ledge plunge into the depths below and end his young life, or not? In the last fifteen minutes of the film, Grace and her movie husband are only visible for a few short seconds, as they stand together on the street in the crowd, arm in arm, gazing up at the hotel.

Fourteen Hours marked Grace Kelly's first film performance. The film's New York premiere was in March 1951, and its US opening occurred in April. It was a flop at the box office, but highly acclaimed by the critics. At the 1952 Academy Awards, Hathaway's drama was nominated for best set design. However, Grace, whose name is listed tenth in the opening credits, was not mentioned in the reviews. Not yet.

Grace's entire screen time only came to three minutes in Hathaway's very successful, atmospheric, tense ninety-two-minute drama, which was predominantly shaped by humanistic ideas as exemplified by the altruistic, empathic traffic cop Charlie Dunnigan. Despite the brevity of her appearance, several of Grace's signature characteristics are utilized and recognizable. These remained consistent throughout her eleven films, a common thread that connect her works: a cool sensibility, restraint in sudden shifts of mood or whim, strong poise and posture, and a keen awareness of her strengths—and all this performed with grace, dignity, and respect.

High Noon
(1952)

Gary Cooper taught me that the
camera is always in the first row.
—*Grace Kelly*[93]

In the spring of 1951, Grace Kelly's agent Edith Van Cleve sent several still photographs to her colleague Jay Kanter, who also worked for MCA as an agent. Immediately, Kanter offered Grace a permanent contract with MCA. Kanter, who was also the agent for Marlon Brando, wanted MCA to exclusively represent her for film and television engagements. However, Grace turned this offer down because she did not want to lock herself into a contract. She wanted to keep her options open; after all, there was still the theater. This suited her much more. But then, in September 1952, she changed her mind and signed a seven-year contract with the Metro-Goldwyn-Mayer Studio, and *Mogambo* became her first MGM production.

Jay Kanter was not only Grace's agent, but he was also married to her friend Judith Balaban Quine. He sent the photos from Edith Van Cleve, along with others, to the producer Stanley Kramer. Besides working as a producer (until 1979), Kramer also had worked as a director, starting in 1955. He mainly made politically and historically oriented films, which met with much acclaim, such as *Judgment at Nuremberg* (1961) and *Guess Who's Coming to Dinner* (1967). Stanley Kramer's (1913-2001) films always grappled with latent or explicit racism. They were shaped by a deep dedication to the implementation and preservation of democracy and justice. Within this social context, one must situate the film *High Noon*.

Prior to *High Noon*, producer Stanley Kramer, director Fred Zinnemann, and screenwriter Carl Foreman had collaborated on the film *The Men* (1950), which was twenty-six-year-old Marlon Brando's first movie.

Stanley Kramer showed the photos of Grace Kelly to his director Fred Zinnemann, who promptly wanted to meet the young actress. What Zinnemann did not know at this time was that, solely based on the photographs and without consulting anyone else, his producer had on his own authority decided to cast Grace in the role of the pious pacifist, Quaker Amy Fowler Kane. Kramer had already even signed the contract. At the time of this meeting, Grace was in Denver for a theater engagement at Elitch Gardens Theatre. From there she flew to Los Angeles in early July, and Zinnemann was taken with her unusual (for Hollywood) appearance.

Fred Zinnemann (1907–1997) had been born in Austria-Hungary, and he grew up in the Third District of Vienna. In 1929, he immigrated to America, just like his other exiled colleagues Fritz Lang, Ernst Lubitsch, and Billy Wilder, who had been born in either Berlin or Vienna. Zinnemann was the director of such movie classics as the adaptation of Anna Seghers's novel *The Seventh Cross* (1944), *The Nun's Story* (1959) with Audrey Hepburn in the title role, and the film version of Frederick Forsyth's *The Day of the Jackal* (1973). His films, some of which deal intensively with the Third Reich and its fatal influences, such as *The Search* (1948), reflect a humanist perspective, as exemplified by *The Seventh Cross* and *The Nun's Story*. This humanism was again revealed in *High Noon*, which more closely resembles an intimate play than it does a typical western. As in other socio-critical works by Zinnemann, in this film, he explored a variety of themes, including the concept of the engagement of the individual to benefit a larger group, and the happiness derived from such an altruistic sacrifice.

Generally speaking, Fred Zinnemann is credited with the discovery of later Hollywood stars, such as Marlon Brando, Montgomery Clift, and even Grace Kelly. This was definitely the case for the first two actors. Marlon Brando's very first film project was Zinnemann's *The Men*, and the young Montgomery Clift was seen for the first time ever in *The Search*. With Grace Kelly, one must be more specific. Excepting her three-minute appearance in Hathaway's *Fourteen Hours*, *High Noon* was Grace's first larger supporting role, earning her fifth billing on the cast list.

However, her role as Amy Kane, which in the broader context was relatively small, did not yet win the lasting attention of the press and the public. This first came after her next two films, John Ford's *Mogambo* and Alfred Hitchcock's *Dial M for Murder* (1954).

Fred Zinnemann described the role of Amy in simple terms: "We simply needed an attractive, virginal-looking and inhibited young actress, the typical Western heroine."[94] Grace Kelly was ideally suited for the role of the newly married, very young Quaker Amy Kane. According to Zinnemann, Grace Kelly seemed to fit the part of newlywed Amy Kane "perhaps because she was technically not ready for it, which made her rather tense and remote."[95] Grace was nervous. At their first meeting, she sat there shyly, since Zinnemann's name demanded respect. Perhaps she was a little afraid. She was also only twenty-one years old. Except for the two days of filming for *Fourteen Hours*, she had no Hollywood film experience. She wore white gloves to this fairly short introductory conversation, and she answered most of the director's questions falteringly with only "yes" or "no." Zinnemann himself was a man of few words and did not care for lengthy conversations, but as he recalled, the situation was too much for her. "Our conversation soon came to a halt," and he sent her "with a sense of relief [...] on to Foreman's office."[96] For the time being, he bid Grace farewell and sent her on her way with a word of advice that she should learn how to talk with people and to lead a conversation whenever she was introduced to someone.

Composer Dimitri Tiomkin described Grace as someone who often seemed out of place on the set of *High Noon*: "Nobody could foresee Princess Grace."[97]

Finally on July 19, the American press announced that Stanley Kramer Productions had scheduled the filming of *High Noon* for late August and early September. Gary Cooper was cast in the main role, and he would be acting alongside movie newcomer, Grace Kelly. However, it was not until August 10, only eighteen days before the advertised production start date, that Grace received a telegram with the final confirmation from producer Stanley Kramer. At the time, she was in Denver for an acting appearance. The telegram read as follows: "Can you report Aug. 28, lead opposite Gary Cooper, tentative title *High Noon.*"

Carl Foreman wrote the screenplay for *High Noon*, basing it on the eight-page short story "The Tin Star" by John W. Cunningham. Stanley Kramer Productions was responsible for producing the film for the United Artists Studio, the smallest of the major US studios. (In 1961, United Artists started producing the James Bond film series to worldwide acclaim and popularity.) With a budget of $750,000 and twenty-eight days for filming, *High Noon* was a low-budget production by Hollywood standards. The filming lasted from September 5 to October 13, 1951. The interior scenes were shot at Motion Picture Center Hollywood, and the difficult, very hot and dusty exterior scenes were shot off-site. Besides Columbia Ranch on the film lot in Burbank, not far from the Warner Bros. Studios, the outside shots were filmed at the historic site of the Mother Lode near Sonora, about 300 miles northwest of Los Angeles. Particularly for the two supporting actresses, Grace Kelly and Katy Jurado, who had to wear heavy period costumes, the more intense scenes were difficult to endure.

High Noon had a run time of eighty-five minutes, and its story was told in real time while strictly adhering to the classical dramatic order of unity of time, place, and action. The story begins at about 10:40 a.m. and ends shortly after 12:00 p.m. The time experienced by the viewer is practically synchronized with that of the actors. During the course of the movie, Will Kane's gaze and that of the others constantly returns to a particular clock. Time is "perceived as an enemy, shown by obsessive use of clocks [...]; clocks looming larger as time slips by, pendulums moving more and more slowly until time finally stands still, gradually creating an unreal, dreamlike, almost hypnotic effect of suspended animation."[98] This is how Fred Zinnemann himself described it.

The film tells the story of Marshal Will Kane (Gary Cooper), who only moments after his marriage to the young Quaker Amy Fowler (Grace Kelly), learns that the dangerous outlaw Frank Miller (Ian MacDonald) is free again. Kane had put him in prison five years ago, and Miller had sworn revenge. Miller is on his way on the noon train to the western town of Hadleyville in order to meet Kane, and to terrorize and shoot up the frontier town. Miller's three fellow outlaws are already at the Hadleyville train station and are waiting in the grueling heat for their leader. Kane has just promised his wife, who abhors any form of violence, that today, Sunday, the day his term as sheriff ends, he will lay down his tin star and never use a gun again. The wedding guests advise them to immediately leave Hadleyville before noon arrives. However, just after they leave town Kane turns back; he wants to surrender himself to Frank Miller. Amy then decides to wait for the noon train and to depart with the luggage. However, at the moment that she wants to board the train, a shot is fired. Amy turns around. In the meantime, a confrontation between the two enemies is unavoidable. Thus, it comes to a final showdown, in the course of which Amy is the one who, despite all of her religious beliefs, shoots one of the bandits in the back and kills him. Ultimately, this leads to Kane's rescue. After the four gangsters are defeated in a street devoid of any people, Amy and Kane are surrounded and celebrated by the town's citizens. However, Kane now throws down his sheriff's star at the feet of those who refused to help or support him in any way. For a second time, he leaves the town with Amy. This time they do not return.

This unusual western had its New York premiere on July 24, 1952, and opened across the United States on July 30. *High Noon* set a high standard for its entire genre, becoming one of the most successful and honored films of the 1950s. Even today, Fred Zinnemann's black-and-white drama counts as an undeniable western classic of its genre. In March 1953, *High Noon* was honored with four Oscars. Gary Cooper won his second Academy Award for Best Actor, and another award went to Elmo Williams and Harry Gerstad for their distinctive, stylistic editing. Finally, two awards were given for the film's score. Dimitri Tiomkin received a golden statuette for Best Music, and both he and lyricist Ned Washington won the award for Best Original Song. The film was also nominated for Best Film, Best Director, and Best Screenplay. Prior to the hosting of the Academy Awards, the film had also been nominated for a total of seven Golden Globes, winning four Globes at the 1953 Golden Globe Awards.

The movie was hailed as a great success by both the press and the public. Even for Hollywood, it is rare when art and commerce, the box office and the critics, are in accord. For United Artists, this low-budget production was, in hindsight, an important film.

Only one person was not satisfied with herself and viewed her achievement very critically. This was a trait that often reared its head during the course of her six-year film career. It was a defining attribute that was already evident in Philadelphia. This self-criticism was not motivated by the reviews that only discussed her in one or two lines, or by Gary Cooper's enormous success because of the film, which gave new life to his flagging career. The cause seems to have been that, even in the earliest viewings of the films, she found her screen presence to be simply bad, flat, and expressionless: "Everything was so clear working with Gary Cooper. When I look into his face, I can see everything he is thinking. But when I look into my own face, I see absolutely nothing."[99]

To the contrary, when asked by Hollywood gossip columnist Hedda Hopper, Gary Cooper recognized the potential, talent, and effectiveness of his young costar: "She was very serious about her work, had her eyes and ears open. She was trying to learn, you could see that. You can tell if a person really wants to be an actress. She was one of those people you could get that feeling about, and she was very pretty. It didn't surprise me when she was a big success."[100]

Although Grace Kelly appears in many scenes throughout *High Noon*, there are two that are particularly dialogue-heavy and critical to the film. Both scenes epitomize her role as the young, shy yet determined Quaker, Amy Kane. This mixture of uncertain timidity and firm determination also corresponded with Grace's actual personality.

The first scene takes place in the Marshal's office. As he frequently does throughout the film, Kane glances up at the clock, which shows the time to be 10:50. In seventy minutes, the train will arrive at the station. It is a crucial moment: Will he finally leave the town with Amy, who has already packed the wagon and turned it around, or will he face his enemy? Kane mistakenly believes that people will stand beside him and help him. Kane doesn't realize that trusting his fellow townspeople will turn out to be a fatal error. Amy and Kane have been married less than an hour, and already they must decide their future together:

Will: "You know I've only got an hour and I've got lots to do. Stay at the hotel until it is over."

Amy: "No, I won't be here when it's over. You're asking me to wait an hour to find out if I'm going to be a wife or a widow. I say it's too long to wait! I won't do it! I mean it! If you won't go with me now, I'll be on that train when it leaves here."

Will: "I've got to stay."[101]

After this, she looks at him mutely, stonily, before walking out the door. She climbs into the horse wagon and drives away, as he stares after her. Exactly at this moment, the singer Tex Ritter begins to sing the melancholy theme song, "Do Not Forsake Me, Oh My Darlin.'"

This is Grace Kelly's first long scene of dialogue. Amy's final words, before she leaves the sheriff's office, could be considered a monologue, a despairingly hopeful plea.

The second scene takes place at 11:45. It involves a visit between Amy and Helen Ramirez, who had previously been romantically involved with Will Kane. Helen lectures her on the moral duty of a wife, in this case, one who had lost her family in a similar fight for justice:

Helen: "What kind of woman are you? How can you leave him like this? Does the sound of the guns frighten you that much?"

Amy: "I've heard guns. My father and my brother were killed by guns. They were on the right side but that didn't help them any when the shooting started. My brother was nineteen. I watched him die. That's when I became a Quaker. I don't care who's right or who's wrong. There's got to be some better way for people to live. Will knows how I feel about it."[102]

In this sequence, Grace Kelly plays her part with visible and audible excitement; her voice shakes and vibrates. Also here, she combines in her portrayal an innocent naïveté and a determined vehemence. Despite her youthfulness, Amy has already experienced deep loss in her life, and it has taught her how to survive; she knows exactly what she wants and what she does not. This, too, was true for Grace herself.

It is interesting to observe, over the course of her short acting career, the parallels that existed between the women that Grace played in her movies and the woman she was in her own life. A great distance separates Louise Anne Fuller of *Fourteen Hours* and Amy Fowler Kane of *High Noon* and certainly also Linda Nordley of *Mogambo* from Lisa Carol Fremont of *Rear Window* (1954) or Francie Stevens of *To Catch a Thief*. These female characters ultimately reveal the transformation that Grace herself underwent during these critical years of her life. It was a process whereby she became a woman, gaining self-awareness and emancipation.

Between January and March 1956, Grace made her eleventh and final film, Charles Walters's *High Society* (1956). Her engagement to Prince Rainier III of Monaco had been announced in early January, and the great, festive fairy-tale wedding lay before her in April. She was again a mixture of shyness and determination, as she had been when she played Amy Kane. However, now she knew exactly what she wanted. She had freed herself from Philadelphia and the constraints of that place, and she had matured into a lady whose style and elegance were neither artificial or insincere, but were instead true and authentic. In the world of appearances—which included both the microcosm of Hollywood and the jet-setting culture of Monaco—Grace's great concern was, first and foremost, to be true to herself, to represent her actual nature, and to not become lost in mere appearances.

By the time that *High Noon* was filmed, Gary Cooper (1901–1961) was a world-renowned success—a legend—although by 1956 his star had begun to wane. He had acted in films such as Sam Woods's adaptation of Ernest Hemingway's novel *For Whom the Bell Tolls* (1943) and Robert Aldrich's *Vera Cruz* (1954). Toward the end of his career, he starred with Audrey Hepburn in Billy Wilder's wonderfully poetic, black-and-white, Parisian film, *Love in the Afternoon* (1957).

The 6'3" giant was fifty at the time of filming, while Grace was eight months shy of twenty-two. Twenty-eight years lay between them, something that did not disturb Grace in the least. The majority of the men with whom she had affairs—affairs which lasted anywhere from a few weeks to several months—were at least twice as old as her, if not older. Although this is only one among several reasons for her choices, the unreciprocated, unerringly loyal love for her father Jack Kelly surely had an effect on her relationships with men.

Throughout her life, "Gracie" sought recognition and support, protection and security, from her larger-than-life father. However, Jack Kelly failed her in all of this, and as a result, she suffered an entire life trying time and time again to compensate for this lack of affection. This was especially recognizable in her relationships with much older men. "I prefer older men. They are more interesting. I like people who know more than me," as she once significantly commented about herself.[103] However, the wound never went away: "Her father must have been a monster," Robert Dornhelm supposed.[104]

During the stressful and tense filming of *High Noon*, Cooper's health was not good. He suffered from back pain, arthritis, and a stomach ulcer. Two months before filming began, he had an operation. His often uncompromising, almost painful physicality as Sheriff Will Kane in the final version of the film may reflect his actual state of health. Additionally, he was also psychologically plagued by his temporary separation from Rocky, his wife of many years. Cooper had married Veronica "Rocky" Balfe, who acted under the stage name Sandra Shaw, in 1933, and despite several tumultuous patches in their relationship, he remained married to her until his death in 1961. Another burden was the ending of Cooper's two-year affair with the young Broadway actress Patricia Neal with whom he had previously starred in King Vidor's *The Fountainhead* (1949) and Michael Curtiz's *Bright Leaf* (1950). This relationship had been both turbulent and somewhat destructive to both of their careers.[105] They had been "plunged, for more than two years, into a maelstrom of guilt, regret, fleeting happiness and underlying despair."[106]

In *High Noon*, Cooper, the myth of the upright man, came across as sorrowful and broken, and this was obvious to everyone on the set. Perhaps Grace Kelly seemed to him a perfect diversion. They spent evenings and weekends at the Chateau Marmont, or cruising through Hollywood in Cooper's silver Jaguar. Grace's younger sister Lizanne commented on their alleged affair: "Grace was infatuated with Gary Cooper. She was in awe of him, very star-struck."[107]

There was also a rumor that, during filming, Grace had an affair not only with Gary Cooper, but with director Fred Zinnemann as well.[108] In contrast to Alfred Hitchcock, neither Zinnemann, nor John Ford on the set of *Mogambo,* took special care with Grace; they gave her hardly any directorial direction and did not spend much time working on her portrayal. This rumored affair seems unlikely in light of the somewhat tense relationship between the director and the actress, in addition to Grace's noticeable reticence and reserve on set. Instead, the rumor seems more likely to be the product of the overactive imaginations of Hollywood sensationalists. Despite that, Hollywood author and friend of Cooper's, Robert Slatzer, both reported and corroborated the story of the two affairs. As Stanley Kramer quite explicitly commented, Grace seemed to deliberately keep to herself on set.[109]

Furthermore, Gene Lyons was waiting for her in Denver. In the summer of 1951, Grace had acted with him in ten performances, including T.S. Eliot's comedy *The Cocktail Party* (1949), over ten weeks for the Elitch Gardens Theatre. The work together was grueling but fun, and despite initial quarrels and some hesitation, Gene Lyons fell in love with Grace, having already separated from the actress Lee Grant. He was set to return to New York, to television, as was Grace.

The action in *High Noon* is played out against the melody of Dimitri Tiomkin's melancholy title song. Sometimes the instrumental version of the song is played, and sometimes Tex Ritter's sonorous rendition of the lyrics can be heard. Besides the guitar, the song is dominated by the unique, catchy rhythm of the Hammond Novachord, the first analog, polyphonic synthesizer, which was invented in 1939. Tiomkin's song, with its double connotations—that of individual fate combined with the fate of the community—functions as the theme song for *High Noon*:

> *Do not forsake me, oh my darlin'*
> *On this, our weddin' day*
> *Do not forsake me, oh my darlin'*
> *Wait, wait along*
> *(...)*
> *Oh, to be torn twixt love and duty*
> *Supposin' I lose my fair-haired beauty*
> *Look at that big hand move along*
> *Nearin' high noon*
> *(...)*
> *Do not forsake me, oh my darlin'*
> *You made that promise when we wed*
> *Do not forsake me, oh my darlin'*
> *Although you're grievin', I can't be leavin'*
> *Until I shoot Frank Miller dead*[110]

Born in Ukraine, Dimitri Tiomkin (1894–1979) immigrated to the United States in 1925, after completing his studies at the St. Petersburg Conservatory of Music. He created a timeless composition in his award-winning score for *High Noon*. Other musical scores by Tiomkin include those for King Vidor's *Duel in the Sun* (1946) and Howard Hawks's *Red River* (1948). The score for *Shadow of a Doubt* (1943) was Tiomkin's first composition for a Hitchcock film. Other compositions by Tiomkin were used in *Strangers on a Train* (1950), *I Confess* (1953), and Grace Kelly's first movie for Hitchcock, *Dial M for Murder*. "Do Not Forsake Me, Oh My Darlin'" was later translated into German under the title *"Sag, Warum willst Du von mir gehen."* Both Bruce Low and Peter Alexander produced recorded versions of this song.

In the first lines of the first verse, one can already feel the double layers of fear under which the protagonist now lives. There is the fear of being abandoned because he has sacrificed what he loves most for the communal good. But there is also the fear that the community, whose well-being he has protected for so long, will turn its back on him and likewise leave him. "Oh to be torn twixt love and duty" is the central focus of Ned Washington's lyrics. This short, simple sentiment describes the entire, complex dilemma in which Sheriff Will Kane finds himself throughout the entire movie. His young wife Amy also finds herself in the same predicament. This dilemma is, first of all, a moral one, but it is also a sociopolitical issue: the individual versus the group. Hadleyville represents a society that looks away as soon as something appears on the horizon that could possibly disrupt the existing system or threaten the established balance of power. Will Kane, as the individual, is ultimately abandoned by the community, experiencing a kind of excommunication. Thus, the threat comes not only from outside the community but also from the inside. Nonetheless, this is the figure who tries to represent the rights of the community and who is prepared to make a great personal sacrifice. Kane becomes the lonely outcast, an outlaw in the true sense of the word—the one outside of the law.

Several scenes in Fred Zinnemann's anti-western clearly reveal this loss: the double abandonment of the antihero, Will Kane. When Kane stands in Hadleyville's Main Street, directly in front of the sheriff's office, under the blistering sun, no one can be seen far and wide. Sweat beads on his careworn face and forehead under his black cowboy hat. The camera first shows him in a tight close-up. Only his face can be seen. Then, the camera pulls back slowly, and the scene in the frame grows larger. At the same time, the camera pans backward, and the crane then pulls up to gain a bird's eye view of the scene. Up there, the shot is held. It is a shot that shows the entire street and most of the town. This long camera sequence takes place in the seventieth minute of the film and lasts thirty-five seconds, without a single cut.

It is an extremely powerful image of a completely abandoned person. Across this cinematic scene lies a deep sadness. It is a picture of an individual who can rely on only himself. There is no one else there. This is Fred Zinnemann's tableau of desolation. *High Noon*'s entire visual vocabulary is very clear, bleak, and sober. It underlies a logical, formal reduction (thanks to cinematographer, Floyd Crosby) and rejects traditional aesthetics. The impression of absolute simplicity prevails, which is intentionally emphasized by the coarse-grained, black and white used in the film.

While writing *High Noon*, screenplay writer Carl Foreman had the trials of the dark McCarthy Era fresh in his mind. "*High Noon* was about Hollywood and no other place but Hollywood," Foreman commented later.[111] Arthur Miller's play *The Crucible* (1953) also pulled heavily from this chapter in American history.

These proceedings during the early 1950s resulted in an oppressive reality: The McCarthy Era was named after the Republican Senator Joseph Raymond McCarthy (1908–1957). It lasted for almost a decade from 1947 to 1956, and coincided with the early years of the Cold War. This period was also known as the Second Red Scare. It was colored by radical anti-Communism, which gave rise to the harsh persecution of both actual and suspected Communists, left-wing activists, intellectuals, and civil rights supporters.

Although Senator Joseph McCarthy was only politically active and powerful in the early 1950s, following the second trial of Franklin D. Roosevelt's adviser Alger Hiss, this entire era of paranoid persecutions was named after him. In this period, the US government tracked and persecuted the American Communist Party, as well as its leaders, members, and numerous supposed sympathizers and supporters. After both Harry Dexter White, a senior Treasury Department official, and Alger Hiss were accused of being Soviet agents, loyalty tests became obligatory for government officials and civil servants. FBI founder and director J. Edgar Hoover personally oversaw these examinations of government employees. Since that time, the McCarthy Era has become a metaphor for political persecution and the stigmatization of nonconformist thinkers. A modern-day witch hunt. A metaphor whose relevance is timeless.

Between 1938 and 1942, Carl Foreman (1914–1984) had been a member of the Communist Party. In April 1951, while he was working on the screenplay for *High Noon*, he was required to appear and testify before the House Un-American Activities Committee (HUAC), as were many of his Hollywood friends. However, the hearing was postponed and eventually rescheduled for September 24, during the filming of *High Noon*. In addition, exiled intellectuals, such as Thomas Mann, Hanns Eisler, and Bertolt Brecht, also had to testify before the HUAC. Charlie Chaplin fell under suspicion as well. While visiting Europe in 1952, he was denied a valid visa to return to the United States. He was forced to move to Switzerland, where he bought a house on Lake Geneva where he resided until his death. America's political landscape at this time was deeply ambivalent and rapidly changing. Distrust was rampant.

Cooper himself made a voluntary statement to the HUAC in October 1947 when they had begun to investigate Communist attitudes in Hollywood.[112] At that time, Cooper was a so-called "friendly witness," similar to Walt Disney, who voluntarily testified as well. Ironically, Disney even collaborated with the FBI as a contact, while he himself was under suspicion, a strange situation.

For screenplay author and co-producer Foreman, the crude witch hunt by HUAC was ultimately his undoing. He soon left his American homeland and immigrated to England.

Filmed between early September and mid-October, 1951—the honeymoon period of the McCarthy Era—*High Noon* clearly reflected the actual political events taking place around the country. There is the town of Hadleyville (Hollywood). There is the murderer Frank Miller (McCarthyism), who along with his three men wants to cause confusion and suffering. And there is Sheriff Will Kane, the guardian of the peace, who even without his tin star is willing to intercede on behalf of the townspeople. Lastly, there is Kane's wife, Amy. She is the one who tips the balance, deciding at the last moment to side with her husband by shooting one of the bandits in the back. The citizens of Hadleyville are the crowd, the masses, and ultimately, the paranoid mob. They withhold from Kane, their protector, all support and cooperation. Loyalty and integrity—even that of old companions and supporters—disintegrate suddenly. No one will stand by his side as deputy. Everyone is afraid, so instead they gather in the saloon and discuss everything to death. It is a form of denunciation. Prematurely, the barber orders four coffins in the back room of the carpenter's shop.

Soberly and clearly, *High Noon* reveals the public's loss of moral values. The witch hunts of the McCarthy era vibrate with this loss. In this respect, the film has never grown old. It is not merely a relic of its generation; it has not lost any of its effectiveness or power. In 1992, exactly forty years after the filming, Fred Zinnemann summarized its importance in a single sentence: "It is a story that still happens everywhere, every day."[113]

One thing that connects *High Noon* with Grace Kelly's next film *Mogambo* is that director John Ford conceived of a similar contrasting pair of women. In *High Noon*, Grace, with her fair, blonde Nordic appearance and white wedding dress and bonnet, contrasts with the black-haired, darker complexioned Katy Jurado, who only appears in black. In *Mogambo*, Grace and the darker, more voluptuous Ava Gardner embody this contrast. Despite this superficial distinction, the inhibited Amy Kane and the uninhibited Helen Ramirez, each in her own way, are both self-reliant, independent women who develop psychologically throughout the film, as is especially the case with Amy. The scene between the two women has led many to interpret the film through a feminist lens.[114]

The Mexican actress Katy Jurado, who was the only other woman on the set of this western drama besides Grace, recalled the filming of *High Noon*: "For Grace Kelly, it was her big break, and for me, it was my first American picture here in Hollywood. I was two years older than she was. I had seven years [of experience] making pictures in Mexico. There was something so different between Grace and I. We could not really explain [why] we could not be very close. But I could see [that she was] a girl with a lot of dignity and a lot of character, because she wanted to be somebody in movies and she worked very hard on that picture. She looked weak and very tiny—but she was a very strong person. I think she was one of the strongest movie stars I worked with. She knew what she wanted—and she did it."[115]

Several months passed between the opening of *High Noon* and Grace's arrival in Africa in late fall 1952 to film *Mogambo* with Clark Gable. During this respite, she spent part of the time at her apartment in New York and part of it in Philadelphia and Ocean City with her family. She acted in a few plays: the comedy *To Be Continued*, which first played in Boston and then in Broadway's Booth Theater (as is often the custom); and *For Love or Money* and *Accent on Youth* in a playhouse in her hometown. She also did a few live television spots. This was the last summer in which she spent significant time in Philadelphia.

She also spent time with Gene Lyons (1921–1974) in New York. Together they attended the premiere of *High Noon* in July 1952. It is clear that Lyons and Grace were both convinced that she was not meant for Hollywood, which explains why she again turned to theater. At this time, Lyons was mainly working on Broadway and live television. They studied their lines together, helping each other prepare for auditions and parts. Their private and professional lives were a seamless fit. Grace's connection with Gene Lyons was not greatly different from the one she had had with Don Richardson. Their relationship was close, intense—they had been very much in love with each other since their time in Denver.

However attractive he was, the eight-years-older, Irish Lyons had a second love—whiskey—as had been the case with the title character in Fitzgerald's play *The Rich Boy*. And just as the female lead, played by Grace, rejects him despite their feelings for each other, over time Grace increasingly turned away from Gene. She once again confirmed (and not for the last time either) the critical objections and fears of her parents. Through his alcohol addiction, Gene Lyons destroyed his promising career. His last part was a supporting role in the television series *Ironside* (1967–1974) before he died at the young age of 53 on July 8, 1974. As Don Richardson before him and Oleg Cassini after him, he was one of Grace's first romantic partners.

In Spring 1952, probably in April, Grace received a phone call just as she was leaving her apartment in the Manhattan House at the corner of 66th Street and 3rd Avenue. She was on her way to an acting lesson with Sanford Meisner. Meisner was a renowned acting teacher at the Neighborhood Playhouse School of Theatre, where he taught between 1935 and 1990. His career resembled that of Lee Strasberg and Stella Adler with whom he had worked at the Group Theatre, an independent theater group founded in 1931. All three were prominent New York practitioners of the naturalist theories of Russian acting teacher and director Konstantin Sergeievich Stanislavski. However, the implementation and approach of the so-called Meisner Technique differed substantially from Strasberg's method acting. Beginning in fall 1951, Grace took lessons from Meisner several times a week in order to become more self-assured and to improve her acting skills—especially after the disappointment she felt toward what she considered to be an immature portrayal of Amy in *High Noon*.

The unexpected call took Grace by surprise. It was an invitation to do a screen test for *Taxi* (1953) that very day. For this reason, despite previous preparation for the part, she was not ready for the moment. She was neither dressed nor styled for the role. Instead of a dress and her signature white gloves, she was made up for a casual gathering with friends in a blouse, a tweed skirt, and flats. She had no makeup on, and her hair was tightly pulled back. This was how she presented herself to director Gregory Ratoff, who was shooting the film for Twentieth Century-Fox. Ultimately, Grace did not receive the role of Mary Turner in *Taxi*. The part was given—against Ratoff's wishes (he wanted Grace at all costs)—to an English actress named Constance Smith, who was under contract with Fox at the time. The film was not a success. However, the black-and-white audition tape must have been impressive, because it soon helped Grace book several roles of incomparably greater significance. Due to the internal studio viewing of the *Taxi* auditions, Grace was hired by John Ford for *Mogambo* and afterward by Alfred Hitchcock for *Dial M for Murder*.

Mogambo
(1953)

> Mogambo *had three things that interested me: John Ford,*
> *Clark Gable, and a trip to Africa with expenses paid.*
> *If* Mogambo *had been made in Arizona I wouldn't have*
> *done it.*
> —*Grace Kelly*[116]

In 1924, a new Hollywood studio was founded: Metro-Goldwyn-Mayer (MGM). For a quarter of a century, Louis B. Mayer was an extremely influential studio head until the early 1950s, when he was replaced by Dore Schary.

Grace Kelly's fairly disastrous seven-year contract with MGM fell during Schary's time. In October 1952, Grace signed the contract that in the coming years would become a regrettable pain in the neck. It was John Ford's project *Mogambo* (and Ford's enthusiasm for Grace's color test for the project) that finally motivated her to sign for the first and last time with a studio. Until then she had consistently refused to sign a contract because she did not want to limit herself to a single studio or group, and she was very wary of multiyear obligations.

However, before signing the contract Grace presented to the studio her conditions—a move that was very unusual at this time, especially for such a young, unknown actress, having only acted in a single supporting film role. The studio executives soon knew that they were dealing with an unconventional, autonomous individual. Things would not be easy with this girl. During the September 1952 negotiations between her future studio, MGM, and her agency, MCA, Grace dictated that every other year she would be allowed a break so that she could have the opportunity to return to the theater. She also insisted on keeping her residence in New York, contrary to the usual requirement to move to Los Angeles or Hollywood where she could be summoned, and controlled, at the whim of the studio. And in an extraordinary move for Hollywood, Dore Schary's MGM accepted her conditions.

Once the contract was signed, Grace received a starting salary of $750 per week—more than she had ever earned as a model.

The Metro-Goldwyn-Mayer British Studios Ltd. in London was responsible for the production of *Mogambo*. This meant that *Mogambo* was actually a British production and Grace would need a work permit, which caused a roadblock for her involvement in the project. Furthermore, there was resistance among some of the British MGM executives to the casting of yet another American in the film. Despite this and some protest by the British trade union, Grace was ultimately permitted to work on the project. Excepting Gable and Gardner in the two main roles, the Dublin-born Denis O'Dea in the role of the Catholic bush priest, and the local and indigenous tribesmen cast in the movie, all the supporting roles were filled with English actors. Except for Grace, of course.

The filming under John Ford lasted four long months from the turn of the year through the entire winter: November 17, 1952, to March 20, 1953. Outdoor scenes were shot in eastern African territories, which during the 1950s were still primarily British colonies: Kenya (Nairobi, Thika, Naivasha Lake), Tanzania (Kagera River, Serengeti Desert), and Uganda (Isoila). A few scenes were also filmed in the French Congo, also known as the Congo Democratic Republic (Okalataka). Indoor scenes, which began filming in February 1953, were located in the MGM Studios in the southern English town of Borehamwood. Founded in 1914, the Elstree Studio Lot is located north of London in the County of Hertfordshire.

For the outdoor scenes, the film team, actors, technicians, doctors, and cooks all traveled to Africa. They were a group composed of several hundred people (estimates range from 300 to 475). On site, there were several dozen tents, a hospital, a restaurant, a leisure tent with a dartboard and a ping-pong table, and a portable movie theater with two 16 mm projectors, which showed a different movie every day. In addition, a landing strip was built for the pilots who were transporting technical equipment and food from Nairobi. This production operated at a scale typical of only Hollywood's most monumental films. Home base was the New

Stanley Hotel in Nairobi, where the actors, director, and various crew members stayed.

Everyone met each other here at the New Stanley Hotel. Grace was by far, at the age of twenty-three, the youngest of the entire cast of *Mogambo*. Gardner and Gable already knew each other, since they had worked together on the films *The Hucksters* (1947) and *Lone Star* (1952). Filming *Mogambo* was stressful, lengthy, and complicated; it brought together actors with extremely different, sometimes clashing, sensibilities.

"*Mogambo* is a soulful remake of *Red Dust*."[117] *Red Dust* (1932) had been made exactly twenty years before under the direction of Victor Fleming for MGM. In that movie, Clark Gable played the part of an adventurer caught between two vastly different women. One of them, played by Jean Harlow, is a brash, provocative blonde. In Ford's remake this part was acted by Ava Gardner. The other, played by Mary Astor, corresponded to Grace Kelly's role. In *Red Dust*, Gable manages a rubber plantation; in *Mogambo* he is a big game hunter and trapper. He manages his own wild game reserve and lodge, and resembles—in both his manner and clothing—Ernest Hemingway. The location of the story was changed from Indochina to Africa.

Both screenplays were written by John Lee Mahin and based on Wilson Collison's play, although *Mogambo* was enhanced with elements of Hemingway's style and themes, as borrowed from his short story, "The Short Happy Life of Francis Macomber" (1936).

John Ford employed two cameramen: Robert L. Surtees and the Englishman Frederick A. Young. During the course of *Mogambo*, John Ford had Surtees take several close-up shots of Grace Kelly during the especially emotional scenes. These scenes relate to Linda Nordley's (Grace Kelly's role) growing attachment for Victor Marswell (Clark Gable), and the close-up shots of Grace's face reveal Linda's inner conflict. One of these scenes takes place on the veranda of Marswell's lodge. After getting caught in a downpour while walking by herself in the jungle, Linda is brought back to the lodge by Marswell. On the way back, she briefly leans back against a tree; sweat and rain run down her neck. She stands there in a short-sleeved blouse and a gray skirt, topped by a brightly patterned Hermés handkerchief, and gazes at Marswell with astonishing directness. When they finally reach the door of the veranda, behind which is the Nordleys' room, Marswell suddenly grabs the handkerchief from her neck—a uniquely explicit moment.

Another scene between Clark Gable and Grace takes place at the top of a waterfall on the riverbank. Here they kiss, and Grace clings closely to the much taller Gable. Despite the arguable triviality of the plot, these are scenes of latent eroticism, an eroticism that can be felt throughout the entire love-triangle drama. The penetrating look with which Grace responds to Gable's actions, the intense gaze of her wide blue eyes, is demanding and full of a cool lasciviousness.

Bound by John Lee Mahin's screenplay, Grace had to deliver some unfortunately banal lines, such as: "I didn't know that monkeys could climb trees," when the expedition group reaches the forest in which the gorillas live and she sees them in person for the first time.[118] Ava Gardner had markedly different lines.

However, *Mogambo* was not an insignificant achievement in Grace's film career. In 1954, she was nominated for an Oscar, as Best Supporting Actress, and a Golden Globe.

John Ford (1894–1973), Grace Kelly's third director, is a legend in the American film world. Ford's career began in 1917, during the early years of film production, with his thirty-minute, silent movie *The Tornado,* and ended with *Seven Women* in 1966. Overall he made 112 feature-length films, along with numerous mid-length and short films. It would be accurate to call him one of the greatest western directors of all time. Films such as *Rio Grande* (1950), *The Quiet Man* (1952), *The Searchers* (1956), and *The Horse Soldiers* (1959) are not only important standouts in Ford's body of work, but are also considered classics in the canon of cinematic masterpieces.

A flat cap, cigar or pipe, glasses, and an eye patch—these are the hallmarks of the notoriously bad-tempered director, who rarely gave direction and who did not treat his actors with great respect. In the western genre he tended to work with the same actors (John Wayne, for example, was a favorite) on multiple films. Thus, he had even less experience dealing with actresses. Grace had difficulties with the fifty-eight-year-old director, similar to the ones she faced with Fred Zinnemann while filming *High Noon*. Zinnemann too had little use for giving direction or even speaking at all. The only difference was that Ford was much more impolite and gruff than Zinnemann had been. Some on the set even described the ill-tempered Ford as a tyrant and an egomaniac.

In his autobiography, the actor Donald Sinden, who played Grace Kelly's very British and oblivious husband, described how John Ford directed him and Grace on their first day of filming:

> Linda and John Nordly arrive. The steamer docks, and on the riverbank stands Victor Marswell to greet the anthropological couple. Without a single rehearsal, without any kind of direction or discussion about how their characters should act or what they could be feeling, Grace and Sinden find themselves on the deck of the steamer while Gable waits on the wooden pier.
>
> Then John Ford's voice is heard over the loudspeaker: "Grace—Donald—get below deck. OK. Donald—come on deck. Look around at the scenery. Call Grace. Put your arm around her. Point out a giraffe over on your right. Get your camera out—quickly. Photograph it—the giraffe. Smile at him, Grace. Grace—look at that hippopotamus on your left. Get Donald to photograph it. A crocodile slides into the water. You're scared, Grace—you're scared! OK. You're coming onto the pier. Look around. What's in store for you? Natives run down to meet you. OK! OK! Cut! Print it!"[119]

Here is the plot of *Mogambo*: Eloise Y. Kelly (Ava Gardner), a glamorous New York dancer and showgirl, is invited to travel to Africa by an Indian maharajah. However, no one awaits her there, as the maharajah has already left. She goes somewhat unwillingly to Kenya to the lodge and wild animal reserve of big game hunter, Victor Maswell (Clark Gable). At first, he is not at all happy about this unexpected visitor. Through clinched teeth,

95

Marswell offers the prima donna one of his guest rooms. Eloise quickly falls head over heels in love with the attractive loner. Marswell's corpulent, cheerful comrade and business partner John Brown-Pryce, "Brownie," (Philip Stainton) recognizes this at once. However, Marswell is not taken with his guest's direct-ness, and so he sticks Eloise on the steamer to take her home. In the meantime, the British Nordleys arrive at Marswell's lodge: the anthropologist Donald Nordley (Donald Sinden) and his wife Linda (Grace Kelly). Victor Marswell is immediately fascinated by the young blonde woman and feels attracted to her. Her distant gentility stands in stark contrast to Eloise's blunt vulgarity. Before too long, Eloise Kelly shows up again on Marswell's veranda with her mountain of luggage, but this time her dress is muddy and damp. The steamer got stuck. She is delighted beyond words. As Leon Boltchak (Eric Pohlmann), another employee of Marswell's, notes: now there are two women staying at the lodge. This has never happened before. There is something ironic in the fact that throughout the entire movie, Ava Gardner is called by her character's last name: "Kelly"!

The dynamic between the lodge's residents is predictable: Eloise is increasingly jealous of her competition, Linda, and Marswell finds himself caught between the two women. After Donald Nordley recovers from the illness he contracted after his arrival, he arranges for an expedition into the jungle to study, film, and record the behavior of gorillas. Marswell is not thrilled by Nordley's proposal, since he knows the difficulties and risks that go along with such an expedition. In addition, the aging wild game hunter feels guilty toward Nordley for the obviously growing attraction between him and Linda. Marswell and Linda meet in secret, but Eloise sees them. An attempt to clear things up with Nordley fails when Marswell sees Nordley's total clue-lessness. Marswell is unwilling to confront the work-absorbed husband with the truth. As the situation threatens to escalate, Eloise sets up a one-on-one, rather inebriated conversation in Marswell's tent. Linda then storms into the tent, deeply hurt and despairing, grabs Marswell's gun, and shoots him in the shoul-der. With this shocking turn of events, Linda returns to her husband, full of regret, and Marswell and Eloise finally become a couple.

The conflict between the protagonists represents the classic love triangle trope. A similar drama played out in real life: Donald Sinden only had eyes for Grace Kelly, who had clearly fallen for Clark Gable. However, Gable was only interested in Ava Gardner. When Gardner rejected him, Gable turned to Grace for a short time. Grace's friend Rita Gam spoke of "a romantic night in the middle of the jungle."[120] Just like in the film, the romantic entanglements would lead to confusion and hurt.

Mogambo was the first time that MGM costume designer Helen Rose and Grace Kelly worked together. Later, Rose was responsible for two other MGM productions in which Grace appeared: *Green Fire* (1954) and *High Society*. Rose also designed the wedding dress that Grace wore to her wedding in Monaco. In *Mogambo*, Grace wore short-sleeved blouses and long skirts, pants and safari jackets. There was something charming in the fact that she, in her pale uniform-like khaki costumes, was the only one to wear a safari hat.

In one evening scene, during which the three men hold a dinner in honor of their three guests, Grace as Linda wears a violet evening gown that resembles, in shape, the red dress she would wear in her subsequent movie, *Dial M for Murder*. Short-sleeved with a low neckline and a long pleated skirt, she attracts all eyes to her in this evening gown. During the course of the supper, she sets off a playful, ambiguous conversation between Marswell and the envious Eloise. Although Linda is the one whose appearance has prompted a turning point in the plot, she says very little.

During the time of the filming, an American by the name of Rupert Allan was staying in London, having traveled there for *Look* magazine to cover the coronation of Queen Elizabeth II. One evening, after a day of filming, Allen was introduced to Grace in the London Savoy Hotel by Morgan Hudgins, the press agent for MGM Studios. He would later become Grace's longtime personal PR adviser and eventually the Monegasque General Consul and Ambassador in Los Angeles.

Allen recalled a significant event that epitomized Grace's romantic dreaminess, one that was later told to him by Clark Gable about the filming of *Mogambo*: "She turned to him and he saw that she was crying. And he said, 'Why are you crying, Grace?' And she said, 'It's so beautiful. I'm reading *The Snows of Kilamanjaro* by Hemingway. And I looked up and I was just reading about this crazy leopard I think they found way up in the snows of this high mountain—the highest mountain in Africa. And I looked up from my book, thinking about what a beautiful picture it was—Hemingway. And then I saw a lion walking along the seashore. And it was just too beautiful.' "[121]

As Metro-Goldwyn-Mayer proudly announced, "*mogambo*" means "passion" in Swahili. However, this word can also carry the connotation of danger. Both of these meanings are applicable to John Ford's adventure epic. Among the most visually spectacular scenes—especially considering when the movie was filmed—are the scenes involving animals, which were filmed by the second unit camera team under the guidance of legendary big game hunter Frank "Bunny" Allen. Besides the scenes of giraffes, elephants, hippopotamuses, and panthers, the high points of these extraordinary wild animal shots are the extensive scenes of the gorilla area. Described as "an evocative adventure film with striking animal shots which capture masterfully the jungle milieu and atmosphere," *Mogambo* is most certainly very different from Ford's mostly western repertoire.[122]

On October 1, 1953, *Mogambo* premiered in New York's Radio City Music Hall. On October 9, it opened in cinemas across the country and went on to be a box office success. The film was both a financial and critical triumph; it was nominated as Best Film of 1954 for the renowned British BAFTA awards. Above all, the African drama was a great success for Ava Gardner. She celebrated her thirtieth birthday during filming, on December 24, 1952, and soon found herself at the peak of her acting career. Previously she had made *The Snows of Kilimanjaro* (1952) under director Henry King, and she would go on next to make Joseph L. Mankiewicz's *The Barefoot Contessa* (1954).

For *Mogambo*, she was nominated as Best Actress for the 1954 Academy Awards.

At the time of the filming, Clark Gable (1901–1960) was fifty-one years old. Since 1924, he had acted in a variety of classics, including Frank Capra's *It Happened One Night* (1934) and, most famously, Victor Fleming's *Gone with the Wind* (1939). The role of Rhett Butler in Fleming's monumental adaptation of Margaret Mitchell's novel was undoubtedly the role of his lifetime. In 1954, his contract with MGM ended, and *Mogambo* was his next to last film, followed only by Gottfried Reinhardt's espionage drama *Betrayed* (1954). The studio did not wish to extend his contract. The affront against this star served as an unmistakable indication that, in the eyes of MGM, his market value was sinking. Furthermore, the charmer's private life was at a low point. He increasingly drew back from society and was often in a bad mood. From this point on, Gable was no longer bound to any studio, and on subsequent films he began to require a share of the film profits in addition to his normal salary. As a result, he became one of the highest paid actors of the 1950s and consistently rejected the contract renewal offers made by a regretful MGM. Gable's next film was *Soldier of Fortune* (1955), which he made for Twentieth Century-Fox under director Edward Dmytryk. Gable himself proposed Grace as his costar, but by that time she was already committed elsewhere. Instead, Susan Hayward was eventually cast in the role.

Eccentric both on and off the camera, Ava Gardner was visited several times during the filming by her husband Frank Sinatra, including Christmas in 1952. Both of them, as well as Grace and Gable, celebrated Christmas together, with Sinatra playing, and singing, the part of a fully costumed Santa Claus. Time and time again, there were emotional scenes and fierce arguments between the married couple, with Ava Gardner arguing especially loudly. Sometimes plates and cups flew through the air, and the atmosphere in the Gardner-Sinatra tent (each cast and crew member had his or her own tent) was a sure sign that an emotional drama was playing itself out. While Ava was on set, Sinatra was bored. New tensions and differences were constantly developing, ones that the team and the actors could not help but witness. To Grace's dismay, her tent was set up right next to Gardner's. Furthermore, Sinatra's jealousy appeared to be justified since his wife had allegedly had an affair with Frank "Bunny" Allen, who was responsible for the handling of the wild animals on set. To make things worse, during Sinatra's visit he was impatiently waiting for word on his casting as Angelo Maggio in Fred Zinnemannn's Columbia production of *From Here to Eternity* (1953). When he finally got the role after New Year's, his flagging career was given a boost. The marriage between Ava Gardner and Frank Sinatra, however, finally ended in 1957, after lasting six years.

Generally laconic and uncomfortable, director Ford had the following to say about his female star Ava Gardner: "She was an experienced actress. She was upset over Sinatra, but she did the work."[123] One time she caused an uproar when she appeared naked in a canvas bath tub in front of the native workers. In reaction, she ran stark naked through the camp, laughing. As trouble between Sinatra and Gardner escalated—although they had spent their first day married on safari—and as both Grace and Ava wooed Clark Gable in front of the camera, the two very different women became friends behind the scenes. A few years later, between January and March of 1956, Grace and Frank Sinatra would appear together in *High Society*, the last film of her artistic career.

Rumors of an affair between Grace Kelly and Clark Gable—some even spoke of marriage—were everywhere in the wake of *Mogambo*'s premiere.[124] This was a media development that would be repeated over and over again during Grace Kelly's acting career. Grace was quite displeased with this dark side to fame, which troubled her anew each time it happened. She hardly knew how to dispell the growing media attention to her family in Philadelphia. While Grace valued discretion and privacy, the press was interested in every conceivable, salacious detail of her private life. There was even talk of Grace proposing to Gable. In terms of actual events, the situation between Grace and Clark Gable was far from this fantasy: "She had a flirtation with Gable."[125] This account (which very much downplayed the affair) was given by her future fiance, Oleg Cassini, with whom Grace was romantically involved in 1954 and 1955. On the other hand, Grace's young sister Lizanne provided this commentary: "Grace was crazy about Clark."[126]

Gable, the "King of Hollywood," enjoyed an unsavory reputation as a notorious ladies' man. On the other hand, during the *Mogambo* filming, Clark Gable was in the midst of divorce proceedings from his fourth wife, Lady Sylvia Ashley, who had once been married to Douglas Fairbanks. Although unsubstantiated even to the present day, the story is that Grace fell in love with the graying Hollywood star that she had long admired, who was thirty years older than she. They supposedly had a short affair. She frequently accompanied him on the safaris he took on their free days, choosing to wake up extremely early for these while the other actors slept in to recover from the stress of filming. According to Donald Sinden, "They were together most of the time."[127] During the filming, Grace called Gable "Ba," which is Swahili for "father." Grace was the only one on set who already spoke some Swahili when the filming began. In the New Stanley Hotel in Nairobi, she would often order the actors' meals in the native language.

In reference to her filming in Africa, Grace once made the ambiguous statement that when one spends months in the African bush, there is so much that one cannot do there. Whatever the case, after the conclusion of months of filming in Africa, the situation was different. At the Elstree Studios near London, the inside scenes took place in a distinctly different atmosphere. In England, Gable acted decidedly cool toward Grace, who was inevitably hurt and irritated. However, since he was in the middle of divorce proceedings, he wanted to avoid any whiff of scandal in London where the press was harder to avoid. He acted friendly yet distant and professional, nothing more. In addition, Ma Kelly arrived from Philadelphia in February 1953. For three whole weeks, she kept an eye on her twenty-three-year-old daughter. The headlines about a possible affair between her Gracie and the twice-as-old Gable had not failed to reach Philadelphia. Margaret Majer-Kelly also wanted to personally meet the "King of Hollywood."

At the conclusion of *Mogambo*'s filming, Grace's agent Jay Kanter invited her to his wedding, which occurred on April 15, 1953, in New York. He introduced Grace to his new wife, Judith Balabin Quine. Three years later, Judith was one of Grace's six bridesmaids. The two women would remain friends until Grace's death.

In 1953, Grace again acted in a live television performance. The NBC program *The Way of the Eagle* aired live on June 7, 1953. Grace costarred with the French actor Jean-Pierre Aumont. Later they would grow close when they both visited Aumont's homeland, in Paris and in Cannes. However, for now there was no relationship for Aumont and Grace beyond the television stage. Six days after the program, Grace flew from New York to Los Angeles. In that same week, Grace Kelly was introduced to Alfred Hitchcock in Hollywood. The *Master of Suspense* was searching for his next heroine. She was supposed to be blonde and to exude a coolness that masked an inner fire and glow.

In terms of her film career, this would be the meeting of her life.

—Alfred Hitchcock
"A lot of people think I'm a monster."

There was no dark side.
—Patricia Hitchcock[128]

Alfred Hitchcock once described his childhood: "At family gatherings, I sat in my corner and said nothing. I looked around and observed a lot. So I've always been and so I am today. I was anything but communicative. I was always alone. I cannot remember having had a playmate."[129]

The primal emotion of fear runs through the entire life and work of Alfred Hitchcock. Next to love, it is the most basic existential motivation of all people and one of Hitchcock's central artistic themes. This feeling accompanied him his entire life.

As a boy, Alfred was a loner. Already at a young age, he was acquainted with the feelings of being alone, of not being understood, of being the outsider. He experienced fear during his childhood in the East London suburb of Leytonstone. Perhaps it is not surprising that later he sought to frighten viewers around the world.

There is a story that deals with trust, or rather distrust, which, according to Alfred Hitchcock, took place when he was six years old. Young Alfred loved to take the new public buses into London. He also enjoyed studying the schedule of the buses and the horse-drawn streetcars that were replaced in 1906 with new electric streetcars. He was also intrigued by city maps and ship routes. (In 1939, when he immigrated to America with his wife Alma and daughter Patricia, he memorized a map of New York City.) During one of his exploratory trips through London in 1905, evening came, and he discovered that he did not have enough money for his return trip. Forced to walk, he did not reach home until 9:00 p.m. His father, an "excitable man," opened the door.[130] Wordlessly, William Hitchcock handed his youngest son a piece of paper and carried him directly to a nearby police station. There

Alfred handed the paper to an officer named Watson. The policeman read the paper handed to him by little Alfred and promptly put the boy into a jail cell, locking him up for about five minutes. There the local cop delivered to young Alfred the now famous line: "This is what we do to naughty boys."[131]

This prison anecdote is legendary; Alfred Hitchcock told it repeatedly throughout his life, with almost notorious obsession, at every possible opportunity. There were slight variations, such as the length of his time in the cell, and the story was always accompanied by an appraising grin focused on his listener. In his next-to-last public appearance ever, to accept a Life Achievement Award from the American Film Institute on March 7, 1979, in Beverly Hills, under painful physical stress and pumped full of medication, he told his best version of the police anecdote. French director and Hitchcock expert Claude Chabrol once reflected on the story: "He repeatedly told this prison story. At the beginning, [he was locked up for a whole] night, then it was three hours. He changed it markedly in order to show that it was a game."[132] Whether or not Hitchcock had fabricated the story, something about it had to be true because he spent his entire life painfully afraid of the police. Policemen, as well as prisoners and prison cells, appear over and over again in his films as a recognizable motif.

The life of Alfred Hitchcock (1899–1980), arguably the most important film director of his generation, was a life lived in and among fears, defined by neuroses and obsessions. There is no doubt that he was a genius. He was shy and withdrawn, fearful and uncertain, some say. Gentle and kind, affable and eloquent, well-read and educated, polite and always humorous. A British gentleman. Others say he was a monster, that he took diabolical pleasure in terrifying others or at least in frightening them in macabre, twisted ways. He supposedly felt no empathy for others and had no friends; the only person he truly trusted was his wife Alma Reville. Even his relationship with his only daughter Patricia was allegedly not a simple one. He was a multifaceted, complex man—difficult to understand and analyze, whether in terms of his ambiguity or in terms of his cinematic thrills and nightmares. He once commented on himself, playfully smug and self-deprecating: "People think I'm a monster—they really do! I've been told that!"[133]

On June 8, 1972, during one of his US television appearances on the legendary 1970s program *The Dick Cavett Show*, the master corrected the moderator Dick Cavett, who interviewed him in depth on his life's work. The correction came in reference to his famous, rumored statement that "actors are cattle." Sitting stoically in his chair, the man known by the entire world as "Hitch" had the following to say: "Well, I think at the time I was accused of calling actors cattle, and I said that I would never say such an unfeeling rude thing about actors at all. What I probably said was that all actors should be treated like cattle...In a nice way, of course."[134] He then smiled slyly, almost imperceptibly, quite pleased with himself. Nothing seemed to worry him—even exposing his industry to ridicule on live television. The amused public laughed and applauded, loud and long. Hitchcock was, at his core, an entertainer.

Alfred Hitchcock made fifty-three movies in about fifty years— an extensive and influential body of cinematic work that continues to influence generations of directors and other artists. His films are famous and familiar worldwide. They live in the collective consciousness of popular culture and are honored members of the global canon; these include *Rebecca* (1940), *Notorious* (1946), *Strangers on a Train* (1951), *Vertigo* (1950), *Psycho* (1960), and *The Birds* (1963). At some point, Hitchcock became a universally recognized brand for both himself as a person and his creative work.

During the first half of the 1950s, Alfred Hitchcock made three films with Grace Kelly: *Dial M for Murder*, *Rear Window*, and *To Catch a Thief.* This period was one of his most radiantly productive periods, one that he considered a high point: "At the time...I was in top form."[135]

Hitchcock once said that before he even started filming, he had finished a movie in his mind. In contrast, the filming was a necessity that he would have gladly spared himself. These are films of fear. Nightmarish cinematic imagery. "Mental pictures," is how

French philosopher Gilles Deleuze described the admirable brilliance of Alfred Hitchcock's films.

Not inconsequential are also two television series of the late 1950s and early 1960s. He always delivered both the prologue and epilogue of the thirty- to sixty-minute episodes himself. His extremely bizarre, absurd manner, as well as his cult-status cameos in his own projects, contributed to his enormous popularity and clout. The public waited anxiously for each of his regular cameos, so he had to place these early in his films so that the viewers would pay attention to the plot and stop watching for his appearance. This is a singular phenomenon in all film history; no other director is as publically recognizable as Hitchcock. Everyone thinks that they know something about Alfred Hitchcock, about the man in a proper black suit with a white shirt and black tie. This Victorian facade helped him maintain an appearance of the sense of control and security that eluded him internally, despite his incredible fame and his immense worldwide success.

In his wonderful seventy-five-minute interview on *The Dick Cavett Show*, Hitchcock told a humorous story about his deep-seated obsession with fear (his humor always held a kernel of truth): "I think my mother scared me when I was three months old. You see, she said BOO! It gave me the hiccups. And she apparently was very satisfied. All mothers do it, you know. That's how fear starts in everyone."[136]

Alfred Hitchcock, the inventor of suspense and the MacGuffin (a driving element in a plot that is ultimately revealed as arbitrary and irrelevant), was a deeply lonely person, an outsider everywhere he went. He was a man who trusted few, who entrenched himself behind his wit and macabre taste. He was an extremely sensitive person on the inside; a calm and stoic Buddha on the outside. He spent his entire life afraid of the world and of people, and, not least of all, afraid of himself. In contrast, he had also once said, "People like the feeling of fear, when they know that they need not fear for themselves." This is precisely what his films are built on as they subtly manipulate the viewers.

The following two anecdotes reveal Hitchcock's unique sense of humor. In the early 1950s, the Hitchcocks had been living in

Hollywood for a decade. Although he was not the most sociable of people, occasionally Hitchcock would host a small, elegant party. Two such parties remain legendary examples of his quirky sense of humor: "I once gave a dinner-party where all the food was blue. Everything was blue... It was a full meal, blue chicken soup, blue trout, blue chicken, blue ice cream, and when you broke open your roll the bread was blue inside. And I did not comment on that at all." "I also gave a dinner-party for my wife, at Chasen's Restaurant, where they had a back garden in those days. And we had a table for 14 people. And I got central casting to give me an aristocratic old lady. We had her hair done beautifully, dressed her well, and sat her at the head of the table. And the guests arrived and said, 'Who is the old lady?' And I said 'I don't know, I never met her before.'"[137]

When Alfred Hitchcock died on April 29, 1980, at his home in Bel Air of kidney failure and heart disease—after years of depression, alcoholism, illness, feelings of being misunderstood, and existential weariness—the world lost a cinematic visionary.[138]

Dial M for Murder
(1954)

> *The collaboration with Hitchcock was a fantastic*
> *experience... As an actress I learned an incredible amount*
> *about the development of motion pictures. Hitchcock gave*
> *me a whole lot of confidence.*
> *—Grace Kelly*[139]

> *My mother was both influenced and touched by Hitchcock.*
> *They were very close.*
> *—Prince Albert II of Monaco*[140]

Dial M for Murder introduced Grace Kelly to Alfred Hitchcock. It would become the most important collaboration of both their careers. A longtime, stable, and respectful friendship grew from this project, one that lasted through to the end of their lives.

Hitchcock made three films with Grace: *Dial M for Murder* (1954), *Rear Window* (1954), and *To Catch a Thief* (1955).

Of the eleven films that Grace Kelly made during her unfortunately short acting career (1950 and 1956), the three Hitchcock films are without a doubt her finest, most important works. Each film received great acclaim. As an actress, Grace Kelly was never more captivating or beguiling than she was in *To Catch a Thief*. This intimate picture, filmed on Hollywood's largest film set, could be considered the epitome of their collaboration. It marked the artistic, creative pinnacle of Hitchcock's directorial career, although other significant works would follow: *Vertigo*, *Psycho*, *The Birds*, *Marnie* (1964), and *Frenzy* (1972). For Grace, working under Hitchcock on *To Catch a Thief* resulted in her finally coming fully into her own as an actress. She projected complete self-assurance, composure, and a distinct elegance that completely discarded all immaturity and naïveté.

Alfred Hitchcock and Grace Kelly first met during the second week of June 1953 in Burbank, Los Angeles. The appointment was set up by MCA Agent Jay Kanter. It must have been a very special moment, full of expectations. On that June morning, Grace Kelly, in any case, was extremely nervous.[141] She was timid, perhaps even a little afraid. "I could not think of anything to say to him. In a horrible way it seemed funny to have my brain turn to stone."[142]

She had just turned twenty-three, and now she was being introduced to a world famous director, who only a few weeks after this introduction turned fifty-four, on August 13, 1953. Hitchcock called himself Hitch. He had done this since June 1919, when at the young age of twenty he published a Kafkaesque, nightmarish short story titled "Gas" in *The Henley* magazine under this name. Already in his youth, he had adamantly rejected his other nickname, "Cocky." This reveals the extreme ambivalence that he had his entire life to the two syllables of his last name. "Hitch" means to hook or knot onto something. As an adjective, "cocky" implies arrogance. In later years, he gleefully instructed new coworkers, even actresses, when they hesitated at what to call him: "Call me Hitch—hold the Cock!" This was one of his classic, ambiguous jokes, which masked his longtime sexual abstinence and asceticism.

Even in Grace Kelly's presence, while working together for the first time on the filming of *Dial M for Murder* in the Warner Studios in Burbank, he would make the occasional innuendo or tell a naughty story. Once, when he was standing with Ray Milland, he turned to Grace after telling Milland an off-color joke and said, gleefully, "Are you shocked, Miss Kelly?" She responded: "Oh no, Mr. Hitchcock. I attended Catholic girls' school. I've been hearing such things since I was thirteen."[143] That tickled the humorous master very much.

"Hitch was wonderful. He was very secretive and mysterious. He was very shy," Grace recalled.[144] The ties between the two of them quickly became tighter, although boundaries were never crossed, despite the avid claims made to the contrary. The rotund, relatively unattractive director making untoward advances on his extremely attractive, seemingly delicate, thirty-year-younger main actress, would have fit the stereotype that many assumed Hitchcock fulfilled. He was seen by some as an obsessive misogynist, who

110

futilely and with growing despair tried to become involved with his string of blonde actresses.

However, he did not do this. To the contrary, for him, Grace Kelly was a protégé. Unlike Fred Zinnemann and John Ford who did not pay much attention to her on their sets, Hitchcock contributed much to her career. She valued and applied his guidance over the coming years through to the making of her final film, *High Society*. "With Hitch, everything was different. He had endless patience with me."[145]

The *Master of Suspence* had seen Grace previously in her screen test for the black-and-white film *Taxi* (1953) made by Gregory Ratoff. Some stories claim that Hitchcock also saw her in John Ford's African adventure-love story *Mogambo* (1953) and in Fred Zinnemann's black-and-white western *High Noon*. *High Noon* had been filmed in the fall of 1951 and had opened in the summer of 1952, so it is possible that Hitchcock saw it. However, *Mogambo* did not finish filming until late March 1953 and did not open until September of that year. By this point, Hitchcock was well into filming *Dial M for Murder*, which had begun on August 5. Hitchcock could have only seen some of the early raw cuts of Ford's *Mogambo,* and this would have only been the case if the studio had let him view the color film internally. There was no way that he could have seen the completed film before he had decided to cast Grace Kelly. Anyhow, Hitchcock was not a director who spent much time watching the works of his colleagues. In recorded interviews with the director, it was very clear that he was rarely acquainted with the films that were produced at the same time as his own, even years later.

Brigitte Auber, who acted in *To Catch a Thief* beside Grace Kelly and Cary Grant, recalled the following story: "One time we were eating on set, and I asked Hitch if he also enjoyed dining with other directors. He said, 'No.' The other directors simply did not interest him. It was an almost charming commentary."[146] Brigitte's was an unconventional attitude, just like Hitchcock.

Regardless of which Grace films Hitchcock may have seen, he did not simply find a main actress for his next film. He discovered

Grace Kelly—the blonde, delicate, cool Hitchcock heroine par excellence. He became her mentor, and she, his muse.

During August and September 1953, Alfred Hitchcock filmed his thirty-ninth film. *Dial M for Murder* was based on an identically titled stage play written by British author Frederick Knott. This was his first published play, and he wrote the screenplay as well. During his long life, Knott only wrote three plays. The other two were *Wait Until Dark* (1966), which was filmed in 1967 by Terence Young with Audrey Hepburn playing the lead role of a blind young woman targeted by conmen, and *Write Me a Murder* (1961). All three of these plays were highly successful on Broadway. With 552 performances, *Dial M for Murder* was by far the most successful of the three.[147] The play was first aired in 1952 as a BBC television movie, and after seeing the program, London producer James P. Sherwood, who was looking for a new play, brought it to the stage. Under director John Fernald, Knott's play premiered on June 19, 1952, in London's Westminster Theatre. On October 29, 1952, the play opened in America at the Plymouth Theater, New York, under the direction of Reginald Denham. The New York cast included John Williams as Chief Inspector Hubbard and Anthony Dawson as the potential murderer, Captain Lesgate. Both actors reprised their roles in Hitchcock's film. Hitchcock saw one of the productions of the three-act play and decided to bring Knott's play to the screen. The film rights were sold to Warner Bros. for a modest $2,800.

Even as a film, *Dial M for Murder* retains its theatrical feel. The enclosed chamber-play-styled film was Hitchcock's final production for Warner Bros. Studio. Reluctantly, MGM loaned the contracted Grace to Warner, the news of which the Hollywood press announced in late July. At the urgent wish of Jack Warner, the studio boss, the film was made using new 3-D technology, which was very popular at this time; it was seen as a means to distinguish movies from television (which was rising in popularity). Another 3-D film made at this time was Andre De Toth's horror film *House of Wax* (1953) with Vincent Price, also produced by Warner Bros. Like *Dial M for Murder, House of Wax* was filmed in Warnercolor, and when it premiered in April 1953, it was the first large-scale, 3-D production of its kind. Another 3-D film was MGM's Cole Porter musical *Kiss Me, Kate*, directed by George Sidney. Its worldwide premiere was in New York in November of that same year.

Hitchcock resisted Warner's efforts, but was eventually forced to accept them. His argument was that 3-D would be a passing fad, and he labeled the new technique, which did not interest him in the least, as "anti-cinematographic." In the end, his prediction was right. When *Dial M for Murder* finally premiered in May 1954 in New York, the 3-D hype was noticeably fading. In the cinemas, the film was ultimately shown in the usual "flat" two-dimensional format.

For the otherwise experimental Hitchcock, the heavy equipment with its monstrously large, clunky cameras was, in the context of the small studio stages, more hindering than it was helpful. After all, the movie, which was made in a span of thirty-six days, took place in a single room. Only a very few scenes were shot in other locations. Due to his skepticism of the new 3-D technology and its tricks, Hitchcock utilized hardly any visual effects. The new medium is only evident, almost incidentally, in the small details. For example, in the foreground one can see vases or a table seemingly enlarged and closer to the viewer. In two scenes, an arm stretches out toward the audience, out of the picture to a certain extent. Hitchcock happily denigrated the movie and ironically commented that, "I would also like to shoot an entire film in a phone booth."[148] Nonetheless, *Dial M for Murder* is among the director's better works, and was the first of several films of his that were set entirely in claustrophobically small spaces.

In the completely enclosed, spatially limited atmosphere of the chamber play and its minimalistic style, *Dial M for Murder* resembles two of Hitchcock's earlier films. The first is the anti-war drama *Lifeboat* (1944). It was a similar experiment, filmed exclusively in a studio in a large water tank with no exterior shots. Based on a novella by John Steinbeck, this unusual film was made for Twentieth Century-Fox and was one of Hitchcock's few political movies—"a microcosm of the war." Nine people with vastly different backgrounds and natures are stuck together on a lifeboat, "like a pack of dogs."[149] They are survivors of a shipwreck caused by a German attack. The other film is the philosophical work *Rope* (1948), which in some ways marks a break and a new start on Hitchcock's part. It was Alfred Hitchcock's first Technicolor film and the first of two movies that he himself produced. Furthermore, *Rope* was the first of four films made with James Stewart. It was also a stylistic and technical experiment, something that Hitchcock always loved. Thus, in 1948, he took Patrick Hamilton's 1929 play, which had been adapted as a screenplay by Arthur Laurents, and filmed it in practically one take. He did this by filming continuously and chronologically, using one 10-minute roll of film after the other. The eighty-minute film takes place in New York, and the fictional plot takes place in real time. Besides an establishing shot, that shows the viewer the wide fenestrated facade of the penthouse apartment, the plot moves forward with little to no cuts. When a roll ended, Hitchcock would let the camera either pan out or zoom in closer to one of the actors in frame.

Dial M for Murder features a love triangle in which the institution of marriage is portrayed as a breeding ground for distrust and moral—as well as financial—betrayal. The story takes place in London. The wife, Margot Wendice (Grace Kelly), has taken a lover, American crime author Mark Halliday (Robert Cummings, who had previously acted in Hitchcock's *Saboteur*, 1942). Margot's husband, former tennis player Tony Wendice (Ray Milland), wants to have her murdered by a former classmate, Captain Lesgate, a.k.a Charles Alexander Swann (Anthony Dawson), who is in financial difficulties and is, consequently, easily corruptible. Tony is not motivated by jealousy or any other emotion, but instead, is solely interested in getting his hands on Margot's money before she can divorce him and possibly marry Mark. Everyone is cheating on everyone else. Everyone can be exploited. The incorruptible, very British, Chief Inspector Hubbard was played by John Williams, who later played a British insurance agent concerned about Grace Kelly's film mother's (Jessie Royce Landis) stolen jewelry in *To*

Catch a Thief. Hubbard eventually explains everything in the final scene, triumphantly combing his mustache after Tony Wendice is ultimately taken away.

After *Rope* and the historical costume drama *Under Capricorn* (1949), *Dial M for Murder* was Hitchcock's third color film, and it is quite remarkable how carefully he considered color in even the smallest details. The most noticeable instance of this was Grace Kelly's wardrobe by costume designer Moss Mabry. In the opening scene, she is together with Ray Milland, who gives her a short, light kiss before he sits down at the breakfast table, where she is reading the *Times*. Grace is wearing a pale dress in a very faint rose color. They are both silent. No dialogue. Then, unnoticed by Tony, her face brightens behind the newspaper, which reports that the steamer *Queen Mary* will soon arrive in Southhampton. Among those on board is the "American mystery writer," Mark Halliday of the United States. There is still no conversation. Cut. Wielded by Hitchcock's longtime cameraman Robert Burks, the camera again shows Grace Kelly kissing—this time Robert Cummings as Mark Halliday. This kiss is longer and more passionate than the one with Ray. And this time she is wearing a red dress, one that exposes her neck, shoulders, and the top of her *décolletage*. However, her arms are covered, and she looks enchantingly lovely. It is the dress of one passionately in love. There has been no dialogue up to this point. Cut.

In only a few scenes, Hitchcock has sketched out the basic constellation of characters, avoiding lengthy stories and explanations with tedious dialogue. Including the title and cast list, he needs only two and a half minutes to complete this exposition, and the viewer already knows Margot's/Grace Kelly's entire dilemma, how she is caught between two men. One of the two loves her. The other wants to kill her.

Hitchcock staged another kissing scene so that only the shadows of Grace Kelly and Robert Cummings are cast against the apartment door. They hold each other tightly, and the kiss lasts for some time. Then, steps can be heard on the staircase; the apartment is on the ground floor and has a small back garden. As a key turns in the lock and they realize that Margot's husband

Tony must have arrived, the two of them move abruptly away from each other. Out of the one large shadow, there are now two individual ones, which are supposedly positioned an appropriate distance apart. The door opens, and Ray Milland enters the living room. This is a wonderfully choreographed and visually implemented metaphor.

On the night of the plotted murder, Grace wears a bluish-white nightgown. When she is finally arrested after killing her would-be murderer in self-defense, she appears in a stark, buttoned-up gray dress. She is sentenced to death for murder. At the end of the film, on the day before her execution she is wearing a brown coat over a gray dress. Her face is pale—as pale as death. She looks broken; her voice is full of despair, quiet and quivering. Her portrayal is reserved and all the more powerful. Everything about her reveals her fragility.

She allows the viewer to see inside her soul. Before the final concluding turning point arrives, which will mean both her relief and her freedom, her Margot Wendice is a shattered woman. These last fateful and touching moments of *Dial M for Murder* reveal the skill of a mature, grown-up actress.

From rose to red and then to light blue, gray, and brown—the colors represent Margot's metamorphosis. Grace Kelly's costumes reveal Margot's inner state, reflecting her increasingly cloudy and darkening spirits. For the murder scene, Hitchcock initially wanted to dress her in a heavy morning dress made of silk, against which light and shadows could play during the scene. However, the young actress had an idea of her own. She thought that it would not be logical for a woman, who has already gone to bed, to put on something new in the middle of the night when the telephone rings. No, a woman—in this case, Margot Wendice— would simply switch on the light, open the bedroom door, and go to the table that held the telephone.

Persuaded by Grace, Hitchcock shot the scene thus: Margot leaves the bedroom wearing a pale thin, shimmering blue nightgown, which clings closely to the contours and form of her body. The camera fixes itself on her back. There is no one else there, only the viewer, the voyeur in front of the screen. The fact that

Hitchcock let himself be convinced of an alternative costume was an extraordinary, somewhat scandalous development on set. Here was a twenty-three-year-old actress, who till now had only acted in two supporting parts in significant films, ones in which she came across as immature and a little naive and awkward. This was her first mature major role. Yet, she was advising the director on costume decisions. Coming after her refusal to be embarrassed by his naughty stories, Hitchcock was again impressed by Grace's determination to express her opinion to others, perhaps also by her stubbornness and self-assurance—typical Kelly characteristics. As a result of this, Grace had a say in the selection of her wardrobe for both *Rear Window* and *To Catch a Thief*. These were not inconsequential moments for the development of their relationship.

A totally different development during the filming occurred between Grace Kelly and her costar Ray Milland (1905–1986). Grace fell in love with the 6'2" Milland only a few days after they first met. And Milland seemed game to patronize various Hollywood restaurants with the young, blonde beauty at his side. He even seemed proud to be idolized by the new Hitchcock heroine. Milland had starred in many movies, including Fritz Lang's *Ministry of Fear* (1944) and Billy Wilder's *Lost Weekend* (1945). Born in Wales, Milland was forty-eight years old, over twice as old as Grace, and at this point, he had been married for twenty-one years to his wife Muriel "Mal" Milland with whom he had a son, Daniel, and an adopted daughter, Victoria. Unfortunately, the affair was found out, and it seriously threatened the Millands' marriage. They separated temporarily. Murial Milland threatened her husband with divorce, and the public sought to turn Grace Kelly into the homewrecker who had ensnared her older costar. The public saw in her an opportunistic young actress who would shamelessly go to bed with anyone if it would help her career. All of Hollywood thought this to be true. The influential and feared Hollywood columnist Hedda Hopper even went so far as to describe Grace as a nymphomaniac. Throughout Grace's acting career, Hopper would always write disrespectfully about her.

Furthermore, besides the longer affair with Milland, Grace supposedly had short relationships during the filming with screenplay writer Frederick Knott, as well as fellow actor Anthony Dawson.[150] It cannot be ascertained if these stories were based on reality or if they were based on the countless, never-ending libelous rumors. However, considering the relationship with Milland, the other affairs seem unlikely. In any case, Ray Milland returned to his wife Muriel, who forgave him. When he died on March 10, 1986, in Torrance, California, at the age of eighty-one, they had been married fifty-four years. Alfred Hitchcock never commented on any of this.

As French director and avid Hitchcock admirer François Truffaut (1932–1984) once claimed, "It was impossible not to see that the love scenes were filmed like murder scenes, and the murder scenes like love scenes...It occurred to me that in Hitchcock's cinema...to make love and to die are one and the same."[151] Truffaut was cofounder of the legendary avant garde "Nouvelle Vague" movement of the late 1950s and early 1960s, whose members included Claude Chabrol, Eric Rohmer, Jean-Luc Godard, and Jacques Rivette.

Truffaut was right: Hitchcock's death scenes have something exciting and passionate about them. They connect with other areas of life or even provide a transition from one state to another. Similarly his love scenes carry a latent, disquieting quality, as well as elements of finitude and futility. These romantic scenes include Hitchcock's carefully staged, captivatingly detailed kiss scenes. One example of this is the scene between Sean Connery and Tippi Hedren in *Marnie*. Life and death are often bound together with food and/or drink—whether nourishing or poisonous. These function in Alfred Hitchcock's work as key tropes.

The strenuous filming of the murder scene for *Dial M for Murder* took an entire week. In the final film, this scene lasts about one minute and is accompanied by Dimitri Tiomkin's dramatic score. At the end of this stressful week, Grace Kelly found herself covered in bruises. It would not be the first time in which one of Hitchcock's actresses would endure heavy stress; after filming the famous attic scene in *The Birds* from Monday morning to Friday evening, Tippi Hedren suffered a nervous breakdown.

For *Dial M for Murder*, Hitchcock's cameraman Robert Burks shot the central murder scene from every possible angle. He took close-up shots of Grace Kelly's face, of her feet kicking and struggling in the air during the fight, of the scissors that are sitting in the foreground on the desktop. Later he cut these close-up scenes into a montage. Time and time again, Grace Kelly had to turn and fall backward onto the hard desk on which the telephone sat. At first, Anthony Lawson lurks behind the heavy, dark green curtain, and then she turns her back on the curtains to answer the telephone. She repeatedly asks "Hello?" with growing confusion, at which point he jumps out and tries to strangle her with a scarf. Some of the shots, specifically those in which Anthony Dawson almost lies on top of Grace Kelly as he tries to kill her, carry overtones of rape.

In recalling Grace's work with Hitchcock on set, James Stewart (who later starred with Grace in *Rear Window)* commented, "She seemed to know the movement before Hitchcock had anything to say about it. And I think Hitchcock liked that. I think everybody liked that."[152]

During the riveting, brutal murder scene, Margot rams the scissors into the back of Swann (Anthony Dawson), the murderer her husband Tony (Ray Milland) has hired to kill her.

When Swann falls backward onto the floor, he causes the scissors to plunge deeper into his back. Predating the legendary, black-and-white shower scene in *Psycho* by six years, this scene made film history. This murder scene, which would legally be considered an action of self-defense and not an actual murder, is considered to be among the top four most shocking Hitchcock death scenes, along with the gas oven murder in *Torn Curtain* (1966), the shower murder in *Psycho*, and the tie murder in *Frenzy* (1972).

These four murder scenes are the most brutal, starkly violent portrayals in Hitchcock's entire filmography. Over time, it is clear that Hitchcock increased the open brutality, specifically the immediacy of the violence, in his movies. The exaggerated "horror" of the scissors murder scene in *Dial M for Murder* and the even more extreme terror of the shower murder in *Psycho* are exceeded by the crude, cold realism of the gas oven murder scene in *Torn Curtain* and the oppressively realistic tie murder in *Frenzy*. With these scenes, Hitchcock moves far beyond the traditional level of visible and comprehensible depictions of violence.

Many years later, over twenty years after the filming of *Dial M for Murder*, on April 29, 1974, Hitchcock gave a short thank-you speech at an honorary gala event at Lincoln Center. He sat between Grace Kelly and his wife Alma. His sinister concluding sentence, which came on the heels of numerous compliments and film clips, was also playful: "As you have seen on the screen, scissors are the best way."[153]

After *Dial M for Murder*, Hitchcock went on to film six more films for Paramount, beginning in late fall of 1953. *Rear Window*, which began filming in late November 1953, was the prelude to Paramount's golden era. *Psycho* was the conclusion. During this creative period, which he himself described as a time in which his "batteries were fully charged," he made film after film.[154] All told, the 1950s were the most prolific years of his eighty-year life. These were also the years in which he felt the happiest and most fulfilled artistically.

Interestingly, Grace Kelly experienced something similar. Between 1953 and 1955, Grace acted in what could be considered her most important films, advancing from supporting roles to main roles, coming into her own as an actress. At this time she reached the absolute peak of her ability, her acting power, and perhaps even her all-too-short life. In the spring of 1956, everything would change.

In reference to her Hitchcockian debut (for which she was awarded a New York Film Critics Award) Grace later said: "Working with Hitch was wonderful for me."[155]

She'll be different in every movie she makes. Not because of makeup or clothes but because she plays a character from the inside out. There's no one else like her in Hollywood.
—*Alfred Hitchcock*[156]

My mother especially liked Rear Window.
—*Prince Albert II of Monaco*[157]

So far she has only played lead roles. What you're still missing is a portrayal around which an entire film can be composed. That is the ultimate test.
—*Alfred Hitchcock*[158]

Once *Dial M for Murder* was finished, Grace returned to New York as soon as she could. Unlike life in the pretentiously glittering, glamorous dream factory of Hollywood, she felt more at home in New York. As she once commented, in California, the sun always shone unnaturally, and money was the only thing that had value here. It was October. Grace's agent Jay Kanter called and sent her two screenplays for two roles that had been offered to her: *On the Waterfront* (1954) and *Rear Window*. Within a short time, Grace had to decide between the two, since both of the projects would soon start preproduction. It couldn't have been an easy decision.

For *Rear Window*, MGM would again need to lend her to another studio. Since MGM held a seven-year contract with Grace, she would have to be loaned to Paramount, as she had been to Warner for *Dial M for Murder*. On one hand, *On the Waterfront* would permit Grace to stay in New York. On the other hand, Hitchcock had asked specifically for her, and she loved working with the Master of Suspense. Grace's dilemma was made all the worse by the two very different film projects and their two very different female characters. *On the Waterfront* was a raw, realistic, sociocritical, film made in black and white. Marlon Brando had already been cast in the role of Terry Malloy. Edie Doyle, the role offered to Grace, lived in a world that was completely foreign to Grace. *Rear Window* was intended to be filmed in color starring James Stewart. The character of Lisa Carol Fremont was a woman of great elegance, class, and style. Furthermore, she was at home in the New York fashion scene. This was a character close to Grace herself. She would be able to interpret and polish this role more precisely and authentically. In addition, Grace learned that Hitchcock had already authorized the preparation for her costumes. Grace chose Hitch.

Without a doubt, this was one of the most critical, direction-setting decisions of her film career, perhaps even of her life. What would have happened if she had chosen *On the Waterfront*? Her loveliest and most significant film would never have been made, and perhaps Hitchcock's subsequent offer to star in *To Catch a Thief* would never have taken place. Most likely, her life would have gone in a very different direction. Because of *To Catch a Thief*, Grace first encountered the French Riviera, which she later decided to visit for a longer period in the summer of 1954. She returned another time in May 1955 as a guest of the Cannes Film Festival. She stayed in the legendary Carlton Hotel and chose to visit the principality of Monaco, where she met Prince Rainier III for the first time. It could even be said that Grace's decision in October 1953 to film *Rear Window* with Hitchcock ultimately resulted in him losing her as an actress after *To Catch a Thief*.

In the end, *On the Waterfront*, directed by Elia Kazan with Marlon Brando and Karl Malden in the main roles, was a springboard and breakthrough role for another blonde actress. For her first film role, Eve Marie Saint received an Oscar as Best Supporting Actress for her portrayal of Edie Doyle. Five years later, she starred beside Cary Grant in Alfred Hitchcock's *North by Northwest* (1959). Along with Kim Novak in *Vertigo*, Vera Miles in *The Wrong Man* (1956) and *Psycho*, and particularly Tippi Hedren in *The Birds* and *Marnie*, Eve Marie Saint was among the later group of blonde heroines, in whose stead Hitchcock would have gladly cast Grace Kelly. This is how some of the actresses actually felt, as if they were simply Grace Kelly replacements in the films that followed the three Hitchcock-Kelly movies.

In the third week of November 1953, Grace again traveled to Hollywood, for the costume fitting for *Rear Window*. Here she was expected by her director, as well as by the renowned costume designer Edith Head (1897–1981). All told, five different costumes were planned for her in *Rear Window*. Hitchcock had already sketched and authorized everything in great detail, from the form to the style and color. As Edith Head remembered: "Hitchcock told me it was important that Grace's clothes help to establish some sort of conflict in the story. She was to be a typical sophisticated society-girl magazine editor who falls in love with a scruffy photographer, Jimmy Stewart. Hitch wanted her to look like a piece of Dresden China, something slightly untouchable. So I did that. Her suits were impeccably tailored; her accessories looked as though they couldn't be worn by anyone else but her. She was perfect."[159]

At the time that *Rear Window* was filmed, Edith Head, head designer at Paramount, had long been a legend—an authority—in her field. Only 5'1" in height, she always wore glasses and bangs. She rarely smiled and was known for her strict regimen. Between 1924 and 1981, she was listed as costume designer, co-designer, or design assistant for 781 films.[160] However, she herself claimed that she worked on well over 1,100 movies. Undoubtedly this small woman did not lack any self-confidence. Over the years, she significantly shaped the clothing styles and images, as well as the identities, of some of Hollywood's most famous actresses, including Audrey Hepburn, Elizabeth Taylor, Barbara Stanwyck, Gloria Swanson, Bette Davis, Marlene Dietrich, Doris Day, Olivia de Havilland, Shirley MacLaine—and Grace Kelly. At this time in 1950s Hollywood, the unique and delicate Audrey Hepburn functioned, to a certain degree, as the antithesis to the curvy, brunette Elizabeth Taylor, just as the stylish, elegant Grace Kelly embodied the opposite of the more voluptuous, blonde Marilyn Monroe.

However, despite all of these famous names, costume designer Head was certain of one thing: "I've dressed thousands of actors, actresses, and animals, but whenever I am asked which star is my personal favorite, I answer, 'Grace Kelly.' She is a charming lady, a most gifted actress and, to me, a valued friend."[161]

Edith Head first worked with Alfred Hitchcock when she dressed Ingrid Bergman for his romantic espionage film, *Notorious* (1946). She would continue to work with him until his final film *Family Plot* (1976) with only a few exceptions, which include *Psycho* and *Frenzy*. Following Hitchcock's meticulously detailed instructions, she designed the costumes for the initially insecure Kim Novak in her complex double role as Madeleine/Judy in *Vertigo* and for Tippi Hedren in *The Birds* and *Marnie*. For her achievements in the field of costume design, Edith Head won eight Oscars over the course of her long life, including ones for the Audrey Hepburn films *Roman Holiday* (1953) and *Sabrina* (1954), and the movie *All About Eve* (1950) with Bette Davis, Anne Baxter, and a very young Marilyn Monroe. In addition, she received thirty-five Academy Award nominations. For a woman in this field, who during the early years of the 1930s and 1940s provided costumes for several dozen movies a year, this was a singular achievement.

Among her numerous Oscar nominations was the one she received for her costume design for *To Catch a Thief*, especially for the wardrobe she designed for Grace Kelly. However, this time the usually successful Edith Head struck out. As she once stated, "[it was] the single greatest disappointment of my costume-design career."[162] Perhaps this deep disappointment was influenced by her close identification as a costume designer with this movie: "When people ask me who is my favorite actress, who is my favorite actor, who is my favorite director, and what is my favorite movie, I say to them, just look over the roofs of Nice and you'll find all the answers. [*To Catch a Thief*] was a dream for a costume designer."[163]

On November 29, 1953, the first day of shooting *Rear Window* began. In no other film—except perhaps *To Catch a Thief*—is Grace Kelly so breathtakingly charming and lovely as she is here. Under the direction of Alfred Hitchcock, as already could be seen in the previous *Dial M for Murder*, she bloomed, completely unfolding both inside and out. In *Rear Window*, one can see most explicitly what Grace could bring forth under Hitchcock's mentorship. It is as if she turns her most innermost self to the outside. Her fragility is apparent, as is her determination to speak her mind. Although it is not until her surprising portrayal in George Seaton's *The Country Girl* (1954) that she received an Oscar on March 30, 1955, handed to her by her costar and lover, William Holden, *Rear Window* is indisputably the most important film of her career.

The shutters of the three-winged window slowly open, as the title credits scroll by and lively, cheerful music plays. After the final credit, "Directed by Alfred Hitchcock," a view is granted of the entire scene, one of the largest and most incredible film sets that had been constructed to date. A complete New York interior courtyard in Greenwich Village with thirty-one apartments, twelve of which are completely furnished. All of this was constructed in Paramount Studios. This is a microcosm. A reflection of human existence. *Rear Window* is undoubtedly one of the most layered, important, and beautiful Hitchcock films—perhaps in some ways, the quintessential Hitchcock film. John Michael Hayes's screenplay adaptation of Cornell Woolrich's 1942 short story goes far beyond its literary basis. In addition, Hitchcock added elements from the real-life criminal case of Patrick Mahon and Dr. Crippen.

Here the window frame serves as the edges of the film frame. People move around in the background, and the viewer's gaze follows, from the very start, through the window, from inside to outside. The viewer is the observer, the voyeur. After the titles, the camera focuses on the middle window pane, and then the first cut comes. In the courtyard, a black cat runs through the garden, birds fly up, and the camera pans along the apartments. In variously sized shots, the camera (Robert Burks) sets up a long take of the entire set. The camera finally focuses on a close-up shot of the sweating professional photographer L.B. Jeffries (James Stewart, 1908–1997) and a thermometer. It is morning, and the thermometer already registers 90°F. After another cut, the camera returns to Stewart inside his two-room apartment and pans across his plastered leg: "Here lie the broken bones of L.B. Jeffries." The camera then cuts quickly to the back part of the room and glides across Jeffries's exposed work instruments: camera, film, slides, folder numbers with his cover designs. Then a fade-out.

The exposition is, in itself, a little story. Without any commentary, the protagonist is introduced in his bachelor apartment, along with his unfortunate situation, his career, his field, and how he lives. Hitchcock's manipulation of the viewer is already complete at this point. The viewer now sees the courtyard primarily through Jeffries's eyes. Only in a few scenes does he/she stand outside. The subjective view is presented as the objective one. The gaze of the viewer is that of the camera. It is Jeffries's gaze. Through this blending, which combines the viewer's position as audience with that of the act of seeing, an indiscretion is committed from the very beginning. The viewer becomes the voyeur. *Rear Window* is absolutely a movie about voyeurism. About secretive observations, about the external intrusion into the internal private spheres of totally unknown people, even if they are one's immediate neighbors. And Jeffries, the photographer, is to a certain degree a professional voyeur.

The pragmatic nurse Stella (Thema Ritter), who regularly gives Jeffries massages, delivers one of the film's key, anticipatory statements: "I got a nose for trouble. I can smell it ten miles away...I can smell trouble right here in this apartment. First you smash your leg. Then you get to lookin' out the window. See things you shouldn't see. Trouble."[164]

"Jeff if you could only see yourself!" complains Jeffries's fiancée, the extremely attractive model Lisa Carol Fremont (Grace Kelly), in reference to his activities. She says this before she is convinced by his suspicions that Lars Thorwald, a man living in the second floor of the building, has killed his wife, cut her into pieces, and removed her from the apartment in a large packing crate in the pouring rain. With his telephoto lens, what Stella calls his "portable keyhole," Jeffries observes how Thorwald wraps a large saw and a large kitchen knife in newspaper. Several times, Jeffries and Lisa ask each other if they should be doing what they are doing. Jeff says to Lisa, "I wonder if it's ethical to watch a man with binoculars and a long-focus lens." She replies: "Jeff, if someone came in here, they wouldn't believe what they'd see. You and me with long faces, plunged into despair because we find out a man didn't kill his wife. We're two of the most frightening ghouls I've ever known."

Jeffries's old war buddy, Police Detective Tom Doyle (Wendell Corey), views the justification of their activities critically. However, their actions are ultimately the only ones that uncover the actual murder of Thorwald's wife. This is the driving plot element in *Rear Window*: the MacGuffin. The actual subject of the plot is the relationship between Jeffries and Lisa.

The French Nouvelle Vague directors Claude Chabrol and Eric Rohmer, who along with François Truffaut worked as film critics during the 1950s for the renowned *Cahiers du Cinéma* in Paris, appropriately compared the courtyard wall (and its windows into each apartment), over which Jeffries gazes throughout the entire film, to "an ensemble of rabbit cages."[165] And in these cages, which on the other hand also resemble prison cells, loneliness reigns supreme. It is unimportant which social status the residents have, or if they are single or married—none of them seem to be fulfilled or happy. The spectrum ranges from a childless husband and wife, who always sleep on their balcony and lower their dog into the little rose garden in the courtyard via a basket and rope; to the unhappily lonely single woman, Miss Lonelyhearts; to Miss Torso who dances constantly through her apartment and is surrounded by aimless men; to the sculptress who works on unconventional sculptures in the garden; to the young unsuccessful pianist who composes the thematic song "Lisa"; to the young, newly married couple who, at least at first, spend their time behind closed shutters.

In his now legendary fifty-hour interview with François Truffaut in August 1962, which was eventually published in 1966 as a book, Hitchcock commented on Jeffries's view of the courtyard: "You had every type of behavior, you had little stories going in each one . . . [it was] reflecting a little world."[166]

The other side of the courtyard represents, for Jeffries especially, a mirror; these neighbors are a catalog of possibilities related to his own life—with or without Lisa. The reflection here corresponds to the people themselves; it is a dualism that Hitchcock had previously used in *Shadow of a Doubt,* in the symmetry of the two Charlies (uncle and niece), and in *Strangers on a Train* in the connection between Bruno and Guy. Here the theme is varied in its application. L.B. Jeffries, who is called Jeff, is in a relationship with a woman who wants to marry him at all costs. As Lisa enters Thorwald's apartment and finds the wife's wedding ring in a handbag, she slips it on and shows it behind her back, which Jeffries observes from the other side. It is a double hint from her side; the wife seems to have actually been killed, and she, Lisa, wants to marry him, Jeffries. Jeffries is the (presumably) positive protagonist. Lars Thorwald is married to a woman—who from a distance seems to be blonde, slender, and young, like Lisa—who increasingly nags him and of whom he wishes to be free. He is the negative antagonist. As Jeff, who otherwise travels the world as a professional photographer, is bound to a wheelchair and a sofa bed because of his broken leg, Lisa insists on caring for him. This is an exact reflection of what is going on across the way. Thorwald's wife is sick and bedridden, just as he, a traveling businessman, is mobile and on the go. He now must care for his wife. Ultimately, Thorwald is Jeffries's extreme alter ego. Jeffries's observation of the Thorwalds and of the eventual murder functions as a projection of his primal fears.

If one chooses to see it thus, the apartment facade only exists in Jeffries's imagination. Everything—the courtyard and the flats above—is a mental externalization. It represents an imaginary projection, an expression of yearnings and wishes on the one side, and of fears and darkness on the other. Thorwald carries out what Jeffries dares not do. His external immobility reflects his internal immobility, as when he asks Lisa if it would not just be best to leave everything as it is. The Thorwalds and Miss Lonelyhearts of this courtyard world, the lonely pianists and the newly married couple—these are all life options for Jeffries.

Grace Kelly first appears in *Rear Window* as a shadow during the fifteenth minute of the film. Evening is approaching. James

Stewart sits in his wheelchair with his plaster cast and has dozed off. Sounds and voices can be heard from the street and the courtyard. A piano plays. A woman practices singing. The shouts of children echo up from the alley that leads from the street to the courtyard. Then suddenly, as if from nothing, silently and very slowly, Grace's shadow stretches over him, and Stewart, as he senses her approach, opens his eyes. A dazed smile appears on his lips. Hitchcock builds the mood through the use of dreamlike imagery, which he later utilized to a fully avant-garde zenith in his film, *Frenzy*. Except for the muted, diffuse hum of the metropolis, suddenly nothing more can be heard from the courtyard. It is as if a length of wool has been laid around the couple, so that for a moment, nothing can acoustically disturb them. Through this, the sequence of pictures creates an even larger undertow. Hitchcock reveals this in an extremely color intensive (and color-restored) slow-motion sequence. Grace Kelly and James Stewart are each shown by the camera in close-up shots. First, Grace is seen from James Stewart's perspective, frontally, bending down—to him and to us, the viewers—and thereby looking almost directly into the camera. And then, when their lips slowly touch and she kisses him three times, she is shown in profile. These camera takes are portraits of the creamy ivory of her face. Hitchcock "paints" Grace Kelly. In her black and white evening gown, designed by Edith Head, with a necklace of white pearls at her neck and her hair severely drawn back, she exudes a perfectly timeless, classical charm and elegance. It is as if this intimate moment has fallen out of all time and space. In this kiss scene, Hitchcock created one of the most beautiful, innocently poetic, and excitingly erotic kisses in film history.

Rear Window is, among other things, a precise treatment of the act of seeing—the staging of seeing. Thus, it is also about the role of the director, as well as the reaction to, and effect of, seeing. This is seeing and showing in their purest, nonverbal forms. It is not by chance that in Hitchcock's courtyard, Bing Crosby's rendition of "To See You (Is to Love You)," music by Jimmy Van Heusen and lyrics by Johnny Burke, is heard. This song addresses seeing and the (reciprocal) perception of the other. The song starts at the very moment that Lisa and Jeff begin talking about life in general, about their relationship and their differing views about it. If possible, this song—and even more so, the thematic "Lisa" melody—is also a hymn (Hitchcock's) to the character of Lisa (and thus, the actress Grace Kelly). As Lisa stylishly sets out in Jeff's apartment the perfect meal—at least perfect for him—that she had ordered from the fashionable 21 Club, Jeff looks across the parterre at the lonely, searching Miss Lonelyhearts. Crosby's "To See You" is still playing.

In this context, the montage served Hitchcock as a significant design medium. (Hitchcock enjoyed talking about the critical influence on him exerted by the montage principle of the Russian directors Eisenstein and Pudowkin.)

"That's it. [The montage] is the perfect cinematic tool. There is the immovable man who looks outside. This is the first piece of film. The second piece can show what the man sees, and the third shows his reaction. This represents the purest expression of a cinematic idea that we know."[167]

As both a witty chamber play and a deeply transcendental kaleidoscope of the soul, *Rear Window* ends ambivalently. Jeffries lies dozing with two broken legs in his wheelchair. (Thorwald had previously threatened him and pushed him out of the window.) In blue pants and a red shirt, Lisa is not dressed in her usually elegant attire. She sits on the sofa, ostensibly reading a book, but as soon as Jeffries falls asleep, she grabs the fashion magazine *Harper's Bazaar*. Which path (as exemplified by the different tenants across the courtyard) has the indecisive photographer decided? Hitchcock does not reveal this to the viewer.

Hitchcock's fortieth film premiered in New York on August 4, 1954. Grace Kelly attended the event escorted by a certain Oleg Cassini. She appeared publicly with this man with whom she would have an on-again, off-again relationship from 1954 to 1955. It was a serious relationship that led to an engagement and concrete wedding plans.

The son of the Russian diplomat Count Alexander Loiewski and the Italian Countess Marguerite Cassini, Oleg Cassini

(1913–2006) opened his own fashion house in Manhattan after settling in the United States in 1936 and serving military duty in the US army during World War II. Young First Lady Jacqueline Kennedy (1929–1994) officially requested that he work as her personal couturier during the years her husband John F. Kennedy served as President (1961–1963). Over these three short years, he created her unmistakable style, the so-called "Jackie Look," and attended both private and social engagements with the Kennedys on the weekends. Jackie Kennedy's geometric, plainly cut dresses—of which Cassini designed about three hundred for her—and the angular pillbox hats were copied by women around the world. Since 1941, Cassini had been married to the actress Gene Tierney (*Laura*, 1941), and in 1952, they divorced.

Cassini and Grace met each other at an event related to the New York premiere of *Mogambo*, which took place on October 1, 1953. According to Cassini, they actually first met in early 1954. However, the filming of *Rear Window* at the Paramount Studios in Hollywood did not end until January 13, and at its conclusion, Grace immediately started to work on director Mark Robson's *The Bridges at Toko-Ri*, which had already begun filming without her on January 4.

Furthermore, on January 6, Grace Kelly made her final appearance in a television program. *The Thankful Heart,* a sixty-minute episode of *Kraft Television Theatre*, was broadcast live, as always, by NBC from New York.[168] For this, Grace had to travel from Los Angeles to New York. It is not possible to date the meeting between Grace and Cassini any closer than this, although it could have possibly occurred on the day in January 1954 when Grace was in New York to film the live television program.

Usually Grace Kelly worked continuously, flying from one film set straight to another to begin a new project. Unsettled, restless, aspirational, ambitious. She wanted to become famous and successful, according to the people who knew her during this time, at all costs. The year 1954 was to be the most creative and stressful year of her career. Without a break, she made six movies within a span of thirteen months, between August 5, 1953, when the filming of *Dial M for Murder* began, to September 4,

1954, when the filming of *To Catch a Thief* ended. These movies included *Dial M for Murder, Rear Window, The Bridges at Toko-Ri, The Country Girl, Green Fire*, and finally *To Catch a Thief*. A film tour de force. This was an almost inconceivable acting achievement—not to mention a psychological and physical achievement as well. It required absolute composure, complete control, and iron discipline. Except for some Sundays, she was never free. Later, in recalling that time, she commented that she did not know how she survived.

At the end of *To Catch a Thief*, Grace finally took a long-overdue, recuperative vacation for the remainder of 1954. She traveled immediately from Los Angeles to New York. In the winter of 1954–55, Grace moved into a seventh-floor apartment with a private elevator and original furnishings from 1925. From here, she had a view of Central Park. The apartment was located in the exclusive 988 Fifth Avenue building, near the Metropolitan Museum of Art. The rent was also quite expensive. Grace hired the interior designer George Stacey to design her new home, which incorporated the entire seventh floor and was divided into various spaces, rooms, halls, and bathrooms. It was actually more suitable for more than one tenant, but nevertheless she had this apartment designed to her individual wishes. She was especially taken with French furniture from the 1700s, and she wanted to furnish her apartment in this style. Her desk, her chaise lounge, and her chairs were found in various antique shops. George Stacey helped her with this. Grace wanted to finally find her footing, not just professionally, but also geographically. Above all else, privately and emotionally. This was her yearning for a safe harbor. Her desire to find a partner and to be in a solid, stable, long-term relationship grew substantially.

A year later, on June 25, 1955, Grace's younger sister Lizanne married stock market trader and horse trainer, Donald Caldwell LeVine, in the Kelly's home church of St. Bridget's in Philadelphia. Grace was one of Lizanne's bridesmaids. Since her older sister Peggy had already married her first husband George Davis, Grace was the only unmarried member of the Kelly clan. (Peggy and George divorced in 1959, and Peggy later married Eugene

Conlan.) This caused Grace to think even more seriously about her romantic prospects.

On November 12, 1954, Grace celebrated her twenty-fifth birthday. This was an occasion and cause for her to again consider her life. She was aware of the fact that the constant flying back and forth from film site to film site stood in the way of her having a halfway stable private life. She was not doing well that winter. She was listless, tired, exhausted. Although it was not an actual state of depression, in addition to her typical cheeriness, she now also tended strongly toward melancholy. Her normal, radiant, hopeful nature, now had a recognizably gloomy edge.

As a result, Grace rarely appeared before a camera for almost an entire year. Only for *The Swan*, her next-to-last movie, did she enter a film set again, in the fall of 1955.

Because of the number of her movies, the American press called 1954 "A Year of Grace." She even appeared on the cover of the June issue of *Look* magazine. And perhaps either despite or because of her extensive and intensive work as an actress, the year 1954, excepting the personally difficult months in fall and winter, was Grace Kelly's *annus mirabilis*, year of wonders, more so than 1956, the year of her marriage.

When Oleg Cassini saw *Mogambo* with his good friend, Bobby Friedman, Cassini immediately came to the personal, self-assured conclusion that the woman he had just seen up on the screen would be his next liaison, if not much more. Over time, it became clear that since the filming of *Dial M for Murder*, Ray Milland had not been the only man in Grace's life. She had also become seriously involved with the French actor Jean-Pierre Aumont. Soon, William Holden himself would enter Grace's life in the upcoming weeks of January 1954. He too would play a role in Grace's private life.

At the conclusion of the *Mogambo* premiere, Bobby Friedman and Oleg Cassini went out to eat at the well-known French restaurant Le Veau d'Or on 60th Street in Manhattan's Upper East Side. It could only be coincidence, or fate, that only half an hour after he had seen her on the screen, Oleg Cassini recognized her sitting at a nearby table with the French actor Jean-Pierre Aumont

(1911–2001). Cassini, the fashion designer, and Aumont, who was known from various films such as Marcell Carnés' *Hôtel du Nord* (1938), knew each other from Hollywood. And close to Aumont at the table sat Grace Kelly.

"I saw her only in profile. I saw the utter perfection of her nose, the long elegant neck, the silky diaphanous blonde hair. She wore a black velvet two-piece, very demure, with a full skirt and a little white Peter Pan collar. Later, when she stood, I saw that she had a pleasing figure, tall, about five-foot-eight, good broad shoulders, subtle curves and long legs—a very aristocratic girl, not the sort you simply called for a date."[169]

Full of charm and self-confidence, Oleg Cassini went to the table, and after greeting and chatting a little with Aumont, he exchanged a few words with Grace Kelly.

Starting the next day, Cassini sent a bouquet of a dozen red roses to Grace's apartment every day for ten days. He always had the same card and cryptic message sent with the flowers. All it read was "The Friendly Florist." On the tenth day of the rose siege, Cassini was walking past the New York Plaza Hotel. In the display window of a boutique there, he spotted a stuffed animal made to look like the Big Bad Wolf from the Walt Disney animated film, *The Three Little Pigs* (1933). He bought this and sent it to Grace.

On the following day, he called her, and when she answered, he said: "This is The Friendly Florist calling."[170] After a pause on the other end of the line, he heard Grace start laughing. It was now clear to the charming Cassini that he could win Grace. However, he did not know at this moment how many other competitors there were for her hand. There were those who had already been involved with her and wanted to renew old relationships and those who were currently connected to her. These suitors included Jean-Pierre Aumont, Ray Milland, William Holden, and Bing Crosby. And later, while Grace was living in New York, there was David Niven (1910–1983) in the spring of 1955. With Oleg Cassini this made a half a dozen men—and an illustrious group at that.

With London native David Niven, Grace eventually established a close, long-term friendship that lasted until their deaths. According to some sources, this friendship had a romantic element, even after the New York period.[171] However, Robert Dornhelm has denied this. He explained that David Niven and his wife Hjordis enjoyed visiting Monaco and were often guests at various occasions. Sometimes they were officially invited to the palace, and sometimes they were privately invited by the princess. For this reason, Dornhelm could not imagine an affair between Grace and Niven.[172]

Having become quite famous for starring in such films as Otto Preminger's adaptation of Françoise Sagan's *Bonjour Tristesse* (1958) and Blake Edwards's comedy *The Pink Panther* (1963), in early 1962, Niven bought a villa on the French Riviera, on the idyllic Saint-Jean-Cap-Ferrat peninsula located between Nice and Monaco. Cap Ferrat is gloriously surrounded on three sides by the sea and is the location of various expensive mansions, including the Villa Rothschild, a favorite film location. Cap Ferrat is supposedly the most expensive place to live in the world. Grace and Niven became neighbors, and Niven and his wife were frequent guests at the royal palace. Grace died before her friend did. At the time, he was seriously ill and could no longer manage the few miles between Saint-Jean-Cap-Ferrat and Monaco. His wife attended Grace's funeral on September 18, 1982. Less than a year later, on July 29, 1983, Grace's good, longtime friend also died at the age of seventy-three.

The Bridges at Toko-Ri
(1954)

> *What man wouldn't be*
> *overwhelmed by her?*
> *— William Holden*[173]

As soon as Grace wrapped up Hitchcock's *Rear Window*, she had to leave the Paramount studios immediately to start on her next film project. Based on James A. Michener's novel and adapted as a screenplay by Valentine Davis, the war film *The Bridges at Toko-Ri*, under the direction of Mark Robson, was filmed from early January through mid-February.

The plot revolves around events in late 1952 that were linked to the Korean War. Considering the time in which this movie was made, it was highly contemporary subject matter. The war between North and South Korea broke out on June 25, 1950, and ended on July 27, 1953. China fought as an ally to the People's Republic of North Korea, while UNO, and especially the United States, supported the Republic of South Korea. Once again, the Korean War reflected the power balance between East and West, between communism and capitalism. Unfortunately, the state of things at the end of the war matched those that had existed before the war's outbreak. If anything, things were now worse. The division between a northern and a southern part of Korea were now politically cemented in place. Furthermore, the Korean War caused the final split between the former World War II Allies. Almost one million soldiers, as well as three million civilians, perished in this war. A senseless loss.

Grace Kelly played Nancy Brubaker, wife of American attorney Harry Brukaber, who one year ago had been drafted to the 77th Pacific Division. Because of his experiences in the horrors of World War II, Harry loathes anything connected with the military. He is embittered. The young husband and wife have not seen each other for a year. Grace's role is fairly small, lasting about twenty minutes. It is among two roles (if one excludes the two

137

very short appearances in *Fourteen Hours*) that she did not value much in hindsight. The other role was that of the coffee plantation owner Catherine Knowland in the Latin American epic *Green Fire* (1954).

Her costar in *The Bridges at Toko-Ri* was the ladies' man William Holden (1918–1981). Although married since 1941 to actress Brenda Marshall, Holden had a taste for the young, classical beauties who acted alongside him. His marriage lasted until 1970, and it had to survive his numerous affairs. Grace and Holden fell head over heels in love with each other. Previously, the thirty-six-year-old Holden, the youngest of Grace's married lovers, had had a passionate affair with Audrey Hepburn with whom he had acted beside in Billy Wilder's *Sabrina* (1954). In the neighboring studio, Hitchcock had been making *Dial M for Murder* with Grace. Already an alcoholic at this time, Holden transitioned straight from his affair with Audrey Hepburn to Grace Kelly. The relationship between Grace and her new film partner ultimately did not last any longer than the three weeks that Grace stood in front of the camera. It was love at first sight, which from Grace's side quickly cooled after the filming—for the time being that is. Holden's problems with alcohol reminded her of Gene Lyons and of how she did not want to live with the long-term consequences of such a struggle. In contrast to some of the other relationships, the affair with Holden is one of the relationships, like the one with Oleg Cassini, that has been officially substantiated by Grace Kelly's son Prince Albert.[174] What Grace did not yet know was that in a short time she would again meet Holden in the spring of 1954 for the filming of *The Country Girl*. Allegedly Holden and Grace grew closer again, although former fling Bing Crosby was in the movie as well. She and Crosby had been involved with each other a year and a half before. Crosby had also been an alcoholic, in earlier years. What happened in the fictional film paralleled real life. And he too again fell in love with Grace.

The plot of *The Bridges at Toko-Ri* is simple. It is November 1952. Because of the Korean War, Harry Brubaker (William Holden) has been serving with the navy on an aircraft carrier in the Pacific for one year. Brubaker is one of the most prominent fighter pilots. He knows that he must complete the mission given to him by Admiral Tarrant (Fredric March). His mission is to destroy the bridges over the Toko-Ri. Nancy Brubaker (Grace Kelly), caring wife and mother, stays at home. It will not end well. After successfully bombing the bridges, Harry Brubaker and his two comrades are shot down by the Koreans on his return flight. The film does not show how his wife Nancy reacts or what happens to her. It seems as if she is forgotten for the remainder of the film. Except for the quiet moment, the day before his attack at Toko-Ri, in which Harry writes a poignant letter to his Nancy from the ship's cabin. He never returns from this flight.

In part, *The Bridges at Toko-Ri* served as a propaganda film for the US Navy and Air Force, which both endorsed the movie. It is not without reason that the following lines were included in the film's opening credits: "We proudly present this motion picture as a tribute to the United States Navy and especially to the men of the Naval Air and Surface Forces of the Pacific Fleet whose cooperation made this picture possible."[175]

The movie's inside scenes were filmed in the Paramount Studios in Japan on the Yellow Sea, as well as on the *USS Oriskany*, an aircraft carrier. In various longer scenes, military procedure was meticulously depicted, which is why Robson's naval and air force films seem to almost be documentary in nature. The final fifteen minutes of the movie portrays the preparations and implementation of the attack on the Korean bridges. Cinematically, these shots are very realistic. For all this, the film received the 1956 Oscar for Best Visual Effects, as well as two other Academy Award nominations.

The character of the wife Nancy Brubaker is a thankless and relatively small supporting role. Grace Kelly is not seen until the film's twenty-fourth minute. She is down in the Tokyo harbor, where she is waiting for the arrival of William Holden on the aircraft carrier. He has one week of leave, which he can spend with his wife and their two little daughters. There are five scenes in all, in which Grace appears: the reunion at the harbor; the meeting with Admiral Tarrant at the hotel bar; the conversation between Nancy and Harry in bed; the visit of the four Brubakers to the

Japanese Yakuzi Baths; and the farewell at the harbor. She did not have much to work with, acting-wise. The longest and most demanding of the scenes was the conversation in bed. At Nancy's request, Harry talks for the first time in some detail about the war and about his upcoming attack at Toko-Ri. He opens up after first avoiding her questions and preferring to discuss the children's piano lessons. She presses him stubbornly. Before now, Nancy was unaware of the level of risk and danger that will be facing her husband. In this conversation, she first grasps the possible consequences. Already in the fiftieth minute of the film, Grace is seen for the last time, standing on the quay and waving at the departing ship.

For this film, Grace Kelly was again dressed by costume designer Edith Head. In the scenes at the harbor, she is wearing a heavy, light-brown coat with a light hat adorned with a brown hat band and pale, not-quite-white gloves. Underneath she is wearing a dress that is a somewhat lighter brown than her coat. For the first time ever on screen, she appears lying in bed (excepting the short scene in *Dial M for Murder* in which she is seen asleep in bed before the telephone rings and she wakes up). When Harry later returns to the hotel, after having to care for his friend Mike (Mickey Rooney) who had gotten into a fight, she is wearing a thin, pale blue nightgown, which is somewhat more chaste than the one she was wearing in *Dial M for Murder*. In several moderately close shots, the camera shows her listening to William Holden explain his upcoming mission. She looks enchantingly lovely in her attention to the serious topic at hand. Perhaps it is not inconsequential that her film partner and costar was her lover on the other side of the camera. Sometimes the boundaries between fiction and reality are fluid. An inner glow streams from Grace's face. Her eyes are deep blue, her lips are dark red. As always, her face is genteelly pale.

Another first-time occurrence took place in the Japanese Natural Hot Springs Hotel pool. Here she is seen in the water. This appearance caused ripples among both the critics and the public. Her neck, arms, shoulders, and occasionally almost visible chest are bare. When the film premiered in New York at Radio

City Music Hall on January 20, 1955, and then opened across the country, this scene received much attention in the reviews and commentaries. In the scene that takes place in the hotel bar, Grace is dressed in a dark blue evening gown with a plunging neckline. It shines like silk, and around her neck hangs a strand of glowing white pearls. With this image, she comes the closest to the picture of herself that she was always striving to establish. Thus, in this war film, which was otherwise not well suited to her, for a few short moments, she projects something noticeable, something that is commonly called the Kelly Touch.

The Country Girl
(1954)

> *Grace is like a kaleidoscope: one twist,*
> *and you get a whole new facet.*
> —George Seaton[176]

In March 1955, this film earned Grace Kelly an Academy Award for Best Actress. Before that, in January of that same year, she received a Golden Globe as Best Actress in a Drama. Eventually, in 1956, she was also honored with a BAFTA nomination as Best Foreign Actress. Thus, in hindsight, *The Country Girl* can be viewed as her most important film, considering the critical acclaim and honors given within the context of her acting career.

Besides Fred Zinnemann's *High Noon* and her brief appearance in Henry Hathaway's noir *Fourteen Hours*, this is her third and last film made in atmospheric black-and-white.

When MGM announced that it would not loan her again to Paramount, Grace told her agent that she was breaking with Hollywood and returning to New York. The studio could henceforth send her Christmas cards to her home address. This made an impression on MGM. The studio heads, including studio boss Dore Schary, wondered why other studios, particularly Paramount, were trying to poach their actress. Over the six years of her acting career, MGM had actually used her very little. Despite her seven-year contract, Grace only made three of her eleven films with MGM: *Mogambo*, *Green Fire*, and *High Society*. Furthermore, she only agreed to make *Green Fire* so that she could gain permission to film *The Country Girl*. She viewed the former as the low point of her career, as an involuntary concession to Hollywood's studio system. As her sister Lizanne Kelly LeVine recalled, *Green Fire* "wasn't one of her favorite films. She was tired when she started. She had done about six pictures in a row and she had to go to South America... But she did it in order to get the part in *The Country Girl*."[177]

Philadelphia native Clifford Odets (1906–1963), who also wrote the screenplay for the film noir classic *Sweet Smell of Success* (1957), published *The Country Girl* in 1949. The play premiered on November 10, 1950, in the Lyceum Theatre in New York. Odets himself directed the play, and the original set design was conceived by Boris Aronson. In the original cast, the actress Uta Hagen played the role of Georgie Elgin, and for her portrayal, she received a Tony Award as the Best Actress of the year. Undoubtedly Grace Kelly's was measured against this fine performance.

The plot is this: Bernie Dodd (William Holden) has started rehearsals for the rural musical *The Land Around Us,* and the main role must still be cast. His gruff producer Phil Cook (Anthony Ross) has been impatiently sitting through the rehearsals in the lobby of the Longacre Theatre, breathing down Dodd's neck to cast the role. This makes it harder for Dodd to actually cast the actor he wants: Frank Elgin (Bing Crosby), a musical star from the past who was once an idolized singer and actor. However, years have passed since his heyday and Elgin has been forgotten; he has not stood on a stage or at a studio microphone for a long time. And he drinks. Producer Cook is more than a little skeptical, and he lets his director know this on no uncertain terms. However, Dodd stands his ground; Elgin will star in the main role, or nobody will. If the role is given to anyone else, then Dodd will resign as director. Dodd believes in Elgin, although he is pretty much alone in his support. Only Elgin's young wife, Georgie Elgin (Grace Kelly), still believes in her much older husband. The play *The Land Around Us,* with its title song (lyrics for the Harold Arlen and Victor Young compositions in *The Country Girl* were written by Ira Gershwin) could be the chance for him. It could also be his last chance. Frank knows this, as does prudent Georgie. Thus, the success of this musical swings like an invisible sword of Damocles over Frank Elgin, who himself has the greatest doubts of all. The rehearsals become increasingly difficult, since Frank is no longer accustomed to the pressure of show business.

However, he is actually tormented by something very different. His mind constantly returns to a moment of tragedy in his past. It was the moment in which he let his young son slip out of his sight for just a moment, causing the boy to be struck by a car and killed. It happened when a photographer wanted to take his picture outside on the sidewalk in front of the record-shaped logo for Vogue Records Studio. He had just recorded a hit for the studio, "The Search Is Through." During this, his son sits on a chair next to his wife Georgie and gives advice to his father as well. After the photos are taken, his wife starts walking off, so that Frank can spend a little time with his son. As Georgie reaches the studio door, Frank whistles at her and says to his son that he has such an attractive mother. Georgie turns around and a delighted smile spreads across her face. With her white-gloved hands, she jokingly pulls the veil attached to her white pillbox hat across her face. Then she leaves the recording studio. This is the last time she sees her son.

As a precautionary measure, the decision is made to hold the premiere and a short run of performances in Boston prior to the actual opening night in New York. These do not go well, and Frank Elgin again seeks to prop himself up with alcohol. He then admits to director Dodd that he lives under Georgie's strict discipline and that years ago she was the one who drank. He turns everything, including the relationship, on its head. And Dodd believes Frank until the tense, distant relationship between him and Georgie finally results in a loud argument in the visiting room of the prison where Frank Elgin has been held through the night in a drunken stupor. In this conversation, Georgie reveals the truth. She never drank; Frank drinks. She never tried to kill herself after the death of their son, as Frank had told Dodd she had. Frank was the one who attempted suicide by slitting his wrists. Prior to this, Dodd had spoken to Elgin's wife in an increasingly gruff and dismissive manner, since he blamed her for Frank's weak stage performances. Now, he is ashamed. He tells Georgie he is sorry and he kisses her. His vehement rejection of her has turned into attraction. The premiere in New York is a great success. The critics are positive, the public loves it. For the first time since the death of his son, Frank Elgin finds courage again, and he becomes confident in what he does and who he is.

During the subsequent opening party, all three of them—Georgie, Frank, and Bernie—sit in a nearby room, a library. With Grace in the middle, the relational constellation is spatially rendered. She sits in an armchair, while William Holden sits relatively close to her on the edge of the desk. When Bing Crosby enters the room and sits down in the chair across from them, the two of them do not look at each other. Grace's face is turned toward Crosby, Holden has his back to both of them.

"You know, there is only one thing more obvious than two people looking longingly at each other—it is two people avoiding it," comments Frank Elgin. This hits the mark. Georgie must now decide. In the large room next door, a piano starts to play one of Frank's songs, the thematic piece that plays throughout the film and throughout his life, "The Search Is Through." He stands up and goes into the other room, and Georgie follows him quickly, afraid that the song and the memory of his son will again deeply affect and unbalance him. However, this time Frank does not collapse or reach for a bottle. He stands next to the piano player and listens to his song. And gets through it. Clifford Odets's drama deals with survival and perseverance.

It seems that Frank Elgin has overcome this painful, traumatic loss—today it would be called post-traumatic stress disorder.

In the last scene of the film, Dodd pushes the curtains a little to the side. He looks out the window and down the empty, dark street. In the pale glare of the streetlights, he sees Georgie run after Frank. He stops walking, and they embrace. Together they walk on, in the same direction. Bernie Dodd lets the curtains fall back in place and turns to the critical reviews in a freshly delivered issue of the *New York Times*.

From its very start, *The Country Girl* was shaped by various difficulties and complications. Originally Jennifer Jones (1919–2009) was supposed to play the part of Georgie Elgin. She was the wife of David O. Selznick (1902–1965), the powerful Hollywood producer, who was responsible for large productions such as *Gone with the Wind* (1939). He had also produced three of Hitchcock's movies: *Rebecca* (1940), *Spellbound* (1945), and *The Paradine Case*

(1947). However, Jennifer Jones was pregnant, so the part had to be recast. There were those who still argued that Jones could still play the part, David O. Selznick being a huge proponent of her being cast regardless. Nonetheless, Grace was requested. George Seaton and producer William Perlberg, who had previously produced *The Bridges at Toko-Ri*, made sure that Grace secretly received a script, despite the resistance of both studios and agents. Grace read the script for *The Country Girl* and was immediately convinced that she needed to play Georgie. A part with high artistic demands. She recognized all of this right away.

After MGM's initial reluctance to again loan her to another studio, Grace was confronted with another point of resistance: her costar, Bing Crosby (1903–1977).

Claiming his contractual right to have a say in decisions, Crosby the star announced that he did not want Grace Kelly to replace Jennifer Jones. Grace was too elegant, too glamorous—at the very least, much too beautiful. She did not have enough experience. She did not fit the part. However, it was Grace, in contrast to the rest of the cast, who knew the play from its run on Broadway. After all, she lived in New York. Over Crosby's protests, Grace was ultimately cast. Crosby later revised his comments about the casting of the main female role, but his initial reaction seems all the more confusing since he and Grace were supposedly closer than the public ever knew. In 1952, they had most likely been involved with one another, although this liaison was never confirmed. Now, during the filming of this dark, difficult drama about life and love, Crosby especially wanted to continue and intensify their connection with each other. At this time, March 1954, he was two months away from his fiftieth birthday on May 2, making him almost twice as old as the twenty-four-year-old Grace.

On this topic, Grace's sister Lizanne said: "Grace called me one evening and said, 'Bing has asked me marry him.'"[178] Lizanne explained, "Bing was crazy about her, really crazy—he asked her to go out all the time. But she wasn't in love with him. She loved him but she was not in love with him."[179] And just as Bing was very much in love with her, Holden was just the same. Even on the set, everyone knew he was in love with Grace.

Another man who had long been in love with her was, of course, Oleg Cassini. He visited Grace during the filming two or three times. As for Crosby, he was a widower; he had lost his wife Dixie Lee, whom he had married in 1930, to cancer in mid-1952. Over the previous year, he had been involved with actress Kathryn Grant. They had become engaged and set, and then canceled, several wedding dates until they actually did marry in 1957. This situation did not seem to bother Crosby during the spring of 1954. Grace did not know anything about it. They went out in the evenings, were observed in public, and were supposedly seen by eyewitnesses cuddling in restaurants. Unlike with the married Ray Milland, this time Grace did not risk putting herself into a tricky situation. The marriage between Bing and Kathryn Crosby eventually lasted twenty years, until 1977, when he died on October 14.

Until the last minute, Crosby did not actually want to accept the role of the aging, alcoholic singer and actor Frank Elgin who is fighting for a comeback. "No! Absolutely not—I am a singer," Crosby nervously and insecurely declared to director George Seaton.[180] By the mid-1950s, Crosby had reached the final high point of his career with such movies as *Little Boy Lost* (1953), and Michael Curtiz's musical *White Christmas* (1954), as well as his 1956 film *High Society* (1956) in which he again starred with Grace. He seemed to be afraid that his most glittering period would soon be over and that the public would begin to associate him too closely with the role of Frank Elgin: "I've got my audience to think of. I don't want to look like an old man on the screen."[181]

Having already worked with Crosby on *Little Boy Lost*, George Seaton tried to allay the popular performer's fears: "Bing, let's be honest, you're frightened." Crosby seemed about to cry, and he answered: "I can't do it." To this, Seaton responded: "Please have faith in me, I'm frightened too, so let's be frightened together."[182] After this conversation, they supposedly hugged each other and walked to the set. The director recognized the source of Crosby's pronounced fear in playing this part. Usually Crosby played Crosby in his films, most of which were lighthearted musicals. On the screen, later on the television (as in the twenty-seven episodes of the *Bing Crosby Show* [1964–1965]), or even anywhere else, he was simply himself: Crosby. But in Seaton's film, Frank Elgin was a multifaceted and deeply grounded character, whose life had certain darker parallels with Crosby's own. Not an easy task. With great determination , Georg Seaton finally succeeded in convincing Crosby to portray Frank Elgin.

The filming lasted from late February through early April 1954 and took place in Paramount Studios Hollywood. The exterior scenes were shot in New York. The first week of filming was a complete disaster. The actors were insecure. Each of them acted for him or herself, and George Seaton had a difficult time directing the actors such that the necessary mood and atmosphere could be created. Later, Grace recalled the nerves that were in the room that first week, particularly that she and Bing were both quite nervous and distracted, which hindered their attempts to work with each other.[183]

In the end, Seaton decided not to use any of the materials taken that week, including all the takes and designs, and to completely start from scratch again. It was a radical, yet logical, decision that cost the production both time and money. During the filming, however, Grace proved to be highly focused, well prepared, and extremely punctual. She always knew her lines. This almost Prussian, unpretentiously correct manner of working quickly impacted her co-actors and the crew. After five taut weeks, the filming concluded. These went much better once they moved past those early difficulties.

For the first and only time in a movie, Grace Kelly appeared in *The Country Girl* without any makeup for most of the scenes. According to television and film director, Ted Post, "The greatest expression of courage that Grace demonstrated was the throwing away of her mask of beauty and elegance and became somebody who was identified with being just a kind of woman that you could meet on the streets."[184] Her outer appearance stood in stark contrast to that from both of her two previous Hitchcock movies. This was clearly reflected in her clothing, which again was designed by costume designer Edith Head: the costumes were plain and unobtrusive in tone. In some scenes, Grace Kelly was hardly recognizable. As Edith Head explained, "Her figure had absolutely no resemblance to Grace Kelly's. I put her in apron dresses and skirts and blouses that made her look dumpy."[185] In one scene, Georgie Elgin waits on her husband Frank in his dressing room, as he rehearses on stage. From time to time, he comes in to take a highly alcoholic cough medicine to combat his alleged cold. While waiting, Grace sits in an armchair and knits. She wears a pair of glasses. In real life, she sat just this way among friends, at home, or even by her parents, crocheting or knitting. Her German mother Margaret had taught this skill to her and her sisters Peggy and Lizanne at an early age in Philadelphia. Since she was nearsighted, Grace wore glasses; she often wore no makeup and dressed casually in a shirt and jeans. Not the typical Kelly Look. Much more the other Grace. The private one who also liked things simple and plain.

In the final scenes of this romantic drama, and also at the premiere party, which was attended by both of the men who loved her, reality and fiction overlap in a delicately suggestive, nuanced way. She appears in a black evening gown with short sleeves and a wide, deep neckline. Her hair is pinned up, and a short strand of pearls encircles her neck. This is an elegant, distinct look that reminds one of her attire in *Rear Window*. "The end of the film rescues Grace's character from her dull existence, giving her a renewed interest in life. So, I got to dress Grace stylishly for at least a couple scenes," remarked Edith Head.[186]

One of Grace's most impressive scenes in this deep, dark drama takes place during the first third of *The Country Girl*. Frank Elgin has just fed Dodd his wife's erroneous life story. He pauses when he sees a shadow appear at the wings of the stage. It is Georgie, who can only be seen in silhouette. A light shines out from the door behind her. Her face cannot be seen since it lies in darkness. Her sudden appearance is disquieting. At the same time, she projects something statuesque, immovable, almost threatening. As soon as he sees Grace, a single thrilling, charged sound intensifies the moment of fear: "Georgie?" the unsettled, hesitant Frank calls questioningly into the half-darkness. He slowly moves toward her. Georgie approaches him, "Just coming from a movie, passing by." She then asks if she is disturbing anything. It is not clear how long she has been standing there listening. Then she moves forward to the front edge of the stage. As she stands on the stage, looking into the dark, empty audience, quietly contemplative, she muses: "There is nothing quite so mysterious and silent as a dark theater—a night without a *star*." Framed in darkness, Grace's face is lit by a single beam of light that seems to come from the nothingness of the deep theater space. She emphasizes the word "star," referencing both a star in the sky and the star status that Frank Elgin once had. The effect of this intonation is deeply ambiguous. It is almost whispered, murmured.

Grace Kelly loved the theater her whole life, ever since her Uncle George had begun telling her stories about his own plays. She owed her love and affinity for theater and acting to perhaps the only member of the Kelly family who understood, comprehended, and supported her in her endeavors. It is likely that George Seaton's *The Country Girl,* and its theater-centric story would have been all the more significant and meaningful for Grace.

At the close of the movie, Georgie Elgin undergoes a cathartic metamorphosis that is parallel to her husband's. She matures from a brown mouse to an attractive woman who is now sure of herself. She seems newly born. And this helps her understand the internal transformation Frank is experiencing. This is exactly the reason why she decides to remain with her husband, an actor who has just had his first taste of success in a decade, in spite of his notorious alcoholism and the trauma of their collective past. It is why she decides against Bernie Dodd, the successful Broadway theater director, the younger man who showed regret for his judgments and was newly in love with her.

The final scene sequences in *The Country Girl* are very touching, either despite or because of the completely somber and reserved staging by George Seaton. Within Georgie's story, Grace's essential character can be seen. Both are women who do not give up easily, who stand up for both themselves and those they are closest to—even when the situation is hard to bear and requires personal sacrifice, discipline, composure, conscientious responsibility, feelings of duty, as well as, above all, human goodness.

151

The Country Girl premiered in Los Angeles on December 11, 1954, and opened in New York on December 15. It received seven Oscar nominations. Besides Grace Kelly's Academy Award, a second one was given to George Seaton for Best Adapted Screenplay. Although he had also been nominated as Best Director, Seaton had to be content with this one golden statuette. Bing Crosby was nominated for Best Actor, but he did not win, which was a blow to him. His director and great advocate was also disappointed for him; Crosby was a kind of proxy for Seaton himself: "My opinion was that Bing's portrayal was outstanding—he went above and beyond everything he had ever done before."[187]

Other Oscar nominations for the team went to the camera man John F. Warren and producer William Perlberg. However, almost all the Academy Awards for that year in these categories were awarded to Elia Kazan's *On the Waterfront*.

—"The Award for Best Actress:
Grace Kelly for *The Country Girl*"

On Feburary 12, 1955, Grace Kelly received the happy news that she was among the five actresses that the Academy of Motion Picture Arts and Sciences had nominated for the Best Actress of 1954. This must have been a dream come true for her. Although she had previously been nominated as Best Supporting Actress for her role as Linda Nordley in John Ford's *Mogambo*, she had not won.

Prior to this announcement, Grace had spent some time relaxing with her older sister Peggy in Jamaica. She wanted to distance herself from the hardships of the previous work-filled year and to revitalize herself. There she met with photographer Howell Conant, who wanted to do a photo shoot with Grace for an upcoming cover of *Collier's* magazine. This was a second meeting for the two of them—Conant already shot her for *Photoplay* magazine. Grace soon came to trust and respect Conant's work.

Until the end of her life, Howell Conant (1917–1999) would accompany Grace as her personal photographer. He was at the filming of *The Swan* and *High Society* as well as with her on the Atlantic crossing of the *Constitution* from New York to Monaco, and at her wedding in April 1956 in the royal palace in Monaco. Howell Conant's photographs of Grace appeared in *Life* and *Look*, in *Paris Match* and *Collier's,* and many other periodicals.

This particular cover photo for the June 24, 1955, issue of *Collier's* became one of his most famous photos worldwide. It shows Grace as if she has just emerged from the water. She stands there with damp, combed-back hair, and from her ears hang droplets of water, like pearl earrings. She looks directly at the viewer. Her eyes are dark blue, her lips are dark red. Around her flows the turquoise water of the Caribbean up to her bust line. There is something very direct and intimate about her gaze.

Conant accompanied Grace for twenty-seven years. Most of the people who became her friends stayed true throughout her life. Conant also attended Grace's funeral—for the first time, without his camera.

The 27th Academy Awards ceremony took place in Los Angeles on March 30, 1955. Grace wore a floor-length, crystal-blue satin evening gown, along with white pearl earrings and elbow-length white gloves. One of her trademarks. On her left arm, she carried a small handbag that was decorated with a floral pattern. Initially, Grace wanted to have the MGM costume department sew a gown for the Oscar ceremony, since she was still under contract with the studio. However, MGM let her know that she was no longer welcome there. Under the new leadership of Dore Schary, who replaced his predecessor Louis B. Mayer in the early 1950s, things were never comfortable for Grace at MGM. Schary liked to meddle in all the departments and shaped things according to his own personal gusto. Furthermore, he could not particularly relate to Grace. He did not find her either sexy or talented. This was the reason behind flops such as her unpopular film *Green Fire*. The studio that was supposed to bring about mutually beneficial successes for both her and themselves ultimately did not know what to do with her.

She had insistently and regularly rejected the other film offers and screenplays that MGM had sent her over the years, and this individualistic, uncompromising attitude increasingly rubbed the studio the wrong way. Within MGM, it was gruffly said that they had had to loan her out to other studios too often and that Grace had not fulfilled the obligations connected with her seven-year contract, in the eyes of the MGM bosses. This would have considerable—almost threatening—consequences.

In the weeks before the Oscar ceremony, Dore Schary made a statement showing his displeasure for Grace. His assertion was that she owed all her subsequent success to MGM because of *Mogambo* and yet, despite her contract, she had only made two pictures with MGM.[188]

Additionally, the fact that Grace Kelly's winning turn was in a Paramount production really rubbed salt in MGM's wound. Refused a dress, Grace immediately turned to Edith Head, who dropped everything in order to design and sew a dress for the Oscar ceremony according to Grace's detailed instructions and desires. Dressed in the resultant ice blue satin gown, Grace was featured on the April 11 cover of *Life* magazine. It was one of the most popular cover stories ever.

In the categories of Best Actress and Best Actor, five actresses and actors are always nominated. Grace was up against four other actresses: Audrey Hepburn in Billy Wilder's *Sabrina* (1954); Judy Garland for George Cukor's *A Star Is Born* (1954); Jane Wyman for Douglas Sirk's *Magnificent Obsession* (1954); and Dorothy Dandridge for Otto Preminger's *Carmen Jones* (1954).

In particular, Judy Garland and Grace Kelly were rumored to be favorites in industry publications and among the gossipmongers of Hollywood. Audrey Hepburn had won the coveted trophy the year before for William Wyler's *Roman Holiday* (1953).

Ironically, William Holden, who had himself won the Oscar for Best Actor the previous year for his role in Billy Wilder's *Stalag 17* (1953), read aloud the five nominations for Best Actress. He then took the envelope containing the name of the winner: "So, the Award for the Best Performance by an Actress: Grace Kelly, for *The Country Girl*!"[189]

At the reading of her name, Holden beams brightly. They had been lovers once, and now he could give Grace the golden statuette. Grace was one of the few actresses to have won an Oscar after acting in only a handful of films.

Grace's thank-you speech is one of the shortest ever given, only twenty seconds in length: "The thrill of this moment keeps me from saying what I really feel. I can only say thank you with all my heart to all who made this possible for me: thank you."[190] Two sentences, short and sweet—how very Grace-like. She broke out in tears only after she had left the stage, having successfully suppressed them until then.

Even John B. Kelly in Philadelphia watched the awards show on the television. When a reporter called him to ask for his comments on his twenty-five-year-old daughter's astounding achievement, her father only had the following to say: "I thought it would be Peggy. Anything Grace could do, Peggy could always do better.

I simply can't believe Grace won. Of the four children, she's the last one I'd expect to support me in my old age. How do you figure these things?"[191]

It is not known how Grace reacted to this humiliating, published statement by her father about the greatest triumph of her acting career. However, one can imagine what it meant to have her own father react with such tactlessness in light of such an achievement. In the career that she had chosen, there was no higher honor. She had worked under the direction of Fred Zinnemann, John Ford, and Alfred Hitchcock. She had acted beside Clark Gable, James Stewart, and William Holden. She had won an Oscar, as well as numerous other awards. Yet, all her father could talk about was how his daughter Peggy could do everything better. For her parents, especially her father, Grace was always the black sheep among the four Kelly children. She still seemed to be that even now, in the spring of 1955 after the Academy Awards. She would always be seen that way. She had hoped so much that this would change things, but it was futile. Grace Kelly had to continue to try to win the goodwill and favor of her father. It wasn't until 1956, close to the end of his life—four years before his death—when she finally would.

The Oscar dinner party that followed the ceremony was held in Romanoff's on Rodeo Drive, one of the most famous "in" restaurants in Hollywood during the 1940s and 1950s. At this time, Romanoff's was very similar to Chasen's, (which, incidentally, remained in business much longer). Chasen's was Alfred Hitchcock's favorite restaurant, and every Thursday evening, he had supper there with his wife Alma. It was also the location he chose several years later, in the fall of 1961, to offer Tippi Hedren her role in *The Birds* and to give her a silver brooch ornamented with three birds, which she still has today.

On this evening in late March 1955, sitting at the table in Romanoff's, Grace was still holding on to her golden statuette. It was sitting directly in front of her plate, and she showed it time and time again to the photographers who came by her table. Her entire face was lit up. Edith Head also sat at Grace's table. She too had an Oscar sitting beside her, the one she had received for Wilder's *Sabrina*.

Grace left the dinner party before it grew too late. After she had taken her limousine back to the Beverly Hills Hotel, she supposedly set the statuette above the fireplace in her hotel bungalow. She then sat down on the sofa and stared at the trophy. Despite her success, this was a very lonely moment, a very lonely night. Perhaps the loneliest moment of her life. This is one version of the conclusion to Oscar Night 1955.

According to another version, Marlon Brando, who had also just received an Oscar for his role as Terry Malloy in Elia Kazan's *On the Waterfront*, gave Grace his telephone number. Supposedly Grace called Brando, and he came to her bungalow at the Beverly Hills. First, Grace complained to Brando about her costar Bing Crosby and how he had been dead set against her casting in *The Country Girl*. As Grace and Brando eventually drew closer, someone knocked on her bungalow door around 3:00 a.m. No one less than Crosby, who also had been nominated for an Oscar and who had lost out to Brando, stood at the door. The rivals scuffled, and Brando easily won out over the older Crosby. At this time, Brando was thirty, and furthermore, he had taken boxing lessons the previous year in preparation for his role as harbor worker Terry Malloy. Grace had to call the hotel manager and the hotel doctor. Finally, Crosby left Grace's hotel bungalow.

This version of the story comes from the Brando biography, *Brando Unzipped*, by Darwin Porter (New York, 2006). Porter was supposedly told this story by Brando's agent Edith Van Cleve, who for a while also represented Grace Kelly.[192]

It remains unclear which of these two scenarios actually corresponded to the reality of that Oscar night on March 30, 1955.

Green Fire
(1954)

Green Fire *was not a pleasant experience. We worked in a wretched village, with miserable huts full of dirt. The crew suffered too. It was awful.*
—*Grace Kelly*[193]

With the greatest reluctance imaginable, Grace Kelly traveled directly after the conclusion of filming for *The Country Girl* to Colombia to fulfill her contract with MGM by acting in *Green Fire*. On all levels, this was a concession, a sacrifice. From the very start, it was clear that this project was not artistically driven. The filming took place under difficult, trying conditions, and the justification for this project was purely commercial in orientation. On the film poster, the names of Stewart Granger and Grace Kelly were accompanied by an image of a voluptuously endowed, typical Hollywood blonde, which clearly was meant to represent her. She was greatly displeased by this. When the film premiered in New York on December 24, 1954, it was a box office flop, and the critics panned it. It was a twofold disaster for MGM.

Grace spent ten days in Colombia for the filming, and then she was in Culver City to shoot the interior scenes at MGM Studios. For this woman, who now knew where she stood and, even more so, where she wished to go, this felt like a lost period of her life. Gradually, Grace was beginning to recognize her own worth, although doubt continued to gnaw at her—even after the Oscars in March 1955. While she stood at the side of Stewart Granger in the role of coffee plantation owner Catherine Knowland, she already knew where she was going after the filming of this movie: to the French Riviera, to Cannes, Nice, and Monaco. There could have been no conceivably greater contrast between the hot, dusty, strenuous filming in Colombia, and the light-suffused Côte d'Azur with its elegant hotels and even more elegant, noble atmosphere. This upcoming change in location must have given Grace both comfort and hope, while she fulfilled her obligations by working on *Green Fire*.

A native of Budapest, director Andrew Marton (1904–1992) worked on some of Hollywood's most legendary large-scale productions, including William Wyler's monumental epic *Ben Hur* (1959) and Joseph L. Mankiewicz's *Cleopatra* (1963). Parallel to these, he also often directed the second unit for various adventure films—the second unit being the group typically charged with filming footage of the setting: establishing shots, landscape sequences, etc. Ivan Goff and Ben Roberts based their screenplay on a novel by Peter W. Rainier. Armand Deutsch was the producer. The plot is flat and one-dimensional. The characters have no depth or any biographical backgrounds. The suspense is solely established through external actions.

When adventurer Rian X. Mitchell (Stewart Granger) finds a gem that could lead to a large cache of emeralds on Mount Carerre deep in the Andes of Colombia, he has to have it at all costs. Returning from the historic, centuries-old mine, he is attacked and injured both by bandits and then a leopard. Father Ripero (Robert Tafur) finds the stranded man and takes him the short distance to a coffee plantation that sits on the bank of the Magdalena River. Here he is cared for by the stylish plantation owner, Catherine Knowland (Grace Kelly). As soon as he can, Rian takes a river steamer to the capital city in order to convince his old pal Vic Leonard (Paul Douglas) to explore the mine with him. They had been partners for many years, but Vic is tired of adventures and hardships. Rian is finally successful in preventing Vic from departing. Together they return to the plantation, where Catherine waits for them. Rian hires laborers from the local villages to perform the mining work both inside the mine and on the mountain face. Catherine actually needs many of them to work on her coffee plantation since it is harvest time. However, the promise of the mountain is tempting, and the laborers accept Rian's offer. Vic is skeptical, and argues with Rian repeatedly. Also, since first seeing her on the pier, he is quite taken with Catherine and wants to help her with the plantation. However, Rian is obsessed with the idea of unearthing the emeralds—the "Green Fire." This obsession will ultimately be the downfall of Catherine's brother, Donald Knowland (John Ericson), who lets himself be convinced to join Rian's enterprise. At the building site on the mountainside, some large boulders come loose and roll down, and Donald is struck by one of them. Catherine is distraught by her brother's death, and it is Vic who stands beside her. Vic again distances himself from his partner, who simply wants the mining activities to continue. For a second time, Vic and Catherine are both disappointed and hurt by Rian, and they abandon his project.

This makes one wonder all the more why, within a very short time, Catherine and Vic are prepared to forgive Rian. This development is, in a dramaturgical sense, completely unsubstantiated and only seems to be a means to a happy "Hollywood ending." After both an attack by bandits under the evil El Moro and a flood that threatens to destroy the plantation are overcome, Catherine and Rian finally fall into each other's arms. By dynamiting a mountain slope, Rian rescues Catherine's plantation from the flood, and he gives up the search for the green emeralds. A very rushed reformation.

Grace Kelly's co-star here is Stewart Granger (1913–1993). Early on he chose this stage name because he feared that his given name, James Lablache Stewart, would be all too easily confused with that of the actor James Stewart. A native Englishman, Granger's second marriage took place in 1950 to the English actress Jean Simmons (*The Big Country*, 1958). Granger was forty-one when he filmed *Green Fire* with Grace Kelly, and Jean Simmons was pregnant with his child. Originally, the role of the adventurer was intended for Clark Gable, but ultimately it was Granger who took the role. At this time, Granger was at the peak of his career. However, the chemistry between Grace and Granger is, in general, nothing like that which connected her to previous costars.

"I don't think I have ever met anyone who was quite so conceited," Grace once commented about the MGM star, whom the public also deemed a swashbuckler.[194]

Granger swashbuckled his way through several adventure and cloak-and-dagger movies in Hollywood. These included *Scaramouche* (1952) by George Sidney and Curtis Bernhardt's *Beau Brummell* (1954) with its star-laden cast: Peter Ustinov and Elizabeth Taylor, as well as Granger in the title role. In the mid-1960s, Granger became very popular in Germany because of his casting in major roles in Rialto Film's Karl May films. His vanity and egotism, which Grace described, are also clearly recognizable in his role in *Green Fire*. Granger's smarmy portrayal of the adventurer Rian Mitchell practically bristles with self-confidence and may cause the audience's sympathies to meander from time to time between the three protagonists.

For a time, Granger found Grace to be aloof and cool, although he also thought her to be fantastically beautiful. He perceived her as distant—lonely, even. As a costar, he described her as totally different and also as someone who was involuntarily treated differently than anyone else on set. Arrogant or not, he respected her courage.

As Catherine, Grace rides from the coffee plantation to the mountain, to where Rian and his men are attempting to mine the mountainside. She is wearing white gloves. This simple accessory had become an instantly recognizable trademark for Grace, both on screen and off. On the set, Grace insisted on riding herself, instead of having a double do it. This astounded and caused concern among the camera team. If something happened to Grace deep in the Colombian jungle, if she was injured, the filming would be interrupted, if not canceled altogether. However, the ride went off without the slightest hitch. Fellow actor and MGM-contracted actor, John Ericson (who played her brother Donald and who some years before had also attended the American Academy of Dramatic Arts in New York at the same time Grace did) later recalled that to date he had never worked with any actress who seemed as far away from the prima donna mentality as Grace.

162

In the movie, Catherine has a private conversation with Rian one evening on the riverbank. She states, "Who knows. Maybe one day my Prince Charming will come riding down from the mountains."[195] Shortly after this, they kiss for the first time. Considering her future, this passing comment takes on prophetic meaning. Nonetheless, most of the dialogue in *Green Fire* lacks any kind of actual content. Some of Paul Douglas's lines as the worrying, sensible pal Vic are somewhat humorous in nature. While also questioning himself, he is constantly cursing Rian's success at convincing him to stay. Grace had already met Paul Douglas during the filming of *Fourteen Hours*. Douglas had played the New York traffic cop Charlie Dunnigan. In both films, Douglas portrayed conscientious, responsible characters, ones that turned out to be the only wholly sympathetic figures.

According to Grace, *Green Fire* was the only dark mark on the map of her filmography. She described working on the film as "a depressing experience."[196] Stewart Granger later commented that she was often unhappy during filming and was delighted after the final take was finished.

In the middle of filming *Green Fire*, Grace hired a private tutor to help her learn French. She already knew that within a few weeks she would be in the Riviera, standing before Robert Burks's camera. Although there was no contract yet and Metro-Goldwyn-Mayer had not yet granted permission for another loan of its actress to another studio, Grace had no doubt that she would be involved with the next Hitchcock movie. Hitch had secretly informed Grace that he could conceive of no one in the role but her. Some years later, he confirmed that from the very beginning, he had intended Grace for this part, ever since he had purchased the rights to David Dodge's novel. Grace was certain that now she would again, for a fourth time, act in a film for Paramount: "I finished *Green Fire* one morning at eleven, I went into the dubbing room at one—and at six o'clock I left for France."[197]

163

To Catch a Thief
(1955)

She never distanced herself from others. Even so, as soon
as she came on the set, everyone fell silent.
—Cary Grant[198]

He would have used Grace in the next ten pictures
he made. I would say that all the actresses he cast
subsequently were attempts to retrieve the image and
feeling that Hitchcock carried around so reverentially
about Grace.
—John Michael Hayes[199]

In the summer of 1954, filming for *To Catch a Thief* took place on
the Côte d'Azur, followed by Paramount Studios in Hollywood
for all interior scenes. Filming lasted three months, from May 31
through September 4. The first stage of filming incorporated various locations around the Riviera: the elegant Carlton Hotel and
the Villa Goldman in Cannes, sites in Tourrettes and La Turbie,
in Eze and Gourdon, in Nice, in Cagnes-sur-Mer and Monte
Carlo. Of course, some scenes were shot in the colorful Marché
des Fleurs, the historic flower market in the center of Nice. It was
a cinematic sightseeing tour par excellence.

On August 13, after departing from France and resuming filming in Hollywood, the team celebrated Hitchcock's fiftieth birthday on the set of the final costume ball. There was champagne
and a large cake, as was the tradition for the master's birthday. As
always, Hitchcock greeted and reacted to this event with exaggerated surprise and humility. Oleg Cassini was present for this
event, and he provided the following description. When Hitch's
thoroughly British secretary—most likely his long-term, personal assistant Peggy Robertson (1916–1998)[200] whom Cassini
for whatever reason did not name—clapped her hands to gather
everyone for the cutting of the cake, she experienced a Freudian
slip in her very carefully clipped English:

165

"Ladies and gentlemen, could I have your attention for a moment? Would you all come into the other room, please, and have a piece of *Mr. Hitchcake's cock*?"[201] According to Oleg Cassini, this was a hilariously comic moment—at least for the majority of those present...

On a black-and-white photograph from that day, Hitch can be seen blowing out the candles on his cake, while Grace stands immediately to his left and watches with interest. He is holding her with his left hand. It is a very lovely moment. A moment that reveals something very familiar and platonic despite the rumored characterization of Hitchcock's film set. It resonates with something that has nothing to do with the banal cliché of a romantic connection between the director and his main actress. This photograph exemplifies the exceptionally good relationship between Grace's favorite director and his favorite actress. As Grace Kelly once explained about Alfred Hitchcock and his wife Alma Reville, "I feel there is so much affection between him and his wife, that he can do no wrong."[202]

With great excitement, Grace flew to Paris on May 24, 1954. There she went shopping at Hermés and then took the night train (the Blue Train) to Cannes. Alfred Hitchcock picked her up at the train station. However, before leaving for Paris, Grace had sent Oleg Cassini a meaningful postcard from Hollywood after the disastrous filming of *Green Fire* had come to an end. It contained only one sentence: "Those who love me shall follow me."[203] And indeed, Oleg Cassini did follow Grace Kelly. Along with Alfred Hitchcock and his wife Alma Reville, Cary Grant and his wife Betsy Drake, and Grace, Cassini too stayed in the elegant Carlton Hotel.

After the long days on set and even on their days off, the six of them often went out to eat together. Alfred Hitchcock may have been a knowledgeable art collector, but above all he considered himself a pleasure-loving gourmet and wine connoisseur. He always carefully selected the restaurants, as well as the menus. As Oleg Cassini recalled, most of the time, he picked three star restaurants, if not higher.[204] Cassini had never before met someone who took so much joy from eating. At this time Hitchcock was again on a diet—at his heaviest, during the filming of *Rebecca*, he weighed 330 pounds—and he drank only water during the hours of filming. In the evening, he ate lavishly.

"What *didn't* he eat?" quipped the actress Brigitte Auber rakishly, remembering with amusement the various meals had while filming on the Riviera.[205] The evening meals ran like small ceremonies under Hitchcock's attentively strict leadership. At the table, he resided like a self-satisfied master of ceremonies, which paralleled the way he would sit like Buddha in the director's chair on the set, holding all the threads in his hand. He loved to surprise others, but he himself wanted to avoid being surprised at all costs, even by a dish that he had not previously seen or tasted. Unforeseen developments on set were a horror of nightmarish proportions. These dinners for six, whether in the hotel restaurant in the Côte d'Azur or in small, out-of-the-way restaurants in the foothills of the maritime Alps, were unforgettable to everyone involved. Grace would greatly miss these in the coming years.

Five years later, in a very personal letter from April 14, 1959—the first surviving letter from Hitchcock to Grace, preserved in the Palace Archives in Monaco—Alfred Hitchcock recalled their time together on the French Riviera and their various lavish dinners: "I miss the Foie Gras in Cannes. We have all the original recipes, but it is just not the same. How is your weight?"[206]

Besides Hitchcock's nostalgic look into the past, this letter is particularly notable because it speaks to both the professional and the private aspects of his life, what moves him and occupies him. It is a further indication of the close connection between the two artists. The letter goes on to tell about the birth of his third granddaughter, Kathleen, on February 27, 1959, and about Alma's battle with advanced cancer. And finally, Hitchcock wrote about the canceling of the long-anticipated *No Bail for the Judge*, which was to be filmed in London. Audrey Hepburn was Hitchcock's intended actress for this film, and in June, her movie *The Nun's Story* (1959; Director: Fred Zinnemann) had its world premiere in New York. After reading the screenplay, she was very concerned about the lasting, negative impact that a rape scene set in

Hyde Park could have on her image as an innocent doe, a classically stylish woman in Givenchy. Ultimately, Hepburn backed out of the project, and the London Hitchcock-Hepburn film was never produced.

For Grace Kelly, the time spent with Oleg Cassini was the best time during this very relaxed, third and last film made with Hitchcock. She enjoyed Oleg's affection and attention, and she enjoyed the work with her favorite director. The work took place on one of the most beautiful coasts in Europe. She could be herself within the privacy of close friends. It was a small, familiar circle. This summer was singular in Grace's life. There would be no other like it again.

Oleg Cassini died on March 17, 2006, on Long Island, New York, at the age of ninety-two. Until his death, he endlessly praised Grace. Whenever he was interviewed—a prime example being his sit-down with publicist Gero von Boehm—and asked about other things in his life, such as his time as the personal couturier for First Lady Jackie Kennedy, he often changed the subject and returned again and again to *her*—to Grace, whom he described as his great love. Here are some of Gero von Boehm's unpublished notes regarding his interview with Oleg:

September 5, 2001. Mid-morning in Cassini's townhouse, which is like a great stage set. A mixture of Venetian Palazzo (with *fake windows!*), English country house, and Russian royal palace. I believe that his father was an ambassador of the czar to America. Everywhere there are little tables with silver-framed pictures, mostly of himself, however it is immediately noticeable how often Grace Kelly appears. All sorts of altars. Cassini is amazingly lively, but he does not want to divulge much about Jackie [Kennedy]. He keeps talking about Grace, who was the love of his life. He has never recovered from the shock of her completely surprising him by ending their relationship. The ideal woman in every way. Her beauty, her perfect body, her intelligence—she had inspired him as no other woman had. She had driven him to his greatest achievements. He complains about Grace's mother, who had always stood between the two of them.

At least he told the story of Jackie and [her sister] Lee, and how Onassis booted Lee off the boat [the *Christina*] and gave her a small bracelet in farewell. Not particularly meaty, so to speak, was and neither was the conversation about Jackie. He would be better in a film about Grace. However, a wonderful meeting with an incredible man from a long vanished epoch. As a farewell, a book and a somewhat oppressive men's cologne which has long been retired from the markets.[207]

Cassini once significantly said that Grace, his great love, "was two people"—a woman with two sides, with two faces.[208] One of them was reserved, distant, and unapproachable. So it seemed. A woman who entered the public arena, elegant and stoic. However, in private she was incredibly warm, giving everyone the feeling that she cared exclusively for them and them alone. This was a talent that later, as the Princess of Monaco, she used to overcome the initial difficulties with the Monegasque population, ultimately becoming quite beloved in her small country.

On one balmy June evening, Grace and Cassini had an intimate dinner with each other on a pier in the Cannes harbor. During the course of this meal, the conversation concretely turned to the topic of marriage. According to Cassini, Grace told him: "I want to be your wife."[209] And immediately, in the midst of this conversation, she began to sketch out and plan everything: Cassini's introduction to her parents in Philadelphia, the wedding dress, the wedding, their children. The conversation went so far that they considered a wedding for fall of that very year; one possible date was in the first half of October 1954. The actual date would be kept a secret, and the wedding in America would include only a close circle of a few friends. This plan was the polar opposite of the actual, expensive, ostentatious, media extravaganza that occurred in Grace's life only a year and a half later, not far from Cannes, on the Riviera.

However, in this romantic summer, Grace and Cassini failed to reckon with Grace's strict parents. Grace promised Cassini that her mother Margaret would side with her, and her mother would somehow convince father Jack. When both of them returned to the United States and filming began at Paramount Studios

(Cassini often accompanied Grace to the set, driving her there in the morning and picking her up afterward for dinner), Grace wanted to immediately introduce Cassini to her parents, but it would be no walk in the park. The location was to be the Kellys' summer house, a large, white, turn-of-the-century wooden beach house on the New Jersey coast between the quaint towns of Ocean City and Margate City, not far from Atlantic City and thus easily reachable from both Philadelphia and New York. Before this fateful visit, Grace and Cassini met her mother Margaret for lunch in New York in early September.

Cassini called the first meeting with Grace's mother "an absolute disaster." Until the end of his life, Cassini would complain about Grace's mother, claiming, "She would always stand between us."[210] He joined the mother and daughter in Grace's apartment in Manhattan to pick them up for lunch. Already during the joint taxi ride from the apartment to the restaurant, a highly unpleasant, extremely frosty conversation ensued. At first, Cassini tried to humorously lighten the tense, strained situation. "Well, here we are—the *unholy* trio," he said, to which Margaret Kelly responded, "You, Mr. Cassini, may be unholy. I can assure you that Grace and I are not."[211] During the subsequent, no-less-icy luncheon, Margaret Kelly gave Cassini a "long talk about his unworthiness," saying he was "a playboy, a divorced man ... not good marriage material." Mrs. Kelly said, "I can understand why Grace may have been charmed by you, Mr. Cassini. You are charming and educated. You have a lot of experience with women. But we believe that Grace owes it to herself, her family, and her community to rethink this."[212]

The eventual introduction of Cassini to Jack Kelly and Grace's brother Kell sometime later was its own fiasco. The two Kelly men would not even look at Cassini during this torturously long weekend—Cassini himself spoke of spending seven days in the Kelly house[213]—and they refused to answer him even if he posed a direct question to them, acting as if he was not even in the same room with them. They looked right through him. A deeply humiliating situation. A completely ridiculous attitude. At one point, Grace's brother Kell gave the following statement to *Time* magazine: "Generally I dislike the strange men she goes out with.

170

I would like to see her date more athletic men. But she doesn't listen to me."[214] In the same *Time* article, Oleg Cassini described Kell as a "professional skirt chaser."

Fifteen years before, Cassini had had a similar experience with the actress Gene Tierney, but the two of them had still married. Tierney had even sided with him against her parents to defend him. Now, at this point, Cassini, who had been twice divorced—an abomination in the eyes of the Catholic Kellys—and was known for his romantic affairs, was a persona non grata for the Kellys. He was yet another man in their daughter's life whom they found unworthy. None of her lovers so far had any standing in their eyes. And there had already been several of them. But Grace did not protest their judgments. She did not resist her parents' dictates. She remained silent. With this, the wheel of fate turned. In terms of marriage, Cassini began to hesitate. As did Grace. "We missed our moment," Oleg Cassini commented vaguely many years later.[215] Who knows what might have become of Grace Kelly, or of the actress, if she had married the fashion designer Oleg Cassini in the fall of 1954?

Grace Kelly and Oleg Cassini saw each other one last time, after she had married Prince Rainier and was living in Monaco on the Riviera. Their meeting was pure accident, a brief, yet lingering moment. Together with a few friends—including young Philippe Junot, a playboy whom Grace's older daughter Princess Caroline would marry in June 1978—Cassini was crossing the Mediterranean in a yacht. They were docked in Monaco. As Cassini walked along the beach, he suddenly saw Grace sitting on a bench with the New York fashion designer Vera Maxwell. He immediately stopped still, a little shocked, and looked across at her. Grace saw him, nodded at him and said: "Hello, Oleg." And he responded: "Hello, Grace." They looked at one another for a long moment. Then Cassini turned around and went back to the yacht. They never saw each other again.

In looking back over his close relationship with Grace Kelly, which lasted about one and a half years before it finally ended, Oleg Cassini once had this to say: "We loved each other. We were engaged to be married. That is the truth. No more, no less."[216]

171

In terms of film history, *To Catch a Thief* may be one of the most underrated of Hitchcock's films. This is totally unjustified. Even through to the minor roles, the film was excellently cast. Furthermore, the foreground of this seemingly lighthearted mélange of thriller, comedy, drama, and romance, which pulses throughout with undertones of melancholy, conceals a background tension that is anything but light in nature.

Due to a series of jewel thefts in the grand hotels of the Côte d'Azur, the French police come to the conclusion that John Robie (Cary Grant), known as "the Cat," is active again. Before World War II, during which he was involved in the French Resistance, Robie had been a well-known jewel thief. Now he lives alone, having withdrawn to his country home not far from Saint-Paul-de-Vence. He has not practiced his "profession" in fifteen years. However, it is not only the assiduous yet bumbling Kommissar Lepic (René Blancard), of the French Sûreté, who thinks that Robie is again moonlighting as "the Cat." His old Resistance cohorts, with whom he seeks shelter from the French police, blame him for putting them in danger, complaining that he seeks to make a profit while they toil in the shadows. These ex-Resistance friends now run a harbor restaurant in Monaco under the leadership of Bertani (Charles Vanel). Among the servers are old fighter Foussard (Jean Martinelli), who hobbles around on a wooden leg, and his young, awkward daughter Danielle (Brigitte Auber). In order to prove his innocence, Robie the ex-thief hunts for the actual offender. With the help of a very British insurance agent, H. H. Hughson (John Williams, who previously acted in *Dial M for Murder* as the no-less-British Chief Inspector Hubbard), who provides him with both a list of potential insured victims, and a false identity as a lumber businessman named Conrad Burns from Oregon, Robie soon meets the Stevenses. Mrs. Stevens (Jessie Royce Landis) is "the American woman with the diamonds and the daughter,"[217] as Robie smugly labels her in a conversation with Hughson. The aforementioned daughter is Frances Stevens, known as Francie (Grace Kelly). A cool, young blonde, she is statuesque and untouchable in an ice blue gown. Mrs. Stevens knowingly asks Robie: "Mr Burns, you said lumber? How come you haven't made a pass at my daughter?" To this, he responds: "Very pretty; quietly attractive."[218]

In this layered cat and mouse game, Alfred Hitchcock chose to emphasize visual storytelling as opposed to verbal. What is verbalized is usually complex and ambiguous in nature. This begins with the very title of the film, *To Catch a Thief*, which could relate to several different individuals and threads of plot. There is an old saying that goes, "You catch thieves with thieves." And certainly, the title pertains to catching and identifying "the Cat." But really, which other characters couldn't be considered a "Cat" in some way? John Robie was once that, and perhaps he is again. Francie is also a "Cat" who is hunting the supposed jewel thief on a totally different plane—an emotional-erotic one.

Last but not least, there is a third cat, the young Danielle, who emerges at the end of the film high over the roofs during the night of the costume ball. She is the actual jewel thief, stealing under the instructions of Bertani the restaurant owner. And Danielle, too, would have gladly "stolen" Robie in order to run away with him to South America.

The French actress Brigitte Auber (born in 1928), who played Danielle Foussard, vividly remembered the filming of *To Catch a Thief*: "It was extremely pleasant to film, very relaxed. And I liked John Williams an awful lot. What a joy it was to work with such a funny man."[219]

And further: "Grace was very elegant. She was very charming and friendly to everyone—just as well-bred people tend to be. You are raised to be that way, and it creates a certain attitude. But it stayed a little... superficial. Grace had a vocal coach for her role—for her dialogue. She was very conscientious about her work, so she was always with her coach. I rarely had breakfast or lunch with Hitch, but I often spent time with Cary Grant. However, Grace always ate with her coach. In short, she was adorable and charming, but kept her inner thoughts private. She was alone in her corner. Always. Or with her coach."

According to Brigitte Auber, the relationship between Hitch and Grace embodied "a great understanding and was something of great elegance. They were bound by a common spirit. There was, otherwise, nothing else between them... It was a very strong friendship. She knew him completely inside and out. And Hitch always had fun with her. Hitch took great care with Grace during filming. He explained everything to her, sometimes for up to three quarters of an hour. Grace had this adorable side, this cool side that was well-bred—however inside she was not like this at all. This was a girl who wanted to live, who wanted to be loved."[220]

At the time of filming, Grace was twenty-four. Brigitte Auber was twenty-six. However, in the film the character of Danielle Foussard is notably younger than Francie Stevens—an inversion that is completely believable because of the distinct look of each actress. Auber plays a young, athletic, and impertinent French girl, who would gladly begin a new life in South America with Grant. Kelly is an elegant, attractive, cool daughter of a wealthy family, whose mother would like to marry her off. These two character types function dramaturgically as foils for one another. As Robie, Grant eventually must decide between these two feminine polar opposites and the lifestyles associated with them.

Brigitte Auber commented further: "All of the scenes with Grace, Cary, and me around the float, in front of the beach at the Carlton Hotel, were first filmed in the water and then a second time in the studio in a pool. Even those with Cary and me in the boat. First, some of the scenes were filmed on location in the boat, and then everything was done again in the studio against a projection of the sea, the Côte, and the police helicopter that flew around us. I had brought a two-piece swimsuit, but Grace told me that this would not work in the swimming pool. At the time, your naval had to be covered when you wore a swimsuit. So, she took me to large shop, and we bought a one-piece."

The key scene for this romantic triangle takes place in the water by the hotel float. It begins about one-third of the way into the film, around the forty-second minute. This scene reveals much about the interpersonal constellation of characters and about the subtext of distrust among them. Francie and Danielle meet one another for the first time and exchange an ironically ambivalent, smugly heated volley of words. Each attractive in her own way, they are both interested in wooing Robie as a romantic partner:

Danielle: "You performed a beautiful robbery last night."
Robie: "Strictly routine."
Danielle: "You steal a small fortune and then lie on the beach with an American beauty."
Robie: "That's why one needs a small fortune."
Danielle: "Is this your next victim?"
Robie: "She's a useful friend."
. . .
Danielle: "What has she got more than me, except money? And you are getting plenty of that.
Robie: "Danielle, you are just a girl. She is a woman."
Danielle: "Why do you want to buy an old car if you can get a new one cheaper? It will run better and last longer."
Robie: "Well, it looks as if my old car just drove off."
Francie: [swimming up] "No, it hasn't, it's just turned amphibious. I thought I'd come out and see what the big attraction was."
Robie: "Yes."
Francie: "And possibly even rate an introduction."
Robie: [to Danielle] "Oh, uh, you didn't tell me your name."
Danielle: "Danielle Foussard."
Robie: "Miss Foussard—Miss Stevens."
Francie: "How do you do, Miss Foussard. Mr. Burns has told me so little about you."
Robie: "Well, we only met a couple of minutes ago."
Danielle: "That's right, only a few minutes ago."
Francie: "Only a few minutes ago? And you talk like old friends. Ah well, that's warm, friendly France for you."
Robie: [to Francie] "I was asking about renting some water-skis. Would you like me to teach you how to water ski?"
Francie: "Thank you, but I was women's champion at Sarasota, Florida, last season."
Robie: "Well, it was just an idea."
Francie: "Are you sure you were talking about water-skis? From where I sat, it looked as though you were conjugating some irregular verbs."

Robie: "Say something nice to her, Danielle."
Danielle: "She looks a lot older, up close."
Robie: "Ohhh—"
Francie: "To a mere child, anything over twenty might seem old."
Danielle: "A child? Shall we stand in shallower water and discuss that?"
Francie: "Enjoying yourself, Mr. Burns?"
Robie: "Oh yes, it's very nice out here, with the sun and all."
Francie: "Well, it's too much for me. I'll see you at the hotel."
Robie: [laughing nervously] "I'll go with you."
Danielle: "But Mr. Burns, you didn't finish telling me why French women are more seductive than American women."
Robie: "I know what I'd like to tell you!"

Brigitte Auber described this central scene: "There was something quite unpleasant for me in this. I have never understood why I had to say the line that she [Francie] looked old, older when at close proximity. And then the car comparison. You simply don't say such things. There was no reason for it. That shocked me at the time. They told me it was funny. But I did not find it funny. Perhaps I am not American or English enough, but I never understood this."[221]

Brigitte Auber also recalled Hitchcock's legendary storyboards, which either he himself or someone he commissioned prepared ahead of time. Without a completed storyboard, he would not come to the set for filming. It was the same with *To Catch a Thief*: "Everything is written down, everything drawn up. The takes, the details—everything. Where did the shoulder have to be in the shot? Is the shoulder actually this way in the picture? His entire film was completely developed before anything began." Yet despite this creative control, he left most of the tonal and emotional delivery of the lines up to the actors. "He did not provide much direction to the actors. After working under director Jacques Becker (*Rendez-vous de juillet*, 1949), this was somewhat irritating. Becker took care to show an interest in one's disposition. He was one to always talk to you, to provoke you, and to make sure he got the right reaction for his shot. It was wonderful how Becker directed his actors. Hitchcock was the opposite. For example, the scene in the boat. We filmed it once a particular way. Then Hitch said, 'We will film it again.' A few things were changed, and the scene was filmed again. After that, I turned to Hitch and asked him how he would ultimately like the scene to be: 'We have now filmed this twice with Cary and me. What do you want?' And he answered me with a response that I found completely dumb: 'It is all the same to me. You are the character. You can do what you want.' That was nonsense, since you can do 100,000 things with a character in a scene. It was a question of the direction."[222]

Interestingly, considering the genesis of the film, the chosen ending did not correspond with the one that Hitchcock had initially intended to film. The original screenplay for *To Catch a Thief* contained a different conclusion. Brigitte Auber remembered it as follows:

This ending was not the original ending, but the one that the producers demanded. There was no ending as it is now in the film. At the end, after Cary bid Grace and her dear film mother farewell, he and John Williams have tea. Williams, very British and motivated a little by ulterior motives, asks Cary how it went with Grace and if he will see her again. To this, Cary answers that this is now water under the bridge. Then you learn that Grace's mother had grown quite close to Cary, that I am in prison, and that they visit me in prison. And then, like brother and sister, we talk amicably. The film ended here. Cary continues his life as before. He stays there and does not concern himself with America and the American. And: He was the one who "dressed" me as the Cat, who taught me everything, the methods of a thief! One scene of this was filmed: Cary had just shared with me his techniques as a thief. And he said to me: "You did not do that well. I told you to do it this way." To a certain extent, he was the big brother speaking to a younger sister. However, the producers agreed—and they were ultimately right—that one could not make the public interested in a couple, especially considering how beautiful both Cary and Grace were, without offering a happy ending. The original ending was somewhat open-ended, as if everything between them had just been an episode in their lives. That was exactly what Hitch wanted. Hitch had many such ideas, ones that were unconventional and made him, above all, quite delighted.[223]

In *To Catch a Thief*, nothing is as it seems. Many things rise to the surface as deception, falsification, or double meaning. A remarkable game of deception. As is often the case with Hitchcock, the main point turns on identities, true and false, the dynamics of motivations. Here the issues relate directly to authenticity and falsification, to trust and distrust, to being together and being apart.

Early in the film, Robie, fleeing from Lepic, is riding in a bus. He sits on the back row of seats, and to the left of him is a cage containing two birds. When he looks to his right, he sees Alfred Hitchcock in his traditional cameo appearance, staring straight ahead. Robie is on his way to visit his Resistance pal Bertani in his restaurant office in Monaco. Bertani lightly provokes him: "You're as nervous as a cat." And shortly afterward, as Danielle takes him in a boat from the restaurant to Cannes, where he will get out on the beach of the Carlton Hotel to elude the police, the double entendres increase all the more. "Cats don't like water," she quips, as Robie complains about getting soaked in the spray kicked up by the boat (and both of them are wearing matching striped pullover shirts). In another scene, he rides with Francie, who is speeding recklessly around the serpentine curves high over Monaco in her ice-blue convertible Cabrio (at a location only a few miles away from Route de La Turbie, where on September 13, 1982, the fifty-two year old Grace Kelly had her fatal car accident). They are being tailed some distance away by the French Police. On his side of the car, there is a sharp drop-off to the sea, and Grant nervously rubs his damp palms on his pants. In the ensuing exchange, Francie reveals her awareness:

Robie: "Slow down."
Francie: "And let them catch us?"
Robie: "Let who catch us?"

Francie: "The police who were following you."
Robie: "Police following me?"
Francie: "Yes, police following you, John Robie, The Cat."[224]

In this scene, Cary Grant's character, similar to the one he played in *Notorious* when he anxiously sat next to Ingrid Bergman as they raced through the night along a Florida road, resembles an aspect of Hitchcock's own character. As Brigitte Auber recalled of "mon petit Hitch": "Hitch was deathly afraid of riding in cars. When I sat in the driver's seat and drove my large American car, he cried out several times. I have never seen anything like that. And he begged me to drive more slowly. He also rarely traveled by airplane, much preferring to go by ship." Shortly afterward, Robie and Francie sit in the car with their picnic basket, parked at an observation point on one of the sharp curves. Below them, they can see the principality of Monaco, an unforeseeable, fateful coincidence at the time. Francie/Grace presents the scene to Robie and says with deep admiration: "Have you ever seen any place more beautiful?" The view contains the royal palace, the harbor, the casino, the opera house, and St. Nicholas Cathedral where Grace would be married in April 1956 and buried after her death in September 1982.

"You want a leg or a breast?" Francie asks John Robie, intentionally suggestive as she opens their picnic basket. Robie responds to her question as if he already senses their future together: "You make the choice."

Before stopping for the picnic, John Robie had said to Francie Stevens: "You know what you want; you go after it. Nothing stops you." A significant line of dialogue. In hindsight, it sounds a little like something Cary Grant could have actually said to Grace Kelly. It is an apt analysis of her story, her sacrifices: the love affairs—particularly the one with Oleg Cassini—her country, her friends there, her language, her career, Hitchcock.

Producer John Foremen had known Grace since her early acting work in New York. His commentary on her would have fit nicely with Cary Grant's fictional assessment of Francie: "Only Grace Kelly could have created Grace Kelly. It must have been a concept in her head. No one else did. No manager, no agent, no producer, not even her family."[225]

Recalling her design for the extremely opulent ball gown that she designed for Grace to wear in the final scene of the film, Edith Head had the following to say: "Hitchcock told me that he wanted her to look like a princess. And she did." [226] The invitation to the masked ball required that the attendees wear eighteenth-century themed costumes. Edith Head claimed that these were the most expensive costumes that she had ever designed. "Grace wore a dress made of fine gold lamé, a golden wig and a golden mask."[227]

Also, the other costumes and dresses that Edith Head designed for Grace were classically, timelessly elegant, almost royal in appearance. The two women traveled to Hermés in Paris, where they spent hours trying to find suitable, trendsetting white gloves. They tried on all different styles, and at the end, Grace stood in the shop with a large package and a high bill. The only things that Grace ever splurged on were gloves and shoes. Hitchcock told Edith that he was well-aware the story was set in a fashion center of the world. And of course, they were shopping in France—the birthplace of fashion—so he expected Edith to give it her all.[228]

In her first scene, Grace is wearing a yellow bathing suit as she sits in the sand on the Carlton beach. She is also wearing large, white-rimmed sunglasses and a yellow head covering as she applies suntan lotion to herself. This is when she sees Robie/Grant for the first time. She later appears in a bathing dress in the hotel lobby, where her beauty renders the waiting Robie speechless. He is so amazed that Grace/Francie smugly asks, "Shall I ask the social director to introduce us?" To which Grant replies, "No, I was wondering which was the best way out." Grace: "The Mediterranean's this way." They go through the columned hall of the Carlton, toward the entrance, toward the Mediterranean. All the hotel guests in the hall turn to watch them as they pass. Grace's gait in this scene has an almost majestic quality. Edith Head described Grace's beach attire: "She was wearing an enormous sunhat and the most beautiful black and white sundress I have ever created. It was stunning—almost too stunning."[229]

To Catch a Thief is in many ways the inverse of *Marnie*, which Hitchcock made almost ten years later in 1962, and in which he wanted to cast his favorite heroine, Grace. In this film, a woman is the kleptomaniac thief, Marnie Edgar (Tippi Hedren), and she is contracted, caught, desired, and reformed by a man, Mark Rutland (Sean Connery). In contrast, it is Francie who links the stealing and possession of jewels with eroticism. She magically attracts Robie, the man, the (ex-)thief. On the other hand, she formally offers herself to him. "The thrill is in front of you, but you can't get it," she says to him in her hotel room in the evening twilight, while outside the firework display becomes more intense. She has situated herself such that she is only seen from the neck down. The brilliant necklace sparkles around her neck, while her face is in darkness. Like a statuesque torso. Like a promising object of desire. This very cleverly choreographed arrangement serves Hitchcock's purposes well. As she tries to convince him of the similarities between jewel thieves and alcoholics—two kinds of addicts—Robie cuts in: "I have the same interest in jewelry as I do in politics, modern poetry, or women who need weird excitement: None." Grace is exquisitely beautiful at this point. Sitting on the sofa, she lays the necklace around her neck directly across Grant's fingers, which she has already kissed: "Hold this necklace in your hand and tell me you're not Robie The Cat." She is offering herself to him. As stolen goods for Robie to steal, to covet—to love. However, Robie has long realized that the necklace is a fake. "Well, I'm not," responds Francie. The erotic connotations are no longer ambiguous. This culminates in the sentence delivered by the truly eloquent Mrs. Stevens. On the next morning, after the nighttime theft of her own jewels, she almost casually tosses this statement at Francie, who has in the meantime become convinced that John is "The Cat." With petulant conviction, Francie claims, "He's a worthless thief!" To this her mother replies, "Just what did he steal from you?"

The night of love between Robie and Francie is accompanied by an orgasmic fireworks display, which the American censors wanted to completely cut out because of its presumably explicit character. Hitchcock stubbornly defended the scene. The no-less-explicit sofa scene was ultimately shortened some. After all, it was 1954.

To Catch a Thief was based on a 1952 novel with the same title written by David Dodge. This was the second screenplay for Hitchcock written by John Michael Hayes, who had already written the screenplay for *Rear Window* and who would go on to write *The Trouble with Harry* (1955) and *The Man Who Knew Too Much* (1956). Hayes adapted Dodge's novel for the screen by adding sparkling, intelligently humorous dialogue.

To Catch a Thief was filmed in the wide-screen process called VistaVision, Paramount Studios' equivalent to Warner's and Fox's CinemaScope. The film is preserved in a richly faceted and beautiful color spectrum, saturated and vibrant. It is permeated with a glistening light of an almost tactile quality. They are magical images, full of elegance and class and style. Hitchcock purposely had the green-blue shimmering nights photographed through a green filter. The visually atmospheric density evident in the night shots and those taken up on the rooftops, especially the final chase sequence between Cary Grant and Brigitte Auber, reveals this. The film truly glows, and even decades after its creation, it is commonly described as "a feast for the eyes." For his achievements, Hitch's longtime cinematographer Robert Burks (1909–1968) received an Oscar. Burks was one of Hitchcock's most important and loyal collaborators. With the exception of *Psycho,* he was responsible for the cinematography of the black-and-white film adaptation of Patricia Highsmith's *Strangers on a Train* (1951), *Dial M for Murder*, *Rear Window*, *Vertigo*, *The Birds*, and finally *Marnie*.

Furthermore, *To Catch A Thief* received two other Academy Award nominations, for Best Set Design and Best Costumes (Edith Head).

For Grace, this was her third and last project with Alfred Hitchcock. The director would "lose" her only one year later to Prince Rainier III—ironically, it was her stay on the Côte d'Azur, Monaco that spurred this chain of events. However, although it is claimed again and again in different documentaries and biographic publications that the actress and the prince met each other during the filming of Hitchcock's movie in the summer months of 1954, this is not the case. Rather, they met in May of the following year (1955) during the annual Cannes International Film Festival. Grace had been invited as a festival guest to represent *The Country Girl*. She first met the prince because of a photo publicity appointment made by the French weekly magazine, *Paris Match*. They met on the afternoon of May 6, 1955, at 4:00 p.m. at the Prince's Palace of Monaco. The meeting was brief, about half an hour.[230]

By the time *To Catch a Thief* had its world premiere in Los Angeles on August 3, 1955, Prince Rainier III of Monaco and Grace Patricia Kelly of Philadelphia had begun exchanging letters in the months that followed their first (and only) half-hour-long rendezvous at the palace. It was less than six months between the premiere of the final Hitchcock-Kelly film and January 1956, and soon nothing would ever be the same. The would-be princess had found her prince.

However, this was a bitter loss for Hitch, similar to when he "lost" Ingrid Bergman to Roberto Rossellini. She too had made three movies with Hitch. In addition, Grace Kelly in particular, specifically in *To Catch a Thief*, absolutely embodied his ideal of the cool blonde, more so than any of his other actresses before or after. He once said: "Grace Kelly's apparent frigidity was like a mountain covered with snow, but that mountain was a volcano."[231]

The visual actualization of this quip can be found in *To Catch a Thief* in the scene in which Robie (Grant) accompanies Francie (Kelly) through the hall to her room after eating supper in the Carlton Hotel with mother Stevens and the insurance agent Hughson. He takes her to her door, which she unlocks. She takes a step into the room, turns around on the threshold, and looks at him for a long, electric moment. Then she goes to him and kisses him directly on the mouth, laying her left arm across his shoulder. Since they have only just met that very evening, this gesture is totally surprising, coming out of nowhere. Thus, Robie, as well as Hitchcock's viewers, are completely baffled, speechless. Without a word, Grace, ever-elegant, takes a step back, still gazing intensely and penetratingly at Grant. Then she closes the white door directly in his face, still completely silent. "It was as though she'd unzipped Cary's fly."[232] This was how Hitch later described this scene, smugly and with evident pleasure. This scene contains something almost transcendental. For a moment, Grant stands with his face toward the door. During this entire scene, the viewer has only seen him from the back. He finally turns around with confusion written across his face. He is also smiling faintly, and as he walks down the hotel corridor, he thoughtfully wipes Grace's lipstick from his mouth with a white handkerchief. Only Hitchcock could have created such a Grace Kelly. Electrifying. Perfect.

"I've never been very keen on women who hang their sex round their neck like baubles. I think it should be discovered. It's more interesting to discover the sex in a woman than it is to have it thrown at you, like a Marilyn Monroe or those types. To me they are rather vulgar and obvious."[233] Grace remained Hitch's ideal forever.

To Catch a Thief did not necessarily end with a veritable happy ending. Hitchcock formulated it such that, "Cary Grant can convince himself that he wants to marry Grace Kelly. But her mother will live with them. So that's an almost tragic conclusion."[234]

The ambivalent final line belongs to Francie, who hurriedly follows Robie to his country house. As they finally stand on the terrace in each other's arms and kiss, she announces in a very self-satisfied tone: "So this is where you live! Mother will love it up here." Again, completely baffled, Cary Grant looks at her and then past the camera into space. Grace Kelly holds him, her prize, close and tight. The cat has found her mate.

—The First Meeting:
Friday, May 6, 4:00 p.m.

In March 1955, Rupert Allan called Grace Kelly. The PR agent had news for his client. She had been invited as an honorable guest to the International Film Festival in Cannes to represent the US festival entry, *The Country Girl*. Grace turned down the invitation. She did not want to travel again so soon, and she wished to gain some distance from the film industry and from show business. Allan begged her to seriously consider it, since it would be an important occasion. He said he would call again. Grace promised to think about it, though she knew she did not want to go. She wanted to stay in New York and finish furnishing her large, new apartment. She wanted to finally start feeling at home. Allan called Grace again a few days later from Los Angeles. This time he was more insistent. He told her that she had been invited by the French government and would represent her country, America. This went on for days. Rupert Allan came up with more and more arguments, each one more sound and significant than the last. In the end, Grace let herself be convinced. This was not the first time. Shortly after this, against her will, she agreed to do something that would change her life forever.

In early May, Grace flew from New York to Paris. She had been there a year before with Edith Head. Again she had a couple of hours to spend in the city before catching the overnight *Train Bleu* from Paris to Cannes, where it arrived the following morning. Grace Kelly was not the only one traveling by train to the Riviera. Pierre Galante also sat on the Blue Train. He was the film editor for the popular weekly Paris magazine, *Paris Match*. His destination was the film festival. However, under orders from his managing editor Gaston Bonheur, Galante had another goal: a story about an arranged meeting at court between Prince Rainier III and Grace Kelly. This photo shoot in the palace would be titled: "Prince Charming Meets Movie Queen."

Galante succeeded in meeting Grace. He was accompanied by his wife, actress Olivia de Havilland who had once been a star in such films as *Gone with the Wind.* She knew Gladys de Segonzac, a dresser for *To Catch a Thief,* who was also Grace's travel companion to France. Introductions were made. At first, Grace did not suspect what was coming her way. In addition, she had no idea how full her schedule would be during the film festival. Toward the end of the train ride, Galante addressed the issue of Monaco. He asked Grace what she would think about fleeing the festival melee for a few hours, seeing a little of the tiny principality, and having a personal audience with His Majesty Prince Rainier III of Monaco. Grace did not initially agree to this, but she also did not turn the opportunity down right away.

On May 5, the following morning, Grace Kelly arrived in Cannes, where she was met at the train station by Rupert Allan, who took her to the Carlton Hotel. One year ago, it had been Alfred Hitchcock who had met her here.

During her ten-day stay on the Côte d'Azur, as well as during the additional week spent in Paris, Grace again met with Jean-Pierre Aumont. During the days prior to her departure for Paris, he had taken her out to supper in New York and had visited her in her luxurious new apartment on Fifth Avenue. After all, a planned diversion with Jean-Pierre on the Riviera and in Paris was yet another good reason to give in to Rupert Allan's demands. There is documentary television footage in black and white of Grace and Aumont holding hands and strolling through the historic center of Cannes and through La Napoule. They visited a pottery shop, they played boules in a public square. There are even photographs of an intimate meeting, a noon lunch, where they sat next to each other at the table. Captured was a moment in which she pulls his arm up toward her face to kiss his hand—a private moment that was made public and circulated. In Cannes for the festival and in the surrounding area as well, photographers and reporters lurked around every corner.

Eventually in Paris, Grace and Aumont alighted at the Hotel Raphael, not far from the Champs-Élysées. They went to the theater and took walks that May through the City of Love. Finally, they spent a weekend with part of his extended family in Aumont's country house in Malmaison, at the gates of the French capital.

Grace's contact with Cassini was on- and off-again at this time, and she had just met the Prince of Monaco. Now she was flirting with a man, Aumont, with whom she had been involved two years ago. This affair flared back into life for a short while. Again, a romance on the Riviera. And Aumont became increasingly hopeful and even mentioned marriage to various reporters— even he. He was not the first to have this hope. After about two and a half weeks abroad, Grace returned to America from France in the third week of May. While still in the airport, a television reporter asked her about her relationship with Aumont: "Good morning, Miss Kelly, it's a beautiful day here in New York. Our viewers would certainly be very disappointed if I did not ask about rumors regarding your romance with Jean-Pierre Aumont, is it? Would you like to tell us about it?"

Reserved and distant, Grace answered: "Well, I can only say that we are very good friends. I met Jean-Pierre a few years ago in New York and was really looking forward seeing him again in Cannes."

"Is it serious?"

"Oh, no," Grace said.[235]

As far as Grace was concerned, the affair was over. It is said that Jean-Pierre Aumont was deeply in love with her and that he was very hurt and upset by her rejection.

Previously, on May 6 in fact, after Grace had been in Cannes only one and a half days, the royal appointment at the palace in Monaco took place.

When Grace first learned that she was expected to host an official reception for the Americans at the Festival at 5:30 p.m., she wanted to cancel her meeting with the prince. However, she was emphatically told that she could not do this as she had been officially invited to court. As a result, *Paris Match* editor Pierre Galante called the palace and successfully rescheduled the meeting from 4:00 to 3:00. However, before his press appointment with Grace Kelly, Prince Rainier had another appointment at his villa at Beaulieu, where he was hosting a meal. He would make every effort to be punctual. On her part, Grace had that late afternoon appointment in Cannes on her mind. The drive from Cannes to Monaco would take between sixty and ninety minutes each way. Because of this extremely tight schedule, tension and uncertainty reigned.

The next day, a series of obstacles developed. During the festival, which was held in May 1955, there was a labor strike, a typical occurrence at the time—one that regularly brought sectors of the public life to a grinding halt. In this case, the power was cut off. There was no more electricity, even in the elegant Carlton. Thus, Grace, who had just washed her hair, could not use her hair dryer. Also, the newly unpacked dresses that were rumpled from the trip could not be ironed. Thus, on the morning of this ultimately fateful Friday, Grace stood in her hotel room with wet hair and wrinkled clothes. This was right before her audience with the prince and the photo shoot for the title story for a national weekly magazine.

Gladys de Segonzac tried to help, and together they spontaneously improvised a solution. First of all, Grace brushed her hair until it was slightly drier, and then she bound it up into a bun. Her dresser tied her bun with a band of artificial flowers, which at least ornamented the back of her head a little and would replace the hat that was otherwise required at court. By the time she arrived in Monaco, her hair would be halfway dry in the warm temperatures that prevailed this time of year on the Côte. Among her clothes, they finally found one that was not rumpled. It was a black cotton dress with a flowered pattern in red and green. The sleeves were long, and the skirt came in tight at the waist and then spread into a wide skirt. Together with Gladys de Segonzac and Pierre Gallante, Grace left Cannes at 1:30 in a car rented by MGM.

During the drive there along the sunny Riviera, the actress asked the journalist about the upcoming meeting. Pierre Galante described this drive: "She did not know the Prince at all. She asked me if he spoke English and if she had to curtsey. She was very nervous."[236]

In over-exuberance, the Peugeot carrying both photographers for *Paris Match* lightly rear-ended another car at a stop, so there was a further delay. After arriving in Monaco, Grace Kelly and company were initially informed by the palace that the prince was delayed. It was as if fate had his hand in the game.

Eventually, Prince Rainier arrived a good three-quarters of an hour late. It was between 3:45 and 4:00 that he finally entered the palace. He asked Grace if he could show her around the palace. However, Grace responded that she already had seen the palace since she had looked around while they were waiting on the prince. Then, they went into the palace garden. The entire meeting was accompanied by the two *Paris Match* journalists, Pierre Galante and the photographer. They stayed a respectful distance away, so that the "couple" could at least feel a little undisturbed. They took a walk together in the garden. For the entire time, Grace wore only one of her white gloves, the one on her left hand. She had removed the one from her right hand when she had greeted the prince, and she held this for the whole time in her hands. This was a sure sign of her nervousness. After all the previous confusion that had led up to this moment, this awkward gesture seems all the more touching. Photos had already been taken inside the palace, in the Hercules Gallery on the second floor and on the wide, sweeping, white marble staircase that led from the gallery to the interior courtyard. Now more photos of Grace and Rainier were taken as they walked next to each other down the garden paths, as he showed her the view from the Rocher—the cliffs—as he showed her the mature stands of cacti and as he finally took her to the cages of his small private zoo.

"They stood in front of the cage in which a tiger, a gift from the Emperor Bao-Dai of Indochina, was kept. Rainier pet the tiger on its head, just as if he was stroking a puppy. Grace was very impressed by this. One could sense just then that something had sparked between the two of them at that moment," recounted eyewitness Pierre Galante.[237] And *Paris Match* the huge story they'd been hoping for: the film princess had met Prince Charming.

During the return trip from the principality to the festival in Cannes, a visibly taciturn Grace responded to Galante's question about her impression of this half-hour meeting and of the prince. Her answer was brief: "He is very charming." "She had never shown her true feelings, nor did she later," revealed Galante.

However, the two of them could not have learned much about each other during this half hour. It could have been no more than an initial, fleeting impression, from both sides.

As publicist Thomas Veszelits describes the scene, "It was an enchantment of two unbelievably charming people. Grace Kelly, Oscar winner and film star, and Prince Rainier, who looked like Douglas Fairbanks. This greatness. And in the background, the palace."[238] And both of them would not soon forget that walk in the royal garden.

Born on May 31, 1923, in Monaco, the prince would soon be turning thirty-two. Since 1949, at the death of his grandfather Prince Louis II (1870–1949), Rainier III had become the Prince of Monaco. The arranged marriage of his parents, Prince Pierre Grimaldi, born Comte Pierre de Polignac (1895–1964) and his mother, the Monegasque Princess Charlotte Grimaldi de Monaco (1898–1977), ended in divorce in 1933, and since that time, they had made no claims to the Monegasque regency. In 1944, Charlotte, the daughter of Louis II, gave up her right to the throne. Thus, the succession eventually skipped a generation, passing directly from Prince Louis II to Prince Rainier III.

Like his older sister, Princess Antoinette Grimaldi (1920–2011), Rainier was a child of divorce, and he was shaped by a rather unhappy, lonely childhood, which was itself character-ized by frequent, irregular relocations. He was still single in the 1950s and was considered one of Europe's most eligible bachelors. Rainier knew how to meet the opposite sex with charm.

In the years before meeting Grace, he had had various shorter affairs, such as his six-year relationship with the French actress and Cannes native Gisèle Pascal (1921–2007). He saw her perform in the stage play *His Lordship* in 1948, and was captivated by her. This was the year before Rainier took the throne on May 9, 1949. Previously engaged to fellow actor and singer Yves Montand,

Pascal acted in the 1942 black-and-white film *L'Arlésienne* under director Marc Allégret. Alongside Louis Jourdan, this was her first major role in a movie. She followed Rainier to Monaco and lived with him in his villa. Interestingly, in this context, this actress continued to pursue her profession, acting in such films as *Véronique* (1950) and *Bel Amour* (1951). During this time, she was in a long-term, committed, private relationship with Monaco's sovereign. It can be assumed that if she had married Prince Rainier and been named the Princess of Monaco, she would have had to end her artistic career. This is exactly what happened to Grace Kelly later, after the wedding in April 1956.

However, in 1953, Rainier quite abruptly broke off this long-term relationship. On the one hand, it had just come out that Gisèle Pascal had had an affair with Gary Cooper that year, just as Grace Kelly had in the fall of 1951 during the filming of *High Noon*. On the other hand, it appeared that the actress could not have children. "The Parliament advised the Regent, 'to care for the future of the dynasty,' by not marrying Gisèle Pascal."[239] The appeal to his duties as a monarch successfully motivated Rainier to take this step, even if it was against his personal will and feelings. Two years later, Gisèle Pascal married the actor Raymond Pellegrin. She had a daughter, Pascale Pellegrin (who also became an actress) several years later, a development that proved the erroneous conclusions of the medical fertility exam she had been given. Later, Grace Kelly also had to go through the same fertility test, to confirm that the prince's chosen wife could bear children and continue the Grimaldi line.

Since 1953, Rainier had been a bachelor, and he knew that he had to have heirs in order to guarantee the continuing ruling line of the small country: "The regular royal succession (as well as its famous casino, Monte Carlo, and tourism in general) is the basis for Monegasque independence. According to the treaty between Monaco and France (signed in 1918), Monaco will become a French protectorate 'in the case of an unoccupied throne, due to a lack of direct or adopted descendants.'"[240] This succession law was changed in April 2002. As an example of the altered statute, the Monegasque succession can now pass to a princess and not just to a direct male heir. The throne can also now pass through an indirect family line.

For Grace's first visit, Prince Rainier wore sunglasses, a simple, dark suit with outside pockets, a white shirt, and a tie. He seemed older and more sedate, with his mustache and his strong, slightly stocky stature. They were both about the same height, although Rainier was a little taller than Grace. They spoke English with each other. Thanks to the time he spent at two British boarding schools, he spoke fluent, unaccented English. (At the age of eleven, Rainier was sent to Summerfields in St. Leonards-on-Sea on the southern coast of England, not far from Hastings, and then he was directly transferred to Stowe in Buckinghamshire, where he stayed until he was fourteen.) He was a chain smoker and a sports enthusiast. Sports. Cars. Animals. These were three of his significant interests and hobbies. He was a committed amateur actor, and he had graduated from the Paris École Libre des Sciences Politiques in 1944. A pragmatist for the most part, however, "Rainier was not a man of the arts."[241] And he was temperamental, suffering frequent mood swings. Thus, it was difficult for him to maneuver interpersonal relationships. He was an introverted loner with a mind of his own. Later, his tendency to be hot-headed and strict would lead to familial problems.

On December 15, 1955, Prince Rainier, together with Father Francis Tucker, one of his close confidantes in Monaco, landed in New York at the beginning of a multiweek trip across the United States. Of course, the ultimate unofficial destination was Philadelphia. Rainier was met by a mob of television reporters who asked about a potential bride and possible wedding. In front of the rolling cameras, the following dialogue ensued between the nosy press and the reserved and obviously cryptic prince:

Reporter: "Your Majesty, according to many rumors, you are in contact with various women. It could be anyone. The latest rumor: Grace Kelly. Could you comment on this for us?"
Rainier: "No. I simply met Grace Kelly. She visited the palace when she was in Cannes for the festival. That is all."

Reporter: "There are numerous reports that you are actively looking for a wife. Could you say something about this?"
Rainier: "No, I am not. That was falsely reported..."
Reporter: "But if you wanted to marry—what kind of girl would it be?"
Rainier: "I don't know. The best kind!"
Reporter: "And what would that be for you?"
Rainier: "We're getting closer to the issue, right? Well, she would need many good characteristics because I have an awful character."[242]

Over these December days, Grace was at MGM Studios in Culver City in Hollywood to film *The Swan*, her next to last film. She knew that the plan was to meet the prince on December 24 at her parents' house in Philadelphia. This would be her first private meeting with the prince. It had been seven and a half months since she first met him in Monaco.

At that first meeting on May 6, 1955, Grace had been twenty-five years old. The prince was six years older than her. After her death twenty-seven years later, the Paris journalist Pierre Galante had this to say: "The end was tragic. Everything had begun so beautifully. I could hardly believe that she had to leave life this way. That was very hard. My wife once said to me: 'We, too, are guilty of her death because we introduced her to the Prince.' And it was there in Monaco that she met her death."[243]

—Famous, Blonde, American: Marilyn or Grace?

George Schlee, Gardner Cowles, and Aristotle Onassis. A trio of men who hatched a plan in the fall of 1955, a conspiracy of sorts. This plan involved the principality of Monaco as well as its yet unmarried, thirty-two-year-old prince. This plan was focused in particular on the increasingly sinking attraction of Monte Carlo (since the end of World War II) for Europe's moneyed aristocracy as well as American tourists. The financial interests of the Greek shipping magnate Aristotle Onassis, who had invested millions of dollars in Monaco, were also a point of consideration. Onassis was concerned with the well-being of the small principality, but more than that he worried about the effect on his own finances.

Since the early 1950s, Aristole Onassis (1906–1975), multimillionaire and owner of an international shipping company, had a special relationship with the almost ramshackle, money-strapped principality on the Riviera. Since 1951, the casino had operated at a loss. Onassis had invested in construction projects and real estate, in mansions and hotels and entire apartment houses in Monaco. Since 1953, he had held the controlling interest in the Monegasque Société des Bains de Mer (SBM), which had been established in 1863. Although Prince Rainier III had first welcomed the Greek's investments, eventually he grew displeased with the way the public had begun to view Onassis as the actual Regent of Monaco. The SBM operated the casino (which had opened in 1863), the sporting club, and a variety of large, centrally located luxury hotels. These included the Hôtel de Paris, located diagonally across the street from the casino, and the Belle Epoque era Hôtel Hermitage, which was only a short distance away. Later, the latter hotel—Grace's favorite—was threatened with demolition, and she personally intervened in its rescue. Both of these hotels belonged to Aristole Onassis, as did the casino. Essentially, this would be a completely untenable situation in the long-term. In spite of the financial support of the Greek shipping magnate, over time this could only result in the prince's displeasure. In

195

certain circles, Monte Carlo was even know as "Monte Greco" for a while. And the press often called Onassis "the King of Monte Carlo." A thorn in the prince's side.

The undeniable reality, however, is that during the 1950s Monaco again became "the place to be" thanks to two individuals and their unique strengths: the financial power and jet-set popularity of Aristotle Onassis and the prominence and radiance of Hollywood actress Grace Kelly.

Publicist Thomas Veszelits provided a colorful account of this time. "Onassis brought a fantastical life to Monaco. All of the yachts, his yacht and all sorts of other ones. As they said at the time, he was also very raffish, a typical Greek of Turkish heritage. He drank, likely to the point of it being a health condition. All of them loved to take short jaunts out into the Mediterranean. It is not far from Monaco to Mallorca. That is how it all started to develop. Mallorca was the summer residence of the King of Spain. At that time, Juan Carlos was quite young, and he was also a playboy. There is a photo of one of his parties on Mallorca, and on it you can see Onassis and Grace Kelly singing together, and Prince Rainier playing a drum set. That does not look like a bad marriage. It looks like a relatively relaxed one. Pictures reveal much. In archival photographs from the 1960s, they did not look unhappy."[244]

The tension between the prince and the shipping magnate grew, and it was noticeable to those around both of them. During the course of the 1960s, the situation heightened to a personal level. Whenever Rainier and Grace attended the same social events as Onassis and his companion, Maria Callas, Grace tried again and again, in a friendly and polite manner, to patch things between them. Nonetheless, the acquaintance between both men cooled noticeably. Separately, the financial issues, especially those involving the SBM, came to a head. In 1966 and 1967, the stage for a final confrontation was set. In order to again gain complete control of the SBM, Rainier authorized the recapitalization of the SBM's capital stock into several hundreds of thousands of shares. Thus, Onassis would no longer possess the majority interest in the company. The proud, outraged shipping magnate filed a complaint at the highest court in Monaco. Of course, he was unsuccessful in his efforts. In reaction, Onassis eventually disposed of all of his investments, and for this, Monaco paid him a one-time sum of $10 million in March 1967. Again, Monaco was independent.

George Schlee, a New York financier and the husband of fashion designer Valentina Samina, represented well the ambivalent connection between the three men. Schlee spent the winter months with Valentina in New York, where she maintained her exclusive fashion salon in the Sherry Netherlands Hotel in Manhattan. During the summer months, together with Greta Garbo, he crossed the Mediterranean on Onassis's luxury yacht, the *Christina*. Schlee and Garbo were involved with each other for many years, and sometimes Garbo, Schlee, and Valentina would publicly appear together. George Schlee was Garbo's agent and adviser, as well as her constant companion until his death in 1964. At this time, Onassis had instructed him to promote the businesses in Monaco. A basically outrageous plot was thus hatched.

The plan was risky, and if it had not been purely opportunistic in nature, it could have been considered quite naïve. George Schlee had just returned to the United States from his summer trip with Onassis, and he and Gardner Cowles met at Cowles's house in Connecticut. Without previously consulting with or involving Prince Rainier III, the two men were considering to whom they could marry him in order to guarantee the return of prosperity to Monaco by increasing its appeal to the jet-setters of the Western world.

Unanimously, the men decided that it must be an American woman. A famous American. A famous blonde American. Yes, it would be best if she was a famous, blonde, American actress!

The list they supposedly created held the names of some of the later Hitchcock heroines, such as Kim Novak (*Vertigo*)[245] and Eva Marie Saint (*North by Northwest*), as well as Deborah Kerr.[246] However, Grace Kelly's name was not included. Then came the final entry: Marilyn Monroe!

Gardner Cowles, the publisher of *Look* magazine, was the one who allegedly came up with this brilliant idea. He knew Monroe personally. At this time, the curvy blonde star was at the height of her career. Since her screen debut in 1948, she had worked on such films as Henry Hathaway's *Niagara* (1953), Howard Hawks's *Gentlemen Prefer Blondes* (1953), Jean Negulesco's *How to Marry a Millionaire* (1953), and Billy Wilder's *The Seven Year Itch* (1955). Already only a few years later, in 1961, she would make her final film, John Huston's *The Misfits* with Clark Gable and Montgomery Clift. On August 5, 1962, Marilyn Monroe died at the age of only thirty-six in Los Angeles under circumstances that have still never been fully resolved. For years, the official theory has been that she committed suicide. However, for some years now, the theory that she was assassinated has also held some weight, considering Monroe's connection to the Kennedy clan. The objective truth can no longer be established. Thus, another myth came into being—another legend was born.

In fall 1955, Gardner Cowles and George Schlee could come up with no better candidate than Monroe. Behind the scenes, Onassis gave a green light to the plan, and Cowles immediately contacted the actress. At this time, she lived with the photographer Milton H. Greene, whom Cowles also knew. (On November 12, 1953, Grace Kelly's twenty-fourth birthday, Greene had held a photo session with Kelly for *Look*, and he later shot a rarely shown series of photographs of her in April 1954.) They set an appointment, Cowles, Schlee, Greene, and Monroe, at Cowles's house. Outside, by the swimming pool, the two conspirators finally outlined their plan to the oblivious actress: could she imagine being married to the Prince of Monaco?! Marilyn Monroe asked only two questions: "Is he rich?" and "Is he handsome?"[247]

Marilyn was not interested in anything else, and naturally she did not even know where Monaco was, just like Grace Kelly's parents who first confused Monaco with Morocco. After a brief series of questions by Cowles and Schlee as to whether the Monegasque prince would accept her as his bride, she answered on the spot:

"Give me two days alone with him, and of course he'll want to marry me."[248]

Cowles and Schlee seem to have not considered the fact that Monroe was not Catholic, that she had already been divorced twice—in June of the following year, 1956, she would marry for a third time, this time to the American playwright Arthur Miller— and that her image as a raunchy, seductive, curvy blonde was anything but suitable for her future role as a representative of one of Europe's royal houses. When Prince Rainier III later learned about these matchmaking plans, he reacted, understandably, with great irritation.

In looking back, this hastily cobbled idea seems quite absurd. Furthermore, at this time, other things were already working to influence the fate of the prince and the fortune of a famous, blonde, American actress, who had just begun her tenth and next-to-last-film: *The Swan*, in which she played—what else?—a princess.

The Swan
(1956)

I want to be a queen.
—Grace Kelly, as Princess Alexandra

Some of the films that Grace Kelly made during her short acting career seem to foreshadow, in an almost fateful way, the actual occurrences in her life. Again and again, she had to choose between duty and feelings (*High Noon*; *The Country Girl*; *The Swan*) or, sometimes by extension, between two men (*Mogambo*; *Dial M for Murder*; *The Country Girl*; *The Swan*; *High Society*). Again and again, she had to maintain her composure, to remain committed to a moral or ethical stance, or to assume responsibility. Like a common thread, there is a similar conflict in almost every film she made—one that relates to a decisive, existential life decision that had both moral as well as societal consequences.

Perhaps the clearest example, *The Swan* anticipated Grace Kelly's later life as the Princess of Monaco. It is a uniquely prophetic film.

Her final film, *High Society*, also mirrors events in her life, although it seems to align more closely with times prior to her engagement with Prince Rainier, as opposed to Charles Vidor's *The Swan*, in which Grace Kelly portrays Princess Alexandra, daughter of Princess Beatrix (Jessie Royce Landis, who had already played Grace's mother once, in *To Catch a Thief*). Alexandra is a woman who must choose between two men. Even though she really does not have the freedom to choose, she finds herself stuck between her tutor Dr. Nicholas Agi (Louis Jourdan) and his Royal Majesty Crown Prince Albert (Alec Guinness). Albert decides to visit the castle of his cousin Beatrix for several days, and Beatrix's greatest hope is that Albert will discover Alexandra's virtues and ask her to marry him. This would allow the family line to continue and would preserve the castle. And Alexandra would become the wife of the future king. However, as an inconvenience for everyone, Albert only cares about ball sports, duck hunting, and sleeping in. The increasingly despairing Beatrix then puts together a plan to turn Albert's attention to Alexandra. The mother asks her daughter to invite the court tutor Dr. Agi to the evening ball being held in Crown Prince Albert's honor. The idea is that this will make Albert jealous. Up until this point, Albert has only said that Alexandra "was like an icicle, and I was like a fish."[249] This humorous comparison reflects the "cool blonde" image long associated with Grace Kelly. On the other hand, Nicholas Agi, whom Alexandra invited to the court ball in person, interprets the invitation as a returning of his deep feelings for her. And he will soon be proven correct.

For the first time, completely unexpectedly, the young princess has discovered love, specifically for the modest and charming court tutor Agi, who has long been in love with the stylish, unapproachable, somewhat childish princess. However, the circumstances require that she marry Prince Albert and that she learn to love him—just as she would learn to love Prince Rainier. When Agi learns of this plan he leaves the castle, utterly heartbroken. Watching as he goes, Alexandra stays behind. She will marry the crown prince.

There is another interesting parallel in *The Swan*. The principality in the movie is just as tiny as Monaco, whose borders do not even encompass two square miles.

The parallels to Grace's actual life are quite astonishing. Shortly before the official announcement of her engagement with Prince Rainier III on January 5, 1956, in her hometown of Philadelphia, Grace finally ended her relationship, albeit a loose one, with her lover, fashion designer Oleg Cassini. She did this on the Staten Island Ferry.

The moment in which she severed their quite serious connection must have struck Cassini like a bullet. He was shocked; there seemed to be no emotional justification for what she had done.[250] (According to his own statements, he considered his short time with Grace to be "the most magical days I ever had in my entire life."[251])

Cassini asked Grace what she wanted from a man whom she had only met for a half hour eight months before. She did not know him at all. "I will learn to love him," she answered.[252] How quintessentially Grace. The discipline—that Kelly ambition for something higher. These things take priority. All possibilities exist only within that framework.

For Grace, it was the only logical path. Her decision was very much grounded in the expectations of her parents, particularly those of her father Jack. Grace still wanted to earn the respect, admiration, and approval of her father. And indeed, in Prince Rainier Jack Kelly saw, for the first time, a potential marriage candidate for his daughter. However, between the wedding in April 1956 and his death in June 1960, Jack Kelly only visited his daughter in Monaco twice, and in the palace, he felt extremely uncomfortable. Nevertheless, Grace's decision satisfied her family greatly. In addition, she hoped to satisfy her own need to marry and have children, to establish a family, and to put an end to her unbearable restlessness. In considering Oleg Cassini and Don Richardson, Grace also described her upcoming marriage to Prince Rainier III as "the solution." Neither Cassini nor Richardson could understand this; they both saw it as a big mistake. While Grace continued to maintain a friendship with Don Richardson, through letters and telephone calls, she broke all contact with Oleg Cassini. According to Nadia LaCoste, longtime press chief for the palace, "I cannot recall seeing Cassini in Monaco. I only know that at the time, the newspapers wrote that Grace and Cassini had almost gotten married. However, he was never in Monaco..."[253] As in Oleg Cassini's actual life, in the fictional film, court tutor Nicholas Agi had to resign himself to the fact that another was chosen. One who as Crown Prince brought with him the promise to make Princess Alexandra queen through marriage.

Starting in mid-September 1955, Grace was in Hollywood for the preparations for *The Swan*. She found herself in hair and makeup tests, and spent a week in long dress rehearsals in the studio in Culver City under the direction of costume designer Helen Rose. She had previously clothed Grace in the MGM productions, *Mogambo* and *Green Fire*. This time, Grace was especially taken with Rose and her team, who created a white chiffon ball gown for her. The gown was covered with countless, separately attached camellia blossoms. On the day of the fitting, she stood in front of the mirror and exclaimed breathlessly: "It's like a fairy tale."[254] Helen Rose had never before met a star who was so excited to try on a ball gown—one that was fit for a princess.

Eventually, Helen Rose would design the $7,200 wedding dress that Grace wore for her wedding on April 19, 1956. It was produced by Metro-Goldwyn-Mayer, which among other things hoped to use this ingenious promotional tactic to obtain free publicity for *The Swan*. Furthermore, MGM acquired the valuable and exclusive rights for the documentary film, *The Wedding in Monaco* (1956; directed by Jean Masson).[255]

The filming of *The Swan* was opulent and expensive in terms of design. Dore Schary himself produced the film, and filming ran from late September until December 22, 1955.

The literary basis for John Dighton's screenplay was the 1920 play *A Hattyú* by Ferenc (Franz) Molnár. Like director Charles Vidor, Molnár was a Hungarian native, and he was one of the most important Hungarian playwrights of the twentieth century. Molnár's most famous play was *Liliom* (1909). *A Hattyú* premiered in the United States in 1923, with the legendary, openly homosexual Eva Le Gallienne in the role of Princess Alexandra. Prior to Charles Vidor's film version, the play had been adapted for screen already twice before. The first version was made in 1925 with Frances Howard as Alexandra (directed by Dimitri Buchowetzki), and the second was directed by Paul L. Stein in 1930 under the title *One Romantic Night*, with Lillian Gish in the main role.

Grace herself knew this play well. She had already played Princess Alexandra in a one-hour television program for the CBS series *The Play's the Thing*. This aired live on June 9, 1950. Moreover, Grace's beloved Uncle George highly respected Ferenc Molnár's *A Hattyú*. And in terms of this role, what first took place on the screen, then occurred in real life.

Since the end of the silent film era (1928–1929), director Charles Vidor (1900–1959) had been responsible for creating such films as *Cover Girl* (1944), *Gilda* (1946)—probably his most famous movie—and *The Joker Is Wild* (1957). Grace and Vidor (who had come from the old Austrian-Hungarian empire and would die only four years after making *The Swan*) understood each other well. Grace felt comfortable on set with him.

The movie was filmed in Eastmancolor in the wide Cinema-Scope format. The sumptuous backdrop of the castle was designed by art director Cedric Gibbons, and the elegant costumes were created by Helen Rose. The cinematography was done by Joseph Ruttenberg and Robert Surtees, who had also helped film Metro's *Mogambo*. The most enchanting shots of Grace happen during the extensive dance scenes at the evening ball in the castle: Alexandra (Grace) and Agi (Jourdan) seem to float over the parquet, their moods becoming dreamier and dreamier, even though half of the court is watching them. In these dance sequences, Grace is indescribably charming and tender. She looks as smooth and flawless as marble, yet seems quite fragile. Her gaze and her body language are infused with yearning. Much of Grace herself can be seen in this central dance scene, which was elegantly and cleverly choreographed. Even the way in which she moves, her gestures, her graciousness, as well as her facial expressions, reveal the noblesse and sincerity that she would adopt in soon-to-be real principality.

In addition, there are several beautiful close-ups of Grace in *The Swan*. These show her face, smooth and relaxed, beaming and enchanting—yet there is a distinct undercurrent to all this. It is some sort of hesitance. Perhaps even a vague sense of fear. Furthermore, Grace appears frequently throughout the film (she received top billing for this MGM production), but she has relatively little dialogue. Much is communicated nonverbally through glances, small gestures, and various facial expressions.

One background observer of the filming of *The Swan* was the photographer Howell Conant, whom had been commissioned by both Metro-Goldwyn-Mayer and by Grace to take color pictures. During the film breaks, Grace often sat to the side. Most of the time she knitted or was lost in a book. Sometimes she read letters she had received. It can be assumed that most of this mail came from Monaco. She was discrete and silent about this. Even Conant noticed that "she seemed quiet and thoughtful on set." He also noted that, to him "this was the hardworking side of Grace."[256]

Grace's British costar, Alec Guinness, also noticed her demeanor: "Sometimes I saw her waiting in the wings, just staring into space. When I asked her, 'Grace, are you alright?' she came right back, but flinched every time, as though she'd been fully lost in thought."[257] This was Guinness' first American production, following his success in such films as David Leans' adaptation of Dickens' *Great Expectations* (1946) and Alexander Mackendricks' *The Ladykillers* (1955).

One of Alexandra's two younger brothers explains in *The Swan* that "No one ever knows what Alexandra is thinking."[258] And later, when Alexandra seeks comfort from her uncle, Father Carl Hyacinth (Brian Aherne), after she realizes that she and the court tutor cannot be together, her caring uncle says to her: "My child, you forget: You've only ever learned to suppress your feelings. If they suddenly come to the surface for a moment—one could make a mistake." These statements are just as applicable to Grace, as they are to Alexandra.

The interior scenes of *The Swan* were filmed in Hollywood, at MGM Studios in Culver City. During this time, Grace rented a white mansion high in the Hollywood Hills that belonged to the diet king, Gaylord Hauser, who was also Greta Garbo's health guru. Oliver, her black poodle, was also with her. Cary Grant and his wife Betsy had given him to her. After the conclusion of the studio scenes, MGM hired two DC-7 airplanes to fly the cast and film crew to North Carolina. Here they filmed both exterior and interior scenes at the Biltmore House in Asheville, North Carolina, and at Lake Junaluska. The youngest child of millionaire William Henry Vanderbilt, George W. Vanderbilt commissioned architect Richard Morris Hunt to model the Biltmore on the French châteaus of the Loire Valley. The mansion and massive estate were built in the 1890s. This impressive building is the largest of its kind in the United States: 250 rooms, dozens of bedrooms and bathrooms. The team and cast spent six weeks at the house, secluded from the rest of the world. On their evenings off, Grace played Scrabble with Alec Guinness and her film mother, Jessie Royce

Landis. Like Grace, Guinness was also religious; he accompanied Grace to Mass on one of the first Sundays in North Carolina.

More than anyone else on the team, Grace was delighted by the house with its 250 rooms. She would regularly rave about it, calling it "heavenly." It was "like a real palace."[259] She often exclaimed things like, "I love castles!"[260] and "I love it!"[261]

Although the others were impressed with the house, no one felt very comfortable in this rather grandiose site. Could Grace, alone in her noticeable praise, have been thinking about the palace on the Rock of Monaco?[262] It was from here that the prince was advancing his courtship, as he had before, in the form of increasingly regular letters, telegrams, and phone calls. All this after only one short, personal meeting five months before, on May 6, at the royal palace. On the film set, Grace read the letters and telegrams, and she answered them. In this written, indirect way, the two became acquainted with one another.

Grace's film partner, the French actor Louis Jourdan, who played the court tutor Nicholas Agi, recalled this time: "There was an innate aristrocracy, [an] elegance about her. Not only comportment and manners, but also in thinking, in being. It has been a cliché to say that Grace Kelly looked like a princess. But she did."[263]

It comes as no small wonder that Grace herself once said that Princess Alexandra felt like a woman she had inside herself already.[264]

Louis Jourdan also explained, "She had this extraordinary sense of humor—not only and first of all, about herself. Never taking herself seriously."[265]

The following anecdote serves as an example of Grace's humor: During the filming of *The Swan*, a running gag developed between Alec Guinness and Grace Kelly, which is known as the legendary "Tomahawk Anecdote." This gag was maintained by both of them over a span of twenty-five years. Alec Guinness himself gave varying accounts of what happened over the years, but the one he provided in the 1987 television documentary, *The Hollywood Collection: Grace Kelly—The American Princess*, is as good as any: "I got back one night. I'm playing in a show, [I] get into bed and I say to my wife, 'For God's sake, why on earth do we need a cold hot water bottle! Why do we need the hot water bottle at all!' She said, 'I don't know what you're talking about.' And it was this identical tomahawk."[266]

Guinness related that he had almost forgotten about the whole thing until he flew to Hollywood in 1979 to receive an honorary Oscar: "I went to Hollywood to receive a special Oscar which was very nice. I stayed at the Beverly Wilshire Hotel. Clasping my Oscar, I got home at three in the morning or whenever it was…and there in my bed at the Beverly Wilshire Hotel was the tomahawk."[267]

Another anecdote described by Alec Guinness involved the filming of the final scene in *The Swan*, one characterized by wistfulness and parting. However, in Guinness' dry, British humor, the filming sounds anything but sad:

"A touch more wind on Grace's hair," they said one afternoon at MGM as Grace Kelly and I, hand in hand, stood at a plaster balustrade apparently gazing out over a non-existent lake. They turned up the wind machine slightly and it blew dust in Grace's eyes, so she had to retire for an hour to be re-made up. When she returned, the director, Charles Vidor, said, "More wind, fellas, but without the dust," It came with a whoosh and blew off my toupee. Grace cried with laughter and had to be repaired again by the make-up artist. Another idle hour. In the end they resorted to wafting a gentle breeze by waving a small board at us.[268]

At the end of the film, court tutor Nicholas Agi departs, and Princess Alexandra sadly and longingly watches his carriage from the balcony. In the meantime, Crown Prince Albert has followed the princess onto the terrace, and he turns to her:

Prince Albert: "Your father used to call you his swan, so I am told. I think that's a good thing to remember. Think what it means to be a swan: to glide like a dream on the smooth surface of the lake, and never go to the shore. On dry land, where ordinary people walk, the swan is awkward, even ridiculous. When she waddles up the bank she painfully resembles a different kind of bird, n'est-ce-pas?"

Princess Alexandra (timidly): "A goose."

Prince Albert: "I'm afraid so. And there she must stay, out on the lake: silent, white, majestic. Be a bird, but never fly. Know one song, but never sing it until the moment of death. And so it must be for you, Alexandra: cool indifference to the staring crowds along the bank. And the song? Never."[269]

Later, in a similar manner, Grace will not be permitted to fly or sing: She was not allowed to make any more films; she was forbidden from appearing before a camera again as an actress. Her subjects, her spouse, her life circumstances were all against this. This was forcibly driven home to her one last time in 1962, when with a heavy heart she was forced to withdraw the consent she had given her friend and mentor Alfred Hitchcock to star in his psychological drama, *Marnie*. Instead, Tippi Hedren played the title role. For a while, Grace fell into a depression.

A sad, oppressive feeling of departure and anxiety lays across the final scene of *The Swan*. Her face is shadowed by yearning. It is as if she senses what will come next. It is a farewell to the life she knew before. This is true for Alexandra. And it is true for Grace.

In the final moments, Grace Kelly and Alec Guinness turn from the balcony railing, and without even looking at him, she crisply says to him, "Take me inside, Albert."[270]

This is the fateful last line of the film. With it, everything is decided. Etiquette has triumphed over emotion. Decorum over passion. And above all, she maintains her composure—because she wants to become queen.

Almost exactly four months after the conclusion of filming for *The Swan*, the film had its world premiere in Los Angeles on April 18, 1956. On April 26, its East Coast premiere was held at Radio City Music Hall in New York. The poster announced, "MGM presents The Love Story of a Princess," and a crown was perched on the capital letter of the word "Swan." Grace Kelly's painted profile can be seen in the background, and in the poster foreground, a snow white swan appears, with a crown on its head.

Metro-Goldwyn-Mayer did not just accidentally select April 18 as the day for the premiere. On that same day in Monaco, in the throne room of the royal palace, the civil wedding took place. And the actress Grace Kelly became her Royal Majesty Princess Grace of Monaco.

As Brigitte Auber revealed, "At the time, I heard that Americans were very proud of her becoming a princess. For that matter, it had a different meaning than it did in Europe. Here, one is more used to such things. However, an actual, real princess from an American family!"[271] The princess in the making had finally found her prince.

High Society
(1956)

"I don't want to be worshiped—
I want to be loved."
—Grace Kelly as Tracy Lord

On January 5, 1956, just after the turn of the new year, the engagement of Prince Charming and the Hollywood Princess was officially announced. In Philadelphia, Grace's hometown, all the Kellys, as well as Grace and Prince Rainier, gathered at the Philadelphia Country Club, one of Jack Kelly's favorite locales. The engagement was first announced to this small circle. Of course, Jack Kelly insisted on being the one to break the news.

Previously, on December 28, 1955, during a walk together through New York, Rainier proposed and gave Grace an engagement ring ornamented with a sparkling, polished emerald. Supposedly they were walking down the esplanade that runs down the center of Park Avenue. According to the story, Grace's delighted "Yes, yes, yes!" could be heard on the other side of the street. In the film *High Society*, she wore her actual engagement ring.

After the announcement at the country club, everyone returned to the Kelly house at 3901 Henry Avenue. The press had been invited to come here for the afternoon. However, what Margaret Majer-Kelly had to experience in her otherwise spacious house was more than she had ever imagined. Television journalists with their camera teams, newspaper reporters, and a horde of photographers stormed the Kelly house. Things were tipped over, furniture was damaged—some photographers even stood on top of the piano. Late in her pregnancy, sister Lizanne was hidden away upstairs. The house was packed and noisy.

What then proceeded was a mostly improvised press conference. Grace and Rainier descended from the second floor, and the press could hardly contain itself. The newly engaged couple sat on a bench, and close by, separated by a little table, Margaret and Jack Kelly also sat. The four of them were arranged in front of a fairly ugly brick wall. Countless microphones were set up on a table in front of them, and behind these were several large television cameras.

There is documentary, black-and-white footage of this afternoon, as Grace holds Rainier's hand, the sparkling engagement ring on her finger. She was used to the flashbulb chaos of Hollywood and the world of movies. Of premieres, interviews, receptions. However, now it was different. It was no longer about a new film project nor did it skirt around the edge of what was going on in her private life. Now it was exclusively about her future as a princess, one whose private life would be fully public and strictly regimented by court protocols—the extent of which was not yet fully known to her. She even smiled as she and Rainier faced the tension and awkwardness of the situation.

And then the relevant questions were asked:

Reporter: "How are you today?"
Grace: "I certainly do not have to stress that I am very happy."
Reporter: "Miss Kelly, when is the wedding?"
Grace: "There is no certain date yet."
Reporter: "Your Highness, you denied everything at an earlier time. Was this because you were being careful or because you did not know yet?"
Rainier: "I was honest. I did not know."
Reporter: "A surprise?"
Rainier: "Just like for you, I suppose."
Reporter: "Did it surprise you too, Miss Kelly?"
Grace: "Yes."
John B. Kelly: "Of course, he is Prince Charming."[272]

On the following day, the engagement was the headline story of the *International Herald Tribune*. The article was illustrated with a large-scale photograph of Grace and Rainier sitting on the bench in the house on Henry Avenue. The headline over the extensive article read: "Grace Kelly's Romance."

That evening, Grace and Rainier attended a benefit ball at the Waldorf Astoria Hotel in New York. The theme of this year's ball was Monte Carlo. Grace appeared in a Dior gown of white satin with an orchid decoration on the bodice. On this night of January 6, the New York public witnessed Grace in the company of the Prince of Monaco for the first time. Margaret and Jack Kelly were also with them, as well as Rainier's loyal companion and adviser, the Catholic priest Father Francis Tucker, and the young Dr. Robert Donat from Nice.

Originally from Wilmington, Delaware, Father John Francis Tucker (1889–1971) was of Irish heritage, and in early 1951, he was sent by the Vatican to Monaco at the special request of Prince Rainier. Here he worked as parish priest of St. Charles, as court chaplain, and as a friend and confessor for Rainier. Prior to coming to America, Father Tucker had investigated Grace Kelly's Catholic heritage and had found it suitable for his prince. Behind the scenes, Father Tucker, who was a central and significant figure in the principality for twelve years, pulled the strings behind the second meeting between Grace and Rainier, and he acted as the caring and informed mediator between the Old and New Worlds.

Until May 1962, Father Tucker served the prince and the Vatican. At this time, he retired and left Monaco due to advancing age. First, he went to Rome, but eventually he returned to the United States in 1963. On November 2, 1971, he died at the age of eighty-three.

A short time later, on January 10, 1956, Grace and Rainier held another press conference, this time in New York. It was only seven days until the filming was to begin for *High Society*, and at this conference, the question of the possible end of her acting career came up. To the question, "Will you continue your career after the wedding?" Grace answered: "The Prince will decide that." When asked if "Miss Kelly" would make other films, Rainier said: "I don't think so!"[273]

Two issues had to be dealt with next. Grace was required to undergo a fertility test. And through mediators, Jack Kelly and Prince Rainier had to take care of the financial transaction that stood behind the engagement: the dowry paid by the bride's father to the future husband. These were two delicate procedures that were not allowed to be made public.

The fertility test would reveal that Grace was no longer a virgin, and she was afraid, "believed that she was," as Don Richardson once related.[274] This was an embarrassing and uncomfortable situation for her, since she did not know how Rainier would react. She was very worried about this, as confirmed by her friends at the time.[275] Although the examination did not take place in the presence of Dr. Donat, he would be the mediator between the examining physician (a gynecologist from the woman's clinic in Bucks County, Pennsylvania, whom Grace knew) and the Monegasque delegation that sat waiting in the neighboring room of the clinic. The medical findings confirmed that Grace was fertile and could bear an heir for Monaco. Naturally, there was also the unspoken finding that she was no longer a virgin. This situation was not communicated further nor made public. They deliberately did not discuss this second point with Prince Rainier. Grace considered—with input from her New York friends—simply telling him that she had once had a sports accident, should the subject come up. Considering Grace's lack of interest in sports, her friends decided that this lie would not be very convincing. However, the conversation never took place. Perhaps Rainier had already had Grace's premarital relationships investigated, or perhaps he really believed she was yet untouched—a belief which would not have been especially unusual for the prudish 1950s.[276]

Through his mediators, Prince Rainier III of Monaco demanded from Jack Kelly a $2 million dowry. It was the tradition. Grace's father was initially outraged and unwilling to pay such a high sum. He refused to pay anyone to marry his daughter, who furthermore was a Hollywood star. Many discussions were held. Loudly argumentative, Jack Kelly stormed out of several of these negotiations, and Grace was deeply ashamed of her father's uncontrolled behavior. Father Tucker talked to the Kellys, Grace called Don Richardson, and Rainier's mediators spoke with father Jack. In the end, they agreed—internally and unofficially, discreetly and diplomatically—that father Jack would pay $1 million, and Grace herself would pay the other million, for which she sold some of her stocks.[277] The public never heard about this; it was shocking. It was too compromising. It was a development that brought with it the negative perception that the upwardly mobile, ambitious Kellys of Philadelphia had had to pay to marry into European aristocracy.

After both of these hurdles were overcome, there remained one third and—at this time—final point that stood on Monaco's agenda: the marriage contract. And even this was the source of new conversations and new arguments, especially in reference to the paragraph that specified that in the case of divorce, any children would remain with the Regent. This clause shocked Grace and her entire family. However, Prince Rainier's attorneys, who along with Jack Kelly's attorneys in New York drew up the contract in the presence of Grace, Jack, and the prince, would not yield on this point. Grace now knew that if her marriage did not last, regardless of who wanted to end it, she would lose her children. This was very difficult for the future bride and mother to accept. As Grace now saw, the contractual negotiations for her marriage were even worse than those she had had with MGM.[278]

In early 1956, Grace still had one film before her, *High Society*. This was her eleventh and final movie. Filming began on January 17 and ran through March 6, 1956. The locations were to be Bel Air, Los Angeles, and Newport, Rhode Island. On behalf of Metro-Goldwyn-Mayer, the producers were Sol C. Siegel and, interestingly, Bing Crosby through his company, Bing Crosby Productions. In mid-January, Grace once again flew from New York to Los Angeles to prepare for *High Society,* which was being directed by Charles Walters. The New York–born Walters had previously directed *The Glass Slipper* (1955) and *The Tender Trap* (1955). John Patrick wrote the screenplay, which was based on the Philip Barry play *The Philadelphia Story* (1939). The play had opened in Broadway's Schubert Theatre with Katherine Hepburn in the role of Tracy Lord. Shortly after the play's publication, George Cukor adapted the work for screen. The black-and-white film *The Philadelphia Story* (1940) had Cary Grant, James Stewart, and Katherine Hepburn in the main roles. The script was written by Donald Ogden Stewart, who won the Academy Award for Best Screenplay. James Stewart also received an Oscar as Best Actor for the film. For *High Society*, John Patrick and Charles Waters decided to relocate the 1930s screwball comedy to Rhode Island. The screenplay writer and the director, thus, abandoned some of the screwball elements from the earlier version in favor of diverse musical numbers typical of other contemporary, lightly tragic-comedic musicals; Cole Porter music pervades the entire film.

It is music that has become legendary and unforgettable. Cole Porter wrote both the music and the lyrics, which were then arranged and orchestrated by Johnny Green and Saul Chaplin. Among the numbers are such songs as "High Society Calypso" (Louis Armstrong and His All-Stars), "Little One" (Bing Crosby, Louis Armstrong), "Who Wants to Be a Millionaire?" (Frank Sinatra, Celeste Holm), "True Love" (Bing Crosby, Grace Kelly), "You're Sensational" (Frank Sinatra), "I Love You, Samantha" (Bing Crosby, Louis Armstrong), "Now You Has Jazz" (Bing Crosby, Louis Armstrong), "Well, Did You Evah?" (Bing Crosby, Frank Sinatra), and "Mind If I Make Love to You?" (Frank Sinatra). Charles Walters was responsible for the staging and choreography of the separate musical numbers. *High Society* received two Oscar nominations for the 1957 Academy Awards: Cole Porter for Best Original Song for "True Love" and Johnny Green and Saul Chaplin for Best Score for a Musical.

In mid-December, Prince Rainier had hoped to visit his future bride on the set of *The Swan*, but that had not worked out. Now he wanted to visit this next set, and for six weeks, he rented a mansion in Bel Air in Los Angeles, living there until mid-March. He took Grace out for supper and watched her on set. In terms of the plot, it rotates around a love triangle or a love "square" depending on how you view it. The protagonist Tracy Lord must decide between two men (and for a short while, between three men), much as Grace had to choose in her real life between Oleg Cassini and Prince Rainier of Monaco. Perhaps this was not the best film set for Rainier to visit.

On one of the days of filming, Grace, Rainier, and a small group of others went out for lunch. This group included Celeste Holm, who played Frank Sinatra's companion in *High Society*, and the unavoidable MGM studio chief Dore Schary. When Schary asked how large the Riviera principality actually was, he was told that the area encompassed less than one square mile and was smaller than the area covered by New York's Central Park. At the top of his voice, the amused and insensitive Schary declared that even the back lot area of MGM Studios was bigger than this. An uncomfortable situation. Everyone at the table felt embarrassed for this faux pas against Rainier. According to Celeste Holm, it was as if a large chandelier had fallen to the floor.[279]

In light of this boastfulness, it comes as no surprise that in his 1979 book *Heyday: An Autobiography*, as well as in a piece published in the October 20, 1956, issue of *The Saturday Review*, Schary ventured to ascribe Grace Kelly's entire success as a film actress to MGM alone. For this, he credited both John Ford and, of course, himself.[280]

High Society is set in Newport, where there are two big events exciting the snobbish high society there. First is the Newport Jazz Festival, which has attracted C. K. Dexter-Haven (Bing Crosby), a popular jazz composer, as well as Louis Armstrong and his five-member band. Second is the upcoming marriage of Tracy Samantha Lord (Grace Kelly), daughter of a wealthy family, to George Kittredge (John Lund). The wedding plans are fully underway in and around the palatial house. However, it is not an accident that Dexter has arrived at this time. He was Tracy's first husband and—as he admits—is still in love with her. Tracy is not at all happy when her ex-husband suddenly appears on the scene. Furthermore, this is an affront to her future husband, the respectable George. In addition, reporter Mike Conner (Frank Sinatra) and photographer Liz Imbrie (Celeste Holm) arrive, sent to the

Lords' by *Spy*. In exchange for not publishing a humiliating story about Tracy's father's romantic affairs, they have been allowed to cover the upper-class wedding. Now the carousel of characters begins to turn. Over the course of the movie, three men are interested in Tracy. Even reporter Mike finds himself enchanted by Tracy's coolness and noblesse. In one scene, he serenades her with the Cole Porter song "You're Sensational" and gradually becomes increasingly intoxicated. The spontaneous tête-à-tête with an equally inebriated Tracy ends later that evening, the day before the wedding, in the spacious garden. At the end of this romp, Dexter is the one who stands in George's place and marries Tracy a second time. Playing himself, Louis Armstrong, accompanied by his "All Stars" band, functions as an individualized version of a Greek chorus. He interjects musically throughout the film and provides occasional outside commentary.

Filmed in Technicolor and in the VistaVision format, *High Society* opened on July 17, 1956, in the American cinemas. Over the following months, it premiered in other countries as well. Contemporary reviews were generally positive: "A perfectly staged musical…thanks to witty dialogues and peppy music, (highlight: Louis Armstrong) an entertaining genre classic."[281]

As for the MGM film *The Swan*, costume designer Helen Rose was responsible for the dresses and evening gowns for this musical. At the beginning of the film, Grace wears a beige blouse along with beige pants and a wide, dark brown belt. Later she dons a pale blue chiffon dress and a white, Greek-style toga.

In *High Society*, Grace seems pronouncedly feminine. It is a femininity that masks a degree of brokenness. This pain is the result of the chasm between her self-perception and the way she is perceived by others. In Tracy Lord, everyone sees an untouchable, unapproachable, cool, beautiful goddess without a heart—even her own father. Tracy wants only to feel loved, yet she does not feel noticed, recognized, or even seen (when her father talks to her, he wears sunglasses). Tracy Lord's haughtiness only functions to conceal her uncertainty in terms of her approaching wedding—and the unexpected situation of being caught between

218

three men—and of her problematic relationship with her restrictive father. It is a protective shield for her pain.

The film's central scene is divided into three parts, a triptych of sorts that acts as a three-act play condensed into ten minutes and positioned in the middle of the film. In this scene, Tracy Lord finds herself alone in the swimming pool at her family's estate in Newport. Behind the azure pool is a slightly curved, cream-colored building ornamented with white columns. Statues stand here and there. Columns, statues—the scenery is classical. In contrast, Grace is robed in a white, floor-length robe.

Then Dexter-Haven (Crosby), her ex-husband, comes by to give her his wedding gift. Tracy removes her robe, under which she is wearing a bathing suit. The suit is also white and very short; the pleated skirt nicely emphasizes her long legs. The dialogue that follows is full of wordplay and ambivalence, subtext, and nostalgic allusions to Dexter-Haven and Tracy's past. The dynamic is almost identical to her relationship with Oleg Cassini, who described his one and a half—almost two—year relationship with Grace as the "most enchanting years of my life." Just like *The Swan*, fiction closely mirrors reality. After Dexter leaves Tracy at the swimming pool, she sinks wistfully into her memories of their early days together, of the honeymoon spent on *True Love*, Dexter's boat. Dexter has actually given her a miniature model of the boat as a wedding present, and she sails the boat out over the water of the pool. This is the scene that also contains Grace's only musical number.

Then the second part of the scene begins. Her future husband, George, appears at the end of the pool. He discovers a completely distant and dreamy Tracy, who resembles the Grace that her friends often found, sitting for hours cross-legged in front of the fireplace or gazing dreamily out of a window. The third segment pertains to Tracy's relationship with her parents, particularly the difficult, distant one with her father. Seth Lord (Sidney Blackmer) and his wife (Margalo Gilmore)—whose name was even Margaret, just like Grace's own mother—come to the swimming pool. Instantly an argument arises between father and daughter.

All three scenic segments handle, in an obvious way, themes from Grace Kelly's own life. The choice of the right life partner and husband. The external image of unapproachable coolness that starkly contrasted with her internal, sensitive self. The problematic relationship with her father John B. Kelly, who never really saw her as she truly was. Also, another parallel existed: the hurt his wife Margaret faced due to his long history of infidelity. Margaret Majer-Kelly always deliberately ignored his affairs at all cost, since the well-being of her four children was more important to her than the state of her own marriage.

Grace spoke with great enthusiasm about the making of her final film as follows. She had always wanted to do a musical and greatly admired the skills of her costars, Sinatra and Crosby.[282]

Bing Crosby recalled working a second time with Grace, after *The Country Girl*: "She is a great woman with a huge talent…friendly, considerate and nice to everyone. She was great with the crew…she always brought them little gifts…For me she was one of the loveliest women I knew and with whom I have ever worked."[283]

With accordion accompaniment, the song "True Love" that Bing Crosby and Grace Kelly sing as a duet became a classic. Millions of records were sold worldwide. While it was Crosby's twentieth golden record, it was Grace's first and only one.

Both Grace Kelly and Bing Crosby long remembered the not-so-easy making of the world renowned song: "I am very proud of my gold record. Of course Bing basically carried it." She went on to say that her brother even teased her, saying that having her voice on a gold record was one of the "wonders of the modern age." As for her recording session with Bing, he "was completely relaxed [and] all so used to it… For me it was a fairly intimidating experience, with a big orchestra in the studio [with us]…but Bing [eased] my fear and helped me through it. He has a very deep voice, and my voice is rather bright and a bit thin—that was a problem with the recording. Actually, I should have sung the melody, but our vocal ranges were just too far apart, so ultimately I had to sing the harmony instead."[284]

The famous "True Love" scene—the song having been recorded separately in a studio—took place on March 6, 1956. It was the last day of filming for *High Society*. And the last day Grace Kelly would ever perform on a movie set.

Instead of returning directly to New York afterward for the cast party and to prepare for her transatlantic trip to Europe in early April, Grace stayed in Los Angeles for two weeks. For one thing, she wanted to say good-bye to all of her friends and colleagues who lived there. In addition, she still had one obligation. Since she had received the previous year's Oscar as Best Actress, she was to fulfill tradition by giving the statuette to the winner of the Best Actor award at the 28th Oscar ceremony on March 21, 1956. That year it went to Ernest Borgnine for his role in Delbert Mann's *Marty* (1955).

At this occasion, a rare photograph was taken of Grace Kelly and Audrey Hepburn together, as the two distinct style icons waited in one of the backstage changing rooms. As the photograph was taken, they exchanged a glance that was reflected in the large mirror behind them.

This was Grace's final appearance in the West Coast dream factory. It was also her farewell to many of her colleagues.

Her farewell to Hollywood.

From the moment she married, she was no longer
Grace Kelly.
The most captivating aspect of Princess Gracia was that
she completely embraced Monaco. She did so much
for Monaco. She was not only gorgeous, but she had a
heart that was as big as this house. We laughed a lot
with each other—my God, she had a wonderful sense
of humor. She was everything—only not cold. She was
very patient. She took great efforts to learn French. She
was thoroughly a mother, thoroughly a wife. I can still
remember how she sat on the floor and read stories to the
children. And whenever she had time, she herself would
pick the children up from school. She behaved just like
any normal mother.
—Nadia LaCoste, former press chief of the royal palace[285]

—II. THE LATER YEARS

1956–1976
Monaco: A Prince, Three Children, and
a Completely Different Life

> *So far Grace has moved with the ease of a trapeze artist.*
> *However, I wonder whether she may have ended*
> *up too high.*
> *—Alfred Hitchcock[286]*

> *I don't think that Grace was in love. She didn't even*
> *have time to really fall in love [with Rainier]. [In the*
> *past] she was much more in love with other men than*
> *with Rainier... But between the two there was a great*
> *attraction. Even still, I do not know why she decided so*
> *quickly to marry him.*
> *—Lizanne Kelly Levine, Grace Kelly's younger sister[287]*

The year was 1297 and, according to legend, the day was January 8. Francesco Grimaldi knocked on the gates of the medieval fortress that crowned the towering cliff, Le Rocher. It was supposedly late in the evening. Also known as "Malizia" (the malicious one), this Grimaldi, though cloaked in the garb of a Franciscan monk, was descended from a noble Genoan family. Together with his men, he forced his way into the fortress and overpowered the watchmen. The Ghebelline regent, the archenemy of the Grimaldis, was stabbed to death in his bed by Francesco Grimaldi and his cousin Rainier Grimaldi. This is the legend of how a historically Italian family, the Grimaldis of Genoa, came to rule Monaco from this cliff. Their reign has been continuous excepting a few interruptions, which lasted for several decades. Rainier Grimaldi, known as Rainier I (1267–1314), was the first regent. He was seven years older than his impetuous cousin Francesco. A dedicated seaman,

Rainier I's rule was quite brief, because in 1304 the French King Philippe IV named him Admiral of France. Rainier I took off across the sea, and the history of Monaco was henceforth determined by a changing array of Italian and French occupiers and regents. In 1314, during a battle against the German emperor Heinrich VII, Rainier I died a hero's death, leaving behind three children from two marriages. When he was not waging battle on the sea, he enjoyed the company of women and was known to enjoy the world of carnal pleasures among prostitutes. According to legend, around the turn of the fourteenth century, he supposedly seduced a beautiful young Flemish woman and raped her in the castle garden. Afterward, this woman, in tears, revealed to him that she could command the powers of black magic. She cursed Rainier I and all of his descendents: "No Grimaldi will ever be truly happy in marriage!"[288]

This is how the legendary and oft-cited "Grimaldi Curse" came into being. Considering the family history of the Grimaldis it seems to come up time and time again.

Francesco Grimaldi carried a sword concealed under his monk's robes. On the 700th anniversary of the taking of the city, on January 8, 1997, a bronze memorial was dedicated to him, and the statue shows Francesco in his monk's habit with sword in hand. The memorial is located in the broad square in front of the palace, by the right-hand entrance. The sculpture was created by the native Dutch sculptor Verkade Kees, who now resides in Monaco. Prince Rainier III unveiled and dedicated the bronze memorial to his Grimaldi ancestors.

Before the conquering of Monaco by the Grimaldis, the area had been occupied by the Phoenicians, after which it fell under Roman law. The Christianization of the area occurred circa 100 A.D. However, the first written reference to Monaco is much older than this. The Greek historian and geographer Hectaeus of Miletus wrote about "Monoikos Polis Ligustike" ("Monaco, the city in Linguria") in the fifth century B.C.[289] Even earlier than this Hercules supposedly performed a few of his heroic feats there. Even today, Monaco's main harbor is called Port Hercule. And it is not an accident that the gallery that runs along the inner courtyard of the palace, which also leads to the throne room and the large, sweeping, marble staircase, is called the Hercules Gallery.

Since Francesco and Rainier's coup, numerous princes have ruled the area, which stretches two miles along the coast. First was Rainier I and then Charles I—who is considered the first true ruler of Monaco. Later came Jean I, Honoré II, Charles III, and many other princes through to Albert I (reign: 1889–1922). Albert I was extremely beloved by the Monegasque people. He was a deep sea adventurer, a kind of Monegasque Jules Verne—an archaeologist and an oceanographer. With great passion and knowledge, he established one of the great tourist attractions, the Musée Océanographique and its aquariums. This is a colossal, almost monstrous-looking, museum that reaches from the cliff top deep down into the sea. Understandably perhaps, Albert I ran himself into extensive debt. The royal line continued through to Rainier's grandfather Louis II (reign: 1922–1949), Rainier III (1949–2005), and now finally Albert II, who inherited the throne on March 31, 2005, and was crowned on July 12, 2005.

The American writer Somerset Maugham, who owned a villa on the wealthy Cap Ferrat peninsula not far from Monaco, once made the following barbed quip about the principality: "A sunny place for shady people." The subtext to Maugham's quote has been attached to the city-state for many decades, despite the years of efforts, particularly under the reign of Prince Albert II since 2005, to create a much friendlier, brighter, and cleaner image for Monaco.

This sunny place, which among others has the nickname "Manhattan on the Mediterranean," covers an area of less than one square mile. Thus, it is smaller than both New York's Central Park and Munich's English Garden. (Today the principality measures exactly 0.78 square miles. The actual land mass has increased a little between the 1970s and the 2000s due to concerted efforts to increase the area by extensions into the sea, such as the small front part of the Larvotto coastal district with the Grimaldi Forum, a congress and conference center that was built in the 1990s. Another recent project has involved the relatively new western city district of Fontvieille with its heliport and rose garden, as well as the new parts of the harbor at Port Fontvieille.)

Because of the limited land area, new high-rises are increasingly being constructed in Monaco, and after the Vatican in Rome, Monaco is the second smallest country in the world. Situated between Nice and the nearby border to Italy, the principality has a population of 30,400 residents. Of this number, about 7,500 are native-born Monegasque, making them only about 17 percent of the actual population. The rest of the residents in Monaco are primarily French—which comprise the majority at 47 percent—Italian, English, Portuguese, Swiss, and German. The city is divided into ten districts. Two of the most famous districts are Monte Carlo, with its casino, opera house, and the Hôtel de Paris; and Monaco Ville, which contains the Rock and the old city. In Monaco Ville one can also find the palace, St. Nicholas Cathedral, and the Oceanographic Museum. Monaco is the most densely populated country in the world with penthouse apartments selling for over $135,000 per square yard. It is the most expensive real estate there is.

As a longtime purveyor to the court claimed, "We enjoy many advantages here in Monaco. We have very little crime—security is the highest law here—we enjoy a high quality of life. Thus, we naturally have the most expensive real estate."[290]

Monaco is the seat of an archbishop who answers directly to the Holy See, and thus the state church is Roman Catholic. St. Nicholas is the country's cathedral, located high upon Le Rocher, the cliffs. Grace Kelly and Prince Rainier III were married here on April 19, 1956. Approximately 90 percent of the Monegasque people are Catholic, and 6 percent are Protestant. In addition, the principality is home to both Orthodox and Jewish minority groups.

Independent since 1489, Monaco has been a constitutional monarchy since 1911. The current constitution was passed on December 17, 1962, and it was substantially expanded and revised on April 2, 2002. One of the most significant changes for the country was to the critical Paragraph 10, the article that stipulates the royal succession. In the past, the throne would pass to the first direct, legitimate offspring of the prince, or else a male successor of the same status. But now, if a prince has no offspring, his brothers *and* his sisters, as well as their offspring, could take the throne. If an heir to the throne abdicates, his descendents automatically take his place.

A potential successor to Prince Albert would be his older sister, Princess Caroline, followed by her oldest son Andrea. After that, in theory, Albert's other nieces and nephews—his sisters' children—would come into question. The 1918 regulations required that the small principality would fall under the governance of its larger neighbor, France, should no Grimaldi successor exist to take the throne. This was abolished on April 2, 2002, through a second Monegasque-French accord. Now, even if the Grimaldi line dies out, the principality of Monaco will remain a sovereign, autonomous, independent state.

However, when Grace married Prince Rainier, six years prior to the passing of the constitution in December 1962, the old statute from 1918 was still in place. A direct successor had to be born. Rainier had to ensure the succession of the Grimaldis and, through him, the independence of his state. Not insignificantly, his people expected this of him. This explains the fertility test that Grace had to go through. Either way, the newly married couple was under great pressure.

Grace Kelly left her homeland on the morning of April 4, 1956. At Pier 84 of the foggy New York harbor, the *SS Constitution* was docked. This was the ocean liner that would take her across the Atlantic. After a short delay, the liner eventually cast off. Its first destination was Cannes, then Monaco. Her parents and sisters were on board, along with seventy other individuals from her personal social circle, including some of her bridesmaids. Besides the regular passengers on the boat, there were also well over one hundred members of the press. Before the departure, Grace was strongly against the presence of reporters and photographers on board the ship. The atmosphere of the press conference held shortly before the sailing of the liner had bordered on hysteria, and in the midst of this, despite all the tension and uproar, Grace had stood, quiet and poised. Morgan Hudgins, the press agent for MGM Studios, helped Grace deal with the undesired journalists on the ship. The eight days on the ocean liner were perhaps her last days of true freedom, regardless of any serious reflection or melancholy caused by quarreling and a hesitation about what would come next. However, there was still no palace protocol. With her friends, she played charades, as they had loved to do in New York. Of all things, she wore an Oleg Cassini gown of white lace. Champagne, Grace's favorite drink, flowed freely.

The Americans had mixed feelings about letting her go. They were losing their Hollywood star but gaining a Princess of American heritage—an American icon as a member of the European ruling class.

She embodied the dream of so many American girls and young women. Her ascent to royalty contributed greatly to the iconization of her that had already begun even before her marriage.

The *Constitution* reached Monaco on April 12, 1956, at 9:30 a.m. On his new ship, *Deo Juvante II*, the prince met his fiancée out on the water. (The boat's name was Monaco's own Latin motto ("With God's Help"); on the Grimaldi coat of arms, the motto is printed under the red and white shield, which is held by two monks carrying swords.) Eight days had passed since Grace Kelly's departure from New York. Grace changed boats, crossing a gangplank from the large *SS Constitution*, which because of its size and depth could not enter the harbor, to the *Deo Juvante*. She carried her poodle, Oliver—a gift from Cary Grant—who was ornamented with a white bow, from which dangled a long white leash. Somewhat awkwardly, Grace and Rainier merely shook hands: "Carrying her poodle Oliver, Grace walked across the gangway. Rainier extended his hand to her—they did not really know what they should do. Thus, there was a handshake. It was laughable. Grace held Oliver with one hand, and with the other, she held the Prince's hand. If the Prince had hugged her, poor Oliver would have been squished. The entire world waited for a kiss. Instead, there was a 'Hello, welcome to Monaco'— totally unromantic."[291] This account was given by her friend and bridesmaid Judith Balaban Quine. People stood around the edge of the harbor, calling, waving, taking pictures. A twenty-one gun salute was given, and a water plane dropped thousands of red and white carnations (the national colors of Monaco) from the sky. Yet on board the *Deo Juvante* as it entered the harbor, Grace could hardly guess what would happen to her over the approaching days, weeks, months.

Her voyage on the *SS Constitution* was a journey into the unknown. Grace did not really know what to expect in the Monegasque principality on the Riviera. Her few previous stays there had each been very brief. She did not know either the country or its residents, nor did she speak their language. In the end, her step was also a risk. Now, Grace would play a major role in one of the greatest media spectacles that the world had experienced to date. As she crossed the gangway, between 1,500 and 1,800 journalists and reporters of the international press reacted to the giant white hat of Swiss lace that Grace wore. These reactions ranged from disenchantment to anger. The wide hat brim almost completely hid her face. In addition, Grace wore her trademark white gloves and a long, dark coat with three-quarter length sleeves. Directly in front of the gangway, one of the palace's dark limousines was parked, waiting on the dock for her and the prince. Everywhere along the roadsides, the Monegasque people stood, waving flags and cheering.

Finally, she had arrived, their future princess and mother of their nation. However, Grace had only arrived in a physical sense—years would pass before her heart and soul would follow.

During the six days between Grace's arrival and the official marriage ceremony, the couple had numerous official engagements to attend—balls, receptions, appointments, opera performances. Among the invited guests was the shipping magnate Aristotle Onassis, who at this time was already a financially powerful and influential shareholder in the Société des Bains de Mer (SBM), the state-controlled company that functioned as Monaco's largest employer. François Mitterand, then France's young minister of justice, was also in attendance.

Maree Frisby Rambo, one of Grace's bridesmaids and an old friend, described this time: "There were more photographers there than Monegasque natives. And all of them were waiting for someone to break a leg so that they had something to write about. It was deathly dull. They were so happy when all of my jewelry was stolen, since they finally had a story."[292]

On April 11, 1956, at 11:00 a.m., the legal marriage of His Majesty Prince Rainier III of Monaco and Grace Kelly took place in the throne room of the 220-room royal palace of Monaco. Since her departure from New York, Grace had lost thirteen pounds. The stress and tension of the previous days and weeks had caused her to lose her appetite. On that April 18, she seemed very tense. She did not smile even once during the marriage ceremony. She was nervous, and her inner turmoil was evident as she sat on one of two upholstered chairs. Prince Rainier's chair was a good yard away from hers. She had dark rings under her eyes, surely caused by the strain of the previous days.

That afternoon, at 4:00 p.m., the royal palace held a reception for the Monegasque people. Sparkling wine was served, and a large buffet was set up.

On this day, the bourgeois American actress and Hollywood icon became the Monegasque princess. A day of metamorphosis. It was as if the shift in her identity was completed then. She was, henceforth, Her Majesty Princess Gracia Patricia of Monaco. Many of her American friends would talk about her last, great role, the role of her lifetime.

Grace's friend Judith Balaban Quine described the official marriage ceremony: "She came into the room, and I thought that she had never looked so frightened or tense. Normally she was always herself, but not there. She clearly did not feel comfortable in her new skin. I noticed it because whenever she was nervous she would always pull on her fingers, and she did this in spite of her gloves, without a break. Very odd."[293]

Friend Robert Dornhelm described it similarly: "Thus, she accepted this offer, undertaking a role that would last the rest of her life. She very much saw this as a big, new job: she had to act, put on make-up, fix her hair, prepare herself, memorize her lines, talk at receptions, represent the country. She herself saw this as a challenge and accepted this job because she told herself that this way she was set with work for life. It was the ultimate soap opera role that never ended and was always there. It was a golden cage. Of course, she had the security that she would always have work, but it was monotonous work and not enriching. There was stagnation. It was always the same. Variations of the same cover story, whether she had gained weight, if she looked as if she had drunk too much, or if the children were running amok. This was not very fulfilling in the long run."[294]

The official marriage ceremony in the throne room was filmed by four French television cameras as well as one local one for the new, local television channel "Télé Monte Carlo" (TMC). This ceremony, as well as the "Fairytale Wedding of the Century," held on the following day, April 19, 1956, was broadcast around the world.

At 10:30 a.m., John B. Kelly led his daughter Grace up the steps of St. Nicholas and down the nave to the high altar. Here, the Bishop of Monaco, Monsignore Gilles Barthe, the Kelly family's priest, Father Cartin from Philadelphia, and Father Francis Tucker waited for the couple. Then, several minutes later, the prince entered the sacred white building, as was the custom.

Grace's wedding gown was designed by Helen Rose and was given as a gift by MGM. It became a much-copied gown, and it was made of 30 yards of tulle and 290 yards of Valenciennes lace. The dress was covered in pearls. It had a stand-up collar, long sleeves, a long skirt, and a three-yard train. Grace carried a small bridal bouquet of lily of the valley, as well as a little Bible that was covered in the same material as her gown.

In Monaco's cathedral behind the altar, hidden by bouquets and shrubbery, and in the upper areas of the side aisles, eleven television cameras were mounted. Three of them belonged to Metro-Goldwyn-Mayer, four of them to various television stations, and the other four were filming for weekly news coverage. In addition, several microphones were set up directly on the altar.

Everything was to be well-recorded both visually and audibly. The MGM cameras, for the documentary film *Le Marriage à Monaco*, as well as the television cameras, were broadcasting live—a true technical wonder for this time. The wedding between Grace and Rainier was watched by about 30 million people in about a dozen countries. Excluding the crowning of Queen Elizabeth II of England on June 2, 1953, this was the largest television viewing audience ever. For this era, this was a gigantic media spectacle. A mass event. Never before were running cameras allowed to be so close to a church wedding of European royalty. This was also the first time that cameras were allowed to film from the perspective of the priest. From time to time, Grace's and Rainier's faces were shot as intimate close-ups during the ceremony. Every movement of their faces could be seen. No moment remained hidden; no moments of privacy were allowed. Everything was public, everything was aired, everything had already been sold to Metro-Goldwyn-Mayer, the French television stations, and TMC. As friend Rita Gam recalled, "The wedding in Monaco was a very special experience. I am not sure if you absolutely have to do something like this in your life, but for Grace and her guests it was something exceptional. An enormous tension dominated because something very private was suddenly a worldwide media event."[295]

At a later date, Grace commented that both she and Rainier had found the day to be rather awful. They had only registered some of the aspects of the day, and everything seemed muffled and distant, as if they were wrapped in cotton. "The whole thing was a nightmare."[296] And during a 1985 interview on the *Today Show*, daughter Caroline confirmed that "my parents found their wedding to be atrocious."[297]

A luncheon followed the church wedding at 1:00 p.m. The palace's inner courtyard was set up for about 700 wedding guests. These included Grace's good friend and actor David Niven and his wife; Aristotle Onassis and his wife Athina; Gloria Swanson and Ava Gardner (who came without her estranged husband Frank Sinatra); and press agent and journalist Rupert Allan from Los Angeles.

On that same afternoon, the newly married couple departed for their honeymoon along with poodle Oliver. They took a seven-week cruise across the Mediterranean. It was the first time ever that Grace and Rainier had spent time together unobserved and alone, the first time that they had experienced each other just as a couple. The young couple went first to Mallorca and Ibiza. The second part of the cruise skirted the coast of Spain. Grace and Rainier spent day after day on land, visiting Valencia, Madrid, Granada, and Málaga. During this honeymoon at sea, Grace became pregnant for the first time. Finally, on June 6, the *Deo Jovante II* returned to the harbor of Monaco.

Friend Rita Gam described Grace's feelings at this time: "I don't think Grace really believed that she was going to give up acting when she became Princess Grace of Monaco. I think that the reality of that probably struck her somewhere in the middle of the Mediterranean after the honeymoon began."[298] One can then suppose that the offer from MGM's Dore Schary shortly after her wedding was all the more sobering, perhaps even bitter. He asked her to star alongside James Stewart in the upcoming film *Designing Women* (1957). However, she was not allowed to take on any new film projects. The prince had strictly forbidden this. Instead of being a second opportunity for Grace and Stewart to appear before the cameras after *Rear Window*, ultimately Lauren Bacall and Gregory Peck would star in this marital comedy directed by Vincente Minnelli.

"I became a Princess before I had much time to think about it," Grace once said about herself.[299] Interestingly, her husband, Prince Rainier, was sitting right next to her when she revealed this.

The question of "Why?" has come up time and time again in the search for the reasons, from both sides, that led to the so-called wedding of the century. For Rainier, the answering of this question was somewhat simpler than it was for Grace. Rainier was searching for a future Princess of Monaco, and he became taken with Grace's charm and personality. Furthermore, she was Catholic and had been strictly and well raised. "She was an absolute enchantment," asserted Thomas Veszilits.[300]

When once asked to describe the start of things between him and Grace, Prince Rainier claimed: "I do not believe in love-at-first-sight, which is a wishy-washy term I never use."[301]

"Rainier was not a man of the arts."[302] He was a pragmatist with an interest in sports, cars, and the animals in his palace zoo. She was a sensitive soul who loved everything in the realms of culture and the arts. Two polar opposites. These poles helped to expand one another, but also resulted in mutual conflicts. Frequently over the years, misunderstandings of each other dominated. They could not relate to the other's world. According to Robert Dornhelm, in subjectively describing the couple's relationship, Rainier "was sometimes quite harsh. In reality, he caused embarrassment and irritation through his indifference and his lack of consideration."[303] In 1974, Grace herself expressed that while they did not have a lot in common, their shared Catholic faith united them deeply.[304]

Robert Dornhelm described the situation in more detail: "Rainier was sometimes in a good mood, sometimes in a bad mood—Grace and Rainier were certainly not very compatible. However, for Monte Carlo this was a huge win: tourism, the casino, the influx of money—she brought Monaco a high level of prestige. Through her charm, she definitely did much good for the country. Again and again, it was in all the newspapers. Suddenly, everyone started coming to Monte Carlo again. The casino was full again, and the real estate properties again became expensive."[305]

As publicist Thomas Veszelits recalled: "At that time, in the early 1970s, Monaco was not yet over-touristed or extremely exclusive. You had a pretty good chance of seeing Grace Kelly meeting someone at the Hôtel de Paris. It was like her second office. She was very, very present. Of course, Grace Kelly was a workaholic, but she liked the American element that could be met in the bar of the Hôtel de Paris. She really enjoyed the hotel and the intimate atmosphere there. She did not look like she did in the films. On the street, you almost might have failed to recognize her. Naturally, she was very elegant but in public she dressed completely normally. She was a lady, but not like Sophia Loren or Claudia Cardinale, whom one could not fail to recognize."[306]

Veszelits went on to describe the various activities that Grace took on as princess: "Grace Kelly lived Monaco. She was a part of Monaco. She was unimaginably disciplined, one of her completely American attributes. Until midnight, she controlled all of the invitations, whether or not they went out with the mail the following day. She managed the office. She also organized all of the balls. She herself established one ball, the Rose Ball. The Red Cross Ball was already a Monegasque tradition, reaching back to the ancestors in the late 1800s. Then, all of the foundations. She created a very important foundation for the natural feeding of babies: La Leche League—emphasizing breastfeeding and the importance of mother's milk. She became seriously involved with this endeavor and argued that it was wrong to feed babies with artificial foods. Babies must be nourished on their mothers' milk. She must have had an extraordinary reserve of energy. At that time, she took on at least ten or twelve foundations, and on top of that, there were the building organizations."[307] Above all, Grace's extensive charitable and social engagement was extended through her "Le Fondation Princess Grace," which was established in 1964. Since 1983, Princess Caroline has been the patroness of this foundation.

"It was her kindness. She always wanted to make sure that no one got taken advantage of..."[308] This is what Nadia Lacoste remembered about Princess Grace. Born in Romania in the 1920s, Nadia Lacoste first came in contact with the American film industry in the 1940s. After they experienced the terror of the approaching German invasion of Paris, Nadia and her parents had fled Europe. She worked in various studio departments, including the script department where workers cut out countless newspaper articles every day, searching for material that could inspire movie magic. Then, she returned to Paris where she opened an office whose work was unprecedented: she helped build contacts through her knowledge of the major studios in Los Angeles and the press circles of the French metropolis.

Nadia LaCoste and Rupert Allan had known each other in Hollywood. He had been involved in so many aspects of Grace's career, and through him, a connection developed between the Monegasque royal house and the multilingual press journalist.

"I met many of the older actors and her costars. We always met at Rupert Allan's house. He was engaged as the Monegasque general consul and PR man in Los Angeles. There Grace always kept a list—who was still alive and who might like to come to Monaco," Robert Dornhelm explained about Rupert Allan.[309]

After the wedding of Grace and Prince Rainier, to which he had been invited by Grace, Rupert Allan called Nadia LaCoste in Paris: "They need you here, absolutely. No one can speak English." And then: "You must first meet Prince Rainier. He is coming to Paris, presumably with Grace. You must speak with him."[310]

And Prince Rainier came to Paris in the fall of 1956, and Nadia LaCoste met her future, longtime employer for the first time. Rainier hired her on the spot. Her position was unprecedented in Monaco: she would be head of a new press office founded specifically for the royal palace. For a while, she traveled between Paris and Monaco, since she preferred to live in Paris. However, the new press office had to be located in Monaco, even if there was no actual press there. The entire press, both national and international, was located in Paris. Monsieur Olivier of the Monegasque tourism information office was still in charge of all the press contacts. This situation needed to be changed. Thus, Nadia LaCoste moved to Monaco.

Starting in the late fall of 1956 and continuing for several decades, she managed the country's press needs and therefore, held a powerful, central position. There was little in or around Monaco that escaped Nadia LaCoste's awareness. She was one of the most competent and discreet palace insiders. Her son, Thierry LaCoste, now an attorney, grew up with Prince Albert in Monaco. Both boys were the same age. It was Nadia LaCoste who had to provide adequate information to the international press about Princess Grace's tragic accident in mid-September 1982.

Nadia LaCoste further remembered: "At the beginning, I met both of them when they were here in Paris. And they often came here. They frequently spent the months of September and October in Paris. They had many friends here, they went to the theater. I met the Princess, and immediately we realized that we had many

236

friends in common. All of the film stars, whom she knew, I knew as well. That quickly linked us..."[311]

And in terms of Grace's slow acclimation to her role and her place in everyday Monegasque society: "At first, Grace simply tried to find a place for herself in Monaco and to do something for Monaco. However, the children also arrived immediately."[312]

Publicist Rolf Palm explained the early difficulties with the lack of amenities in the royal palace: "At first, Grace Kelly had mineral water shipped from America. And the castle was still fairly shabby. At the time that Grace came to live in the castle, it in no way resembled the level of comfort enjoyed by wealthy Americans. There was much she had to get used to, to learn."[313]

On January 23, 1957, almost exactly nine months after the wedding, Princess Caroline was born at 9:27 a.m. Like both of her other children, Grace gave birth to Caroline in the palace, not in a hospital. The cannon fired a twenty-one gun salute, and every Monegasque knew that Princess Gracia had had a daughter.

On March 14, 1958, only fourteen months after firstborn Caroline's birth, Grace gave birth to the long-awaited male heir, Prince Albert. This time, the cannon fired 101 salutes. Monaco now had its successor.

The birth of Princess Stéphanie fell on February 1, 1965. This was Grace and Rainier's third and final child.

"I think the easier thing came when she had the children. And they did come very quickly. She wanted the children and she loved them. And we had so much fun rough-housing together. Her children and my children are the same age. And they've gone to camp together. Don [LeVine] and I have been over to Monaco several times with the children and they've come here to Ocean City," related Grace's younger sister, Lizanne Kelly LeVine.[314]

Nadia LaCoste described this similarly: "By all means, Princess Grace was family oriented. Her sisters came, her brother, they all came to visit. And she visited them every year. She always took the children. She never traveled alone, for herself. She came from a family that was very close, and that was wonderful since Rainier's life had been quite different. His parents did not stay together. As a child, he had not had a life like hers. It was great because they could build something together, and he was very grateful to finally have a family since he had not had one before."[315]

Sporadically, if their schedules allowed, they carried on this family life outside of the palace and the principality. On some weekends, especially those during the summer months of August and September, they would go to their estate at Roc Agel. This was located above the French town of La Turbie, high up Mont Agel in the Maritime Alps. In 1957, Rainier bought the old farmhouse there and renovated it. By 1959 the family house was ready. Nadia LaCoste recounted: "Sometimes they would spend the weekends there because there was no protocol that had to be followed there. They had a cook, a maid, and a butler. But when she wanted to, she also cooked herself. They were simply a family there. Up there they could live like they would in a normal house. There were also animals. They had horses, cows, and chickens. They drove up there, and it was like a normal family that had a little more money than most..."[316]

The annual weeks in Roc Agel ended in October with a month in Paris. Soon the growing family outgrew Rainier's bachelor apartment there, eventually moving into a spacious apartment in the aristocratic Avenue Foch in the sixteenth arrondissement, the west side of Paris. Their neighbors there included the pianist Arthur Rubinstein and his wife Lena, and the writer Marcel Pagnol, who was later named the honorary consul of Monaco. Later, in the 1970s, Grace stayed there often, particularly during the time that Caroline was in Paris and Grace herself was increasingly distancing herself from Monaco.

In late May or early June 1960, several telephone conversations between Monaco and Philadelphia involving Grace and her mother Margaret took place. Grace was deeply upset; she flew to Philadelphia and stayed there for fourteen days. Her father was lying in a hospital bed and Grace felt she had to be at his side. She was very sad and distressed at this time, but she managed to keep her composure. She wanted to cheer him, not trouble him. As per usual, her own fear was kept in the background. With a heavy heart, she flew back to Nice on June 13. On June 20, 1960, John B.

"Jack" Kelly died at the age of seventy of stomach cancer. He died at home in Philadelphia, in the Kelly house on Henry Avenue. He had had an operation, but it had been unsuccessful. The disease was too advanced. Again, Grace traveled to the United States for her father's burial. Her husband did not accompany her on this trip home. Rainier left Grace alone during these difficult hours.

The death of her father Jack had a distinct affect on Grace. She never experienced the closure—the catharsis—of finally confronting him for his neglect and mistreatment. She had wanted so badly to connect with him, to receive an explicit gesture of love from him, so that she could forgive him the pain he caused. But it never happened; it was too late.

Upon her return from the United States, she was depressed and melancholy. She was often silent and moody. She retreated into herself. Besides the deaths of Grace's grandparents, this was one of the first deaths within the close circle of the Kelly family. Grace was still grieving—about one and a half years after the death of her father—when Alfred Hitchcock offered her the title role in his film *Marnie* in early 1962.The impossibility of pursuing this long-cherished dream again caused her world to collapse.

Robert Dornhelm discussed Grace's alleged controversial behavior within the Monegasque microcosm: "She was shy. She was also shy if there were receptions or something like that. She did not like to shake hundreds of hands. Half of the people whose hands she had to shake had damp hands. Then she herself got damp hands, which was unpleasant for her. She had a disgust of damp hands. Then she said that she had decided to wear white gloves even at these events. Others thought badly of her for this."[317]

And further: "In considering the rumors, the world can breathe more easily: She did not have any affairs—in case that is important to the world. Of course, she was a woman full of life, and there in the palace everything was very artificial and formal and forced. And she came from American culture, which is very free, very open, and direct. And it was precisely this that she no longer had. She longed for this afterward, the freedom to interact casually with her peers and people from her profession. To live, to breathe, to dance, to eat, as she had been accustomed to doing—without pressure to abide by the strict protocol of a royal lifestyle. Her longing to be free makes perfect sense."[318]

As Thomas Veszelits expanded, "If you stood across from Grace Kelly, you would not be able to imagine her having any kind of adventure with someone else, even if the times had been different. She was truly too duty-bound for this. In the end, she had religious reasons to not have an affair with anyone. She could not have reconciled it with her Catholic conscience. Strictly Catholic: thus, it was unthinkable. Also, there was absolutely no private sphere in Monaco. One could not meet anybody there without it being known."[319] It was a life lived inside a gilded cage—on display for all the world to see.

1962
The Case of *Marnie*— and a Crisis of State

> *It was heartbreaking for me to have to leave the picture.*
> *—Grace Kelly in a letter to Alfred Hitchcock*[320]

> *I am certain that if my mother could have, she would have made more films with Hitchcock. She knew that he wanted her for* Marnie—*but she would have also made* North by Northwest.
> *—Prince Albert II of Monaco*[321]

It was March 1962, when Alfred Hitchcock offered Grace Kelly the title role in his next film, *Marnie*. He sent her the first draft of the screenplay as well. Grace immediately and enthusiastically accepted his offer. She was ecstatic. This moment was one of the most fateful in Grace Kelly's life.

Hitchcock had long waited for just the right moment to offer a new film to his favorite actress. Six years had now passed since Grace and Rainier's wedding. Hitchcock hoped that enough time had gone by for him to be able to get her in front of a camera again.

Grace wanted nothing in the world more than this: to finally be able to act on screen again after years of involuntary absence. She had had various offers during the previous years, and in the coming years, she would be forced to give them all up. These included several offers for the role of Mary, mother of Jesus, for Nicholas Ray's *King of Kings* (1961) for MGM and George Stevens's monumental, three-and-a-half hour epic *The Greatest Story Ever Told* (1965).

Joseph Stefano, who had previously written the screenplay for Hitchcock's highly successful *Psycho*, had again been hired by the director to write the screenplay for *Marnie*. At this point, they were a long ways from a finished script, an issue that would play a critical role in the complicated genesis of *Marnie*. Grace was completely committed to playing the main role in Hitchcock's next film adaptation, which was based on a 1961 British novel. The book had been written by the British author Winston Graham, who between 1945 and 2002 wrote numerous mystery novels, as well as the eighteenth-century historical *Poldark* series set in Cornwall. The plot was to be relocated from England to the United States, to Philadelphia, Grace's hometown (and that of Joseph Stefano as well). This geographic shift was not accidental— Hitchcock moved *Marnie* to Philadelphia in order to give Grace an opportunity to visit her family at home. After Grace's acceptance, it was clear for Hitch that *Marnie* would be the screen comeback for actress Grace Kelly. He used this as an argument in discussing casting with his new studio, Universal, and studio boss, Lew Wasserman. Ultimately, the screenplay for *Marnie* was written by Evan Hunter, who had previously adapted Daphne du Maurier's short story "The Birds" for Hitchcock. Hunter was the second screenwriter to work on the project, and he was hired after Hitchcock fired Stefano due to dissatisfaction with the latter's work. While Hunter worked on the screenplay, a photo of Grace Kelly sat the whole time on his desk. He described this in an interview with the *Daily Express*.[322] In agreement with Hitch, Hunter was to develop the character of Margaret "Marnie" Edgar specifically with the former leading lady in mind.

In any case, Hitchcock and Hunter were not in agreement about the characters and the plot. Hunter did not believe the intended explicitness of the rape scene (between Marnie and her newly married husband, Mark Rutland, on board of a steamer during their honeymoon) was necessary. Hunter was specifically worried about the scene's overt violence. Then, just as had been the case with Stefano, Hunter found himself, without justification or means of protest, removed from the project. Now Hitchcock hired the young, inexperienced author Jay Presson Allen to finish the seemingly unlucky screenplay. For Hitchcock, the problems and difficulties with *Marnie* seemed to stretch throughout the entire, prolonged project until its premiere in July 1964. The film was not received well by the public, the critics were mainly negative (some even scathing in their reviews), and filming was stressful and troubled from the beginning.

For Alfred Hitchcock, *Marnie* was a total disaster.

However, at the very beginning of this project, two people were completely delighted to be able to work with each other again. At this time, the plan was to begin filming in the late summer of 1962 and wrap in the fall. The intention was to combine a longer American vacation for the royal family with the filming of the Hitchcock movie. While Prince Rainier and the children Caroline and Albert enjoyed a vacation nearby, Grace would play the role of Marnie Edgar, acting for a fourth time under Hitch's direction. Years later, in a 1989 interview, Prince Rainier confirmed that not only was this the plan, but he had helped come up with it; he was fully on board at first.[323]

At this point, Grace Kelly and Alfred Hitchcock must have felt so close to fulfilling a mutual, long-cherished dream. According to longtime New York friend Rita Gam, "In the back of Grace's mind was always the possibility of going back to being a film star. I think she kept it there for those rainy nights. And when the opportunity rose to do *Marnie*, she leapt at it."[324] And then: "Everyone assumed that she would accept the offer. Nowhere in her marriage contract was it written that films were forbidden to the Princess."[325]

On March 18, 1962,[326] the royal palace in Monaco finally sent an official communiqué to the press announcing to the world that Grace Kelly would soon return to the silver screen.

The news hit like a bomb. A storm of controversy spread through Monaco. The citizens and press of the small principality feared that in accepting this role, the princess would humiliate and degrade their country. Going from European royalty back to the life of a Hollywood starlet was seen as a scandalous demotion. At this point, *Marnie* was the first Hitchcock film since *Psycho*, which had irreparably shocked the world, forever changing and radically influencing how movie audiences viewed films.

Furthermore, an unpleasant public debate centered on the salary that Grace would receive for her role in *Marnie*. The sums cited in the rumors swung between $375,000 to more than $880,000. At one point, she was supposedly going to earn $1 million.[327] However, the outcry focused on the spending of the salary, which the royal house could not claim for itself. In reaction, the palace press office sent out another short explanation as a quick defense. The first official communiqué had failed to include the information that the princess's Hollywood salary would be donated in its entirety to needy Monegasque children, young athletes, and artists. None of it would be kept by the palace.

Not much time passed after the premature and ill-considered publication of the original communiqué before Grace Kelly had to give in to both external and internal pressures. Thus, she had to retract the announcement and renounce her involvement in *Marnie*. It was a difficult decision and one which, in the end, was completely against what she truly wanted. After the cancellation was wrung out of her, she retreated to her palace rooms for days on end and would not emerge. The story was that she shut herself away for an entire week and cried.[328] At night, driven by her inner turmoil, she wandered the endless corridors of the palace alone. Up until that point, she had been full of hope and confidence, and now she had to painfully admit that she would never again appear before the camera, that she would never again act. A key chapter of her life was officially closed. Grace had to bury her dearest dream. The cancellation would be a lasting, traumatic experience. For a while, there was a fear that she would suffer a serious nervous breakdown. It was said that she suffered from depression and insomnia. There are those who claim that during this time, something died in Grace. *Marnie* marked a deep break in Grace Kelly's life.

As friend Judith Balaban Quine recalled, "Grace was unhappy because she had no true task and she was not allowed to work anymore. She felt superfluous. And Rainier absolutely did not understand it."[329]

Four years later, in 1966, Prince Rainier described the situation related to Grace's reaction and her general state after the cancellation of *Marnie*. In his statement he emphasized logistical issues of geography as the root cause: "There have been times when the Princess has been melancholy. I understand [she felt] cut off from [an art she loved]. If we had lived in New York or London or Paris [perhaps] she could have still pursued it."[330]

As Grace's friend Rita Gam commented, "I think the thing that convinced her that she couldn't do it, do that part, which was just another heroine, was that she was a Princess of the Church, and once she believed that [the] dignity [of] being the Princess of the Catholic Church was more important than being an actress, she accepted it. But I think it took a long time."[331] In terms of the Vatican, "a letter from Pope John XXIII was personally sent to Grace as a Catholic princess, demanding that she not make the film."[332]

It was ultimately Tippi Hedren—born in 1930 in Minnesota as Nathalie Hedren—who played the role of Marnie Edgar. This was her second time starring in a Hitchcock film, the first film being, of course, *The Birds*. Without Hitchcock, Hedren the model might never have become Hedren the actress. On Friday, October 13, 1961, a very quiet and rather uncreative year for Hitchcock, Alma and Alfred Hitchcock discovered Tippi Hedren during breakfast. It was pure chance. They saw a seemingly cool blonde on a television advertisement during the *Today Show* on NBC. And it was immediately clear to them: this was the new Hitchcock heroine, the now necessary successor to Grace Kelly.

The black-and-white ad seen by the Hitchcocks was for Sego, a diet milk drink with chocolate flavoring. Before this, Hedren had worked as a model in New York for eleven years, and she had no acting experience. In the ad, she took a drink of Sego, and a boy whistled at her from the sidewalk. *The Birds* begins similarly, and at the age of thirty-two, this was the first role she had ever played. In Chasen's, Hitch's favorite Hollywood restaurant, he announced to her that he wanted her for the main role of Melanie Daniels in *The Birds*. With this, he handed her a brooch ornamented with three birds, a piece that she still has today.

Tippi Hedren described this and the preparations for *Marnie* as follows: "It was like a fairy tale, like Cinderella. Exactly like it... This dream career was simply handed to me on a silver platter... And Alfred Hitchcock was not only my director, but also my acting teacher."[333] And further: "She [Grace Kelly] would have certainly been glad to play this role. But due to reasons of state, she had to decline. One cannot be both the Princess of Monaco and a servant ordered about. Even if it is only in the theater. It simply could not be."[334]

The Monegasque did not want to see their princess back on the silver screen. Besides the other reasons, the plans failed, in all likelihood, because of Prince Rainier's disapproval: "Rainier was not enthusiastic. But I am convinced that she could have changed his mind. However, she respected the feelings of the populace. The Monegasque did not want their Princess kissing some Hollywood star [Sean Connery], even if it was only on screen," opined Grace's younger sister Lizanne.[335]

On the subject of *Marnie*, Grace's son Prince Albert had the following to say: "She never talked about it too much because I think maybe it was sort of a difficult subject for her, as she really would have loved to play that part, but of course, she realized that it would have been awkward and it wouldn't have pleased my father too much, and so I am sure that she regretted that but...I think he wasn't completely opposed to it but, you know, he was kind of...in-between, but I think that he also realized that here in Monaco it probably would not have been very well-accepted and he had to accept that after thinking about it. I think it would have been a very difficult situation for her, and he didn't want to be in that kind of situation either. And he was also at the time having some difficulties with France, as you recall. So I think he didn't want to add fuel to that fire."[336]

Another consideration was a new development: Grace learned that spring that she was again pregnant. At the time of the Monegasque communiqué about *Marnie* in mid-March, she could not have yet known this. However, the pregnancy did not go well, and in June, Grace had a miscarriage. She had three miscarriages in total during the course of the 1960s. Another one occurred in the summer of 1963, and the last one came in July 1967, two years after the birth of Princess Stéphanie on February 1, 1965, during a trip abroad for the World's Fair in Montreal, Canada. During her lifetime, Grace was pregnant a total of six times.

It was also in June 1962 that the decision against her involvement in *Marnie* happened. She informed Alfred Hitchcock shortly thereafter. At this time, Hitchcock was two months into the filming of *The Birds*, which would have its world premiere in New York on March 28, 1963. In May, it was included on the program for the Cannes Film Festival. The director then announced that the filming of *Marnie* would be postponed a year and a half.

To the director's great surprise, Metro-Goldwyn-Mayer contacted Alfred Hitchcock only a few days after the publishing of the Monegasque communiqué. In a letter dated March 28, 1962, studio chief Joseph R. Vogel told him that, as before, Grace Kelly was under contract with MGM, and if she returned to Hollywood, she would have to fulfill her seven-year commitment. According to Metro, the existing and valid contract was still in force for four and a half years. Grace would have to fulfill her contractual obligations if she wished to return to work as an actor. MGM man Vogel continued, the actress's employment was "an untapped asset to our organization."[337] Vogel assert that Hitchcock himself ought to understand that as welcome as her return to the movie industry was, she was lawfully bound to pick up where she left off—an employee of MGM.[338]

After his successful years at Paramount, which ended with *Psycho*, Hitchcock was now attached to Universal, with whom he would remain until the end of his career. His final film was *Family Plot* (1976). Grace could not simply be cast in a Universal production. MGM was willing to make this very clear through its studio lawyers. However, it never came to this, even if Hitchcock, his studio, and their lawyers were of a totally different opinion. If Grace had actually been cast in *Marnie*, there is no doubt that a legal battle would have arisen with MGM and Joseph R. Vogel. As if all of this turmoil was not difficult enough, the political differences between the small principality and its bigger neighbor, France, were escalating, especially during the course of 1962.

Eight weeks prior to the controversy over the palace communiqué, the following developed on the political level. On January 24, 1962, Prince Rainier III met with the French Minister of State, Émile Pelletier, who was also the Monegasque ambassador. Pelletier had urgently requested this meeting. The former Minister of the Interior under De Gaulle, Pelletier demanded that Rainier promptly lift a Monegasque trade suspension, which Rainier refused to do. Rainier had previously passed the suspension to prevent France from investing heavily in and taking control of Radio Monte Carlo (RMC) and Télé Monte Carlo (TMC). The consequence of this move would have been the loss of control over the Monegasque media outlets to France. This was a development that the prince could not permit, and it played itself out against the flourishing economic situation in Monaco during the early 1960s. Approximately fifty international companies had moved their main offices to Monaco due to the prevailing fiscal advantages that were created in the international accord from July 1918. Under the leadership of President Charles De Gaulle, France was no longer open to tolerating these advantages. Furthermore, in 1960, the prince had brought the young American functionary Martin A. Dale to Monaco as his personal adviser. An increasing number of American firms were moving their headquarters to this part of the Riviera. Thus, the proud *Grande Nation*, which for years had distanced itself as far as possible from all things American, feared an all-too-great American influence in the small neighboring principality. Martin A. Dale was even accused of working for the CIA.[339]

On January 24, 1962, in Dale's presence, a loud argument arose between the irritated Prince Rainier and the no-less-miffed Minister Pelletier. Prince Rainier delivered a slap to Monsier le Ministre and directed him to leave the country.[340] President De Gaulle welcomed the late evening altercation, the so-called Pelletier Affair, as an excuse to put massive pressure on the principality that he viewed with great suspicion. De Gaulle threatened Monaco: If the principality did not change its tax laws and bring them in line with the French ones, France would cut off Monaco's electricity, telephone connections, gas, and water at the end of a six-month period ending at midnight on October 11, 1962. Within a very short span of time, life in the principality would be brought to a standstill. This touched on a basic fear among the Monegasque, a fear of France annexing and dissolving their principality.

Ultimately, the bilateral confrontation culminated in President De Gaulle ordering troops of French customs officials and policemen from around Monaco to march on the country on October 12, 1962. The Monegasque could see that they were caught within their national borders. The access roads along the coast were blocked and controlled. Along the center road lines, customs signs were set up, reading "Stop Customs."[341] On the following day, the newspaper headlines announced *Entre Monaco et la France: Cordon douanier depuis minuit* ("Between Monaco and France: Customs Barriers since Midnight").[342] "Close against the border along the streets and steps, an entire French regiment was posted. The Monegasque approached the troops and gave them flowers and every gift imaginable."[343] It was their way to try to turn the opinion of the more-powerful enemy with cordiality.

The problems were grounded in the seven-year Algerian War (1954–1962). Many French Algerians fled their country and took their cash with them. However, many of these Algerian refugees did not flee to France but to Monaco. Under President De Gaulle, Giscard d'Estaing was made minister of finance. As publicist Rolf Palm explained, "There was a television interview with Giscard d'Estaing in which he said, 'I have here several addresses of Frenchmen who allegedly reside in Monaco. Over the past few weeks, I have tried to call them numerous times, and someone has answered. However, I know that they also live in France, in Paris.' Another cause for French resentment was Monaco's lack of value-added tax, and the resulting price differences between Monaco and France. There were companies that sold their products all over France but kept their headquarters in Monaco. The French government was losing money, and this furor ramped up over the passing weeks. The ruckus was set aside one year later. At this point, a new French-Monegasque accord went into effect, and a value-added tax was introduced at the same rate as in France. However, Monaco was allowed to keep the tax monies. Thus, the main point was that the price difference no longer existed. It was also said that the Vatican played a role in the drafting of the French-Monegasque accord. At the time, the Monegasque Minister of Finance was Louis Notari, who was 5'1", and the two Frenchmen, Giscard d'Estaing and De Gaulle, each about 6'6", were said to have been somewhat bamboozled by the little guy."[344]

Prince Rainier felt that he was forced to make concessions to France. During this difficult time, he purposely did not leave the country. On short notice, he convened Parliament and proposed a new constitution, which he signed on December 17, 1962. With the permission of the French government, the constitution was announced, and in its opening paragraph, "the sovereignty and independence of the principality" was affirmed and its territory was declared "inalienable."[345] He also called for an election that October, and for the first time in Monaco, women were given the right to vote, a measure that the princess had also long endorsed. Again, she functioned as a good figure for Rainier to have at his side in negotiating with France; as she had at the previous official state visits, she again captured the admiration of the French President. De Gaulle and his wife had received the Monegasque royal couple in Paris at the Élysée Palace in 1959, and in October 1960, they in turn made an official visit to Monaco. Despite his pronounced anti-Americanism, the President of the Fifth Republic seemed quite impressed by Her Royal Highness Princess Grace. As Thomas Veszelits recalled, "She was a wonderful link between all things French, De Gaulle, and Onassis. Here she stood up for Prince Rainier and helped him greatly in the negotiations."[346]

Finally, on May 18, 1963, the French-Monegasque accord was signed in Paris and immediately went into effect. The legal framework substantially resolved most of the previous differences between the two countries. The concerns about the financial issues were answered: the French residents of Monaco would be taxed according to the French tax laws. The Monegasque and the residents of other nationalities would not be. In terms of the fiscal authorities, it would no longer matter if a French citizen resided in the principality or in the *Grande Nation*. "The solution was very advantageous for Monaco, except for the French who lived there. Now they had to pay taxes to France."[347] In addition, President De Gaulle and his Minister of Finance d'Estaing no longer had to worry that other French companies would move their headquarters to the principality, since they would no longer profit from any tax advantages.

"As such, Monaco with all of its privileges was untouched, thanks to this agreement, which the Vatican helped foster, and thanks to Grace Kelly's sacrifice to no longer make any films."[348]

On June 18, 1962, Grace Kelly finally sat down at her desk in the palace and wrote a personal letter to Alfred Hitchcock. In this, she asked her respected director and longtime friend, her creative mentor, for his understanding of her decision to not take the role in *Marnie*. The letter from Grace to Hitch was written in her clear, girl-like handwriting, and a typescript of this missive also exists:

Dear Hitch, It was heartbreaking for me to have to leave the picture . . . I was so excited about doing it and particularly about working with you again . . . When we meet I would like to explain to you myself all of the reasons which is difficult to do by letter or through a third party . . . It is unfortunate that it had to happen this way and I am deeply sorry. Thank you dear Hitch for being so understanding and helpful. I hate disappointing you . . . I also hate the fact that there are probably many other "cattle" who could play the part equally as well. Despite that I hope to remain one of your "sacred cows." With deep affection, Grace.[349]

And Hitchcock responded. He wrote Grace back one week later, showing the greatest understanding for her difficult rejection and even supporting her decision. He signed his handwritten letter to Grace, as always, with "Hitch": "Dear Grace, Yes, it was sad, wasn't it? I was looking forward so much to the fun and pleasure of our doing a picture again. Without a doubt, I think you made, not only the best decision, but the only one. After all, it was 'only a movie.' Alma joins me in sending our most fond and affectionate thoughts for you. Hitch"[350]

And thus, Hitch let Grace go for a second time. He had to let her go. He never let her know of his deep disappointment. To the contrary, both longtime friends showed discretion. In their correspondence, there were no accusations, blame, or bitterness. The painful decision to turn down the role, which was not desired by either of them, changed nothing in their friendship. Until Hitchcock's death in April 1980, they remained fast friends. Two soul mates.

Instead of *Marnie*, Alfred Hitchcock turned his attention to *The Birds*, the most technically advanced film of his entire fifty-year directing career. It was avant garde and innovative, setting a new cinematographic standard. Only at the conclusion of this film did he return to the *Marnie* project. After a long preproduction phase, and one and half years after Grace left the project, filming of Alfred Hitchcock's forty-ninth film began in the third week of November 1963.

The main roles were played by Tippi Hedren as Marnie Edgar and Sean Connery as Mark Rutland. Before this final casting, Hitchcock had an option for a while on Rock Hudson. In the spring of 1962, Grace Kelly and Rock Hudson had been announced in the main roles of *Marnie*. Both *Hollywood Reporter* and *Variety*, two of the traditional film industry periodicals, had published this casting in May 1962.[351] This occurred during the transitional period of the project, two months after Grace's acceptance and one month prior to her cancellation. Also, the option on Rock Hudson eventually ran out. The main roles had to be completely recast.

The Scottish actor Sean Connery was extremely popular at this time, thanks to the James Bond series based on the novels by British author Ian Fleming. He had previously starred in the films *Dr. No* (1962) and *From Russia with Love* (1963). Directly after *Marnie*, Connery went on to star in *Goldfinger* (1964), arguably the most popular and perhaps best of the Bond films. While filming *Marnie*, pronounced tensions developed between the director and his (ersatz) main actress Hedren. Sometimes they would only communicate with each other through a third person or by written notes.

After both outstanding, previous works, *Psycho* and *The Birds*, which count as two of his finest creations and which are timeless in their influence, *Marnie* was the start of years of creative and commercial failures for Hitchcock. *Torn Curtain*, *Topaz*, and *Family Plot* were great disappointments and represent the swan song for a great oeuvre of fifty-three films. Only *Frenzy* was the exception. He made plans for three other projects that were never completed: *The Three Hostages*, which was based on a novel by John Buchan, who had also written *The Thirty-Nine Steps* (1935); *Mary Rose*, for which Tippi Hedren was to be cast for a third and final time; and *R.R.R.R.*

Not insignificantly, *Marnie* marked the last time that Hitchcock would work with several longtime coworkers: his cinematographer Robert Burks, his composer Bernard Herrmann, his cutter George Tomasini, and production designer Robert Boyle. Tragically, Burks, who had directed the photography for twelve of Hitchcock's films, died along with his wife in a house fire. This was a bitter loss for Hitchcock. Tomasini died around the same time as well. If one counts his advisory position for *The Birds*, Hermann was responsible for the music of eight Hitchcock films. Ultimately, Hitchcock had a falling out with Hermann over the composing of the score for *Torn Curtain*. The studio demanded music that was more commercial in nature than what Herrmann composed. The director fired his longtime composer and friend, and replaced him, under pressure from Universal-MCA, with John Addison. On a personal level, this was a tragic development due to misunderstandings that existed on both sides. Finally, *Marnie* was Hitchcock's last collaboration with Robert Doyle. With the falling away of these central coworkers, Hitchcock suddenly found himself working almost alone. The most essential positions on his staff had to be newly filled, however there simply was no second Robert Burks or second Bernard Herrmann. These were among the most critical columns in the "House of Hitchcock." The difficult time before and after *Marnie* comprised a distinctly disappointing period in Hitchcock's life and work.

For almost a month, the Hitchcocks vacationed in Europe, traveling to Italy, Yugoslavia, and Monaco, where they dined with Princess Grace and Prince Rainier. The Hitchcocks also traveled to Paris where they visited Ingrid Bergman and where Hitchcock agreed to make himself available for François Truffaut's planned fifty-hour interview about his films and artistry. At the conclusion of the European trip came a city tour through the United States to advertise *Marnie*. Hitchcock gave interviews in New York, Washington, and Chicago. Afterward, when the film opened in theaters in July 1964 and the press was united in its negative reaction, for several weeks, he was not seen either on the Universal studio lot or in his bungalow office. He never coped well with failures. The reception of *Marnie* on the heels of his previous film triumphs and the personal dilemma with Tippi Hedren, thus, represented a bigger, in some ways double defeat: an emotional defeat as well as a creative-professional one. And then there was, of course, the commercial failure for Universal Studios.

At the time, the critics claimed that *Marnie* "in its setting, seemed to be a more antiquated type of Hitchcock film with psychoanalytical ambitions. It was cool, and in general, it lacked tension, despite its sophisticated use of color."[352] This perspective is now considered outdated; it has since been revised. Today, *Marnie* is recognized as one of Hitchcock's more important films. The drama is full of both explicit and subtly subversive psychological elements linked to dreams and hallucinations. Freudian symbolism permeates the entire film: Marnie always rides her horse Forio whenever she has stolen something (it is also no accident that she shoots him after a riding accident); her handbag—the first image of the film—is one of her most important tools; various storm scenes with thunder and lightning are explosive with meaning. The narration is poetically dreamy, unstructured, and elliptical, mosaic-like. Contemporary critics accused Hitchcock of the supposedly dilettantish style of the film, such as the easily recognizable background projections against which Marnie rides her horse (in Universal Studios) or the clearly painted backdrop of the harbor landscape on the other side of the street on which her mother's house sits. These are the exact elements that today would be interpreted as intentional metaphors for allegoric fantasies. In *Marnie*, just as in *To Catch a Thief*, theft functions as a replacement for love. Some of the scenes in *Marnie* have an indefinable, latent undertow and a strong, attractive power. The use of color in Robert Burks's camera work—specifically the use of red—is just as noticeable as the edited montage footage; the loaded drama of Bernard Hermann's hypnotic music resembles the romantic score in *Vertigo*. In addition to Hitchcock's earlier work *Spellbound* (1945), about which the master himself once said, "I wanted to make the first psychoanalytic film,"[353] during the early 1960s, *Marnie* was one of the few explicit film treatments of Sigmund Freud's psychoanalysis.

When Truffault asked Hitch what about *Marnie* appealed to him, he answered, "The fetish idea. A man wants to go to bed with a thief because she *is* a thief, just like other men have a yen for a Chinese or a colored woman."[354] Hitchcock's commentaries on his own films were always oversimplifications characterized by his smug understatements. (He once described *Psycho* offhand as a "lighthearted comedy.")

Of course one cannot help but wonder: What would Alfred Hitchcock's *Marnie* have been like if Grace Kelly had been its star?

She was actually the opposite of all that her external image
would have had you believe. In her social interactions, she
was very uncomplicated, laid-back. The opposite of the
unapproachable, cold woman from whom one had
to shy away.
—Robert Dornhelm, Director and Friend[355]

The final six years of Princess Grace's life were defined by the return of her creativity. She found her life finally had some room again for film, as well as the worlds of the theater and literature.

"Slowly the gilded cage began to open a little for her so that she could do more. She could no longer make major motion pictures, but slowly she could breathe again—the children were all more or less grown. She wanted to be involved in creative things of various kinds."[356]

During the second half of the 1970s, Grace performed various poetry readings on stage, traveling in both the United States and England. She was seen in Philadelphia and Washington, in Princeton and Harvard. Conceptualized by John Carroll, one of her programs was called "Birds, Beasts, & Flowers," and she did the readings along with Richard Pasco. Grace also made recordings of this program for both record and cassette. She recited Walt Whitman and D.H. Lawrence, William Blake and Shakespeare, Thomas Hardy and Edward Lear. She was happy about this step, even if it could not come close in comparison to the continuation of her acting career, for which she so longed.

In 1976, Grace met the twenty-nine-year-old Robert Dornhelm. The young director had just completed the work on his film documentary, *The Children of Theatre Street* (1977). Robert Dornhelm had been born on December 17, 1947. His parents moved with him to Vienna when he was thirteen years old. He grew up there. Today, the director Robert Dornhelm divides his time between

Los Angeles and the small town of Mougins, located just north of Cannes.

The first meeting between Grace Kelly and Robert Dornhelm took place in Paris:

I was going into the CBS studio with a roll of film under my arm. I was filing a copy in the editing room, and there she was with one of Prince Rainier's aunts, a Russian princess, a very wealthy, funny lady. Thus, we sat in the editing room of the CBS office in Paris, around the corner from the Champs-Élysées, and I showed her my film. The question was, if she liked it, could she imagine doing the spoken introduction as the narrator for the film. During the viewing, I noted that she was tickled pink by the film. She laughed, and was delighted and excited by these children. After the viewing, she spontaneously invited me to her house. Champagne was opened, and she said: "I will do it." It was incredible, and it made her very happy. It was exactly what she was searching for. She had even opened a ballet school in Monte Carlo, the Ballet Russe de Monte Carlo. This connection afforded a good reason for her participation. She decided on the spot that I should come to Monte Carlo the following week in order to discuss everything.

There I walked around in jeans and a blazer, and this was during Fête Nationale (also known as Bastille Day), during which everyone wears their jewels and medals. I did not trust myself to join her in the loge, which is where she had invited me. I was completely underdressed. Intimidated, I sank myself into an armchair, hoping that no one would notice me. Then, a butler tapped me on the shoulder and said: "The Princess is waiting for you." Thus, with red cheeks, I had to make my way through the pompous, ornamented gentlemen, and they made fun of how I looked like a fish out of water. Afterward, she told me she sympathized with how I felt completely out of place. At the same time, she was amused. She felt sorry for me but not in a negative sense. And she felt closer to me than to all those other men, because she could tell that I was based in reality. Everything else here was about money. This is how we got to know each other.[357]

After this initial meeting, the yet-to-be-filmed opening scenes of the documentary were filmed with Grace. She set up the contextual framework for the legendary St. Petersburg Kirov Ballet and its school, the Vaganova Ballet Academy. The filming took place in Monaco and Paris, including a stunning location on the roof of the Paris Palais Garnier opera house.

"Then suddenly, we were one week away from filming. And I asked her: 'Your Serene Highness, how should I address you on set? Another take, could you now look to the right, Serene Highness?' And she said: 'What about if you call me Grace?' Then I said that I could not do that. I could not simply say: 'Come on, Grace, one more take. The last one sucked.' Or what? And she said: 'Yes, that's exactly what you say. Hopefully it won't suck.'"[358]

During the time before and after the filming of *The Children of Theatre Street*, Robert Dornhelm came to know Grace Kelly, and because the princess trusted the young director, he experienced her in a very authentic way. Their friendship would last for six years, until her death.

"I very often saw her happy. She was full of life—she liked to dance, to go out, to eat well. Occasionally, she liked to drink but only socially, if she was at a party and felt merry. It was absolutely not true that she drank every day. To the contrary, one year she did not have a drink for two months. This was not a problem for her at all. That was not a major concern. Such romantically inclined people as her are, by nature, plagued with melancholy and are dreamy. They always dream about that which they do not have. Even though she had much and she was aware and thankful of that. However, to say that she was happy... There was always a certain melancholy there, a degree of sadness. That was the Irish in her. Of course, she had a joyful nature, but she was often tormented by insecurity and nostalgia..."[359]

The documentary *The Children of Theatre Street* was nominated for an Oscar in 1977. In connection with the film, Grace engaged seriously in finding sponsors. She took part in events to help raise money for the talented children. "We traveled much with the movie, all across Europe. In America, there were also a couple of premieres."

The world premiere of the film took place at the Palais Garnier. At this time, the French press was full of rumors about the first wedding of daughter Caroline to the dubious venture capitalist Philippe Junot on June 28, 1978.

Robert Dornhelm recalled the premiere:

They held a huge reception in the Paris opera house, where the film was shown, with the *Garde d'honneur*, with much pomp. It was funny; I was the director, she was the actress, but we sat far away from each other. And luckily, I said: "I insist on an intermission, if it is shown in an opera house. Operas need intermissions so that people can get a drink and talk to each other." Otherwise, the evening would have been a sad one for me. During the intermission, I went up to her—in the meantime, I had become braver and more emancipated, and had also bought a suit so that I no longer just sat around feeling overwhelmed—and she said that she was looking forward to the supper afterward. Then I said: "Yes, where is the supper?" She: "It is just up there. Why do you always sit down there?" She was in the important loge area with the entire administration of the opera and the bureaucrats of the Ministry of Culture. As film maker, I was lost somewhere in the theater. No one had said anything to me about a supper. That irritated her, and she said: "Sit next to me tonight." I explained: "I was not invited." Then she walked over to Serge Liebermann, the director of the Palais Garnier Opera, and said: "Serge, Mr. Dornhelm doesn't know about the dinner." He responded: "He doesn't know about it because he will not be there. I am sorry but it is for only sixteen people, the Minister, the State President. It is a small affair, very exclusive." She said: "Yes, it is very exclusive. But I am accustomed to directors, such as the one whose film we are celebrating today, coming to their own premiere parties." Liebermann said: "Unfortunately, that is not the case now." And Grace answered: "Certainly not a problem. Now all of you can really spread out, since I am going to celebrate with my director. Understandably, I will spend the evening with him and not with people I don't even know." A total affront. On the following day, her punishment was in the newspaper. She had snubbed the Palais Garnier Opera by not taking part in its premiere festivities.[360]

There were several other such situations in which she showed loyalty to her "less-connected" team members. According to Dornhelm, during their next joint film project, *Rearranged*, she herself decided on location where the team would stay, making sure that the hotel rooms were acceptable: "One would not expect that a princess would inspect the rooms and ask about where the team had eaten. A sign of her loyalty to the team."[361]

Dornhelm described the emotional connection between him and Grace as follows: "I think that I am a dreamer. And also nostalgic. At the time, there was also a very painful personal struggle happening in my life—and she just happened to be there right then. She understood me and sensed the state I was. She accepted my situation, which the work naturally had not made any easier. And then she was so motherly, so caring. That was very good for her, and it appealed to her maternal instinct, even if she was unaware of it. (Her son was in America.) And I was honest with her. I had absolutely no fear of telling her the truth. I said exactly what I felt and what I observed in her. Things that no one else dared to say. She valued that. It was exactly the antidote she needed."[362]

During the 1970s, Grace Kelly increasingly dedicated herself to a "passion" that gave rise to qualms and alienation among many people in her social circle. She began to collect and dry flowers. Later she created designs for pictures, for linens, for wallpaper. In the renowned Drouant Gallerie, situated in the wealthy Parisian street Faubourg Saint-Honoré in the First Arrondissement, an exhibition of Grace's flower arrangements was held from June 9–30, 1977. All of the members of her family, as well as Madame

Pompidou, the wife of the former French president, attended the opening. In addition, an annual flower show was hosted in Monaco, and in 1979, it played a significant role in her final film, *Rearranged*. In 1980, *My Book of Flowers* was published. This richly illustrated book was 220 pages in length, and it contained the histories of various flower species and sorts. The text for Grace's only book was written by the British author Gwen Robyns, who also wrote *Princess Grace*, one of the first biographies about Grace, published in 1976.

"One of her other great contributions was her rescue and renovation of the Hôtel Hermitage. Like the palace, the hotel was very dilapidated. When the great construction boom of the 1960s started, almost everything was demolished. Then the linear style of Michel Pastor came into vogue. To a certain extent, this influenced Grace Kelly's efforts at interior design. Even today, in the halls of the Hermitage you can see this: flower designs in all forms and facets on everything from furniture to wallpaper. And even the imitation Art Nouveau elements in the lobby, are not original Art Nouveau patterns but rather Grace Kelly's stylized additions. And here again her great enthusiasm for flowers can be seen. Everywhere there are flowers."[363] These were the memories of Thomas Veszelits.

Robert Dornhelm was quite critical of this passion: "It was dreadful. I tried to hold her back from it and told her: 'Not only are you using pressed, dead flowers, but this is pure kitsch. Why do you have to sell flower pictures or use your name on bed linens with flower designs on them? This doesn't mean anything.' I tried to tell her this in a harsh tone. If it must be, use living flowers, not cut ones. Pressed flowers are rather morbid since they are dead. But she enjoyed doing this. Perhaps it was again a blending of the dreamy Irish element and the disciplined German element. And perhaps the loneliness in the castle. This talented woman was arranging dried flowers. I thought that someone needed to shake her. And I did that. I said again and again: 'Come on, live, live! You must go out, enjoy yourself, and be happy. Do active things. Not arranging dead flowers.' We had this conversation often."[364]

In her role as princess, Grace traveled to Japan several times, and here she received inspiration for her flower arrangements, which increasingly consumed more and more of her time. In Japan today, Grace Kelly has a cult status. Japanese tourists travel to Monaco to follow in the footsteps of the screen icon and princess—an icon who was so very different in private.

Robert Dornhelm: "Bag Lady—it was a dream of hers. If you live in a castle, you can dream of being a bag lady, running around, unrecognized, with bags. She always liked presents. She was very materialistic. In the first class section of airplanes, she always took with her the little bottles of champagne or cognac or vodka. She was so frugal. She often wanted to go shopping herself and cook or make breakfast for the children, like an American housewife, although there were servants for that. You always want what you do not have."[365]

Robert Dornhelm characterized the outline of Grace Kelly's life as follows: "She was a very simple, modest woman who searched for happiness. The petty bourgeois. She could have lived very modestly and been just as happy. In reality, she yearned for a simple life with a happy family, children with the parents and the siblings staying together. The good American tradition. She dreamed of this, but she never had it. Thus, it was a dream. However, she had definitely dreamed of a normal life. And she had tried to make this extraordinary life in the golden palace as normal as possible. Even in Paris she insisted that she cook breakfast and not the cook who was there. And instead of the butler bringing her meal, she said: 'I can get it myself.' That was a rebellion against the privileges she had. She wanted to be who she was and not a person removed from reality."[366] And further: "She was very controlled. I never saw her upset or in turmoil. Although she was sometimes irritated and would talk about it. However, I never saw her truly excited. She never gave herself over to this bareness. This was her diplomatic side. Life in the castle had had a major impact on her in this. She knew that one did not do this, or if you did, it would come back and haunt you. She was not impulsive at all."[367] Inner composure, integrity, and loyalty.

During the 1970s, Josephine Baker came to Monaco. She had met Grace many years before in New York and remembered this meeting. As Patrick Hourdequin, who has been the director of the Théâtre Princesse Grace since the early 1980s, described: "Princess Grace had a very deep respect for Josephine Baker's artistic side, and Baker had performed for several summers here in Monaco at the Sporting d'Été. These were large revues, like those at the Casino de Paris or the Moulin Rouge, and Josephine Baker was very popular. At this time, she earned a lot of money. She could not have any children. Thus, she decided with her husband, a great musician and trumpeter, to adopt children from various countries, of various religions. It was to be a sign of the world of the future, in which everyone got along with everyone else, regardless of skin color or religion. At this time, this was a revolutionary idea; it was very idealistic and quite beautiful. Princess Grace was very taken with it. Josephine Baker invested much in the education of her children, in their housing. In France, she bought a castle, a very large one, for all of the children, and also for their teachers and personnel. After awhile, things did not go well for her. She was sick. Many times, Grace helped her out financially, and eventually she brought some of the children to Monaco, sometimes putting them up near the castle. Some of them stayed here or in the region as they grew older. One of them was employed as a gardener here. Others left Monaco and went to places like Paris."[368]

Grace Kelly and Josephine Baker, both American in heritage, were good friends: "Josephine Baker's children always spoke very enthusiastically and positively about Princess Grace, who in a ways was a second mother to them."[369] One of Josephine Baker's final performances was given in Monaco, and naturally Grace Kelly was in attendance. Josephine Baker was buried in Monaco's cemetery alongside her husband. The princess took care of this.

In the early 1980s, one project that lay close to the princess's heart was the former theater of Monaco. Once called the Théâtre des Beaux-Arts, the facility opened on February 1, 1932. At this time, the performances were held in English, since most of the people vacationing on the Riviera at this time came from the Anglo-Saxon realm: "The men went to the casino to play, and the women came here to the theater," explained theater director Patrick Hourdequin.[370] However, this period did not last long. The theater director at that time was also the artistic director of the Monegasque SBM and was, thus, also responsible for the Garnier Auditorium of the opera. The close connection between the SBM and all cultural matters in Monaco dated back to this point.

The festive reopening of the renamed Théâtre Princess Grace, located above the harbor, occurred on December 17, 1981. Grace was accompanied by Rainier and Caroline, and among the guests in attendance were the three actors, Dirk Bogarde, Valentina Cortese, and Edwige Feuillère. Bogarde was the one who dubbed the theater and even Monaco as a whole as "Grace's Place."

Prior to this point, Grace had thoughtfully guided the design of the theater, her theater. The princess visited the site every two weeks: "She herself actually selected everything, she took care of even the smallest of details, tending to both the *côté publique* and the *côté artistique*. At the time, I learned much from her."[371] She searched out the champagne-colored chairs for the theater lobby and, together with an English designer, worked out the Art Deco-style, blue theater logo. She also initiated a practice that is usually a normal part of theater administration. She did not want everything, from the programs to the coat check, to have a fee. Instead, she wanted theater visits to be affordable for everyone.

One evening Grace recited English-language poems on the stage of the Théâtre Princess Grace. "It was very moving to listen to her," Patrick Hourdequin remembered. And how she did not find the acoustics of the auditorium to be good enough yet. She sat with the decorator to design cladding for the walls that would absorb the resonance of the space and create a cleaner tone. Even the large crystal chandeliers in the theater foyer were designed by her and constructed in Murano, near Venice. She was involved with everything in the theater, "and she always worked with great delight with a smile on her lips and a light humor. She was very attentive. She had an unbelievable naturalness about her. She understood how to get along with people, without the slightest bit of pretension or pedantry. Nothing at all, just totally natural."[372]

1979
An Attempted Comeback:
Rearranged (1982)

> *This was a cheerful film. It was a lot of fun for her to shoot.*
> —Prince Albert of Monaco[373]

> *I decided to rearrange things.*
> —Grace Kelly in Rearranged[374]

> *Of course, after her death, they all wanted to have*
> Rearranged, *because it was Grace's final film.*
> —Robert Dornhelm[375]

The princess and director Robert Dornhelm had known each other since 1976. Since then, they stayed in contact, regularly seeing each other, talking on the telephone, writing letters. And often, Dornhelm accompanied Grace on her travels around the world.

After working together on the documentary film *The Children of Theatre Street*, they wanted to work on another project together, one which would entail more than an off-camera commentary for Grace. Robert Dornhelm recalled: "We often looked for things that she could do, things that would make her happy and have something to do with film. Previously, she had been my casting director for another film, one that I never made. It was a project about the history of Raoul Wallenberg, who rescued Hungarian Jews during the Holocaust. She held auditions with actors, when we were testing people for the role. Then, nothing came of it because financing for the project never quite worked out. Afterward she said: 'Perhaps we could do something for my fiftieth birthday.' The Garden Club needed a PR film for the flower show, the prominent competition that was eagerly awaited every year. Aesthetically these were wonderful things. It was an entirely different world, flower arranging. It was an internationally significant event that attracted thousands of visitors."[376]

When the French author Jacqueline Mosigny and her husband, the American actor Edward Meeks, were invited to Monaco for a television event, they were introduced to the princess. Her ears perked up when she learned that Monsigny wrote and Meeks acted. Among his other roles, Meeks had acted in the once popular French television series *Les Globe-trotters* (1966–1968), as well as in various major American and French movies. He also performed alongside Raimund Harmstorf in the male supporting role in the four-part television adaptation of Jack London's *The Sea-Wolf* (1971). In talking to them, Grace mentioned that she would love to act again. Then she asked whether, between the three of them, they might have enough creative power to take on a joint project—perhaps something fictional, for television? Then she told them about the director that she had had in mind the entire time: Robert Dornhelm.

In May 1979, they finally gathered together to film *Rearranged* in Monaco—Grace, Dornhelm, Mosigny, Meeks, cinematographer Karl Kofler, and soundman Willi Buchmüller. It was a small team for a small film.

The Austrian cinematographer Karl Kofler had previously worked on Robert Dornhelm's documentary film *The Children of Theatre Street*. He was responsible for the photography for *Rearranged*, which in the end only existed as a fragment. As he explained, "We always talked about continuing to work on it. None of us suspected that this was the end. We were always talking about plans [to make more films with her]. She really wanted to make a comeback."[377]

Rearranged opened with aerial shots of Le Rocher, of the cliffs and the royal palace. After this short introduction, the story then moved to the Nice-Côte d'Azur airport. Professor Nelson (Edward Meeks) has just landed. As an internationally renowned professor of astrophysics, he has come to Monte Carlo to participate in a scholarly conference. A chauffeur (played by one of the princess's actual chauffeurs, Paul Raimondo) is waiting for him with a car. They drive from Nice to the small principality. In the car, the chauffeur informs the surprised professor that Princess Grace is waiting for him in the palace. Through an internal monologue, the professor hypothesizes and reflects on this new development that took him completely unaware. Professor Nelson is taken directly to the palace garden, where he is introduced to Princess Grace. She has mistaken him for a certain Mr. Wilson, a cosmopolitan travel writer. Thus, a comedy of errors is set in motion.

After arguing some with himself, Nelson plays along with the mistake, after he tries several times to straighten things out. The princess keeps interrupting him, preferring to talk about the approaching flower show and competition. This year the event will honor Sarah Bernhardt. From this point, Nelson acts the part of Wilson, and he finds himself in the middle of various controversies centered on Monaco's annual flower show. He also ends up having to design a flower arrangement to be judged by the jury. The movie was filmed in the Hall du Centenaire, which was subsequently demolished and replaced by the modern Grimaldi Forum conference center. (In 2007, the exhibition *Les années Grace Kelly—Princess de Monaco* began its world tour here; it later traveled to Paris, Moscow, Rome, Toronto, and other cities.) À la Hitchcock, Prince Rainier III makes a brief cameo in the film, as he too gives flower arranging a try. Before this point, the princess and the supposed travel writer walk through Monaco's market at the Place d'Armes, which is situated below the cliff. Here Grace waxes philosophical about plants and flowers. Other scenes were shot in the Hôtel de Paris near the casino, in the Hôtel Hermitage, and in the palace's Salon Bleu, where Grace is seen sitting in an armchair, deeply absorbed in reading. It is at this point that suddenly "Mr. Wilson" appears to again try to clarify things with the princess. This scene is surreal—almost mystical. Particularly considering that in reality, it would have been impossible for a journalist to gain access to the palace's private chambers in order to speak with the princess. In any case, *Rearranged* has something dreamlike about it. It blurs the line between fiction and reality.

The finale focuses on the jury selections in the floral competition and the handing out of prizes to the winners. This scene was filmed in Le Sporting d'Été, a large special events hall located directly on the sea. In another short appearance, Prince Rainier receives one of the prizes. Monaco's then-mayor announces the winners into the microphone.

The double twist of the little film comes at the very end. First, the princess tells "Mr. Wilson" that she knew the entire time who he really was. Since his lecture had been postponed, she explains, "I decided to *rearrange* things."[378]

Furthermore, after this dialogue which takes place in the princess's car, Professor Nelson finds himself again in that same car, complete with chauffeur Paul Raimondo. The plot circles back on itself. They are again en route to the cliffs, to the palace. The entire story was only a daydream.

Throughout the film Dornhelm inserted separate, free-standing scenes that showed Grace walking in the palace garden and examining plants. Her gaze wanders off into space again and again. She stands at the garden wall of the palace and looks down at the harbor of Monaco. Her gaze, her mannerisms, have something indefinably yearning about them. And the camera embraces her, courts her, charms her.

Her last feature film, *High Society*, was made in 1956. Twenty-three years passed between then and *Rearranged*, in 1979. It is amazing—her voice is almost unchanged. It still has the same distinguished clarity, precise articulation, and elegant tone. It was the same exact, fine English that she had used in her films. It was that very specific sound, that very specific soft warmth that she always had. Even her gestures were the same. Prince Albert II commented on *Rearranged*: "For her it was an amusing diversion for a few days. Of course now, in some ways, it is also a serious movie."[379]

Robert Dornhelm described the supposed meaning of *Rearranged* for Grace Kelly: "It was a lot of fun for her. And since she was also the producer, she wanted to take care of everything; she was especially involved. She told me that she had always been afraid of producers. You always had to be nice to them so they would treat you well. And I wrote one or two things for her. We discussed a whole array of films and wanted to make them all—together. One of them was the history of Prince Albert I. Albert was a pacifist, and he founded the Monegasque Red Cross

270

organization and the Oceanographic Institute. He was awarded the National Order of the Legion of Honour. His wife left him, and he had huge debts tied to the institute. He was totally bankrupt. We wanted to make a film about all of this…

"She was often in Los Angeles since she was on the board of directors for Twentieth Century-Fox at the time. (In November 1976, Grace became the first female member of the Fox Board of Directors.) I often went with her to see films."[380]

Disregarding the simple plot of the now highly obscure *Rearranged*, it is, of course, the appearance and presence of Grace Kelly that makes something noteworthy out of this thirty-three-minute film fragment.[381] She imbued it with her own charm and beauty; it was brief yet very unique.

Although it was never intended to be, *Rearranged* became a kind of tribute to Grace Kelly. Not really because of its content or narration. Rather, simply because it was her last performance before a camera, apart from the one-hour interview she did for CBS with journalist Pierre Salinger in the palace garden on July 22, 1982, only seven weeks before her death.

"Unfortunately it is not a good film, but it is a document," Robert Dornhelm commented self-critically.[382] *Rearranged* was definitely a product of its time. It was created in May 1979 during the 12th Annual Flower Show and Competition. Shot on 16 mm film, the movie shows in passing the fashion, colors, style, and accessories, as well as Monaco, of the late 1970s and early 1980s. Artifacts from another era.

Rearranged was not originally planned to be only thirty-three minutes in length. It was meant to be twice as long, or longer. The circumstances, perhaps even fate, prevented this. The English-language fragment, now provided with French subtitles, was restored and preserved by the Archives Audiovisuelles de Monaco in March 2007.

According to Vincent Vatrican, director of the Archives Audiovisuelles de Monaco: "*Rearranged* was found among the cinematographic materials in the palace archives. We had heard much about this prior to 2006, but neither we nor anyone else had seen it. Thus, we viewed it and all of the existing film copies, all of which had a strong red discoloration. This is the case with many films from the 1970s that have not been carefully preserved. We decided to undertake a digital restoration of the film. Afterward, the film was provided with French subtitles. Since then, it has been shown in Monaco at the Garden Club. However, it has not been shown publicly in a movie theater or on television."[383]

During Grace Kelly's lifetime, *Rearranged* was only shown once to a select audience. After that, Rainier III strictly refused to have the film shown publicly until his death in April 2005. Vatrican explained: "As far as I know, Prince Rainier III did not want the film shown after Princess Grace's death."[384] The film vanished into the archives of the royal palace, unbeknownst to the world outside.

Robert Dornhelm could understand why *Rearranged* stayed locked away for decades after its filming: "There were good reasons. It was a light comedy, a comedy of mistaken identities. The protagonist gets into the wrong car and does not land at the hotel, but at the palace, and he does not take part in the conference but ends up arranging flowers instead of talking about stars. After her death, the Prince was of the opinion that this was a film of memories. Of course, after her death, everyone wanted to have it because it was her last film. To have marketed this film, that was so lighthearted anyway, would have been inappropriate. And I think he was right. It was certainly not an important film that suitably showcased her incredible acting abilities. They could have shown excerpts from the film. I would have been very much in favor of this, but ultimately, it was a meaningless film. Now years later, I would probably cut it differently and only use parts of it. We had planned to re-shoot the entire thing. On the day of our appointment in Paris [September 14, the day Grace Kelly died], ABC had made us an offer to create a one-hour film from it. We wanted to discuss this, what we still wanted to film and how we would expand the whole thing to an hour in length."[385]

Generally speaking, it is little known that besides the never aired film *Rearranged*, Princess Gracia Patricia, in private, often picked up a camera and shot movies. "In 2006, we began to prepare the large exhibition *Les années Grace Kelly—Princess de Monaco*. After the death of his father, Prince Albert II gave us the palace film and archival materials so that we might restore and conserve them. Among these were many unpublished private photos and film footage. Privately, Princess Grace had shot quite a lot of film with a small hand camera. There are about one hundred films on both 16 mm and 8 mm film. Many of the films show her three children, but many also show her friends, such as David Niven, Cary Grant, Bing Crosby, and Alfred Hitchcock."[386] All of these life excerpts and parts, frozen on film, make up a compilation: a kaleidoscope of a life.

The shots of Hitchcock were taken during one of Princess Grace's many trips abroad. They were shot on the veranda at his house in California. The Master sat next to Grace and smoked a cigar with apparent pleasure. Grace can be seen talking, as Hitch listens to her. Thus, it is likely that Prince Rainier was the one who captured this moment of reunion between two old friends.[387]

Other shots show Grace and Cary Grant with a group of children playing on the edge of a swimming pool. These images contain something touching in them. In other photos, Bing Crosby was captured at the Grimaldi family's private estate high above Monaco, at Roc Agel. David Niven and John Williams can be seen laughing at the edge of a pool. Although Rainier absolutely did not approve and felt insecure in the face of it, Grace tried to maintain her contacts in Hollywood—the world that was lost to her—at least with the people to whom she felt the closest.

As Nadia LaCoste recalled, "I saw all sorts of actors in Monaco, also some who were friends. However, the two she felt closest to were Cary Grant and Frank Sinatra. Frank Sinatra even sang in Monaco, at a large charity function, the Red Cross Ball, and Rainier loved it: 'Come Fly With Me.' That was in the Sporting d'Été. Cary Grant was often a visitor here, and once he even served on the jury for one of the festivals in Monaco. Whenever any of her friends from Hollywood were on the Côte d'Azur, they were always invited to either lunch or dinner."[388]

Perhaps this was one of Grace Kelly's contradictions. Although she never liked Hollywood, she maintained the friendships she had made there, some even until her death. Hers was a loyalty that never wavered.

1980
The Master Departs:
Farewell to Hitch

*She liked Hitchcock and his wife Alma very much. That
was a lasting relationship.*
—Nadia LaCoste[389]

Over the passing years, Grace and Hitchcock stayed in close contact, writing letters and visiting each other. Hitchcock described
to her his upcoming projects, such as the political thriller *Torn
Curtain* (1966) with Paul Newman and Julie Andrews in the leading roles. Grace sent him photos of baby Stéphanie, and in his
letter he responded with sheer delight—a reaction that might
surprise those who know him only as the master of horror.

In mid-May 1972, Grace and Hitch met at the Cannes Film
Festival. On May 19, the seventy-two-year-old director hosted
the world premiere of *Frenzy* on the festival's main program. This
was his next-to-last film, and he had filmed it in his hometown,
London, in 1971. In two letters dated April 19 and May 3, 1972,
Hitch informed Grace that he would soon be on the Riviera.
Afterward, she invited him to visit her in a letter from May 19.[390]

Hitchcock's letters contained a very detailed description of his
itinerary, accommodations, transit stops, and other information.
He also outlined his extensive publicity tour for *Frenzy*, which
would take him to Paris, London, and New York after his time
in Cannes. There is something almost touching in the way that
Hitchcock shared all of his plans with Grace and how truly concerned he was that under no circumstances should they miss an
opportunity to see each other. Alongside his concern, his typical
ironic sense of humor pertaining to these concise plans can be
read between the lines.

In the late 1970s, Robert Dornhelm visited Alfred Hitchcock,
along with Grace Kelly, at Hitchcock's house on Bellagio Road
in Bel Air, Los Angeles. Dornhelm described the comfortable

relationship between the two of them and commented on the decades' long speculation that Hitchcock had his eye on even this blonde leading lady: "I never sensed this, not even in the slightest. She was good friends with his wife Alma, a film cutter. I never noticed even the smallest bit of tension. It was very familiar, even from his side. It was as if an old family friend had come for a visit. I never sensed an obsession in connection with her. It was all the nicer since he even chatted with me in German. He was very congenial and sympathetic."[391]

On April 29, 1974, almost two years after the premiere of *Frenzy*, Hitchcock was honored by the New York Film Society of Lincoln Center. That year the society dedicated its annual gala to the old master, who was increasingly gaining recognition and honor within the academic world. Together with his wife Alma and Grace Kelly, Hitchcock attended the gala at Lincoln Center. He was also accompanied by his admirer and follower, the French director François Truffaut. Hitchcock was honored with a compilation of film excerpts, at the conclusion of which he gave a brief commentary.

This was the context of his much-cited, legendary sentence: "As you can see, the best way to do it is with scissors." This was a playful reference to *Dial M for Murder*, which had starred Grace in the main role and which had been included in the honorary film montage.

Grace gave a short talk in honor of her director and friend, who along with his wife Alma listened attentively: "I think the qualities I most admired while working with Mr. Hitchcock were his incredible patience and good humor. I have watched him in trying [...] situations that would set many directors screaming in rage—but Hitch always remained calm and in control of the situation."[392]

In conclusion, the heavyset Master of Suspense delivered his prerecorded thank-you speech, as always in a tone of dry, humorous-ironic ambivalence:

Good evening. They say that when a man drowns, his entire life flashes before his eyes. I am indeed fortunate for having just had that same experience without even getting my feet wet.

First of all, I wish to express my deep satisfaction for this honour. It makes me feel very proud indeed.

As you will have seen, murder seems to be the prominent theme. As I do not approve of the current wave of violence that we see on our screens, I have always felt that murder should be treated delicately. And, in addition to that, with the help of television, murder should be brought into the home, where it rightly belongs. Some of our most exquisite murders have been domestic—performed with tenderness in simple homey places like the kitchen table or the bathtub.

Nothing is more revolting to my sense of decency than the underworld thug is able to murder anyone, even people to whom he has not been properly introduced. After all, I'm sure you will agree that murder can be so much more charming and enjoyable—even for the victim—if the surroundings are pleasant and the people involved are ladies and gentlemen like yourselves.

Finally, I think I can best describe the insidious effect of murder on one's character by quoting a paragraph from Thomas De Quincey's delightful essay "Murder as One of the Fine Arts." He said: "If once a man indulges himself in murder, very soon he comes to think little of robbing; and from robbing he comes next to drinking and Sabbath-breaking, and from that to incivility and procrastination. Once begun on this downward path, you never know where you are to stop. Many a man dates his ruin from some murder or other that perhaps he thought little of at the time."

They tell me that murder is committed every minute, so I don't want to waste any more of your time. I know you want to get to work.

Thank you.[393]

One week after this festive occasion, Hitch wrote Grace a letter in which he thanked her. Once again, the mutual respect maintained between the two of them is evident: "I can't thank you enough for the effect of your presence. It made the crush of the all-embracing crowd so much more pleasant to endure."[394]

On March 7, 1979, the American Film Institute awarded Alfred Hitchcock with its Lifetime Achievement Award.[395] This was another belated honor for him. As had been the case with Charlie Chaplin, he had scandalously never received an Oscar. The event was aired on television, and everyone who was anyone in Hollywood was there. All of the great Hitchcock stars were there, including Ingrid Bergman, who acted as hostess for the evening, Tippi Hedren, Janet Leigh, Anthony Perkins, Sean Connery, Henry Fonda, and even Cary Grant and James Stewart. The latter two actors, both of whom were the only ones who had each starred in four Hitchcock films, sat directly next to the honoree at his table.

There was a standing ovation when his name was read and the spotlight illuminated his spot. With an occasional pained expression on his face, he laboriously made his way through the waiting crowd to his table, where the waiting Alma showed him his seat next to hers. Despite their physical difficulties, both of them insisted on participating in this event. The most painful aspect of these images is the visible age of both of them, particularly Hitchcock. There is something lost and wistful in the way that Alma and Alfred Hitchcock sat at their large, covered table in the midst of all the other dinner tables set up for this opulent gala affair. At times, they seemed to no longer be part of this world.

François Truffaut was also one of the presenters and congratulators that evening. He had planned the fifty-hour interview with this personally revered director during the 1960s, and he recalled this experience in his speech. However, the Master of Suspense seemed to be completely untouched and unmoved by all of these accolades of recognition, respect, and admiration. His expression remained stoic throughout.

Finally, it was Alfred Hitchcock's turn to say thank you. With great effort, he stood up from his chair, falling back into it once. He rose again and his prerecorded thank-you speech began to play, but not before he once again told his legendary tale of his five-minute incarceration at the age of six.

The most moving moment of this speech was certainly his thank-you to all of his colleagues and collaborators, which he expressed in a specific thankyou to four people in his life: "I beg to mention by name only four people who have given me the most affection, appreciation and encouragement...and constant collaboration. The first of the four is a film editor, the second is a scriptwriter, the third is the mother of my daughter Pat, and the fourth is as fine a cook as ever performed miracles in a domestic kitchen...and their names are Alma Reville."[396]

A declaration of love. The speech was deeply touching. The pragmatic, hardworking woman, now old and weary and ill, hid her face behind her hands. Behind her perennially oversized glasses, tears could be seen running down her cheeks. It was clear in this moment that Hitch and Alma, Alma and Hitch, would each be lost without the other. Norman Lloyd, actor in *Saboteur* and *Spellbound* as well as coproducer of Hitchcock's television series, once said, "She was his soul." They had been married for fifty-three years and had made fifty-three feature films together.

Patricia Hitchcock once had the following to say about her mother Alma Reville: "My mother has never gotten enough credit for the part she played. For instance, when my father wanted to make another movie...[based on] a story, a book—he would have her read it first, to see if she thought it would make a good picture. If she said no, he didn't even go on with it. It was the same way all the way through with writers, with actors. She was always the first one—she didn't see a lot of the rushes [the unedited prints of a movie scene], because she wasn't there every day to see the finished product. In fact she saw *Psycho* right before they sent it out, and they asked her 'What do you think?'—and then she said 'you can't send it out.' And they said 'Why?' And she said 'Because Janet Leigh takes a breath when she is supposed to be dead. Nobody had caught it except her. She used to be a film cutter too. But she never got enough credit. [...] But when she died, the *Los Angeles Times* said: 'The Hitchcock touch had four hands, and two of them were Alma's.' And it's true, it's true."[397]

On May 9, 1979, Alfred Hitchcock closed his large bungalow office on the Universal Studios lot. It was the end of an era. It was the conclusion of a unique, fifty-five-year directing career. It was also a self-admission of sorts. The work on *The Short Night* was stopped, although the screenplay would later be published.[398] Alfred Hitchcock would not make any more films. Against his wishes, *Family Plot* became the conclusion to his body of work.

Afterward, Hitchcock contacted Claude Chabrol and asked him if he was interested in turning *The Short Night* into a film. Sean Connery was the first choice for the leading male role, but because of the rape scene that occurs at the beginning of the film, he was not interested. Hitchcock wanted to cast Liv Ullmann in the leading female role, but she was unavailable because of a musical engagement in New York.

Claude Chabrol recalled: "He sent me his last screenplay shortly before his death. And in it, there was a pretty bad scene: the hero raped this woman, but he truly raped her. The hero! How can this be? This is the hero of the film. You simply can't do that. Neither could Sean Connery. The writing was truly, truly not good anymore..."[399]

In August, shortly after Hitchcock's eightieth birthday, Ingrid Bergman visited him at his home in Bel Air. What she saw there was a broken man who could no longer hide his age. Alfred Hitchcock was deeply sad at this point. The old director and the cancer-stricken actress, who like Grace had made three films under Hitchcock—*Spellbound* (1945), *Notorious* (1946), and *Under Capricorn* (1949)—talked about death. He was fearful of death. An absolutely morbid, very melancholy mood lay across this reunion, which would also be a final farewell for these two people.

Two years later, Ingrid Bergman died on her sixty-seventh birthday, August 29, 1982, in London. Only two weeks later, on September 13, Grace was killed in an accident. Two of Hitchcock's most important heroines, probably the two most important in his entire body of work, died within fourteen days of each other during the disastrous, dark year of 1982. This was also the year of

Romy Schneider's premature death at the age of forty-three, on April 29 in Paris.

On December 31, 1979, Queen Elizabeth II named Hitchcock a Knight Commander of the British Empire. Since he could no longer travel to England, he was knighted in absentia by the British General Consul in Los Angeles. Janet Leigh, Cary Grant, and Lew Wasserman were in attendance. Now he was Sir Alfred Hitchcock, and even on this occasion, he made jokes. He called himself "The Short Knight," playing on the title of his latest film project. And when a journalist asked him why this honorable recognition had taken so long, he replied laconically: "I guess she forgot."[400]

Alfred Hitchcock's last public appearance took place on March 16, 1980, when he was again present for the honoring gala of the American Film Institute. It was the tradition that the previous year's recipient would hand out the prize. This time, the honoree was James Stewart. Hitchcock's speech was recorded at the Beverly Hilton Hotel, and afterward, he was taken back home. He did not attend the evening gala. At this time, his condition and constitution were declining rapidly. His liver and kidneys no longer functioned, and his heart had stopped responding to the pacemaker that had been installed a few years before. The end was in sight.

And this end was very still, very quiet. His kidneys failed, as had happened to his mother. On the morning of April 29, 1980, at 9:30 a.m., Alfred Hitchcock died at his home in Bel Air, in his own bed. His family was with him. It is said that he went peacefully.

The funeral took place in the Church of the Good Shepherd in Beverly Hills, celebrated by the Jesuit priest Thomas Sullivan, a longtime acquaintance of Hitchcock. Then amazingly, the casket went missing! A final joke by the Master. Even at this point, he wished to control everything. Nothing could be left to chance. It was a Catholic service with a Jesuit priest—formal and correct— but the casket was missing. Previously Hitch had decided to be cremated. As he had stipulated, his ashes were to be scattered on the Pacific, along the California coast. On May 8, 1980, in London's Westminster Cathedral, a funeral mass was held for the native Englishman.

Two years later, Alma Reville, Hitchcock's wife and lifelong companion and coworker, followed him. She died on July 6, 1982. Her funeral was held in St. Paul the Apostle Church in Westwood, and Alma's ashes were also scattered on the waters of the Pacific. It is perfectly understandable that she wanted to follow her Hitch even into death.

Two and a half years before her own death, Grace Kelly lost her directing master, friend, and mentor. More importantly, he had been a longtime companion, and was most likely the most important individual in her entire acting career.

—Faith, Love, Hope:
Catholicism, Astrology, Scorpio Parties

*Grace was always very drawn to spiritual matters. She
wanted to be one with nature, with people, yes, even the
whole universe. She felt a strong desire for harmony.*
—Judith Balaban Quine[401]

"We were educated by nuns. We were very devout—Grace certainly more than I was. And she stayed that way. Our entire family
was very religious, especially my father. Thus, it was also clear
that my mother would convert to Catholicism when she married
him," Grace's younger sister Lizanne related.[402]

From her earliest years, Grace was inclined toward every form
and expression of faith. This affinity for spirituality and astrology,
paranormal and supernatural experiences, to everything immate-
rial and sacred, lasted her entire lifetime. This might also be one
of the pillars that gave form to her character.

It is telling that Grace maintained contact throughout her
life with the nuns who had educated her at Ravenhill Academy
in the Philadelphia East Falls neighborhood. She continued to
exchange letters and phone calls with Sister Frances who said,
"[Grace] had always prayed for her children, and she asked me
again and again to pray for her. And she called me whenever
Caroline had a test or she had to make a difficult decision. She
trusted strongly in God, and prayer was our way of mutually supporting each other."[403]

When the head of the Catholic Church, Pope John Paul II,
wanted to give her a medal, Grace turned it down. According
to Robert Dornhelm, "She did not want to receive a medal from
the pope indicating that she was a model mother. That was too
much for her. Although she truly respected the pope, she did not
want a medal. She said that she had not earned it. It implied too
many things that were not justified. This really surprised me. She
said that she would not feel right about it. She felt she still had

to truly prove herself. She did not think that she had raised her children perfectly."[404]

Born on November 12, Grace's astrological sign was Scorpio, with Scorpio rising—a double Scorpio.

The twelve astrological signs are tied to the four elements: fire, earth, air, and water. As one of the three water signs, Scorpios are passionate, decisive, and intuitive. However, they are also prone to jealousy, strong mood swings, and a tendency toward depression.

The realm of the abstract—"poetry and the stars"—were important to Grace. As Robert Dornhelm explained, "Astrology and horoscopes, as well as palm reading, were big topics for her. I don't know how serious these all were, but they were there." And again: "On Sundays, she frequently went to church. She did not drink alcohol for the month before Easter, or even longer. She fasted. Every year. And she would not let herself be dissuaded from this."[405]

Like a recurring theme, Grace's piety was rooted in her Catholic upbringing, and it remained constant through her life. Already at an early age, she had distinguished herself from the rest of her family through her pronounced artistic and creative inclinations. While her parents and siblings were faithful Catholics, Grace expanded far beyond the close boundaries they respected.

Grace was superstitious, and she believed in fate. Through her deep sensitivity and intuition, she believed greatly in the fated course of life.

Books about astrology, horoscopes, and the Zodiac signs were scattered all around her New York apartment, and when she met someone new, regardless of gender, she often asked for his or her Zodiac sign. Thus, Grace tried as much as possible to avoid associating with anyone who was a Virgo. She was convinced that under no circumstances could Virgos and Scorpios get along. And Scorpios could also not get along well with Geminis. In Grace's opinion, these were two signs that could never be in harmony. Ironically, the man she married was a Gemini.

Grace regularly requested that predictions be sent to her from the American astrologer Carroll Righter in California. Righter advised Ronald Reagan over a period of forty-five years, and as the most outstanding of all American astrologers, he was featured on the cover of the March 21, 1969, issue of *Time* magazine under the headline, "Astrology and the New Cult of the Occult." His other prominent clients included Marlene Dietrich, Hildegard Knef, Natalie Wood, and Hitchcock heroine Joan Fontaine (*Rebecca*). Over a period of about twenty years, Grace had Righter send her predictions about the future, about what the coming days would bring for her. This correspondence was based on a mixture of naïveté, gullibility, dreaminess, and romanticism. In part, this mixture aligned well with one of Grace's two sides: her dreamy side, the irrationality of which opened the door for everything tied to the occult and astrology.

Together with her friends, including Carolyn Reybold (who was one of her bridesmaids) and her husband Malcolm Reybold, Grace read the astrology book *The Pursuit of Destiny* while living in New York.

In addition, Grace engaged in Tarot card readings, and was interested in table-turning and Ouija boards.[406] Once she even sought out a Gypsy woman to have her prophesy read. "Astrology was important to her. I was even with her one time when she visited a palm reader. Incognito. And the woman was very disquieted. She was an Irish woman, and she had a six- or seven-year-old son, called Red because of his red hair. The little boy was running around, and she said had him leave because she sensed that this was not a normal hand, although she had no idea who Grace was. It was totally incognito, and no one would have believed that Grace had gone into a little five-dollar palm reading tent. The fortune teller had a feeling, since these kinds of people can sense things. It was a little uncanny for her, and she had a hard time with it. She did not risk asking any direct questions, but she had noticed something. Grace was quite amused at how she had unsettled her," recalled Robert Dornhelm.[407]

And further: "Grace went to Lourdes twice (once in 1961, and again in 1979 with her son Albert). And she wanted to pilgrimage along the Santiago di Compostela road. She thought that the Catholic Church was very practical. You could do penance, and then everything was good again. That fit her world view. She had often joked that the good thing was that you could and should sin so that you could be forgiven."[408]

At one point, when Robert Dornhelm accompanied Grace Kelly to London where she was a guest at a flower arranging event, the following occurred: "Once, in London, I brought Grace some feathers, and I said: 'At least take these pheasant feathers. They have such beautiful colors, and you can add them to the flowers.' And she just froze—since she was superstitious. She later told me: 'I wish you had not given me that.' Because feathers—pheasant feathers—are bad luck, and are a sign of coming death."[409]

In 1969, Grace turned forty. Shortly before her birthday—an unpleasant occasion which she would have rather ignored—she decided to do something. Carroll Righter held monthly Zodiac parties for the pertinent signs and exclusively invited only those who fell under a particular sign; these parties also featured the appropriate Zodiac animal as a party surprise. Taking a nod from him, Grace decided to celebrate her fortieth birthday with a Scorpio party. She only invited Scorpios and those friends who were married to Scorpios. These people were invited on Saturday, November 15, 1969, to dinner and dancing. The guest count came to sixty, and this international group gathered in the grand Belle Époque hall of the Hotel Hermitage in Monte Carlo. The palatial ball and dining room was decorated ahead of time and Grace had portraits of famous individuals who were also Scorpios hung on the walls. Thus, Grace's guests could view old portraits of the sculptor Auguste Rodin, Queen Marie Antoinette, and the author Edgar Allan Poe. The invitations were sent out in French and English, and on these, the French women and English ladies were asked to dress in the colors of Scorpio, predominantly red but also black and white. Other associated Zodiac signs would be tolerated. The paper invitations bore the inscription *High Scorpia*. In this context, Grace called herself "Her Scorpio Majesty," a title she used again and again at other occasions when she invited her old friends from Hollywood to gather together.

On the following day, at the agreeable time of 12:30 p.m., the guests of the Scorpio party were invited to have breakfast at the swimming pool of the neighboring, extremely expensive Hôtel de Paris, where the guests had also been lodged.

Among those that Grace invited were the actor couple Elizabeth Taylor and Richard Burton. The Welsh Burton was the Scorpio, having been born two days before Grace on November 10, 1925. Born in late February, Liz Taylor was a Pisces. A highly explosive combination. Here in Monaco, a place where wealth and luxury had no bounds, Taylor displayed for the first time the legendary Krupp Diamond, a gift from her husband.

Around the time of her fortieth birthday, Grace gave an interview to *Look* magazine, whose cover she had already graced in the 1950s. At that time, she had been Hollywood's white swan, the cool, elegant lady. Select quotes from this conversation with journalist William B. Arthur, however, about growing old—a process that troubled and occupied her greatly—were marked by an astonishing candor. They revealed her despair: "For a woman, forty is torture, the end. I think turning forty is miserable."[410] And then she continued: "I constantly think of Shakespeare's verse: When forty winters shall besiege thy brow / And dig deep trenches in thy beauty's field / Thy youth's proud livery, so gazed on now / Will be a tattered weed, of small worth held..."[411]

Grace experienced this period around her birthday as another serious breaking point in her life. Her youth was now passed. She now saw herself as middle-aged, and she was the one who had the hardest time with this. The time of her Hollywood films, the time of her beloved New York, and the time of her flawless, transcendental beauty were irrevocably behind her. Neither the decade just behind her, nor the one in front of her, belonged only to herself. After her third and final miscarriage in 1967, the last-born Princess Stéphanie became the spoiled baby in the family. However, the older the three children grew and the busier they became with school, the more independent and less needy they became. Over time, there was more and more free time. Time that needed to be filled. Grace had always hated not having something to do, not having plans or goals to pursue. And thus, she filled the days with organizing things; she increased her number of obligations and appointments. As she took care of her children, she turned her attention to everyone and everything in the small principality. Attentively and lovingly, she tried to address the needs of the people and their interests. There was only one person she always considered last, and this was another motif that ran through her entire life: she failed to consider herself.

In another interview that she gave around her fortieth birthday, Grace revealed that she had never found herself to be "a great beauty." She confessed how horrible she thought it was that she was so recognized for her appearance—"I'd much rather be known for my achievements." One of her biggest regrets was that she hadn't had more time to develop as an actress. She feared being remembered as only a young, beautiful novice. "I can only hope that I have instead evolved as a person," she said.[412] As publicist Thomas Veszelits saw it, "The big problem arose at some point in the early 1970s. The catalyst was her recognition: 'Now I am slowly getting older and older.' Her inclination to the New Age mind-set and to the music of Georg Deuter, a New Age musician from Munich, must be connected with this. Looking in the mirror, she suddenly realized that her youth was slowly vanishing. And with some women, this is a problem. Starting in the 1970s, there was a complete shift. And then large difficulties arose with Caroline. At that time, Grace went to Paris to function as a kind of chaperone for Caroline."[413]

There is another lesser known side to Grace: With her acute sensitivity and her intuitive perception of the thoughts and feelings of those around her—something that often happened without their knowledge—Grace came close to having extrasensory perception (ESP). This circumstance should not be considered completely absurd or simply dismissed. Cary Grant and William Holden expressed at various times that Grace could almost read their minds and seemed to have almost an unnatural understanding for the male psychology. Cary Grant once suggested that Grace had an extraordinary gift for reading his thoughts. Her friend Rita Gam agreed, "Grace had ESP."[414]

Princess Grace's marked inclination toward various spiritual modes was the subject of a documentary film made in 1997, fifteen years after her tragic death. *Secret Lives: Grace Kelly* (1997) was originally a British documentary that aired on the television channel, Channel 4. Originally the British program (1997) was sixty minutes in length, but it was then edited and shortened to fifty-three minutes (2002) and then forty-two minutes (2007).

The documentary film by auteur filmmakers David Cohen and Jennifer Clayton was first aired on December 29, 1997, on Channel 4. This was one week after David Cohen and his colleague David Carr-Brown revealed their presumably spectacular discoveries in the December 21 issue of the *Sunday Times*.

During the summer months of 1982, a friend supposedly drove Grace to a meeting of the Order of the Solar Templars. The friend in question was the French actress and singer Colette Deréal, who had represented Monaco in the 1961 Grand Prix Eurovision de la Chanson and who died in the principality in 1988.[415] An eyewitness saw both women drive past in a gray Jaguar. In the late 1970s, the center of this ominous, secret society was located in southern France, in Beaujolais in a priory in Villié-Morgon.

The British documentary claimed to prove that it was a close, longtime friend of Prince Rainier, someone he had known since childhood, who was the leading figure of these Solar Templars. Jean-Louis "Lou-Lou" Marsan, school friend and Prince Rainier's financial adviser, was named as a key figure in this society. Marsan also died in 1982, in August, only one month prior to the princess's tragic accident. As the film further claimed, Marsan had been a member of the Order of the Solar Templars since 1970. Various members of the upper crust in Monaco, as well as powerful financiers, had belonged to this order, which was dissolved in the mid-1990s. Approximately fifty individuals were members of this southern French society. The French journalist Roger Bianchi explained that Marsan "was one of the most influential individuals in Monaco." He "was fascinated by the philosophy of the Solar Templars and brought it to Monaco." His own villa functioned as a kind of private chapel. However, Marsan was only involved in the purely spiritual aspects of the order.[416]

At the end of her short life, Grace Kelly was supposedly a member of the Solar Templars. This was reported by an allegedly former member of the controversial order, Monsieur Guy Mouyrin. "Mouyrin" was clearly a false name, and in other places, the man called himself Georges Leroux. The documentary filmmakers presented Mouyrin as a witness and questioned him on camera. He described the promises that the secret society made to its members. According to Mouyrin's/Leroux's claims, Jean-Louis Marsan permitted Princess Grace to attend a conference with Luc Jouret, who along with Joseph Di Mambro was a cofounder of the order. (Later, he died in the October 1994 apocalyptic mass suicide of the Solar Templars in Switzerland.) This conference involved acupuncture and other New Age–embraced medicinal practices. To attend, Luc Jouret demanded 20 million Francs, but he never received them. However, at this time, Luc Jouret, a former doctor and homeopath, was staying in Belgium. He first appeared again in Geneva in September 1982. It was not until 1984 that he even first established the part of the Order that he led.

The small Monegasque, purely spiritually oriented, harmless order of Jean-Louis Marsan, called "L'Ordre souverain du Temple solaire" (OSTS), which was officially recognized by Prince Rainier in 1964, had nothing to do with the religiously fanatic Order of the Solar Templars, "L'Ordre du Temple solaire" (OTS). A small but significant difference. One that the documentary film on Channel 4 failed to notice.

Thus, it is highly doubtful that the princess had any contact with all of these things. It is much more likely that the filmmakers followed a false thread, treating unproven, highly speculative claims as serious facts. After the initial airing of the program, the royal palace in Monaco disclaimed the unverifiable claims made in the documentary film in an officially published communiqué in December 1997. The palace expressed its regret that the film and its fantasies were even shown.[417]

1982
Annus horribilis

I would like to be remembered as someone who accomplished useful deeds, and who was a kind and loving person. I would like to leave the memory of a human being with a correct attitude and who did her best to help others ... I don't think I was accomplished enough as an actress to be remembered for that. I'd like to be remembered as a decent human being, and a caring one.
—Grace Kelly in July 1982[418]

A great darkness lay across the city. It was deathly silent. Everyone knew there had been an accident. And then, the lights in and around the casino went out. Then everyone knew that she had died.
—Rolf Palm[419]

There was a lot of pressure on me because everyone was saying that I had been driving the car, that it was all my fault, that I'd killed my mother. It's not easy when you're seventeen to live with that. There was so much magic that surrounded Mom, so much of that dream, that in some ways she almost stopped being human. It was difficult for people to accept that she could do something so human as to have a car accident. People figured I must have caused it because she was too perfect to do something like that. After a while you can't help feeling guilty. Everybody looks at you and you know they're thinking, "How come she's still around and Grace is dead?" No one ever said it to me like that, but I knew that's what they were thinking. I needed my mother a lot when I lost her. And my dad was so lost without her. I felt so alone. I just went off to do my own thing.[420]

In the royally-authorized book *Rainier & Grace*, published by author and journalist Jeffrey Robinson in 1989, Princess Stéphanie is only quoted a few times. By 1989, Grace Kelly had been dead for seven years. Prince Rainier III would reign for another sixteen years, until his death in the spring of 2005. Prince Albert and Princess Caroline were both in their early thirties. At the time she was interviewed by Robinson, Princess Stéphanie was twenty-four years old. The quotations in the book came from this interview. This was the first time she spoke with any member of the press about the accident on that fatal September morning and its far-reaching existential repercussions, especially on her own life. These were statements that corroborated the official version of events that had always been given by the palace. Those versions that do not correspond with the official statements are only speculations, hypotheses, and rumors.

In October 2002, twenty years after her mother's death, the princess gave another interview to the French periodical *Paris Match*. Stéphanie was now thirty-seven years old. In this rare interview, she related the moments before the crash. She explained that from the passenger seat she had pushed the automatic gear shift to the park position and had yanked up the parking brake but the car would not stop. She did not want to comment on what they had been discussing in the car. This was something between them and them alone. Although others may blame her for the death of her mother, she does not feel guilt over it any longer. She added that even twenty years after her mother's death, she still suffers from a double trauma: not only had she lost her mother when both women were far too young, but she was present at her mother's side for the harrowing accident that took her life.[421]

It is an indisputable fact that the only person yet alive who truly knows what happened in that Rover 3500 on that sad morning of September 13, 1982, is Princess Stéphanie.

The morning of September 13, 1982, was glorious. The sun was shining. It was the start of a new week. Princess Grace had many upcoming plans. She was supposed to meet Robert Dornhelm in Paris the following day to discuss the reworking of *Rearranged*, as well as other joint film projects. And Stéphanie was also supposed to go to Paris. On Wednesday, September 15, she was to start her first course in fashion design at the Chambre Syndicale de la Haute Couture. However, on this family weekend at Roc Agel, Stéphanie had announced to her shocked parents that she did not plan to start her intended education. Instead, she wanted to attend a car racing school with her boyfriend Paul Belmondo, the son of legendary actor Jean-Paul Belmondo. Her ambition now was to become a race car driver. Grace and Rainier could hardly believe it. Furthermore, Grace had always been strongly opposed to car driving. As Robert Dornhelm recalled, "The daughter was there because of Belmondo. Then there was an argument about whether she would go to the course. That was the next thing. The scandals were a foregone conclusion. They (Grace and Stéphanie) argued at the end—this part I knew about. The fight about the racing school, it definitely occurred. This was not a new argument there [at Roc Agel]."[422]

On the other hand, Albert had just graduated from Amherst University in Massachusetts. He would soon be starting his training in finance and communication with the Morgan Guaranty Trust in New York and the luxury brand Moët-Hennessy in Paris. After this time, he would serve with the French Navy for seven months, until April 1983. Caroline was set to depart soon for London to spend time at the therapeutic resort, Forest Mere, in Hampshire. One day after her planned visit to Paris, Grace had a poetry reading scheduled at Windsor Castle that the Queen of England was set to attend. It was a time of departures.

Robert Dornhelm had arrived on September 10, and he spent that emotionally charged weekend of September 11–12 with the royal family at their estate on Roc Agel, high above Monaco. On Sunday, he departed to travel to Paris: "I had met with her for a couple of days prior, up at Roc Agel. Very steep, narrow serpentine roads. It is several hundred meters up to La Turbie, and the road grade is about ten degrees. It takes half an hour to get up there."

The close friends were supposed to see each other again in two days in Paris. Grace was excited and full of energy and initiative to both start and finish various things.

However, on the other hand, according to Dornhelm, since her return from the cruise to Scandanavia on the SS *Mermoz*, which she took with Rainier, Caroline, and Albert, she was "not happy—ailing even." In addition: "I can verify that she was not doing well beforehand. That her health was not in good shape. She had a sinus infection from the air conditioning on the ship. She had headaches and earaches. There was too much to eat, and she did not feel well. The ship journey had not been very enjoyable, even up in Greenland and at the fjords of Norway. Besides that, she had gained weight. At our last meeting, she was very depressed, very defeated. I tried to cheer her up."[423]

It was about 9:45 a.m.

Grace and Stéphanie left the house at Roc Agel and started the drive down. They turned onto the narrow road that passed the Mont Agel Golf Course. Chauffeur Christian Silvestri stayed back at the house. The princess sat at the wheel, the daughter in the passenger seat. On the backseat were all the gowns and dresses, including one by Dior, which Grace did not want to get rumpled. The Dior dress became the one in which she was clothed three days later for the viewing of the open casket at the royal palace.

As theater director Patrick Hourdequin explained, "There were five or six chauffeurs in the palace, but Princess Grace only trusted Christian Silvestri. He was actually supposed to drive the car, the automatic Rover. However, the clothes were all across the backseat. And so the Princess said, 'No, Christian, it won't work for you to drive. You can see my daughter has to sit up front since in the back are the dresses. If you like, you can follow us by running after the car.'—That was her sense of humor."[424]

The tragedy took place on the dangerous, extremely curvy Route D 37. Several sharp hairpin turns come one after the other. The cliff begins right at the edge of the road.

As he follows behind the brown Rover 3500 on the small serpentine road which leads from La Turbie, high in the French highlands, down to Monaco, the truck driver Yves Raimondo notices at some point that he can no longer see the brake lights of the car in front of him.[425] At this speed and incline, the red brake lights should have been burning for a while already. Suddenly the car begins to skid and skirts along the rock wall. Observing all of this, Raimondo honks repeatedly. For a moment, the car seems to right itself. It speeds up down the hill, and the next sharp, hairpin turn is already in sight. There is still no indication that the driver of the Rover 3500 is slowing down to brake. Then, Yves Raimondo witnesses how the Rover at full speed races out over the curve. The car plunges off the steep, 130-foot cliff and comes to rest in a clump of trees and bushes in a private garden. A pile of steel. A wreck.

It was about 10:05 a.m.

About thirty-six hours passed between this moment and the time of her death.

Princess Stéphanie, who survived the plunge into the chasm, crawled out of the left side of the car and begged the first people hurrying toward her to call for help. It was her *Maman*, her mother, who was lying in the car. Someone needed to call her father, *mon pére*, the prince, right away.

"It was horrifying. I will never forget it. The car landed on the property of Monsieur Jacques Provence. He then moved away from this property; he could no longer stay there. At this time, he was the creative director for the Loews Monte Carlo Hotel, which is known today as the Fairmont Monte Carlo. Monsieur Provence was having breakfast in his garden with his wife when he heard a loud crash at the other end of his garden. He immediately recognized Stéphanie. He never discussed this much. He was intelligent. He had the foresight to call the police and fire department here in Monaco, although the accident took place on French soil. He did not want any kind of false stories to circulate," remembered Patrick Hourdequin.[426]

Furthermore: "There was a man here, probably a farmer, Sesto Lequio, whom everyone here in Monaco saw on the French television. He presented himself as an eyewitness and told stories to the press. However, he seemed to be mainly interested in the money. Nonetheless, it was the house and garden of Jacques Provence, whose wife Josette was completely destroyed and traumatized by what happened."[427]

The statements made by this Sesto Lequio were, in part, the source for many of the lasting speculations and legends over the years. As he later claimed, he himself helped Princess Stéphanie out of the wreck, out of the driver's side. Supposedly still conscious, the princess whispered in Lequio's ear these words, or something to that effect: "They should believe that I was driving."[428] Later, the relatively unreliable witness Lequio retracted part of his story, the part about Grace's final words. He stuck by the rest of his story, just as did Monsieur Michel Pierre, the owner of the neighboring property and another "witness." However, Jacques and Josette Provence, who called the police after Stéphanie climbed out of the wreck and came toward them, never talked about what happened.

First, cars stop above. People scurry around. One farmer calls for two rescue vehicles, which soon arrive at the scene. Grace Kelly lies across the interior of the car, her head toward the rear, her legs near the front. One of them seems twisted. Her eyes are glassy, she is non-responsive and clearly unconscious. On her forehead is a gaping wound. The emergency personnel must pull her through the bushes, and she is immediately placed into one of the ambulances and transported to her namesake hospital, Hôpital Princesse Grace. Her daughter lies in the other ambulance.

Captain Roger Bencze, French police commissioner from Menton, which lies east of Monaco, arrived at the accident site. The accident happened within Menton's police jurisdiction. Bencze would go on to lead the investigation from the French side.

It was 10:30 a.m.

Shortly before Bencze's arrival, Prince Rainier and his son Albert reached the site. They witnessed the initial emergency care given to Grace and Stéphanie in the ambulances prior to their transport to the hospital.

At the hospital, Grace Kelly was examined by Dr. Charles Louis Chatelin, the head of surgery, and her first emergency operation lasted four hours. Her crushed chest cavity was opened, as was her abdomen. Her internal bleeding had to be stopped. Furthermore, there were breaks in her thighs, her clavicle, and her ribs. These all had to be treated. The bleeding from her head wound was heavy, and the brain damage was determined to be lasting and severe. Thus, Dr. Chatelin in consultation with Dr. Jean Duplay, director of neurosurgery at the Hôpital Pasteur in Nice, decided that a CT scan of her brain was urgently needed in order to gauge the severity of the damage to the cranium.

However, the only CT machine in the entire principality was not located in this hospital high up on the northwestern mountainside. Only after Grace's death would this hospital have the most modern equipment in the region. Publicist Rolf Palm shared his memories of this time: "At that time, the medical technology was not as advanced as it is today, and this hospital had hardly anything. The hospital had never had a CT machine. The only one belonged to the private physician, Monsieur Mourou, at Boulevard des Moulins 4. And then there was another problem. The office was located on the third floor. First they tried to take the unconscious Grace up the elevator to the doctor. In that narrow elevator, they would have had to prop upright the stretcher to which she was strapped. After seeing that this was impossible, they carried her up the stairs, trying to keep the stretcher as horizontal as possible."[429] Valuable time was lost. By the time the scan was completed, thirteen valuable hours had passed since the accident.

As Patrick Hourdequin explained: "At that time, we lived on Place des Moulins, directly on Boulevard de Moulins, where Dr. Mourou's office was. And I remember how they blocked the boulevard and carried her body into the house. It was dreadful. However, no one really knew at this point what was going on."[430]

In the meantime, Roger Bencze had examined the wreck carefully. The car had been removed relatively quickly from the accident site, and with permission from the palace, the Monaco police chief and the district attorney from Nice were also present for the examination.

It was about 4:30 p.m.

In his protocol, the official investigation file, Captain Bencze wrote that the brakes worked perfectly fine—this finding was subsequently contradicted time and time again. He also found that the automatic gear shift was on "D" for drive and not on "P" for park or on "Mountain" for steep inclines. The hand brake had never been pulled.[431] The seat belts had not been used; neither of them were strapped in. Furthermore, the Rover did not have any headrests, which is why Grace was tossed about in the car interior. In terms of its physical state, prior to the accident and the resultant massive damages, the car functioned properly and was in good condition. Also, despite the claims by Sesto Lequio and others, at no point was the car on fire.

It was about 1:30 p.m.

A palace spokesperson—presumably an inexperienced one who had taken over the duties during the summer when the palace was closed and the royal family was on vacation or at Roc Agel—sent out a communiqué that explained that Princess Gracia had broken her leg and suffered from a few minor, external injuries and was being treated in a hospital. A seemingly innocent communiqué that initially did not upset anyone. Not even the Kellys in the United States. A broken leg and a few scratches do not imply a life or death situation. However, this was exactly the situation Grace was in from the moment the Rover crashed through the guardrail. These were circumstances that were hopeless from the very beginning. Later, the palace communiqué and other statements gave rise to the speculations. Why did someone let this go out when the information was so far from the actual truth? The answer may be, in part, that for a long while the supervising physicians did not inform the family and the palace about the seriousness of the situation. Thus, at the time that the communiqué was drafted, it could be that no one knew anything more.

The night between September 13 and 14 is a night of uncertainty, a night of trepidation and hope for one husband, Prince Rainier III, and his two children, son Albert and daughter Caroline. The third and youngest child, Stéphanie, is completely unaware of this. She is in the hospital, suffering from a serious vertebrae injury and concussion, and Rainier wishes to spare her the shock. It is several days later when she first learns the full measure of the tragedy. Only after the burial, in the company of her family, will she be taken to the grave of her mother in St. Nicholas Cathedral.

According to Nadia LaCoste, "At first, Stéphanie did not know that her mother had died. It was kept a secret from her while she was in the hospital. After all, they had been given different rooms. The doctors thought that she should first be informed when she was better able to cope with the situation. I still recall how it was of utmost importance that Stéphanie should know nothing. That was the primary concern. She should have every opportunity to get better..."[432]

On the next day, neither the Monegasque people, nor the world at large, know exactly what has happened to the princess.

Now the doctors finally share with Prince Rainier how things truly stand with his wife. They had operated on her the day before, opening her chest cavity as well as the abdominal wall. The bleeding from her head wound is very heavy. Her brain damage is serious and permanent. The electroencephalogram to which she is connected and which is measuring her brain waves has, over the course of the day, indicated no brain function. She lies in a coma from which she will never awake. Since 6:00 a.m., she has been, for all intents and purposes, clinically dead. There is no hope.

At this point, the brain damage that could be seen on the scanner images was too serious and extensive. In addition, most of the spots were inoperable. The primary problems were the cerebral bleeding and a contusion to the frontal lobe, as well as bleeding behind the right side of the brain. Even if she were, contrary to expectations, to wake up from the coma, in all likelihood, she would lack almost all mental capabilities.

The family comes to bid farewell. After son Albert and daughter Caroline have said their good-byes, Rainier stays behind, alone with his wife. They had spent twenty-six years together. At noon, Rainier gives the doctors permission to turn off the life support machines, which have until now kept his wife's body functioning. It is a difficult decision in a lonely hour.

On September 14, 1982, at 10:35 p.m., the actress Grace Kelly, the Princess of Monaco, Gracia Patricia, dies. At the age of fifty-two, she is much too young.

Only at this point does the world learn of what has occurred.

Interrupting her vacation in Germany, Monaco's longtime palace press chief Nadia LaCoste left her husband behind and returned straightaway to Monaco: "I was on vacation when I heard—I simply could not believe it!"[433]

And now LaCoste had to provide her press office with palace communiqués for the hosts of international journalists, reporters, photographers, and television teams that arrived in the principality: "I still remember how the newspaper reporters tried to climb into my office through a window. My press office was located above the park between the casino and the tourist information bureau. On the park side, the windows were protected by tall bars. They were really pretty high. They tried to climb over them because they wanted to get into my office. It was unbelievable how many of them were over there in the park. Each time, whenever there was something to announce, I went outside and simply shared it with them. It was a nightmare..."[434]

Parallel to these developments, Robert Dornhelm had already left Monaco after the weekend he had spent at Roc Agel. "We had made off to meet on the day of her death. At her place in Paris."[435] On Tuesday, September 14.

On Monday, September 13, he had waited for a sign from Grace. No calls. No news. Nothing.

"I waited on her. That evening, the call came through that she had been in an accident. That she had broken her leg, but everything was in order and under control. It was the secretary from one castle or another. Then six hours later, in the middle of the night, a phone call from America woke me up. At first, I was irritated. It was a friend, Bram Roos, the producer of the planned *Wallenberg* film: 'I am so very sorry, and it is so awful, and I don't

300

know how to tell you.' And I said: 'What?' 'About Grace.' 'Yes, I know that she broke her leg.' 'No, oh God, she's dead.' Then I said: 'I hate the American media. How can you say that to a friend?! She hasn't died. She broke her leg.' 'Wake up.' I did not want to believe this. Then he said: 'No, it was in all the media, in all the news, it is everywhere. They could not show that if it weren't true.' I said: 'It can't possibly be true. I wanted to meet her tomorrow.' "[436]

The fact that all of these rumors circulated in the immediate aftermath of the tragic event resulted in a difficult existential burden that has accompanied the Grimaldis ever since. As Nadia LaCoste argued, "In a certain sense, it is easy to say: 'She did this and that, and therefore, she lost control of the car.' No, the actual wonder is that Stéphanie survived at all."[437]

On a related note, Thomas Veszelits provided commentary: "Grace Kelly's death is no mystery. A mystery arose from it— just as it did with Lady Di. An accident is always something incomprehensible. If she had died of cancer, that would have been an entirely normal death. However, these accidents. There again as the fatal parallel to Lady Di—again, an accident. Was the driver drunk? Did he drive too fast? Did he have to flee from the paparazzi? After Grace Kelly's fatal accident, it was just as inexplicable. And why did the brakes fail? There were rumors at that time that Rainier was being blackmailed by the Mafia. These pre-dated the accident, but then suddenly they escalated. There are things that simply cannot be fathomed. There are these three great mysteries: John F. Kennedy's murder, Grace Kelly's accident, Lady Di's accident. The amazing thing is that these three individuals set television records. Television was still in its infancy, so Kennedy's burial, which was aired worldwide, became the first great media event of its kind. The second great media event was the burial of Grace Kelly that was aired from the cathedral in Monaco. The third was finally Lady Di's in 1997."[438]

And further: "She was simply hungover. They had drunk, as they always did on those weekends, and this time they had also argued because Stéphanie wanted to suddenly become a race-car driver, thanks to the Belmondo son. The Princess never saw that curve. Furthermore, she was a verifiably bad driver. If you overlook these hairpin curves, there is simply nothing you can do about it anymore. It happened with lightning speed. At that time, the curve was also not secured. The guardrail was only two iron posts and some stone blocks, and to come across them—it was simply and plainly an accident due to the residual effects of alcohol. This conjecture builds on the police report: no blood test was ever performed. Normally, even during the 1980s, blood tests were done after accidents. Although the accident took place on French soil, because it was the Princess, the police from Monaco were immediately there. They sent the French home and said that they themselves would take care of things. Furthermore, the wrecked car rested on Monegasque soil, in that garden. It was also claimed that the brakes failed. This information was contained in the first protocol. The accident investigation by Rover, the English company, also indicated that. Of course, it must have terrified the Princess when the brakes failed in that car. The first press releases gave brake failure as the cause of the accident. That is what was written in the first police report."[439]

The discrepancy between the details contained in the police investigative report and the various witness accounts continue to perplex today.

Nothing can be substantiated.

The discussion about whether or not Grace Kelly would have hypothetically allowed her daughter Stéphanie to drive has not yet vanished, even today, regardless of the official assertion that Grace was in the driver's seat. It is known that at Roc Agel, Rainier and Grace permitted daughter Stéphanie to drive the few yards between the yard and the driveway. However, Stéphanie was not allowed to drive outside of the property.

As Thomas Veszelits said, "It is proven that there was no change in the driver. Stéphanie herself was injured, so it was not possible to change places. She was not driving. She denied that numerous times, choosing to personally speak about it. The media and the press hyped this up too much."[440]

And Rolf Palm explained: "Over the previous years, Grace Kelly had undergone intense cortisone treatments. Cortisone has various side effects. In this case, it was cerebral apoplexy, an aneurysm. A vein burst in her head. This was also not the first car that had fallen off the cliff. The gardener's first reaction was: 'What? Again?'" And further: "Grace was not the type to have permitted that. Based on purely psychological reasons and on her character, it is totally impossible that she allowed Stéphanie to drive the car. Grace would have never let that happen."[441]

Nadia LaCoste concurred with this: "She would never have let Stéphanie take the wheel. In addition, she was much too upset. If they had wanted to teach Stéphanie to drive, she would never have done that on *this* road. And the dreadful thing was that she herself should not have been driving. But she wanted to go to Paris, and she had the dresses from Roc Agel that she wanted to take back to Monaco. She had those packed on the back seat, and she told the driver: 'I will drive down myself. Come with the other car.' So that the clothes could be stored nicely, she drove. On the drive up [before the weekend], the palace chauffeur had driven. Normally, they would not have been driving themselves. She did not like to drive at all. Thus, you can talk of fate..."[442] In addition, "I never read anything about a stroke. And I never heard of one. At the time, I talked with the doctors, and none of them mentioned anything like that. It was caused by the accident."[443]

"What changed in reality? Absolutely nothing. She is dead. She was truly a devoted mother, a mother who sacrificed herself for her children."[444]

In the chapel of the Prince's Palace, high on a rocky point, Gracia Patricia's open coffin, surrounded by candles and countless white flowers and watched over by two palace guards, is visited by countless people who wish to have one last look at her. They have come to say farewell to their princess, the mother of their country. It is also a farewell to a legendary actress and beauty icon.

A longtime palace merchant was quoted, saying quite poetically, "She is physically not here, but she lives among us."[445]

She was laid out for three days, September 15–17. Since her head had been shaved in the hospital for the CT scans and for any potential brain surgeries, an artificial blonde wig covered her head. It also helped to conceal her serious head wound. Her appearance, with the wig (which was pulled too far down on her forehead) disconcerted her siblings and her former brides-maids, Judith, Rita, Maree, and others. A rosary was clasped in her folded hands. She was wearing a long silk dress, the pale Dior ball gown that had been on the backseat of the Rover on the day of the accident.

On September 18, the coffin is ceremoniously carried several hundred yards to the Notre-Dame-Immaculée Cathedral, Saint Nicholas, and at regular intervals, a bell sounds a single tone. This solemn sound echoes through the streets, landing heavily upon the slow, advancing funeral procession.

Rainier followed the casket, flanked by Albert and Caroline. His gait slightly resembled a ponderous stagger. An indescribable weight rested across everything. It was an image of a visibly grief-stricken man. As Robert Dornhelm remembered, "Rainier was a broken man. The pictures that you see—they are truly distressing, and they speak volumes."[446] Those pictures of the father and two of his children—also the way in which they sat together as a trio in the cathedral in front of her casket. Rainier repeatedly reached for his handkerchief, and once Caroline laid her hand on his arm, and he briefly looked over at her. These pictures traveled around the world and were burned into collective memory.

Approximately 100 million people around the world sat in front of their television screens. To date, this was one of the larg-est audiences ever. This was the onset of a kind of worldwide mourning and empathy. A global phenomenon.

Among the eight hundred invited funeral guests were included dignitaries from around the world, including Nancy Reagan, Danielle Mitterrand, and Princess Diana. Politicians and mem-bers of the upper aristocracy, many of whom had remained absent from the 1956 wedding, much to Rainier's chagrin. The salvaging of Monaco's once tarnished reputation by Grace Kelly was made clear once more at her own funeral: "It was a ceremonial act, an official goodbye."[447] Longtime friends arrived, such as the deeply shaken Cary Grant and Sam Spiegel as well as her friends from America, her former bridesmaids. Once again they stayed in the Hôtel de Paris. And some of her family came, the Kellys of Philadelphia: Grace's sisters, Peggy and Lizanne, and their brother, Kell. Seven years before, in 1975, mother Margaret Majer-Kelly had suffered a serious stroke, and since that time, she had been mentally incapacitated. Never, even up to her death in January 1990, did she ever register the fact that her world-renowned daughter had died. None of them wanted to believe that Grace, their *little Gracie*, was dead. Disbelief and paralysis were widespread.

"It was not real to me," related Robert Dornhelm.[448] After receiving the news in Paris, he traveled to Nice, and like most of the funeral guests, he was flown from there by helicopter to the heliport in Monaco.

In accord with Rainier's wish, on September 21, Gracia Patricia of Monaco was laid to rest in the cathedral choir. She was the first princess to be buried there.

Stéphanie did not attend the burial, since at this time she was still in the hospital in a plaster cast. Paul Belmondo was with her. She had to live with the knowledge that not only was her mother dead but she, Stéphanie, would not have the opportunity to say farewell to her. It was doubly traumatic.

And then the haunting questions arose. Could the events have happened other than they did? Could Grace have taken the clothes at another time so that Christian Silvestri could have driven the car? As Nadia LaCoste commented, "It was dreadful, but such is fate. She could have laid the clothes out and said: 'Alright, tomorrow we will send another car for them...'"[449] The torturous "what if" questions would haunt Grace's family and friends for many years.

Born on February 1, 1965, as the youngest of the three children, Princess Stéphanie of Monaco was only seventeen years old at the time of the accident, and for many years, she seemed to lack inner peace. Her numerous, mostly unhappy romantic relationships seem to point to this. Also, her repeated attempts to establish herself in the creative-artistic realm have, in the end, never lasted. She worked in fashion; she designed her own swimsuit collection; she worked for Dior; she worked as a model.

She also tried to become a pop singer, recording the album *Ouragan* in 1986. The LP actually landed on the international top ten list. With the album's catchy single "Irrésistible," she made it onto the charts of several European countries. In France, the song stayed on the charts for twenty-nine weeks; in Germany, it lasted for eighteen weeks. One other song from the album, "One Love to Give," also climbed the hit charts. In 1991, she released a second, not nearly as successful album under the simple title, *Stéphanie*. That year, she also recorded the song "In the Closet" with Michael Jackson, which was included on his album *Dangerous*.

In recent years, Prince Stéphanie has engaged in the fight against AIDS; she established the Fight AIDS Monaco organization, of which she is president. In the context of this work, she contributed to the 2006 benefit song "L'or de nos vies," the proceeds of which were given to the Monegasque foundation.

The fateful events of that September day in 1982 have been with her ever since.

Again and again, in connection with the death of Grace Kelly and the repercussions suffered by Princess Stéphanie—as well as in reference to her father, Prince Rainier, who lived alone as a widower until his death in April 2005, choosing not to remarry—the Grimaldi curse is mentioned. The curse that first appeared in the late thirteenth century.

Robert Dornhelm had the following to say about Grace Kelly's death: "I marveled at the fact she went so young, but actually I was not really surprised. Because of the fear that what she stood for, what she had done, would become watered down. For her to become an old woman, living unhappily in the castle and possibly becoming bitter and unfulfilled, that would not have suited her. She was a star, in the sense that she always absorbed the light that shone on her and in turn, she glowed back. The fact that she died so young fits well with the myth. Although she always joked that once she was old she could finally ride the Métro without being recognized, the issue of growing old was only talk. I never really believed that it would happen. It was part of her romanticism to imagine being someone else."[450]

Only seven weeks before her unexpected death on July 22, 1982, Princess Grace gave her final interview. She sat outside in the garden palace and talked for an hour with journalist Pierre Salinger. The interview was for *20/20* on ABC.

When Salinger surprised her at one point with a question about how she would like to be remembered in the future, she answered: "I would like to be remembered as someone who accomplished useful deeds, and who was a kind and loving person."[451]

And it was as if her words contained a quiet premonition of a premature farewell.

The grave of Grace Kelly, Princess Gracia Patricia of Monaco, can be found in the Cathedral of St. Nicholas high up on Le Rocher. The steps to the cathedral command a stunning view of the azure blue sea and the horizon. Grace and Prince Rainier III were married there. Now they are both buried there, side by side.

Groups of tourists from all around the world come time and time again to the cathedral. They are led through the sacred building, which is now part of the *Parcours Princesse Grace*, the Grace Kelly Trail, in Monaco. This path crosses the principality, and along it, twenty-five photographic panels have been installed at various places. In the cathedral, the tourists finally come to rest at one spot; at the end of the choir gallery on the left side are the royal graves.

Here lies Grace Kelly.

In simple Latin letters, one can read:

GRACIA PATRICIA
PRINCIPIS RAINERII III UXOR
OBIIT ANN. DNI. MDMLXXXII

Here, at this gravestone, ends the life story of the girl from Henry Avenue in Philadelphia. The American girl who became a princess.

The pre-Christian, Roman poet Titus Plautus supposedly once said, "He whom the gods love dies young."

The gods must have loved Grace Kelly.

—AFTERWORD

Conversation with Prince Albert II of Monaco

—Thilo Wydra:
What comes into your mind first, Your Highness, as her son, when you think about your mother, Princess Grace?

—Prince Albert II:
Of course—and I do think I am speaking for my sisters as well—what comes into our mind straightaway mostly is our mother. She was a princess also, she was an incredible and generous person, gave her time to others. She was also very involved with humanitarian and charitable activities. That's also very much there—but how we remember her straightaway is, of course, how she was as a mother. And she was very loving, very careful—it's her generosity which was part of her character and her spirit. What a wonderful life we had with her. The incredible thing, and I'm sure we will come back to it in the conversation, but it still amazes me how many lives she touched with her personality, her generosity—still today. That still has a meaning, it still has value, the fact that people identify with her, still do. This incredible connection that, I think, got through the generations. She is still relevant. She still means something to the younger generations.

Could you define the attitude, which your mother had toward life? It seemed to be a very special, graceful attitude.
Graceful—yes. It's hard to put it into words, and it's hard to really describe it in the right way. But of course she was…she really knew how to listen to people and how to connect with people. As you said, in a very graceful way, in a very touching way. And I don't think that anybody who's…that I have known…wears her name like she did. She really had grace and kindness in her attitude towards people. So, yes, she really knew how to listen to people, how to comfort them, she loved sharing things about her

education, with other children, with other women or with other people. Learning more about their lives, listening to their problems. She really revelled in that, she was... that also gave her a lot of energy and meaning, this contact with other people.

Actually one could gain the impression that she was a very sensitive person, who could feel the emotions of other people, who could realize their feelings or thoughts. And at the same time, besides her sensitivity, she seemed to be very strong, of a strong will. Which, at first glance, seems to be a contradiction, but which might not be at all.

Absolutely. She had that inner strength, that ability to stand on her own and to stand by her convictions, but yet she was incredibly sensitive to the world around her, to other people, to other people's unhappiness or stress or... I think that's why she loved her work for very charitable organisations. She tried to help other people in a very genuine way. But also to other friends of hers, if they had problems in their lives, she also tried to, very discreetly, but... so she had that great sensibility, this loving nature.

Do you know where this nature came from? Also this wish to help people, to be there for others?

I think it is most probably through her upbringing, values that she had already in her family—my grandparents. My grandmother was also a very strong character, she was also very intent to the need of others... and for my mother, those were really great, strong memories that also shaped her. But I think my mother, because of the fact that she was exposed to a lot of other cultures as well, she managed to travel to other parts of the world even before marrying my father and becoming Princess Grace of Monaco, she already had a keen sense of what the world was about. And how she could help.

Highness, you just mentioned your grandparents, John B. Kelly, who was Irish, and Margaret Majer, who was German. So, apparently, there are several contacts to Germany—can you remember your grandmother, Margaret?

Yes, very well. In fact, I was one of the last of the family to have seen her. She was in a nursing home. So I went there once, before she passed away. But she was an incredible lady, too. Very strong, very sort of no-nonsense with us kids. We visited her mostly in the summer time. She would always welcome us and cook for us, and be there for us, but she'd discipline us, too, so...

Did your mother tell you very much about her parents, your grandparents?

Yes, but more about my grandfather, about John B. Kelly, because I hardly knew him. He died when I was two years. So unfortunately—and I always regretted not to have known him better and not to have been able to have some conversations with him. He's a legendary figure, not only in our family, but throughout the United States. But he was also a very generous man, also had that spirit of entrepreneurship. Making it, on his own, in a country where he wasn't born yet he built his career pretty quickly. And I think also that that side, the Irish side of the family is also very important. We are all very proud of that heritage, as we are of the German side, too. But I think that also adds to the fact of the character of, you know, being generous, and Irish people are usually very generous in spirit and heart and so on, so that's an added dimension to it.

So—it's a good mixture. Did your mother speak German a little bit?

Yes, a little bit. You know, I think she explained it, of course my grandmother tried to teach them German. I think there was a War Resistance at that time. So, especially when the War Years came, it was a different attitude. But I think that's why she encouraged us, her kids—Stéphanie not so much, although she understands a bit, but Caroline and myself—so she encouraged us to speak German, also probably because she gave that up too soon. So I wound up saying a few words once in a while, in German, to my grandmother...but she didn't want to speak it, she didn't want to have a single conversation. But also because she lost a bit of practice over the years. She sort of humored us once in a while.

Did your mother speak to you about her former strong wish to become an actress?

Yes, a little bit. She would start by saying that it was because of her interest in the theatre. And at first it was—as it is for a lot of actors—that wonderful thrill of performing in front of live audiences, so she really enjoyed that part, the theatre acting, her theatre years. And, of course, she went to the American Academy of Dramatic Arts. During that full time she was exposed to a lot of different roles, a lot of different, great theatre experiences...I think she really enjoyed studying plays, learning lines, and acting, and both the other actors and the directors wanted her to continue. But it's true that at first...well, I was told when I asked my grandmother, that no one in the family seriously believed that she would become an actress. She was sort of shy, and she had a great disposition, but not really a typical personality for an actress. And I think it helped her also to overcome her shyness.

Would you call it something like a kind of "vocation"?

Well, I think it's something...I think...it became pretty apparent rapidly that she would embrace that career. So, I don't think she would have done anything else than that with her life.

Did she speak about the movies she used to shoot?

Yes, and I did ask her a few questions about it. I was probably the one of the three children that asked her the most about it. What was it like? What was Clark Gable like? What was James Stewart like? And Cary Grant. And of course I met Cary Grant, and Alfred Hitchcock. Yes, you know, it was interesting. Because also I was interested, even more so when I started taking film criticism courses when I was at Amherst. I did some film and literature courses there. She was happy that I took interest in that. But I probably had more questions after, as I was taking these courses. She wouldn't want...I think it's because she wouldn't want to bore us with it. Although she was very proud of what she did, she wanted to emphasize more her activities now, more than stories of the past. But she was very happy to share some of these...great memories...

You met Alfred Hitchcock personally?

Yes. But I was probably still too young to appreciate him. He was always very kind to us children and he had a great sense of humour. Incredible personality—always very calm, very British, very dry sense of humour, but incredibly kind.

Can you kind of make out why this relationship—on a working level and as a deep friendship—between your mother and Alfred Hitchcock, where this came from, where the roots of this are to be found?

I think it's because—and this was referred to several times in interviews with Alfred Hitchcock or his critics or his biographers—that this was his ideal leading lady. One, that was very blonde, very innocent, but fragile...and sometimes referred to as a cold lady... But that's what he liked. But also because he was able to show that...of course, my mother, but the other leading ladies as well, Kim Novak, Tippi Hedren...that they also have a personality, they could also be strong. I think he liked those contrasts, that things and people are really not secure in a way, are not always what they appear. That's a great strength of vision to be able to show that, to want to show that.

Do you know if the friendship between your mother and Alfred Hitchcock lasted until Hitchcock's death in 1980?

Oh yes, very very much so. She was so...well you saw there some of the letters that were shown in the exhibition—but there were other, more personal letters that we didn't show. But, you know, of course they stayed very, very close. And she was very affected by Hitchcock. I am sure that if she could have, she would have made more movies with him. You know he was thinking about her for *Marnie*, but also she was supposed to be in *North by Northwest*.

Did your mother tell you something about the Marnie *conflict from 1962?*

She never talked about it too much because I think maybe it was sort of a difficult subject for her, as she really would have loved to play that part, but of course, she realized that it would have been awkward and it wouldn't have pleased my father too much, and so I am sure that she regretted that but...

Did your father, Prince Rainier, support her in this aim or was it rather kind of difficult for him?

I think he wasn't completely opposed to it but, you know, he was kind of...in-between, but I think that he also realized that here in Monaco it probably would not have been very well-accepted and he had to accept that after thinking about it. I think it would have been a very difficult situation for her, and he didn't want to be in that kind of situation either. And he was also at the time having some difficulties with France, as you recall. So I think he didn't want to add fuel to that fire.

You just mentioned Hitchcock's North by Northwest *as well...*

Yes—Hitchcock had thought of her for that role...but, she was a mother then, and it was difficult for her for other reasons also. I think she would have wanted that. Maybe not as much as *Marnie*, but...

Two shorter questions: Do you have a favorite movie of your mother? And, second, did she have a favorite of her own?

I'll start with her. I think she was very pleased with her performance in *The Country Girl*, but I don't think it was her favourite movie. I am not sure, which one was...I think she liked herself in different scenes in different movies. I think she also liked— [and that's my favorite]—overall she liked *Rear Window*. That's not why it's my favourite movie, because I like them all, not only because of her, but it's a study of, you know, voyeurism and social behaviour, and psychological intensity.

Claude Chabrol once said that this court and the apartments at the other side of it do offer several proposals of how to lead your life—and James Stewart and Grace Kelly are confronted with these various proposals.

Oh, yes, absolutely, very interesting—fascinating!

What would be important for you to be written in a book about your mother? What would be your wish?

Well, I think it's great...thank you for making this tribute to my mother and showing some aspects of her life and her personality that aren't as well-known as others. And I know that it's very heart-warming to us that there is such a [regard] still towards my mother around the world; I think she would be very proud, very fortunate to have you write a book that shows her as the incredible being that she was.

—APPENDIX

Endnotes

All the author's interviews were recorded on cassette. All the documents quoted throughout this book were reproduced or copied.

1   Yann-Brice Dherbier/Pierre-Henri Verlhac (Hrsg.): Grace Kelly. Bilder eines Lebens. Berlin 2006, S. 18.

2   J. Randy Taraborrelli: Grace Kelly und Fürst Rainier. Ein Hollywoodmärchen in Monaco. Frankfurt am Main 2004, S. 41..

3   Television Documentary. The Hollywood Collection: Grace Kelly—The American Princess. 1987.

4   Suzanne Lander (Editor). Grace Kelly. Eine Hommage in Fotografien, Berlin: Schwarzkopf + Schwarzkopf, 2009, p 23.

5   In some sources, he is referenced under the name Yves Phily.

6   James Spada: Grace. Das geheime Vorleben einer Fürstin. Berlin 1996, S. 375.

7   Conversation between the author and Prince Albert II of Monaco. Royal Palace, Monaco, November 28, 2011.

8   Wendy Leigh. True Grace: The Life and Times of an American Princess. New York: St. Martin's Griffin, 2007, p. 11.

9   Heppenheim Municipal Archives, Archival Documents: Genealogy. "Weitere Nachträge zur Ahnenliste der Fürstin Grace Patricia von Monaco geb. Kelly"; Ernst Löslein: V., Zur Ahnenschaft von Margaretha Berg. Volume 8, Folder 4, April 1967, p. 694–702.

10 Conversation between the author and Harald E. Jost, Heppenheim Municipal Archives. August 2, 2011, in Heppenheim.

11 Ibid.

12 Stadtarchiv Heppenheim, Archiv-Unterlagen: Auszug aus dem Taufregister des Jahres 1870.

13 Ibid. "Konvolut Grace Kelly." Notice to the Mayor. Supplement to Short Notice Nr. 5957 v. 23. 3. 1956; 26. 3. 1956, p. 2.

14 Ibid. Excerpt from the Baptism Register of 1870.

15 Ibid. "Konvolut Grace Kelly." Notice to the Mayor. Supplement to Short Notice Nr. 5957 v. 23. 3. 1956; 26. 3. 1956, p. 1.

16 Ibid. p. 1 ff.

17 Conversation between the author and Harald E. Jost, Heppenheim Municipal Archives. August 2, 2011, in Heppenheim.

18 Heppenheim Municipal Archives, Archival Documents. "Konvolut Grace Kelly." Letter from the Foreign Office, Bonn, dated May 2, 1956.

19 Ibid. "Konvolut Grace Kelly." Typescript of the Kelly Visit, dated April 21, 1958. p. 1 ff.

20 Ibid.

21 Ibid. Bergsträßer Anzeiger vom 16. 3. 1999, Nr. 62.

22 Ibid. Typescript of the Kelly visit, dated April 21, 1958. p. 1 ff.

23 Sources for this information include: Website www.findagrave.com/cgi-bin/fg.cgi?page=gr&GRid=17693 755: Grabstein der Familie Kelly – Margaret Majer, Dec. 13, 1898 – Jan. 6, 1990/Website: www.genealogylookups.com/gedcoms/psmonaco/fam00050.htm.

24 Sarah Bradford: Gracia Patricia. Fürstin von Monaco. Bergisch Gladbach 1985, S. 31.

25 Sources for this information include: Website www.findagrave.com/cgi-bin/fg.cgi?page=gr&GRid=7467 719: Grabstein der Familie Kelly – John Brendan Oct. 4, 1889 – June 20, 1960/Stadtarchiv Heppenheim, Archiv-Unterlagen: Genealogie. C. Frederick Kaufholz: Die deutschen Ahnen der Fürstin von Monaco, Grace Patricia geb. Kelly; Band 7, Heft 1, Januar/Februar 1964, S. 2; Wendy Leigh: True Grace. The Life and Times of an American Princess. New York 2007, S. 6.

26 Conversation between the author and Prince Albert II of Monaco. Royal Palace, Monaco, November 28, 2011.

27 Donald Spoto. High Society. The Life of Grace Kelly. New York: Harmony Books, 2009. p. 16.

28 Conversations between the author and Robert Dornhelm. Mougins near Cannes on May 13. and 21, 2011, Munich on September 7, 2011.

29 Ibid.

30 Wendy Leigh. True Grace: The Life and Times of an American Princess. New York, 2007, p. 11.

31 Ibid.

32 Conversation between the author and Mary Louise Murray-Johnson. Heidelberg on August 3, 2011.

33 Ibid.

34 Conversation between the author and Prince Albert II of Monaco. Royal Palace, Monaco, November 28, 2011.

35 Gant Gaither: Fürstin von Monaco. Bern/Stuttgart/Wien 1957, S. 9.

36 Zitiert nach: Gwen Robyns: Gracia Patricia, Fürstin von Monaco. München 1981, S. 28.

37 Wendy Leigh: True Grace. The Life and Times of an American Princess. New York 2007, S. 10 ff.

38 Among others: TV Documentary, Legenden—Grace Kelly, ARD/MDR 2002.

39 Gregor Ball: Grace Kelly. Ihre Filme – ihr Leben. München 1983, S. 22.

40 Website: www.findagrave.com/cgi-bin/fg.cgi?page=gr&GRid=7 467 719: Gravestone of the Kelly family with birth and death dates (Often the birth

dates of the parents, as well as of Grace Kelly's older sister, Margaret K. "Peggy" Kelly Conlan, are wrongly identified in the literature.)

41 Conversation between the author and Mary Louise Murray-Johnson. Heidelberg on August 3, 2011.

42 Gwen Robbins, Grace Patricia, Princess of Monaco. Munich 1981, S. 5, untitled and undated, probably very early forties, from her time at the convent school in Ravenhill, Philadelphia, written around the age of eleven or twelve years.

43 James Spada. Grace: The Secret Lives of a Princess. Thorndike, Maine: Thorndike-Magna, 1987.

44 Conversations between the author and Robert Dornhelm. Mougins near Cannes on May 13 and 21, 2011, Munich on September 7, 2011.

45 Ibid.

46 Conversation between the author and Mary Louise Murray-Johnson. Heidelberg on August 3, 2011.

47 Ibid.

48 Conversation between the author and Prince Albert II of Monaco. Royal Palace, Monaco, November 28, 2011.

49 James Spada: Grace. Das geheime Vorleben einer Fürstin. Berlin 1996, S. 29.

50 Television Documentary. The Hollywood Collection: Grace Kelly—The American Princess, 1987.

51 Conversations between the author and Robert Dornhelm. Mougins near Cannes on May 13. and 21, 2011, Munich on September 7, 2011.

52 Television Documentary. The Hollywood Collection: Grace Kelly—The American Princess, 1987.

53 Gwen Robyns: Gracia Patricia, Fürstin von Monaco. München 1981, S. 26.

54 Conversation between the author and Mary Louise Murray-Johnson. Heidelberg on August 3, 2011.

55 Approximate translation of German subtitles. Television Documentary. Secret Lives: Grace Kelly (Gracia Patricia—Der Preis des Ruhms), Channel 41997/ORF 2007/3sat 2011.

56 Frédéric Mitterrand (Editor). Les années Grace Kelly—Princesse de Monaco (Exhibition Catalog). Milan: Grimaldi Forum Monaco, 2007, pp. 37–43.

57 Ibid.

58 Conversation between the author and Mary Louise Murray-Johnson. Heidelberg on August 3, 2011.

59 Sarah Bradford: Gracia Patricia. Fürstin von Monaco. Bergisch Gladbach 1985, S. 65..

60 Conversation between the author and Prince Albert II of Monaco. Royal Palace, Monaco, November 28, 2011.

61 Gant Gaither: Fürstin von Monaco. Bern/Stuttgart/Wien 1957, S. 10.

62 James Spada: Grace. Das geheime Vorleben einer Fürstin. Berlin 1996, S. 60.

63 Conversations between the author and Robert Dornhelm. Mougins near Cannes on May 13. and 21, 2011, Munich on September 7, 2011.

64 Sarah Bradford: Gracia Patricia. Fürstin von Monaco. Bergisch Gladbach 1985, S. 67.

65 James Spada: Grace. Das geheime Vorleben einer Fürstin. Berlin 1996, S. 41.

66 Approximate translation of German subtitles. Television Documentary. Secret Lives: Grace Kelly (Gracia Patricia—Der Preis des Ruhms), Channel 41997/ORF 2007/3sat 2011.

67 Yann-Brice Dherbier/Pierre-Henri Verlhac (Hrsg.): Grace Kelly. Bilder eines Lebens. Berlin 2006, S. 32.

68 Approximate translation of German subtitles. Television Documentary Secret Lives: Grace Kelly (Gracia Patricia—Der Preis des Ruhms), Channel 41997/ORF 2007/3sat 2011.

69 Ibid.

70 Conversations between the author and Robert Dornhelm. Mougins near Cannes on May 13 and 21, 2011, Munich on September 7, 2011.

71 J. Randy Taraborrelli: Grace Kelly und Fürst Rainier. Ein Hollywoodmärchen in Monaco. Frankfurt am Main 2004, S. 31.

72 Conversations between the author and Robert Dornhelm. Mougins near Cannes on May 13 and 21, 2011, Munich on September 7, 2011.

73 James Spada: Grace. Das geheime Vorleben einer Fürstin. Berlin 1996, S. 354.

74 Ibid.

75 Conversations between the author and Robert Dornhelm. Mougins near Cannes on May 13 and 21, 2011, Munich on September 7, 2011.

76 James Spada: Grace. Das geheime Vorleben einer Fürstin. Berlin 1996, S. 53.

77 Ibid. p. 51.

78 Conversations between the author and Robert Dornhelm. Mougins near Cannes on May 13 and 21, 2011, Munich on September 7, 2011.

79 See Appendix, Filmography, p. 337.

80 According to James Spada: "In all, she appeared in over sixty television shows in two years…" Both the span of years and the number of appearances are inaccurate. James Spada. Grace: The Secret Lives of a Princess. Thorndike, Maine: Thorndike-Magna, 1987, p. 88. Sarah Bradford claimed the following: "Grace acted in some one hundred television plays." Sarah Bradford. Princess Grace. New York: Stein and Day, 1984, p. 58. See Appendix: Filmography.

81 Donald Spoto: High Society. The Life of Grace Kelly. New York 2009, S. 50.

82 Conversations between the author and Robert Dornhelm. Mougins near Cannes on May 13 and 21, 2011, Munich on September 7, 2011.

83 Yann-Brice Dherbier/Pierre-Henri Verlhac (Hrsg.): Grace Kelly. Bilder eines Lebens. Berlin 2006, S. 42.

84 Conversation between the author and Prince Albert II of Monaco. Royal Palace, Monaco, November 28, 2011.

85 Jan Knopf (Hrsg.): Bertolt Brecht. Die Gedichte. Frankfurt am Main 2007.

86 Conversations between the author and Robert Dornhelm. Mougins near Cannes on May 13 and 21, 2011, Munich on September 7, 2011.

87 Approximate translation of German subtitles. Television Documentary. Secret Lives: Grace Kelly (Gracia Patricia—Der Preis des Ruhms), Channel 41997/ORF 2007/3sat 2011.

88 Television Documentary. The Hollywood Collection: Grace Kelly—The American Princess. 1987.

89 Conversations between the author and Robert Dornhelm. Mougins near Cannes on May 13 and 21, 2011, Munich on September 7, 2011.

90 Conversation between the author and Prince Albert II of Monaco. Royal Palace, Monaco, November 28, 2011.

91 James Spada: Grace. Das geheime Vorleben einer Fürstin. Berlin 1996, S. 68.

92 Fourteen Hours, 1951. DVD Fox 2006.

93 Suzanne Lander (Hrsg.): Grace Kelly. Eine Hommage in Fotografien. Berlin 2009, S. 79.

94 Fred Zinnemann: An Autobiography. London 1992, S. 100.

95 Ibid.

96 Ibid.

97 Dimitri Tiomkin. Please Don't Hate Me. Garden City: Doubleday & Company, 1959, p. 234.

98 Fred Zinnemann: An Autobiography. London 1992, S. 109.

99 James Spada: Grace. Das geheime Vorleben einer Fürstin. Berlin 1996, S. 83.

100 Hector Arce: Gary Cooper. An Intimate Biography. New York 1979, S. 210.

101 http://www.filmsite.org/high.html (Visited February 20, 2014)

102 http://en.wikiquote.org/wiki/High_Noon (Visited February 20, 2014)

103 Suzanne Lander (Hrsg.): Grace Kelly. Eine Hommage in Fotografien. Berlin 2009, S. 78.

104 Conversations between the author and Robert Dornhelm. Mougins near Cannes on May 13. and 21, 2011, Munich on September 7, 2011.

105 René Jordan: Gary Cooper. Seine Filme – sein Leben. München 1981, S. 138.

106 Ibid.

107 James Spada. Grace: The Secret Lives of a Princess. Thorndike, Maine: Thorndike-Magna, 1987, p. 105.

108 James Spada: Grace. Das geheime Vorleben einer Fürstin. Berlin 1996, S. 81/ Wendy Leigh: True Grace. The Life and Times of an American Princess. New York 2007, S. 55.

109 Ibid.

110 High Noon, 1952. ("Do Not Forsake Me, Oh My Darlin'," 1952. Composer: Dimitri Tiomkin, Lyricist: Ned Washington, Performed by: Tex Ritter).

111 Robert Lacey: Grace. London 1994, S. 115.

112 Larry Swindell: The Last Hero. A Biography of Gary Cooper. Garden City 1980, S. 272 f.

113 Fred Zinnemann: An Autobiography. London 1992, S. 97.

114 Siehe hierzu auch: Philipp Drummond: Zwölf Uhr mittags. Mythos und Geschichte eines Filmklassikers. Hamburg/Wien 2000, S. 104 ff.

115 Television Documentary. The Hollywood Collection: Grace Kelly—The American Princess. 1987.

116 Suzanne Lander (Hrsg.): Grace Kelly. Eine Hommage in Fotografien. Berlin 2009, S. 88.

117 René Jordan: Clark Gable. Seine Filme – sein Leben. München 1986, S. 146.

118 Mogambo, 1953. DVD Warner 2004.

119 Donald Sinden. A Touch of the Memoirs. London: Hodder & Stoughton, 1982.

120 Television Documentary. Die Fürsten von Monaco. 2. Teil: Grace Kelly und Rainier, ZDF, June 16, 2009.

121 Television Documentary. The Hollywood Collection: Grace Kelly—The American Princess. 1987.

122 Translation. Lexikon des internationalen Films. Volume L—N. Hamburg: Reinbek bei, 1995, p. 3896.

123 John Daniell: Ava Gardner. Ihre Filme – ihr Leben. München 1987, S. 81.

124 René Jordan: Clark Gable. Seine Filme – sein Leben. München 1986, S. 150.

125 Oleg Cassini: In My Own Fashion. New York 1987, S. 241.

126 James Spada. Grace. Das geheime Vorleben einer Fürstin. Berlin 1996, p. 88.

127 Donald Sinden: A Touch of the Memoirs. London 1982.

128 Conversation between the author and Patricia Hitchcock. Berlin, Feburary 1997.

129 François Truffaut: Truffaut/Hitchcock. München 1999, S. 17.

130 Ibid.

131 Ibid.

132 Conversation between the author and Claude Chabrol. Berlin, February 9, 2009.

133 François Truffaut: Truffaut/Hitchcock. München 1999.

134 Television show. The Dick Cavett Show, ABC, June 8, 1972. DVD Sony BMG 2006.

135 François Truffaut: Truffaut/Hitchcock. München 1999, S. 184.

136 Television show. The Dick Cavett Show, ABC, June 8, 1972. DVD Sony BMG 2006.

137 Ibid.

138 Thilo Wydra: Alfred Hitchcock. Leben – Werk – Wirkung. Berlin 2010.

139 Suzanne Lander (Hrsg.): Grace Kelly. Eine Hommage in Fotografien. Berlin 2009, S. 92.

140 Conversation between the author and Prince Albert II of Monaco. Royal Palace, Monaco, November 28, 2011.

141 Donald Spoto: High Society. The Life of Grace Kelly. New York 2009, S. 109.

142 Wendy Leigh: True Grace. The Life and Times of an American Princess. New York 2007, S. 71.

143 Donald Spoto: High Society. The Life of Grace Kelly. New York 2009, S. 118.

144 Jeffrey Robinson: Rainier and Grace. London 1989, S. 299.

145 Donald Spoto: High Society. The Life of Grace Kelly. New York 2009, S. 118.

146 Conversation between the author and Brigitte Auber. Paris, May 20, 2010.

147 Los Angeles Times, Elaine Woo: Obituaries, Frederick Knott, 86. 22. 12. 2002.

148 François Truffaut: Truffaut/Hitchcock. München 1999, S. 178.

149 Ibid, p. 128 ff.

150 Wendy Leigh: True Grace. The Life and Times of an American Princess. New York 2007, S. 71.

151 François Truffaut: Truffaut/Hitchcock. München 1999, S. 295.

152 Television Documentary. The Hollywood Collection: Grace Kelly—The American Princess. 1987.

153 Ibid., p. 295.

154 François Truffaut: Truffaut/Hitchcock. München 1999, S. 184.

155 Donald Spoto: High Society. The Life of Grace Kelly. New York 2009, S. 113.

156 Suzanne Lander (Hrsg.): Grace Kelly. Eine Hommage in Fotografien. Berlin 2009, S. 102.

157 Conversation between the author and Prince Albert II of Monaco. Royal Palace, Monaco, November 28, 2011.

158 James Spada: Grace. Das geheime Vorleben einer Fürstin. Berlin 1996, S. 113.

159 Edith Head/Paddy Calistro: Edith Head's Hollywood. Santa Monica 2008, S. 138.

160 Ibid, p. 247.

161 Ibid, p. 137.

162 Ibid, p. 140.

163 Ibid., p. 138f.

164 Rear Window, 1954. DVD Universal 2001.

165 Claude Chabrol/Eric Rohmer: Hitchcock. Paris 1957. 1986, S. 126.

166 François Truffaut: Truffaut/Hitchcock. München 1999, S. 180.

167 Ibid, p. 178.

168 See Appendix, Filmography.

169 Oleg Cassini: In My Own Fashion. New York 1987, S. 238.

170 Ibid.

171 Wendy Leigh: True Grace. The Life and Times of an American Princess. New York 2007, S. 186 f.

172 Conversations between the author and Robert Dornhelm. Mougins near Cannes on May 13 and 21, 2011, Munich on September 7, 2011.

173 James Spada: Grace. Das geheime Vorleben einer Fürstin. Berlin 1996, S. 120.

174 Yann-Brice Dherbier/Pierre-Henri Verlhac (Hrsg.): Grace Kelly. Bilder eines Lebens. Berlin 2006.

175 The Bridges at Toko-Ri. USA 1954. DVD Paramount 2003.

176 Suzanne Lander (Hrsg.): Grace Kelly. Eine Hommage in Fotografien. Berlin 2009, S. 112.

177 Television Documentary. The Hollywood Collection: Grace Kelly—The American Princess. 1987.

178 James Spada: Grace. Das geheime Vorleben einer Fürstin. Berlin 1996, S. 120.

179 Sarah Bradford: Gracia Patricia. Fürstin von Monaco. Bergisch Gladbach 1985, S. 130.

180 Charles Thompson: Bing. London 1976, S. 162.

181 Donald Spoto. High Society. The Life of Grace Kelly. New York: Harmony Books, 2009, p. 156.

182 Ibid.

183 Ibid.

184 Television Documentary. The Hollywood Collection: Grace Kelly—The American Princess. 1987.

185 Edith Head/Paddy Calistro: Edith Head's Hollywood. Santa Monica 2008, S. 137.

186 Ibid.

187 Charles Thompson: Bing. London 1976, S. 164.

188 Robert Lacey: Grace. London 1994, S. 195.

189 Television Documentary. Grace face à son destin (Grace—Film Star and Princess), France 3 2006/Arte 2011.

190 Ibid.

191 Wendy Leigh. True Grace. The Life and Times of an American Princess. New York: St. Martin's Griffin, 2007, p. 95.

192 Ibid, p. 95f.

193 James Spada: Grace. Das geheime Vorleben einer Fürstin. Berlin 1996, S. 129. – Wendy Leigh: True Grace. The Life and Times of an American Princess. New York 2007, S. 88.

194 Robert Lacey: Grace. London 1994, S. 168.

195 Green Fire, 1954.

196 James Spada: Grace. Das geheime Vorleben einer Fürstin. Berlin 1996, S. 129.

197 Robert Lacey: Grace. London 1994, S. 169.

198 Yann-Brice Dherbier/Pierre-Henri Verlhac (Hrsg.): Grace Kelly. Bilder eines Lebens. Berlin 2006, S. 50.

199 Suzanne Lander (Hrsg.): Grace Kelly. Eine Hommage in Fotografien. Berlin 2009, S. 120.

200 Los Angeles Times: "Peggy Robertson. Personal Assistant to Hitchcock," February 12, 1998.

201 Oleg Cassini: In My Own Fashion. New York 1987, S. 253.

202 Paul Duncan: Kelly. Köln 2007, S. 64.

203 Oleg Cassini: In My Own Fashion. New York 1987, S. 248.

204 Ibid, p. 253.

205 Conversation between the author and Brigitte Auber. Paris, May 20, 2010.

206 Letter from Alfred Hitchcock to Grace Kelly, April 14, 1959. Archives of the Royal Palace of Monaco.

207 Unpublished notes of publicist Gero von Boehm on meeting Oleg Cassini in his apartment in New York on September 5, 2001.

208 Oleg Cassini: In My Own Fashion. New York 1987.

209 Ibid.

210 Unpublished notes of publicist Gero von Boehm on meeting Oleg Cassini in his apartment in New York on September 5, 2001.

211 Oleg Cassini: In My Own Fashion. New York 1987, S. 259.

212 Ibid.

213 Television Documentary. Legenden—Grace Kelly, ARD/MDR 2002.

214 Oleg Cassini: In My Own Fashion. New York 1987, S. 261.

215 Television Documentary. Grace face à son destin (Grace—Film Star and Princess), France 3, 2006/Arte, 2011.

216 Oleg Cassini: In My Own Fashion. New York 1987, S. 268.

217 To Catch a Thief, 1955. DVD Paramount 2003.

218 Ibid.

219 Conversation between the author and Brigitte Auber. Paris, May 20, 2010.

220 Ibid.

221 Ibid.

222 Ibid.

223 Ibid.

224 Ibid.

225 Gwen Robyns. Gracia Patricia, Fürstin von Monaco. München: Heyne-Verlag, 1981, S. 10.

226 Edith Head/Paddy Calistro: Edith Head's Hollywood. Santa Monica 2008, S. 139

227 Ibid.

228 Ibid.

229 Ibid.

230 For more details, see the chapter "The First Meeting: Friday, May 6, 4:00 p.m.," p. 185.

231 Suzanne Lander (Hrsg.): Grace Kelly. Eine Hommage in Fotografien. Berlin 2009, S. 23.

232 Robert Lacey: Grace. London 1994, S. 177.

233 François Truffaut: Truffaut/Hitchcock. München 1999, S. 188.

234 Ibid, p. 189.

235 Television Documentary. Grace face à son destin (Grace—Film Star and Princess). France 3, 2006/Arte, 2011.

236 Approximate translation of German subtitles. Television Documentary. Secret Lives: Grace Kelly (Gracia Patricia—Der Preis des Ruhms). Channel 41997/ORF 2007/3sat 2011.

237 Ibid.

238 Conversation between the author and Thomas Veszelits. Munich, June 16, 2011.

239 Der Spiegel. "Der Erbfolge-Krieg." Nr. 10/1953, March 4, 1953, p. 21 ff.

240 Ibid.

241 Conversation between the author and Thomas Veszelits. Munich, June 16, 2011.

242 Approximate translation of German subtitles. Grace face à son destin (Grace—Film Star and Princess). France 3, 2006/Arte, 2011.

243 Approximate translation of German subtitles. Television Documentary Secret Lives: Grace Kelly (Gracia Patricia—Der Preis des Ruhms). Channel 41997/ORF 2007/3sat 2011.

244 Conversation between the author and Thomas Veszelits. Munich, June 16, 2011.

245 Jane Ellen Wayne: Grace Kelly's Men. The Romantic Life of Princess Grace. New York 1991, S. 243.

246 Wendy Leigh: True Grace. The Life and Times of an American Princess. New York 2007, S. 110.

247 Bertrand Meyer-Stabley: La véritable Grace de Monaco. Paris 2007, S. 136.

248 This statement by Marilyn Monroe is quoted in various versions in the source materials. See: Gwen Robyns. Gracia Patricia, Fürstin von Monaco. München: Heyne-Verlag, 1981, S. 186. James Spada. Grace: The Secret Lives of a Princess. Thorndike, Maine: Thorndike-Magna, 1987, S. 289.

249 The Swan, 1956. DVD Carousel 2010.

250 Television Documentary. Legenden—Grace Kelly, ARD/MDR 2002.

251 Donald Spoto: High Society. The Life of Grace Kelly. New York 2009, S. 179.

252 Oleg Cassini: In My Own Fashion. New York 1987, S. 267.

253 Conversation between the author and Nadia LaCoste. Paris, November 21, 2011.

254 James Spada: Grace. Das geheime Vorleben einer Fürstin. Berlin 1996, S. 175.

255 For more information, see the chapter titled "Monaco: A Prince, Three Children, and a Completely Different Life." p. 223.

256 Howell Conant: Grace. Die unveröffentlichten Photographien von Howell Conant. München 2007, S. 66.

257 James Spada: Grace. Das geheime Vorleben einer Fürstin. Berlin 1996, S. 177.

258 The Swan, 1956. DVD Carousel 2010.

259 James Spada: Grace. Das geheime Vorleben einer Fürstin. Berlin 1996, S. 176.

260 Gwen Robyns: Gracia Patricia, Fürstin von Monaco. München 1981, S. 177.

261 Robert Lacey: Grace. London 1994, S. 216.

262 James Spada: Grace. Das geheime Vorleben einer Fürstin. Berlin 1996, S. 177 f. – Randy Taraborrelli: Grace Kelly und Fürst Rainier. Ein Hollywoodmärchen in Monaco. Frankfurt am Main 2004, S. 88 ff.

263 Television Documentary. The Hollywood Collection: Grace Kelly—The American Princess. 1987.

264 Donald Spoto: High Society. The Life of Grace Kelly. New York 2009, S. 220.

265 Television Documentary. The Hollywood Collection: Grace Kelly—The American Princess. 1987.

266 Alec Guinness. Blessings in Disguise. Mosel: München 1986, S. 362 ff.

267 Ibid.

268 Ibid, p. 339.

269 The Swan, 1956. DVD Carousel 2010.

270 Ibid.

271 Conversation between the author and Brigitte Auber. Paris, May 20, 2010.

272 Television Documentary. Grace face à son destin (Grace—Film Star and Princess), France 3, 2006/Arte, 2011.

273 Approximate translation of German subtitles. Television Documentary. Legenden—Grace Kelly, ARD/MDR 2002.

274 Suzanne Lander (Hrsg.): Grace Kelly. Eine Hommage in Fotografien. Berlin 2009, S. 53.

275 Randy Taraborrelli: Grace Kelly und Fürst Rainier. Ein Hollywoodmärchen in Monaco. Frankfurt am Main 2004, S. 128.

276 Ibid, p. 125 ff.

277 Ibid, p. 134.

278 Ibid., p. 134 ff.

279 Television Documentary. Legenden—Grace Kelly, ARD/MDR 2002.

280 Dore Schary: Heyday: An Autobiography. Boston/Toronto 1979, S. 261.

281 Lexikon des Internationalen Films. Band O – R. Reinbek bei Hamburg 1995, S. 4190.

282 Charles Thompson: Bing. London 1976, S. 169.

283 Ibid, p. 167 f.

284 Ibid, p. 170.

285 Conversation between the author and Nadia LaCoste. Paris, November 21, 2011.

286 Yann-Brice Dherbier/Pierre-Henri Verlhac (Hrsg.): Grace Kelly. Bilder eines Lebens. Berlin 2006, S. 108.

287 James Spada: Grace. Das geheime Vorleben einer Fürstin. Berlin 1996, S. 188.

288 The old, early 14th-century curse is expressed differently across a variety of sources.

289 Jean des Cars: La saga des Grimaldi. Paris 2011, S. 10 f.

290 Conversation between the author and Alexander Moghadam, court purveyor of oriental carpets. May 20, 2011, Monaco.

291 Approximate translation of German subtitles. Television documentary. Die Fürsten von Monaco. 2. Teil: Grace Kelly und Rainier. ZDF, 16. 6. 2009.

292 Ibid.

293 Ibid.

294 Conversations between the author and Robert Dornhelm. Mougins near Cannes on May 13. and 21, 2011, Munich on September 7, 2011.

295 Approximate translation of German subtitles. Television documentary. Die Fürsten von Monaco. 2. Teil: Grace Kelly und Rainier, ZDF, 16. 6. 2009.

296 James Spada: Grace. Das geheime Vorleben einer Fürstin. Berlin 1996, S. 225.

297 Ibid.

298 Television Documentary. The Hollywood Collection: Grace Kelly—The American Princess. 1987.

299 Ibid.

300 Conversation between the author and Thomas Veszelits. Munich, June 16, 2011.

301 J. Randy Taraborrelli: Grace Kelly und Fürst Rainier. Ein Hollywoodmärchen in Monaco. Frankfurt am Main 2004, S. 127, 129.

302 Conversation between the author and Thomas Veszelits. Munich, June 16, 2011.

303 Conversations between the author and Robert Dornhelm. Mougins near Cannes on May 13 and 21, 2011, Munich on September 7, 2011.

304 James Spada: Grace. Das geheime Vorleben einer Fürstin. Berlin 1996, S. 279.

305 Conversations between the author and Robert Dornhelm. Mougins near Cannes on May 13 and 21, 2011, Munich on September 7, 2011.

306 Conversation between the author and Thomas Veszelits. Munich, June 16, 2011.

307 Ibid.

308 Conversation between the author and Nadia LaCoste. Paris, November 21, 2011.

309 Conversations between the author and Robert Dornhelm. Mougins near Cannes on May 13 and 21, 2011, Munich on September 7, 2011.

310 Conversation between the author and Nadia LaCoste. Paris, November 21, 2011.

311 Ibid.

312 Ibid.

313 Conversation between the author and Rolf Palm. Monaco, May 20, 2011.

314 Television Documentary. The Hollywood Collection: Grace Kelly—The American Princess. 1987.

315 Conversation between the author and Nadia LaCoste. Paris, November 21, 2011.

316 Ibid.

317 Conversations between the author and Robert Dornhelm. Mougins near Cannes on May 13. and 21, 2011, Munich on September 7, 2011.

318 Ibid.

319 Conversation between the author and Thomas Veszelits. Munich, June 16, 2011.

320 Correspondence between Alfred Hitchcock and Grace Kelly. Letter from June 18, 1962. Archives of the Prince's Palace of Monaco.

321 Conversation between the author and Prince Albert II of Monaco. Royal Palace, Monaco, November 28, 2011.

322 John Hamilton: Hitchcock's Blonde. Grace Kelly and Alfred Hitchcock. Bristol 2009, S. 200.

323 Jeffrey Robinson: Rainier and Grace. London 1989, S. 196.

324 Television Documentary. The Hollywood Collection: Grace Kelly—The American Princess. 1987.

325 Approximate translation of German subtitles. Television Documentary Secret Lives: Grace Kelly (Gracia Patricia—Der Preis des Ruhms). Channel 41997/ORF 2007/3sat 2011.

326 Various sources give conflicting dates of either March 18 or March 19, 1962. However, the evidence seems to show that the announcement was sent on March 18.

327 See: Sarah Bradford: Gracia Patricia. Fürstin von Monaco. Bergisch Gladbach 1985, S. 251. – J. Randy Taraborrelli: Grace Kelly und Fürst Rainier. Ein Hollywoodmärchen in Monaco. Frankfurt 2004, S. 271/John Hamilton: Hitchcock's Blonde. Grace Kelly and Alfred Hitchcock. Bristol 2009, S. 203.

328 Wendy Leigh: True Grace. The Life and Times of an American Princess. New York 2007, S. 197.

329 Approximate translation of German subtitles. Television Documentary Secret Lives: Grace Kelly (Gracia Patricia—Der Preis des Ruhms). Channel 41997/ORF 2007/3sat 2011.

330 Peter Hawkins: Prince Rainier of Monaco. His Authorised and Exclusive Story. London 1966.

331 Television Documentary. The Hollywood Collection: Grace Kelly—The American Princess. 1987.

332 Jeffrey Robinson: Rainier and Grace. London 1989, S. 197.

333 Approximate translation of German subtitles. Television Documentary. Legenden-Alfred Hitchcock. ARD/WDR 2009. Unpublished interview with Tippi Hedren, WDR Archive, 2008/2009.

334 Approximate translation of German subtitles. Television Documentary Secret Lives: Grace Kelly (Gracia Patricia—Der Preis des Ruhms). Channel 41997/ORF 2007/3sat 2011.

335 Ibid.

336 Conversation between the author and Prince Albert II of Monaco. Royal Palace, Monaco, November 28, 2011.

337 James Spada: Grace. Das geheime Vorleben einer Fürstin. Berlin 1996, S. 310.

338 Donald Spoto: High Society. The Life of Grace Kelly. New York 2009, S. 261.

339 Frédéric Laurent: Monaco. Le Rocher des Grimaldi. Paris 2009, S. 72 f.

340 Jean des Cars: La saga des Grimaldi. Paris 2011, S. 462 f.

341 Conversation between the author and Rolf Palm. Monaco, May 20, 2011.

342 Frédéric Laurent: Monaco. Le Rocher des Grimaldi. Paris 2009, S. 74 f.

343 Conversation between the author and Rolf Palm. Monaco, May 20, 2011.

344 Ibid.

345 Frédéric Laurent: Monaco. Le Rocher des Grimaldi. Paris 2009, S. 108 f.

346 Conversation between the author and Thomas Veszelits. Munich, June 16, 2011.

347 Conversation between the author and Rolf Palm. Monaco, May 20, 2011.

348 Ibid.

349 Correspondence between Alfred Hitchcock and Grace Kelly. Letter from June 18, 1962. Archives of the Prince's Palace of Monaco.

350 Correspondence between Alfred Hitchcock and Grace Kelly. Undated letter. Archives of the royal palace of Monaco.

351 John Hamilton: Hitchcock's Blonde. Grace Kelly and Alfred Hitchcock. Bristol 2009, S. 209.

352 Lexikon des Internationalen Films. Band L—N. Hamburg: Reinbek bei, 1995, p. 3714f.

353 François Truffaut: Truffaut/Hitchcock. München 1999, S. 135.

354 Ibid, p. 257f.

355 Conversations between the author and Robert Dornhelm. Mougins near Cannes on May 13 and 21, 2011, Munich on September 7, 2011.

356 Ibid.

357 Ibid.

358 Ibid.

359 Ibid.

360 Ibid.

361 Ibid.

362 Ibid.

363 Conversation between the author and Thomas Veszelits. Munich, June 16, 2011.

364 Conversations between the author and Robert Dornhelm. Mougins near Cannes on May 13 and 21, 2011, Munich on September 7, 2011.

365 Ibid.

366 Ibid.

367 Ibid.

368 Conversations between the author and Patrick Hourdequin. Théâtre Princesse Grace; Monaco, June 9 and November 29, 2011.

369 Ibid.

370 Ibid.

371 Ibid.

372 Ibid.

373 Conversation between the author and Prince Albert II of Monaco. Royal Palace, Monaco, November 28, 2011.

374 Rearranged, 1979/1982. DVD, Les Archives Audiovisuelles de Monaco, 2011.

375 Conversations between the author and Robert Dornhelm. Mougins near Cannes on May 13 and 21, 2011, Munich on September 7, 2011.

376 Ibid.

377 Conversation between the author and cinematographer Karl Kofler. August 12, 2011.

378 Rearranged, 1979/1982. DVD, Les Archives Audiovisuelles de Monaco, 2011.

379 Conversation between the author and Prince Albert II of Monaco. Royal Palace, Monaco, November 28, 2011.

380 Conversations between the author and Robert Dornhelm. Mougins near Cannes on May 13 and 21, 2011, Munich on September 7, 2011.

381 Other, older sources ascribe varying lengths of time to Rearranged. The author's viewing of the film on location in the Archives Visuelles de Monaco on November 30, 2011, was documented using a time code, and the film length was documented at thirty-three minutes.

382 Conversations between the author and Robert Dornhelm. Mougins near Cannes on May 13 and 21, 2011, Munich on September 7, 2011.

383 Conversation between the author and Vincent Vatrican, Les Archives Audiovisuelles de Monaco. Monaco, November 30, 2011.

384 Ibid.

385 Conversations between the author and Robert Dornhelm. Mougins near Cannes on May 13 and 21, 2011, Munich on September 7, 2011.

386 Conversation between the author and Vincent Vatrican, Les Archives Audiovisuelles de Monaco. Monaco, November 30, 2011.

387 Ibid.

388 Conversation between the author and Nadia LaCoste. Paris, November 21, 2011.

389 Ibid.

390 Ibid.

391 Conversations between the author and Robert Dornhelm. Mougins near Cannes on May 13 and 21, 2011, Munich on September 7, 2011.

392 Grace Kelly's speech manuscript from April 29, 1974, Lincoln Center, New York. Archives du Palais Princier de Monaco.

393 Donald Spoto: Alfred Hitchcock. Die dunkle Seite des Genies. München 1986, S. 618 f.

394 Correspondence between Alfred Hitchcock and Grace Kelly. Letter from May 6, 1974. Archives of the Prince's Palace of Monaco.

395 Thilo Wydra: Alfred Hitchcock. Leben – Werk – Wirkung. Berlin 2010.

396 Alfred Hitchcock's speech. AFI, Los Angeles, March 7, 1979.

397 Conversation between the author and Patricia Hitchcock. February 1997, Berlin.

398 David Freeman: The Last Days of Alfred Hitchcock. New York 1984.

399 Conversation between the author and Claude Chabrol. Berlin, February 9, 2009.

400 Charlotte Chandler: Hitchcock. Die persönliche Biografie. München 2005, S. 394.

401 Approximate translation of German subtitles. Television Documentary Secret Lives: Grace Kelly (Gracia Patricia—Der Preis des Ruhms). Channel 41997/ORF 2007/3sat 2011.

402 Ibid.

403 Ibid.

404 Conversations between the author and Robert Dornhelm. Mougins near Cannes on May 13 and 21, 2011, Munich on September 7, 2011.

405 Ibid.

406 Robert Lacey: Grace. London 1994, S. 110.

407 Conversations between the author and Robert Dornhelm. Mougins near Cannes on May 13 and 21, 2011, Munich on September 7, 2011.

408 Ibid.

409 Ibid.

410 J. Randy Taraborrelli: Grace Kelly und Fürst Rainier. Ein Hollywoodmärchen in Monaco. Frankfurt am Main 2004, S. 326.

411 James Spada: Grace. Das geheime Vorleben einer Fürstin. Berlin 1996, S. 320.

412 Donald Spoto: High Society. The Life of Grace Kelly. New York 2009, S. 253.

413 Conversation between the author and Thomas Veszelits. Munich, June 16, 2011.

414 Ibid.

415 Television Documentary Secret Lives: Grace Kelly (Gracia Patricia—Der Preis des Ruhms). Channel 41997/ORF 2007/3sat 2011.

416 Ibid.

417 Thilo Wydra, "Voller Widersprüche," Der Tagesspiegel, June 9, 2011.

418 James Spada: Grace. Das geheime Vorleben einer Fürstin. Berlin 1996, S. 376.

419 Conversation between the author and Rolf Palm. Monaco, May 20, 2011.

420 Jeffrey Robinson: Rainier and Grace. London 1989, S. 214.

421 Paris Match, October 10, 2002. BBC News, Europe, October 11, 2002. Jon Henley, "Stephanie: 'I Was Not at Wheel when Grace Was Killed,'" The Guardian, October 10, 2002.

422 Conversations between the author and Robert Dornhelm. Mougins near Cannes on May 13 and 21, 2011, Munich on September 7, 2011.

423 Ibid.

424 Conversations between the author and Patrick Hourdequin. Théâtre Princesse Grace, Monaco, June 9 and November 29, 2011.

425 In some sources, he is referenced under the name Yves Phily.

426 Ibid.

427 Ibid.

428 J. Randy Taraborrelli: Grace Kelly und Fürst Rainier. Ein Hollywoodmärchen in Monaco. Frankfurt am Main 2004, S. 440.

429 Conversation between the author and Rolf Palm. Monaco, May 20, 2011.

430 Conversations between the author and Patrick Hourdequin. Théâtre Princesse Grace, Monaco, June 9 and November 29, 2011.

431 J. Randy Taraborrelli: Grace Kelly und Fürst Rainier. Ein Hollywoodmärchen in Monaco. Frankfurt am Main 2004, S. 465.

432 Conversation between the author and Nadia LaCoste. Paris, November 21, 2011.

433 Ibid.

434 Ibid.

435 Conversations between the author and Robert Dornhelm. Mougins near Cannes on May 13 and 21, 2011, Munich on September 7, 2011.

436 Ibid.

437 Ibid.

438 Conversation between the author and Thomas Veszelits. Munich, June 16, 2011.

439 Ibid.

440 Ibid.

441 Conversation between the author and Rolf Palm. Monaco, May 20, 2011.

442 Conversation between the author and Nadia LaCoste. Paris, November 21, 2011.

443 Ibid.

444 Conversation between the author and an anonymous source. The statements were recorded.

445 Conversation between the author and Alexander Moghadam, court purveyor of oriental carpets. May 20, 2011, Monaco.

446 Conversations between the author and Robert Dornhelm. Mougins near Cannes on May 13 and 21, 2011, Munich on September 7, 2011.

447 Ibid.

448 Ibid.

449 Conversation between the author and Nadia LaCoste. Paris, November 21, 2011.

450 Conversations between the author and Robert Dornhelm. Mougins near Cannes on May 13 and 21, 2011, Munich on September 7, 2011.

451 20/20. ABC News, July 22, 1982. DVD ABC News Classics Productions, 2007.

CHRONOLOGY

1929   Grace Patricia Kelly was born on November 12 in Philadelphia, as the third of four children. Her parents were the Irish-American building contractor and millionaire John Brendan Kelly and the German-American athletic instructor Margaret Majer. They were married on January 30, 1924. Margaret Majer's parents, Grace Kelly's grandparents, were German emigrants: grandmother Margaretha Berg was born in Heppenheim on the Bergstrasse, and her grandfather Carl Majer was from Immenstaad on Lake Constance.

1935   Father John B. Kelly ran for the office of Mayor of Philadelphia and lost.

1936   Grace started school at Ravenhill Academy of the Assumption in Philadelphia.

1941   First acting lessons with the Old Academy Players in East Falls, Philadelphia, as well as her first acting appearance at the age of twelve.

1943   Attended the Stevens School in Germantown, Philadelphia

1947   High school graduation. Summer trip to Europe. Beginning of studies at the American Academy of Dramatic Arts in New York. She lived in the Barbizon Hotel. First side job as a photography model and her first television advertising appearance.

1948   November 3: first involvement with a live television broadcast for NBC. Between 1948 and 1956, Grace Kelly acted in 42 live television programs, including *The Swan*.

1949   Conclusion of acting studies. November 16: theater debut on Broadway in August Strindberg's play *The Father* alongside Raymond Massey (69 performances).

1950   16 live television performances for CBS and NBC.

1951   Movie debut in *Fourteen Hours* (director: Henry Hathaway). Various roles in about three dozen live television broadcasts. Further acting lessons with Sanford Meisner at New York City's Neighborhood Playhouse School of Theatre.

1952   *High Noon* (director: Fred Zinnemann). Seven-year contract with Metro Goldwyn Mayer.

1953   *Mogambo* (director: John Ford). Nomination for an Oscar and a Golden Globe as Best Supporting Actress. June: first meeting with Alfred Hitchcock.

1954   The busiest year in her career. *Dial M for Murder* (director: Alfred Hitchcock). *Rear Window* (director: Alfred Hitchcock). *The Bridges at Toko-Ri* (director: Mark Robson). *The Country Girl* (director: George Seaton). *Green Fire* (director: Andrew Marton). Met the Russian-Italian fashion designer Oleg Cassini.

1955	March 30: Oscar for her leading role in *The Country Girl*. *To Catch a Thief* (director: Alfred Hitchcock). May 6: arranged meeting between Grace Kelly and Prince Rainier III of Monaco through *Paris Match* magazine during her attendance at the Cannes Film Festival. Christmas: first meeting since May, Prince Rainier visited Philadelphia and New York.
1956	January: Grace Kelly's final parting with Oleg Cassini. January 5: Official engagement announcement for Grace Kelly and Prince Rainier III of Monaco. April 4: Transatlantic crossing on the *Constitution* from New York to Monaco. April 19: Wedding of Grace Kelly and Prince Rainier III in St. Nicholas Cathedral, Monaco. Henrietta Award by the Hollywood Foreign Press Association as favorite actress. *The Swan* (director: Charles Vidor). *High Society* (director: Charles Walters), her final film. October 15: official visit to President Dwight D. Eisenhower at the White House in Washington, D.C.
1957	January 23: birth of daughter Caroline Louise Marguerite. April: official visit to Pope Pius XII.
1958	March 14: birth of son Albert Alexandre Louis Pierre. May: Grace Kelly becomes lifelong president of the Monegasque Red Cross organization.
1959	Between 1959 and 1964, Grace Kelly suffered three miscarriages. June: official visit to Pope John XXIII. October: official visit to France. November: official visit to Italy.
1960	October 23: official visit by General Charles de Galle in Monaco. November: official visit to Switzerland.
1961	May 24: lunch with President John F. Kennedy in the White House. June: official visit to Ireland. July: pilgrimage to Lourdes.
1962	March 18: Announcement of involvement in Alfred Hitchcock's next film, *Marnie*. June 18: Grace Kelly's letter to Alfred Hitchcock informing him of her decision not to act in *Marnie*. October 12: Charles de Gaulle orders border policemen and customs officials to surround the principality.
1963	May 18: French-Monegasque accord. June: founding of the charitable children's organization, AMADE (Association Mondiale des Amis de l'Enfance).
1964	November 10: death of Prince Pierre.
1965	February 1: birth of daughter Stéphanie Marie Elisabeth. April 27: reception of the Monegasque royal couple by General Charles de Gaulle at the Élysée Palace in Paris. Founding of the Fondation Princesse Grace.
1966	Celebration of the centennial of Monte Carlo's founding.
1967	Official visit to Canada.
1968	Grace Kelly established the Garden-Club de Monaco.

1969	November 12: celebration of her 40th birthday with a large party. December 4: Chair of the UNICEF gala.
1970	January 13: reception of the Monegasque royal couple by Prsident George Pompidou in the Élysée Palace.
1971	Participation in Frank Sinatra's theater farewell in Los Angeles (this only lasted for two years). Took part in the anniversary celebration in Persepolis of Persia's 2,500-year existence.
1972	May: the principality's national museum was dedicated.
1974	Celebration of Rainier III's 25th anniversary as regent. April 29: guest at New York's Lincoln Center for the gala honoring Alfred Hitchcock.
1975	Became international chair of the Irish American Cultural Institute.
1976	Member of the 20th Century-Fox Board of Directors. September 6: first poetry reading in Edinburgh. First meeting with Robert Dornhelm.
1977	Voiced the narration for Robert Dornhelm's documentary film *The Children of Theatre Street*. Exhibition of her dried flower arrangements in Paris.
1978	Participation in the Aldeburgh Festival. Tour through the U.S. Made two recordings. June 29: Wedding of daughter Caroline to Philippe Junot.
1979	November 12: large gala at St. James Palace, London, in honor of her 50th birthday.
1980	June: second exhibition in Paris. Publication of her book, *My Book of Flowers*, in the U.S. Announcement of the separation of Caroline and Philippe Junot.
1981	March 16: appearance at the Chichester Festival. April: celebration of 25th wedding anniversary. Participated in *Night of 1000 Stars* in New York.
1982	*Rearranged* (director: Robert Dornhelm), until today the film is only an incomplete fragment of 33 minutes. September 13: accident shortly after 10:00 am. September 14: Gracia Patricia died at 10:35 pm in Hôpital Princesse Grace. September 18: burial in St. Nicholas Cathedral, Monaco.
2005	April 6: death of Prince Rainier III at the age of 82.
2009	November 12: 80th birthday of Grace Kelly.
2011	July 1 and 2: official and church weddings of Prince Albert II of Monaco and the one-time Olympic swimmer, Charlene Wittstock in Monaco. Raised in South Africa, Charlene is of German heritage.
2012	September 14: 30th anniversary of Grace Kelly's death.

FILMOGRAPHY

Compiled by Hans-Michael Bock (Cinegraph):
Expanded by Thilo Wydra

This filmography includes the feature films in which Grace Kelly was involved, as well as the television programs in which her casting has been verified. Short appearances in various television shows, the Oscar Award ceremonies, and talk shows have not been included.

The second part of this filmography presents an array of biographical documentaries about Grace Kelly/Princess Gracia that were filmed and compiled after her death. In addition, a list of feature films in which she appears as a character is included.

Most of her television performances fell during the early years of the American television industry. Due to technical limitations, the studios could not broadcast live programs that were longer than thirty or sixty minutes in duration. A digital recording was not possible at this time; the only television programs that survive from this period entailed recordings taken directly from a monitor. Furthermore, newspapers and magazines commonly published very few details about cast and crew. Like the German networks, the American networks were little concerned with carefully documenting their broadcasts. Thus, despite the handbooks about American television and the now numerous websites and archives, the information about these broadcasts is quite fragmentary. Two television programs are documented in only one single source.

I would like to thank the following individuals for their support in this research: Vincent Vatrican (Les Archives Audiovisuelles de Monaco), Lothar Schröder (beta bande, Cologne), Doris Wetzel (Point du Jour International, Paris), Margaret Deriaz (BFI, London), Markku Salmi (London), and Lindsey Merrison (Avening/Berlin).

Besides the IMDb (http://www.imdb.com/) and rovi (http://www.allrovi.com/movies) databases, the following sources were consulted:

— AFI Catalog of Feature Films (http://www.afi.com/)
— bbfc – British Board of Film Classification (ex: Censors) (http://www.bbfc.co.uk/)
— BFI Film & TV Database (http://www.bfi.org.uk/)
— The Classic TV Archive (http://ctva.biz/index.htm)
— The Museum of Broadcast Communication (http://www.museum.tv/)
— epguides.com (http://epguides.com/)
— tv.com (http://www.tv.com/)
— Wikipedia (in various languages).

The following abbreviations are used:

DIR	Direction, Director
ASST DIR	Assistant Director
WRI	Writer
CAM	Camera
CAO	Camera Operator
OEF	Optical Effects
SPE	Special Effects
ART	Art Direction
SET	Set Design
COS	Costumes
MAK	Make-up
HAIR	Hair Design
MUS	Music
LYR	Lyrics
MDI	Music Direction
SON	Songs
MT	Music Titles
CHO	Choreography
DAN	Dancers
PCO	Production Company
PRO	Producer
EXP	Executive Producer
ASP	Associate Producer
FIL	Filming Period
LOC	Film Location
DUR	Duration
FOR	Format
©	Copyright
BBFC	British Board of Film Censors
FBR	First Broadcast
WPR	World Premiere

Unless otherwise noted, the following is true for the television programs:
Location: New York
Format: b/w, 1:1.33, sound

1948. Kraft Television Theatre: Old Lady Robbins.
WRI: Albert G. Miller.
Announcer: Ed Herlihy. CAST: Ethel Owen (Lady Robbins), Grace Kelly.
PCO: J. Walter Thompson Agency; *for:* National Broadcasting Company Inc.
(NBC), New York. DUR: 60 min. FBR: November 3, 1948, NBC.

— Live TV Program, Series Kraft Television Theatre, *Season 2, Episode 7.*
— Sponsor: Kraft.

1950. The Philco Television Playhouse: Bethel Merriday.
DIR: Delbert Mann. WRI: William Kendall Clarke. *Source: Bethel Merriday* (1940), novel by Sinclair Lewis.
CAST: Grace Kelly (Bethel Merriday), Oliver Thorndike, Warren Stevens, Mary K. Wells, Frank Stephens, Katherine Meskill, Mary Patton.
PCO: Showcase Productions, Inc.; *for:* National Broadcasting Company, Inc. (NBC), New York. PRO: Fred Coe. DUR: 60 min. FBR: January 8, 1950, NBC.
— Live TV Program, Series The Philco Television Playhouse, *Season 2, Episode 19.*
— Sponsor: Philco (Philadelphia Storage Battery Company).

1950. Ripley's Believe It or Not: The Voice of Obsession.
Cast: John Hudson, Hildy Parks, Grace Kelly.
PCO: National Broadcasting Company, Inc. (NBC), New York. DUR: 30 min. FBR: January 11, 1950, NBC.
— TV Program, Series Ripley's Believe It or Not, *Season 2, Episode 2.*

1950. Westinghouse Studio One: The Rockingham Tea Set.
DIR: Franklin J. Schaffner. WRI: Worthington Miner, Mathew Harlib. *Story:* Virginia Douglas Dawson.
Announcer: Paul Grenson. *Cast:* Louise Allbritton (Celia Arden), Judson Laire (Dr. Waller), Katherine Emmet (Mrs. Anna Gregory), Grace Kelly (Sara Mappin), Nell Harrison (Lizzie), Richard McMurray (David Barr), Catherine Willard (Mrs. Arden), Amanda Randolph (Maid).
PCO: CBS Television; *for:* Columbia Broadcasting System (CBS), Inc., New York. PRO: Worthington Miner. DUR: 60 min. EBR: January 23, 1950, CBS.
— Live TV Program, Series Westinghouse Studio One, *Season 2, Episode 20.*
— Sponsor: Westinghouse Electric Corporation.

1950. The Philco Television Playhouse: Ann Rutledge.
WRI: Joseph Liss. *Source:* radio play by Norman Corwin.
Cast: Stephen Courtleigh (Abraham Lincoln), Grace Kelly (Ann Rutledge).
PCO: Showcase Productions, Inc. *for:* National Broadcasting Company, Inc. (NBC), New York. PRO: Fred Coe. DUR: 60 min. FBR: February 12, 1950, NBC.
— Live TV Program, Series The Philco Television Playhouse, *Season 2, Episode 24.*
— Sponsor: Philco (Philadelphia Storage Battery Company).

1950. Actors Studio: The Apple Tree.
Host: Marc Connelly. *Cast:* Grace Kelly, John Merivale, Patricia Kirkland.
PCO: The Actors Studio; *for:* Columbia Broadcasting System (CBS), Inc., New York. DUR: 60 min. FBR: March 3, 1950, CBS.
— Live TV Program, Series Actors Studio, *Season 2, Episode 22.*

1950. Cads, Scoundrels and Ladies: The Lovesick Robber.
Cast: Grace Kelly (in the one-act play, *The Lovesick Robber*).
PCO: National Broadcasting Company, Inc. (NBC), New York. DUR: 60 min.
FBR: April 25. 1950, NBC.
— *Live TV Program.* Drama Special – *composed of various one acts*
[The only source for this program is the English-language Wikipedia site].

1950. The Play's the Thing: The Token.
Host: Marc Connelly. *Cast:* Mark Roberts, Grace Kelly, Lucy Vines.
PCO: The Actors Studio; *for:* Columbia Broadcasting System (CBS), Inc., New
York. DUR: 60 min. FBR: May 26, 1950, CBS.
— *Live TV Program, Series* The Play's the Thing *(until March 1950, known as
Actors Studio), Season 2, Episode 28.*

1950. The Play's the Thing: The Swan.
DIR: David Pressman. WRI: Melville C. Baker. *Source:* Play *A hattyú*
(1920) by Ferenc Molnár.
Host: Marc Connelly. *Cast:* Grace Kelly (Princess Alexandra), George Keane
(Prince Albert), Alfred Ryder (Dr. Nicholas Agi), Dennis Hoey (Father
Hyacinth), Leopoldine Konstantin (Princess Maria Dominica), Jane Hoffman
(Princess Beatrix), Frances Ingalls, Gene Lyons, Richard Malek, David Rosen,
Herbie Walsh.
PCO: The Actors Studio; *for:* Columbia Broadcasting System (CBS), Inc., New
York. PRO: Donald Davis. DUR: 60 min. FBR: June 9, 1950, CBS.
— *Live TV Program, Series* The Play's the Thing *(until March 1950, known as
Actors Studio), Season 2, Episode 29.*
— *1955/56 film remake with Grace Kelly in the same role.*

1950. Comedy Theater: Summer Had Better Be Good.
Source: Story by Ruth McKenney.
Cast: Grace Kelly.
PCO: Columbia Broadcasting System (CBS), Inc., New York. FBR: July 9, 1950,
CBS. [p. 366]
— *Live TV Program, Series* Comedy Theater, *Season 2, Episode 29.*
[The only source on this program is the English-language Wikipedia site].

1950. Lights Out: The Devil to Pay.
DIR: William Corrigan. WRI: Frederick Lonsdale.
Host: Frank Gallop. *Cast:* Jonathan Harris, Grace Kelly, Theodore Marcuse.
PCO: National Broadcasting Company, Inc. (NBC), New York. PRO: Herbert B.
Swope Jr. DUR: 30 min. FBR: July 17, 1950, NBC.
— *Live TV Program, Series* Lights Out, *Season 1, Episode 45.*
— *Sponsor: Admiral Corporation.*

1950. Big Town: The Pay-Off.
DIR: David Lowell Rich.
Cast: Patrick McVey (Steve Wilson), Mary K. Wells (Lorelei Kilbourne), Grace Kelly.
PCO: Gross-Krasne Inc., Hollywood; *for:* Columbia Broadcasting System (CBS), Inc., New York. DUR: 30 min. FBR: October 5, 1950, CBS.
— *Live TV Program, Series* Big Town, *Season 1, Episode 1.*

1950. The Clock: Vengeance.
DIR: Grey Lockwood. WRI: Phyllis Coe, Milton Subotsky. *Source:* Short Story by Honoré de Balzac.
Narrator: Larry Semon. *Cast:* Grace Kelly, Torin Thatcher.
PCO: National Broadcasting Company, Inc. (NBC), New York. PRO: Herbert B. Swope Jr. DUR: 30 min. FBR: October 20, 1950, NBC.
— *Live TV Program, Series* The Clock, *Season 2, Episode 4.*

1950. The Web: Mirror of Delusion.
Host: Jonathan Blake. *Cast:* Hugh Franklin, Grace Kelly, Anna Lee, Mary Stuart.
PCO: Mark Goodson-Bill Todman Productions; *for:* Columbia Broadcasting System (CBS), Inc., New York. PRO: Mark Goodson, Bill Todman. DUR: 30 min. FBR: November 1, 1950, CBS.
— *Live TV Program, Series* The Web, *Season 1, Episode 18.*

1950. Somerset Maugham TV Theatre: Episode 5.
Source: Story by W. Somerset Maugham.
Host: W. Somerset Maugham. *Cast:* Leo Penn (Fred Manson), Grace Kelly (Gracie Carter).
PCO: CBS Television; *for:* Columbia Broadcasting System (CBS), Inc., New York. DUR: 30 min. FBR: November, 15 1950.
— *Live TV Program, Series* Somerset Maugham TV Theatre, *Season 1, Episode 5.*

1950. Danger: The Sergeant and the Doll.
Host: Richard Stark. *Cast:* James Westerfield, Laura Weber, Grace Kelly, Bert Conway.
PCO: CBS Television; *for:* Columbia Broadcasting System (CBS), Inc., New York. DUR: 30 min. FBR: December 19, 1950, CBS.
— *Live TV Program, Series* Danger, *Season 1, Episode 13.*

1950. The Philco Television Playhouse: Leaf out of a Book.
Cast: Grace Kelly, Vicki Cummings, Lauren Gilbert, Claudia Morgan.
PCO: Showcase Productions Inc, *for:* National Broadcasting Company, Inc. (NBC), New York. PRO: Fred Coe. DUR: 60 min. FBR: December 31, 1950, NBC.
— *Live TV Program, Series* The Philco Television Playhouse, *Season 3, Episode 17.*
— *Sponsor: Philco (Philadelphia Storage Battery Company).*

341

1950/51. Fourteen Hours.

DIR: Henry Hathaway. WRI: John Paxton. *Source:* Story "The Man on the Ledge" (1949) by Joel Sayre. CAM: Joe MacDonald. OEF: Fred Sersen, Ray Kellog. ART: Lyle Wheeler, Leland Fuller; SET: Thomas Little, Fred J. Rode. COS: Edward Stevenson.

MAK: Ben Nye. *Editor:* Dorothy Spencer. *Sound:* W. D. Flick, Roger Heman. MUS: Alfred Newman.

Cast: Paul Douglas (Charlie Dunnigan), Richard Basehart (Robert Cosick), Barbara Bel Geddes (Virginia Foster), Debra Paget (Ruth), Agnes Moorehead (Mrs. Cosick), Robert Keith (Mr. Cosick), Howard Da Silva (Deputy Chief Moksar), Jeffrey Hunter (Danny Klemptner), Martin Gabel (Dr. Strauss), Grace Kelly (Mrs. Louise Anne Fuller), Frank Faylen (Waiter), Jeff Corey (Sgt. Farley), James Millican (Sgt. Boyle), Donald Randolph (Dr. Benson).

— PCO: *Twentieth Century-Fox Studios, Beverly Hills; for:* Twentieth Century-Fox Film Corp., New York. PRO: Sol C. Siegel. *Filming Period:* Early June – Early August 1950; *Reshooting:* Starting in early January 1951. *Filming Location:* 20th Century-Fox Studios;

AA: Manhattan (Broadway, Wall Street). DUR: 91 min, 8203 ft = 2500 m. FOR: 35mm, s/w, 1:1.33, Western Electric. (C): April 20, 1951, LP918. *Premieres:* March 5, 1951, New York (Astor); April 27, 1951, Los Angeles.

— *Working Title:* The Man on the Ledge.

— *Academy Awards 1952:* Oscar Nomination (Production Design, black and white) for Lyle R. Wheeler, Leland Fuller, Thomas Little, Fred J. Rode.

1951. The Prudential Family Playhouse: Berkeley Square.

DIR: Donald Davis. WRI: John L. Balderston. *Source:* Story by Henry James.

Cast: Richard Greene (Peter Standish), Grace Kelly (Helen Pettigrew) Rosalind Ivan (Lady Ann Pettigrew), Mary Scott (Kate Pettigrew), Augusta Dabney, Michael McAloney, Don McHenry, Richard Aherne, Cele McLaughlin.

PCO: CBS Television; *for:* Columbia Broadcasting System, (CBS) Inc., New York. PRO: Donald Davis. DUR: 60 min. FBR: February 13, 1951, CBS.

— *Live TV Program, Series* The Prudential Family Playhouse, *Season 1, Episode 10.*

— *Sponsor: Prudential Insurance Company of America.*

1951. Nash Airflyte Theatre: A Kiss for Mr. Lincoln.

DIR: David Pressman. WRI: Alvin Sapinsley. *Source:* Story by Louise Kennedy Mabie.

Host: William Gaxton. *Cast:* Richard Greene, Grace Kelly, Bruce Gordon, Sarah Cunningham, Sarah Floyd.

PCO: CBS Television; *for:* Columbia Broadcasting System, (CBS) Inc., New York. PRO: David Pressman. DUR: 30 min. FBR: February 22, 1951, CBS.

— *Live TV Program, Series* Nash Airflyte Theatre, *Season 1, Episode 23.*

— *Sponsor: Nash Airflyte Automobile.*

1951. Armstrong Circle Theatre: Lover's Leap.

Host: Nelson Case. *Cast:* Alan Abel, Larry Buchanan, Michael Keith, Grace Kelly, Charles Mendick, Donald Murphy, Leslie Nielsen.

PCO: Talent Associates Productions; *for:* National Broadcasting Company, Inc. (NBC), New York. DUR: 30 min. FBR: June 5, 1951, NBC.

— *Live TV Program, Series* Armstrong Circle Theatre, *Season 2, Episode 37.*

— *Sponsor: Armstrong Cork Company.*

1951. Armstrong Circle Theatre: Brand from the Burning

Host: Nelson Case. *Cast:* Thomas Coley, Grace Kelly, Joseph Sweeney, Lester Lonergan, Aileen Poe, Tom McElhaney, Morton L. Stevens.

PCO: Talent Associates Productions; *for:* National Broadcasting Company, Inc. (NBC), New York. DUR: 30 min. FBR: November 27, 1951, NBC.

— *Live TV Program, Series* Armstrong Circle Theatre, *Season 3, Episode 11.*

— *Sponsor: Armstrong Cork Company.*

1951. The Philco Television Playhouse: The Sisters.

DIR: Gordon Duff. WRI: Robert Alan Aurthur.

Cast: Grace Kelly, Leslie Nielsen, Dorothy Peterson, Natalie Schafer.

PCO: Showcase Productions Inc; *for:* National Broadcasting Company, Inc. (NBC), New York. PRO: Fred Coe. DUR: 60 min. FBR: December 30, 1951, NBC.

— *Live TV Program, Series* The Philco Television Playhouse, *Season 4, Episode 6.*

— *Sponsor: Philco (Philadelphia Storage Battery Company).*

1951/52. High Noon.

DIR: Fred Zinnemann. WRI: Carl Foreman. *Source:* Short story "The Tin Star" in *Collier's* (1947) von John W. Cunningham. CAM: Floyd Crosby. *Production Design:* Rudolph Sternad; ART: Ben Hayne; SET: Murray Waite. COS: Joe King, Ann Peck. MAK: Gustaf Norin. *Hairstylist:* Louise Miehle. *Screen Clerk:* Sam Freedle. *Editor:* Elmo Williams; Harry Gerstad (Superv.). *Sound:* Jean Speak, John Speak. MUS, MDI: Dimitri Tiomkin. LYR: Ned Washington. SON: Tex Ritter. MT: "High Noon".

Cast: Gary Cooper (Will Kane), Thomas Mitchell (Jonas Henderson), Lloyd Bridges (Harvey Pell), Katy Jurado (Helen Ramirez), Grace Kelly (Amy Fowler Kane), Otto Kruger (Judge Percy Mettrick), Lon Chaney Jr. (Martin Howe), Henry "Harry" Morgan (Sam Fuller), Ian MacDonald (Frank Miller), Eve McVeagh (Mildred Fuller), Morgan Farley (Minister), Harry Shannon (Cooper), Lee Van Cleef (Jack Colby), Robert Wilke (James Pierce), Sheb Wooley (Ben Miller).

— PCO: Stanley Kramer Productions, Inc.; *for:* United Artists Corp. (UA), New York. PRO: Stanley Kramer. ASP: Carl Foreman. *Filming Period:* September 5 – October13, 1951. *Filming Location:* Motion Picture Center Hollywood; AA: Columbia Ranch (Burbank), Sonora.

DUR: 85 min, 7641 ft = 2329 m. FOR: 35mm, s/w, 1:1.33, Western Electric. (C): August 30, 1952, LP1846; BBFC: 27.3.1952, U, AFF035 697. *Premiere:* July 24, 1952, New York (Mayfair).

— *Academy Awards 1953: Oscars (Best Actor) to Gary Cooper, (Film Editing) to Elmo Williams & Harry Gerstad, (Music) to Dimitri Tiomkin, (Original Song) to Dimitri Tiomkin & Ned Washington; Oscar Nominations: Best Picture, (Director) to Fred Zinneman, (Best Screenplay) to Carl Foreman.*

— *Golden Globes 1953: (Best Cinematography – Black and White) to Floyd Crosby, (Best Motion Picture Actor – Drama) to Gary Cooper, (Best Motion Picture Score) to Dimitri Tiomkin, (Best Supporting Actress) to Katy Jurado, Nominations (Best Motion Picture – Drama), (Best Screenplay) to Carl Foreman, (Most Promising Newcomer – Female) to Katy Jurado.*

1952. CBS Television Workshop: Don Quixote.

DIR: Sidney Lumet. WRI: Alvin Sapinsley. *Source:* Novel *El ingenioso hidalgo don Quixote de la Mancha* (1605/1615) by Miguel de Cervantes y Saavédra.
Cast: Boris Karloff (Don Quixote), Grace Kelly (Dulcinea), Jimmy Savo (Sancho Panza).
PCO: CBS Productions; *for:* Columbia Broadcasting System, (CBS) Inc., New York.
DUR: 30 min. FBR: January 13, 1952, CBS.
— *Live TV Program, Series* CBS Television Workshop, *Season 1, Episode 1.*

1952. Hallmark Hall of Fame: The Big Build Up.

DIR: William Corrigan. WRI: Jean Holloway. *Story:* Michael Foster.
Host: Sarah Churchill. *Cast:* Richard Derr (Mark), Grace Kelly (Claire), Vinton Hayworth (Harry), Elinor Randel (Kathi), Parker McCormick (Miss Glockler), Harry Mehaffey (Sidman).
PCO: Hallmark Hall of Fame Productions; *for:* National Broadcasting Company, Inc. (NBC), New York. PRO: William Corrigan. *Filming Location:* NBC Television Studios Burbank. DUR: 30 min. FBR: January 20, 1952, NBC.
— *Live TV Program, Series* Hallmark Hall of Fame, *Season 1, Episode 4.*
— *Sponsor: Hallmark Cards, Inc., Kansas City, Missouri.*

1952. Danger: Prelude to Death.

Host: Richard Stark. *Cast:* Grace Kelly, Carmen Mathews.
PCO: CBS Productions; *for:* Columbia Broadcasting System, (CBS) Inc., New York.
DUR: 30 min. FBR: February 5, 1952, CBS.
— *Live TV Program, Series* Danger, *Season 2, Episode 21.*

1952. The Philco Television Playhouse: The Rich Boy.

DIR: Delbert Mann. WRI: Walter Bernstein. *Source:* Story "The Rich Boy" (1926) by F. Scott Fitzgerald.

Cast: Grace Kelly (Paula), Robert Pastene, Gene Lyons (Anson Hunter), Phyllis Kirk (Dolly), Kathleen Comegys (Mrs. Legendie), David White (Cary Sloane), Mary Jackson (Aunt Edna), Tom Pedi (Joe), Geoffrey Lumb (Uncle Robert), Henry Hart, Robert McQueeney, Eric Sinclair, Elinor Randall, Stratton Walling. PCO: Showcase Productions Inc; *for:* National Broadcasting Company, Inc. (NBC), New York. PRO: Fred Coe. DUR: 60 min. FBR: February 10, 1952, NBC.
— *Live TV Program, Series* The Philco Television Playhouse, *Season 4, Episode 9.*
— *Sponsor: Philco (Philadelphia Storage Battery Company).*

1952. Lux Video Theatre: Life, Liberty and Orrin Dudley.
DIR: Richard Goode. WRI: John Whedon.
Cast: Jackie Cooper (Orrin Dudley), Grace Kelly (Beth), Roy Fant (Pa), Edith Meiser (Ma), Maurice Manson (Mayor), Evelyn Wall (Mrs. Jeffers), Tom Glazer (Guitarist), Chet Stratton.
PCO: J. Walter Thompson Agency; *for:* Columbia Broadcasting System, (CBS) Inc., New York. *Filming Location:* CBS Studio 41, New York City. DUR: 30 min. FBR: February 18, 1952, CBS.
— *Live TV Program, Series* Lux Video Theatre, *Season 2, Episode 26.*
— *Sponsor: Lux Soap (Unilever).*

1952. Lights Out: The Borgia Lamp.
DIR: Laurence Schwab (?).
Narrator: Frank Gallop. *Cast:* Hugh Griffith, Grace Kelly, Robert Sterling.
PCO: National Broadcasting Company, Inc. (NBC), New York. PRO: Herbert B. Swope, Jr. DUR: 30 min. FBR: March 17, 1952, NBC.
— *Live TV Program, Series* Lights Out, *Season 3, Episode 30.*
— *Sponsor: Admiral Corporation.*

1952. Robert Montgomery Presents: Candles for Therese.
Story: I. A. R. Wylie. MUS: John Gart (Series Theme).
Host: Robert Montgomery. *Cast:* Grace Kelly (Therese), Robert Sterling, Jacques Aubuchon, Nils Asther, Marcel Hillaire.
PCO: Neptune Productions; *for:* National Broadcasting Company, Inc. (NBC), New York. EXP: Robert Montgomery. DUR: 60 min. FBR: June 2, 1952, NBC.
— *Live TV Program, Series* Robert Montgomery Presents, *Season 3, Episode 27.*
— *Sponsor: Lucky Strike.*

1952. Kraft Television Theatre: The Cricket on the Hearth.
Announcer: Ed Herlihy. *Cast:* Grace Kelly, Russell Hardie.
PCO: J. Walter Thompson Agency; *for:* National Broadcasting Company, Inc. (NBC), New York. DUR: 60 min. FBR: June 11, 1952, NBC.
— *Live TV Program, Series* Kraft Television Theatre, *Season 5, Episode 40.*
— *Sponsor: Kraft.*

1952. Suspense: Fifty Beautiful Girls.
Host: Rex Marshall. *Cast:* Grace Kelly, Joseph Anthony, Robert Keith, Jr. [= Brian Keith], Rusty Lane.
PCO: CBS Productions; *for:* Columbia Broadcasting System, (CBS) Inc., New York.
DUR: 30 min. FBR: July 1, 1952, CBS.
— *Live TV Program, Series* Suspense, *Season 4, Episode 41.*

1952. Armstrong Circle Theatre: City Editor.
Host: Nelson Case. *Cast:* Louise Allbritton, Grace Kelly, Shepperd Strudwick.
PCO: Talent Associates Productions; *for:* National Broadcasting Company, Inc. (NBC), New York. DUR: 60 min. FBR: July 1, 1952, NBC.
— *Live TV Program, Series* Armstrong Circle Theatre, *Season 2, Episode 41.*
— *Sponsor: Armstrong Cork Company.*

1952. Goodyear Television Playhouse: Leaf Out of a Book.
Cast: Grace Kelly, Nita Talbot, Lauren Gilbert, Claudia Morgan.
PCO: Showcase Productions; *for:* National Broadcasting Company, Inc. (NBC), New York. PRO: Fred Coe. DUR: 60 min. FBR: July 6, 1952, NBC.
— *Live TV Program, Series* Goodyear Television Playhouse, *Season 1, Episode 20.*
— *Sponsor: The Goodyear Tire & Rubber Company.*

1952. Kraft Television Theatre: The Small Hours.
Cast: Katherine Meskill, Lauren Gilbert, Grace Kelly.
PCO: J. Walter Thompson Agency; *for:* National Broadcasting Company, Inc. (NBC), New York. DUR: 60 min. FBR: August 29, 1952, NBC.
— *Live TV Program, Series* Kraft Television Theatre, *Season 5, Episode 49.*
— *Sponsor: Kraft.*

1952. Armstrong Circle Theatre: Recapture.
DIR: Garry Simpson.
Host: Joe Ripley. *Cast:* Darren McGavin, Grace Kelly, Barbara Baxley, John Stephen.
PCO: Talent Associates Productions; *for:* National Broadcasting Company, Inc. (NBC), New York. DUR: 30 min. FBR: September 2, 1952, NBC.
— *Live TV Program, Series* Armstrong Circle Theatre, *Season 3, Episode 48.*
— *Sponsor: Armstrong Cork Company.*

1952. Westinghouse Studio One: The Kill.
DIR: Franklin J. Schaffner. WRI: Reginald Rose. *Source:* Novel *The Mountains Have No Shadow* (1952) by Owen Cameron. *Set Construction:* Willard Levitas.
Cast: Dick Foran (Jeff Clark), Nina Foch (Carrie Brown Huddleston), Grace Kelly (Freda Clark), Paul Langton (Marsh Huddleston), Harry Townes (Dave Walters), Don Hanmer (Al Huddleston), Carl Frank (Link), George Mitchell

(Abner), Joe Maross (Nebro), Alan Devitt (Cap Manny), Frank Marth (Bubber "Bub" Huddleston), James Coots (Sheriff), Arthur Junaleska (Billy), Lynn Loring (Carol Clark), Sigrid Olsen.
PCO: CBS Productions; *for:* Columbia Broadcasting System, (CBS) Inc., New York.
PRO: Donald Davis. DUR: 60 min. FBR: September 22, 1952, CBS.
— *Live TV Program, Series* Westinghouse Studio One, *Season 5, Episode 1.*
— *Sponsor: Westinghouse Electric Corporation.*

1952. Lux Video Theatre: A Message for Janice.
DIR: Richard Goode. WRI: S. H. Barnett. *Story:* Walter C. Brown.
Cast: Jackie Cooper (Dave Carter), Grace Kelly (Janice), George Chandler (Newspaper Man), Royal Beal (Mr. Towers), Peggy Allenby (Mrs. Towers), George Hall (Desk Clerk), Evelyn Wall (Maid), Anne Roberts.
PCO: J. Walter Thompson Agency; *for:* Columbia Broadcasting System, (CBS) Inc., New York. *Filming Location:* CBS Studio 61, New York. DUR: 30 min. FBR: September 29, 1952, CBS.
— *Live TV Program, Series* Lux Video Theatre, *Season 3, Episode 6.*
— *Sponsor: Lux Soap (Unilever).*

1952/53. Mogambo.
DIR: John Ford. WRI: John Lee Mahin. *Source:* Play *Red Dust* (1928) by Wilson Collison. CAM: Robert Surtees, Freddie Young. CAO: Graham "Skeets" Kelly, Cecil Cooney; KAS: Neil Binney, Kelvin Pike; *Additional* CAM: Stephen Dade. *Technicolor Color Consultant:* Joan Bridge. ART: Alfred Junge. COS: Helen Rose. MAK: Colin Garde. *Hairstylist:* Maud Onslow. ASST DIR: Wingate Smith, Cecil Ford, John Hancock. *Editor:* Frank Clarke. *Sound:* A. W. Watkins. MUS: Afrikanische Musik. *Safari Leaders:* Carr Hartley, Frank Allen. – *Gorilla Scenes:* DIR: Yakima Canutt; CAM: Jack Whitehead; CAO: Freddie Cooper, Jackson Drury, Doug Wolf.
Cast: Clark Gable (Victor Marswell), Ava Gardner (Eloise Y. Kelly), Grace Kelly (Linda Nordley), Donald Sinden (Donald Nordley), Philip Stainton (John Brown-Pryce), Eric Pohlmann (Leon Boltchak), Laurence Naismith (Skipper), Denis O'Dea (Father Josef), Samburu Tribe of Kenya Colony, Wagenia Tribe of Belgian Congo, Bahaya Tribe of Tanganyika, M'Beti tribe of French Equatorial Africa, Bruce Seton (Wilson).
PCO: Metro-Goldwyn-Mayer British Studios, Ltd. (M-G-M), London; *for:* Metro-Goldwyn-Mayer Corp. (M-G-M)/Loew's Inc., New York. PRO: Sam Zimbalist. *Filming Period:* November 17, 1952–March 20, 1953. *Filming Location:* M-G-M Studios, Boreham Wood, Elstree.
Outdoor Scenes: Tansania (Kangera River), Uganda (Isoila), French Congo (Okalataka), Zaire, Kenya (Nairobi, Thika, Naivashasee). DUR: 115 min, 10 440 ft = 3184 m.

FOR: 35mm, Technicolor, 1:1.33, Western Electric. (C): September 4, 1953, LP3755; BBFC: September 23, 1953, U (with cuts), AFF046 003. *Premieres:* September 23, 1953, San Francisco; October 1, 1953, New York (Radio City Music Hall); October 9, 1953, Release.

— *Remake of* Red Dust, *1932 (M-G-M), DIR: Victor Fleming, with Clark Gable, Jean Harlow, and Mary Astor.*

— *Academy Awards 1954: Oscar Nominations (Best Actress) to Ava Gardner, (Supporting Actress) to Grace Kelly.*

— *Golden Globes 1954: Golden Globe (Supporting Actress) to Grace Kelly.*

— BAFTA *Awards 1954: Nomination BAFTA Film Award (Best Film).*

1953. Lux Video Theatre: The Betrayers.

DIR: Fielder Cook. WRI: Charles L. Emmons.

Presenter: James Mason. *Cast:* Robert Preston (Tom), Grace Kelly (Meg), Bruce Gordon (Labrutte), Doris Rich (Mrs. Curtis), Richard Carlyle (Detective), Louis Lytton (Mac).

PCO: J. Walter Thompson Agency; *for:* Columbia Broadcasting System, (CBS) Inc., New York. *Filming Location:* CBS Studio 61, New York. DUR: 30 min. FBR: May 14, 1953, CBS.

— *Live TV Program, Series* Lux Video Theatre, *Season 3, Episode 36.*

— *Sponsor: Lux Soap (Unilever).*

1953. The Philco Television Playhouse: The Way of the Eagle.

Cast: Jean-Pierre Aumont, Grace Kelly.

PCO: Showcase Productions, Inc; *for:* National Broadcasting Company, Inc. (NBC), New York. DUR: 60 min. FBR: June 7, 1953, NBC.

— *Live TV Program, Series* The Philco Television Playhouse, *Season 5, Episode 24.*

— *Sponsor: Philco (Philadelphia Storage Battery Company).*

1953. Kraft Television Theatre: Boy of Mine.

WRI: Dana Lee Thomas.

Announcer: Ed Herlihy. *Cast:* Henry Jones, Grace Kelly, Martin Newman.

PCO: J. Walter Thompson Agency; *for:* National Broadcasting Company, Inc. (NBC), New York. DUR: 60 min. FBR: June 17, 1953, NBC.

— *Live TV Program, Series* Kraft Television Theatre, *Season 6, Episode 37.*

— *Sponsor: Kraft.*

1953. Ed Sullivan hosts: Toast of the Town.

Host: Ed Sullivan. *Cast:* Grace Kelly & Ralph Meeker (in "The French Lesson" from the musical *Good News* by Ray Henderson [Music], Laurence Schwab & B. G. DeSylva [Lyrics]); John Forsythe & David Wayne (scene from the Broadway play *The Teahouse of the August Moon* by John Patrick); Eugene List (Pianist) & Dimitri Mitropoulos (Conductor) (Chopin's "Polonaise in A Major").

PCO: Columbia Broadcasting System (CBS), Inc., New York. DUR: 60 min. FBR: October 18, 1953, CBS.
— *Live TV Program, Series* Toast of the Town, *Season 7, Episode 6.*
— *Title after 1955: The Ed Sullivan Show.*

1953/54. Dial M for Murder.

DIR: Alfred Hitchcock. WRI: Frederick Knott. *Source:* Play *Dial M for Murder* (1952) by Frederick Knott. CAM: Robert Burks. CAO: Wesley Anderson.
ART: Edward Carrere; SET: George James Hopkins. COS: Moss Mabry; Lillian House (Ladies' ward), Jack Delaney (Men's ward). MAK: Gordon Bau, Otis Malcolm. *Hairstylist:* Gertrude Wheeler. ASST DIR: Mel Dellar, Carter Gibson. *Script Supervisor:* Rita Michaels. *Editor:* Rudi Fehr. *Sound:* Oliver S. Garretson, Robert Wayne, Stanley Martin. MUS, MDI: Dimitri Tiomkin.
— *Cast:* Ray Milland (Tony Wendice), Grace Kelly (Margot Wendice), Robert Cummings (Mark Halliday), John Williams (Inspector Hubbard), Anthony Dawson (Capt. Lesgate, a. k. a. C. A. Swann), Leo Britt (Storyteller), Patrick Allen (Pearson), George Leigh (Williams), George Alderson (Detective), Robin Hughes (Police sergeant), Sanders Clark (Detective), Guy Doleman (Detective), Thayer Roberts (Detective), Jack Cunningham (Bobby), Robert Dobson (Police photographer), Maj. Sam Harris (Man in phone booth), Robert Garvin (Banquet member), Ben Pollock (Banquet member), Richard Bender (Banquet member), Michael Hadlow. – *Speakers:* Dennis Martin, John Farrow, Gerald Hammer.
— PCO: Warner Bros. Studios, Burbank [Warner Bros. – First National]; *for:* Warner Bros. Pictures Inc., New York. PRO: Alfred Hitchcock. *Filming Period:* August 5 – September 25, 1953. *Filming Location:* Warner Bros. Studios, Burbank. DUR: 105 min. FOR: 35mm, WarnerColor, 1:1.85, RCA Sound System. (C): September 29, 1954, LP4758. *Premiere:* May 28, 1954, New York (Paramount).
— *Filmed in 3-D Format "Natural Vision" for 2 projectors.*
— *However, already for its premiere in New York, the film was presented "flat."*
— *Grace Kelly was loaned by MGM to Warner Bros.*

1953/54. Rear Window.

DIR: Alfred Hitchcock. WRI: John Michael Hayes. *Source:* Short Story "It Had to Be Murder" (1942) by Cornell Woolrich. CAM: Robert Burks. OEF: John P. Fulton. *Technicolor Color Consultant:* Richard Mueller. ART: Hal Pereira, J. Mc-Millan Johnson; SET: Sam Comer, Ray Moyer. COS: Edith Head. MAK: Wally Westmore (supv). ASST DIR: Herbert Coleman, Lloyd Allen, *Script Supervisor:* Irene Ives. *Editor:* George Tomasini.
Sound: Harry Lindgren, John Cope; Loren L. Ryder (Sd dir).
MUS: Franz Waxman. MT: "That's Amore" (Harry Warren/Jack Brooks), excerpt from the ballet *Fancy Free* by Leonard Bernstein; *Songs:* "Lisa" (Waxman), "Mona Lisa" (Jay Livingston/Ray Evans), "To See You" (James Van Heusen/Johnny Burke), excerpt from the opera *Martha, oder Der Markt von Richmond* (Friedrich von Flotow/Libretto: Friedrich Wilhelm Riese). *Technical Advisor:* Bob Landry.

Cast: James Stewart (L. B. "Jeff" Jeffries), Grace Kelly (Lisa Carol Fremont), Wendell Corey (Thomas J. Doyle), Thelma Ritter (Stella), Raymond Burr (Lars Thorwald), Judith Evelyn ("Miss Lonely Hearts"), Ross Bagdasarian (Composer), Georgine Darcy ("Miss Torso"), Sara Berner (Woman on fire escape), Frank Cady (Fire escape man), Jesslyn Fax ("Miss Hearing Aid"), Rand Harper (Newlywed), Irene Winston (Anna Thorwald), Haris Davenport (Newlywed), Marla English (Party girl), Kathryn Grant (Party girl), Alan Lee (Landlord), Anthony Warde (Detective), Fred Graham (Detective), Edwin Parker (Detective), Don Dunning (Detective), Benny Bartlett (Friend of "Miss Torso"), Harry Landers (Young man), Iphigenie Castiglioni (Bird woman), Ralph Smiley (Carl, waiter), Len Hendry (Policeman), Mike Mahoney (Policeman), Jack Stoney (Ice man), Sue Casey (Sunbather), Jonni Paris (Sunbather), Bess Flowers (Woman with poodle), Jerry Antes (Dancer), Barbara Bailey (Choreographer), Dick Simmons, Charles Harvey, Bob Sherman, Nick Borgani, James A. Cornell, Alfred Hitchcock (Man winding clock in composer's apartment).

PCO: Patron Inc./Paramount Pictures, Inc., Hollywood; *for:* Paramount Pictures Corp., New York. PRO: Alfred Hitchcock. *Production Manager:* C. O. Erikson. *Filming Period:* November 27, 1953–January 13, 1954, *Reshooting:* started on February 26, 1954. *Filming Location:* Paramount Studios Hollywood. DUR:112 min. FOR: 35mm, Technicolor, 1:1.66, Western Electric. (C): September 1, 1954, LP3992. *Premiere:* August 4, 1954, New York (Rivoli); *Release:* September 1954.
— *Academy Awards 1955: Oscar Nominations (Director) to Alfred Hitchcock, (Original Screenplay) to John Michael Hayes, (Camera) to Robert Burks, (Sound) to Loren L. Ryder*

1954. Kraft Television Theatre: The Thankful Heart.

WRI: Jack Roche. *Story:* Herbert A. Francis.
Announcer: Ed Herlihy. *Cast:* Leora Thatcher, Grace Kelly, John Stephen, Florenz Ames.
PCO: J. Walter Thompson Agency; *for:* National Broadcasting Company, Inc. (NBC), New York. DUR: 60 min. FBR: January 6, 1954, NBC.
— *Live TV Program, Series* Kraft Television Theatre, *Season 7, Episode 19.*
— *Sponsor: Kraft.*

1954. The Bridges at Toko-Ri.

DIR: Mark Robson. WRI: Valentine Davies. *Source:* Novella *The Bridges at Toko-Ri* (1953) by James A. Michener. CAM: Loyal Griggs; *2nd unit* CAM: W. Wallace Kelley, Thomas Tutwiler; *Aerial Photography:* Charles G. Clarke. OEF: John P. Fulton; *Process Photography:* Farciot Edouart, W. Wallace Kelley. *Technicolor Color Consultant:* Richard Mueller. ART: Hal Pereira, Henry Bumstead; SET: Sam Comer, Grace Gregory. COS: Edith Head. MAK: Wally Westmore. ASST DIR: Francisco Day, James Rosenberger, Richard Caffey. *Script Supervision:* Stan Scheuer. *Editor:* Alma Macrorie; *Sound Editor:* Howard Beals. *Sound:* Hugo Grenzbach, Gene Garvin, Bud Fehlman.

MUS: Lyn Murray. *Technical Advisor:* Commander Marshall U. Beebe U. S. N. *Cast:* William Holden (Lt. Harry Brubaker), Grace Kelly (Nancy Brubaker), Fredric March (Rear Adm. George Tarrant), Mickey Rooney (Mike Forney), Robert Strauss (Beer Barrel), Charles McGraw (Cmdr. Wayne Lee), Keiko Awaji (Kimiko), Earl Holliman (Nestor Gamidge), Richard Shannon (Lt. Olds), Willis B. Bouchey (Capt. Evans).

— PCO: Perlberg-Seaton Productions Inc./Paramount Pictures Inc., Hollywood; *for:* Paramount Pictures Corp., New York. PRO: William Perlberg, George Seaton. *Production Manager:* Charles Woolstenhulme, William Mull. *Filming Period:* Early January – Mid-February 1954. *Outdoor Scenes:* Kanagawa (Japan), Yellow Sea, Aircraft Carrier *USS Oriskany*. DUR: 103 min, 9288 ft = 2831 m. FOR: 35mm, Technicolor, 1:1,85, Western Electric. (C): December 1, 1955, LP4377; BBFC: November 30, 1954, AFF005 442. Premiere: January 20, 1955, New York (Radio City Music Hall).

— *Grace Kelly was loaned by MGM to Paramount.*

— *Academy Awards 1956: Oscar (Special Effects) to Paramount Studio, Oscar-Nomination (Editing) to Alma Macrorie.*

1954. The Country Girl.

DIR, WRI: George Seaton. *Source:* Play *The Country Girl* (1950) by Clifford Odets. CAM: John F. Warren. OEF: John P. Fulton. ART: Hal Pereira, Roland Anderson; SET: Sam Comer, Grace Gregory. COS: Edith Head. MAK: Wally Westmore. ASST DIR: Francisco Day; *Script Supervisor:* Stanley Scheuer. *Editor:* Ellsworth Hoagland. *Sound:* Gene Merritt, John Cope. MUS: Victor Young; *Songs:* Harold Arlen; LYR:
Ira Gershwin. MT: "The Search Is Through," "It's Mine, It's Yours (The Pitchman)," "The Land Around Us," "Dissertation on the State of Bliss (Love and Learn)" (Arlen/Gershwin). CHO: Robert Alton (Mus seq staged by).
Cast: Bing Crosby (Frank Elgin), Grace Kelly (Georgie Elgin), William Holden (Bernie Dodd), Anthony Ross (Phil "Cookie" Cook), Gene Reynolds (Larry).

— PCO: Perlberg-Seaton Productions/Paramount Pictures, Inc., Hollywood; *for:* Paramount Pictures Corp., New York. PRO: William Perlberg, George Seaton. *Production Manager:* Harry Caplan. *Filming Period:* Late February – Early April 1954. *Filming Location:* Paramount Studios, Hollywood, *Outdoor Scenes:* New York. DUR: 104 min, 9362 ft = 2854 m. FOR:35mm, s/w, 1:1.85, Western Electric. *(C):* December 15, 1954, LP4495; BBFC: January 12, 1955, A, AFF007 367. *Premiere:* December 11, 1954, Los Angeles; December 15, 1954, New York (Criterion); March 1955, Release.

— *Grace Kelly was loaned by MGM to Paramount.*

— *Academy Awards 1955: Oscar (Best Actress) to Grace Kelly, (Screenplay) to George Seaton, Oscar Nominations (Best Actor) an Bing Crosby, (Art Direction/ Set Decoration, black and white) to Hal Pereira, Roland Anderson, Sam Comer & Grace Gregory, (Camera, black and white) to John F. Warren, (Director) to George Seaton, (Best Film) to William Perlberg.*

— *Golden Globes 1955: Golden Globe (Best Actress – Drama) to Grace Kelly.*
— BAFTA *Awards 1956: Nomination (Foreign Actress) to Grace Kelly.*

1954. Green Fire.

DIR: Andrew Marton. WRI: Ivan Goff, Ben Roberts. CAM: Paul Vogel. *Color Consultant:* Alvord Eiseman. ART: Cedric Gibbons, Malcolm Brown; SET: Edwin B. Willis, Ralph Hurst. SPE: A. Arnold Gillespie, Warren Newcombe. COS: Helen Rose (Grace Kelly's Costumes), Walter Plunkett. MAK: William Tuttle. *Hairstylist:* Sydney Guilaroff. ASST DIR: Joel Freeman, Reggie Callow. *Editor:* Harold F. Kress. *Sound:* Wesley C. Miller (supv), Frank MacKenzie. MUS: Miklos Rozsa; LYR: Jack Brooks. MT: "Green Fire."
Cast: Stewart Granger (Rian X. Mitchell), Grace Kelly (Catherine Knowland), Paul Douglas (Vic Leonard), John Ericson (Donald Knowland), Murvyn Vye (El Moro), José Torvay (Manuel), Robert Tafur (Father Ripero), Joe Dominguez (Jose).
— PCO: Metro-Goldwyn-Mayer Studios (M-G-M), Culver City; *for:* Metro-Goldwyn-Mayer Corp. (M-G-M)/Loew's Inc., New York. PRO: Armand Deutsch. *Unit Manager:* Jay Marchant. *Filming Period:* Mid-April – Late May 1954. *Filming Location:* M-G-M Studios, Culver City; *Outdoor Scenes:* Columbia (Barranquilla, Rio Magdalena, Berge near Bogotá), California (near Bel Air). DUR: 100 min, 9017 ft = 2748 m. FOR: 35mm, Eastmancolor, CinemaScope, Western Electric. *(C):* November 29, 1954, LP4304. Premiere: December 24, 1954, New York (Mayfair); December 29, 1954, Release.

1954/55. To Catch a Thief.

DIR: Alfred Hitchcock. *2nd unit* DIR: Herbert Coleman. WRI: John Michael Hayes; *Contract Writer:* Alec Coppel. *Source:* Novel *To Catch a Thief* (1952) by David Dodge. CAM: Robert Burks. *2nd unit* CAM: Wallace Kelley. CAO: William Schurr; *Camera Assistant:* Leonard South, James Grant, George Gall, Gene Liggett. OEF: John P. Fulton; *Process Photography:* Farciot Edouart. *Technicolor Color Consultant:* Richard Mueller. ART: Hal Pereira, Joseph MacMillan Johnson; SET: Sam Comer, Arthur Krams; *Props:* Robert McCrillis, Joe Keller. COS: Edith Head; *Wardrobe:* Grace Harris, Ed Fitzharris. MAK: Wally Westmore (supv), Harry Ray, Bud Bashaw. ASST DIR: Daniel McCauley, Paul Feyder, Ralph Axness, Al Mann. *Script Supervisor:* Claire Behnke. *Editor:* George Tomasini. *Sound:* Harold Lewis, John Cope, Paul Franz. MUS: Lyn Murray. *Technical Adviser:* Vincent McEveety.
Cast: Cary Grant (John Robie, also known as Conrad Burns), Grace Kelly (Frances "Francie" Stevens), Jessie Royce Landis (Mrs. Jessie Stevens), John Williams (H. H. Hughson), Charles Vanel (Bertani), Brigitte Auber (Danielle Foussard), Jean Martinelli (Foussard), Georgette Anys (Germaine); [Alfred Hitchcock (Passenger sitting next to woman with bird cage)].
— PCO: Paramount Pictures, Inc., Hollywood; *for:* Paramount Pictures Corp., New York. PRO: Alfred Hitchcock. *Filming Period:* May 31–September 4, 1954,

352

Reshooting: September 14-15, 1954, December 1-2, 1954. *Filming Location:* Paramount Studios Hollywood; *Outdoor Scenes:* French Riviera, Cannes (Carlton Hotel, Villa Goldman), Tourrettes, La Turbie, Eze, Gourdon, Nice, Cagnes-sur-Mer, Speracedes; Monte Carlo (Hotel Metropole); Mt. Wilson, Canada; Long Beach, California. DUR: 106 min. FOR: 35mm, Technicolor, Vista-Vision, Western Electric. (C): August 22, 1955, LP5277; BBFC: August 11, 1955, A (with cuts), AFF013 820. *Premiere:* August 3, 1955, Los Angeles; August 4, 1955, New York (Paramount).

— *Grace Kelly was loaned by MGM to Paramount.*

— *MPAA required the following changes: "in all prints . . . the following alteration will be made: In the love scenes between Cary Grant and Grace Kelly in Miss Kelly's hotel room, the lovemaking on the sofa will be terminated by a dissolve before the couple lean back towards the corner of the sofa." Furthermore, the fireworks display that followed was to be cut out, which Hitchcock refused to do.*

— *Academy Awards 1956: Oscar (Camera, Color) to Robert Burks, Oscar Nominations (Art Direction/Set Decoration, Color) to Hal Pereira, J. McMillan Johnson, Sam Comer, Arthur Krams, (Costumes, Color) to Edith Head.*

1955/56. The Swan.

DIR: Charles Vidor. WRI: John Dighton. *Source:* Play *Á Hattyú* (1920) by Ferenc Molnár; Play *The Swan* (1923), *Translation and Adaptation:* Melville C. Baker. CAM: Joseph Ruttenberg (exterior), Robert Surtees (interior). CAO: Jack Swain, Ned Belford, John Pasternak, Hubert Jansen, Eric Carpenter. *Color Consultant:* Charles K. Hagedon. ART: Cedric Gibbons, Randall Duell; SET: Henry Grace, Edwin B. Willis. COS: Helen Rose. MAK: William Tuttle. *Hairstylist:* Sydney Guilaroff. *Editor:* John Dunning. *Sound:* Jim Brock; Dr. Wesley C. Miller (Superv.).

MUS: Bronislau Kaper. CHO: Angela Blue. *Technical Advisor:* Graf Carl Lonyay. *Fencing Instructor:* Jean Heremans.

Cast: Grace Kelly (Princess Alexandra), Alec Guinness (Prince Albert), Louis Jourdan (Dr. Nicholas Agi), Agnes Moorehead (Queen Maria Dominika), Jessie Royce Landis (Princess Beatrix), Brian Aherne (Father [Carl] Hyacinth), Leo G. Carroll (Caesar), Estelle Winwood (Symphorosa), Van Dyke Parks (George), Christopher Cook (Arsene), Robert Coote (Capt. Wunderlich), Doris Lloyd (Countess Sibenstoyn), Edith Barrett (Elsa, Beatrix's maid).

— PCO: Metro-Goldwyn-Mayer Studios (M-G-M), Culver City; *for:* Metro-Goldwyn-Mayer Corp. (M-G-M)/Loew's Inc., New York. PRO: Dore Schary. *Filming Period:* Late September – Mid-December 1955. *Filming Location:* M-G-M Studios, Culver City; *Outdoor Scenes:* North Carolina, Asheville (Biltmore Estate of George W. Vanderbilt), Lake Junaluska. DUR: 108 min, 9710 ft = 2960 m. FOR: 35mm, Eastmancolor, CinemaScope, Western Electric. (C): March 26, 1956, LP6238. *Premiere:* April 18, 1956, Los Angeles; April 26, 1956, New York (Radio City Music Hall).

1956. Screen Snapshots: Hollywood, City of Stars.
DIR, WRI: Ralph Staub.
Narrator: Ralph Staub. *Assistants:* Gary Lewis, Ronald Lewis; *Contributors (Archival Material):* June Allyson, William Bendix, Grace Kelly, Alan Ladd, Jerry Lewis, Dean Martin, James Stewart, Elizabeth Taylor, Esther Williams.
PCO: Columbia Pictures Corporation; *for:* Columbia Pictures Corp., New York. PRO: Ralph Staub. DUR: 9 min. *Premiere:* March 22, 1956.
— *Short film documentary.*

1956. High Society.
DIR: Charles Walters. WRI: John Patrick. *Source:* Play *The Philadelphia Story* (1939) by Philip Barry. CAM: Paul C. Vogel. SPE: A. Arnold Gillespie. *Technicolor Color Consultant:* Charles K. Hagedon. ART: Cedric Gibbons, Hans Peters; SET: Edwin B. Willis, Richard Pefferle. COS: Helen Rose. *Editor:* Ralph E. Winters. *Sound:* Lowell Kinsall; Dr. Wesley C. Miller (Superv). MUS, LYR: Cole Porter. MDI: Johnny Green, Saul Chaplin. MT: "High Society Calypso," "Little One," "Who Wants to Be a Millionaire?," "True Love," "You're Sensational," "I Love You, Samantha," "Now You Has Jazz," "Well, Did You Evah?," "Mind If I Make Love to You?" CHO: Charles Walters (Music numbers staged).
Cast: Bing Crosby (C. K. Dexter-Haven), Grace Kelly (Tracy Lord), Frank Sinatra (Mike Connor), Celeste Holm (Liz Imbrie), John Lund (George Kittredge), Louis Calhern (Uncle Willie), Sidney Blackmer (Seth Lord), Louis Armstrong (and His Band), Margalo Gillmore (Mrs. Seth Lord), Lydia Reed (Caroline Lord), Gordon Richards (Dexter, Haven's Butler), Richard Garrick (Lords' Butler); Armstrongs Band: Barrett Deems (dr), Edmond Hall (cl), Billy Kyle (p), Arvell Shaw (bs), James Young (tro).
— PCO: Sol C. Siegel Productions Inc. & Bing Crosby Productions; *for:* Metro-Goldwyn-Mayer Corp. (M-G-M)/Loew's Inc., New York. PRO: Sol C. Siegel, Bing Crosby. *Filming Period:* January 18 – March 6, 1956. *Filming Location:* Bel Air, Los Angeles, CA, Newport, RI. DUR: 107 min, 9591 ft = 2923 m. FOR: 35mm, Technicolor, VistaVision, Westrex. *(C):* July 16, 1956, LP6945. *Premiere:* July 17, 1956, Release.
— *Academy Awards 1957: Oscar Nominations (Original Song) to Cole Porter for "True Love," (Music, Musical Picture) to Johnny Green & Saul Chaplin.*

1956. Le mariage de Monaco.
DIR: Jean Masson. ASST DIR: Jacques Demy. COS: Helen Rose (Wedding Dress), Priscilla Kidder (Bridesmaids). MUS: Stan Kenton, Daniel White.
Cast: Rainier III de Monaco, Grace Kelly.
PCO: Citel Monaco/Compagnie Française de Films, Paris; *for* Principauté de Monaco. PRO: Jean Masson. *Production Manager:* André Hugues. DUR: 30 min. FOR: 35mm, Eastmancolor, CinemaScope 1:2.35, Sound.
— *Short documentary film made on behalf of the Prince of Monaco.*

354

1958/59. Zwischen Glück und Krone. (Between Happiness and the Crown.)
DIR: Rudolf Schündler. WRI: Dieter Fritko, Kurt Gereich. CAM: Erich Küchler.
OEF: Theodor Nischwitz. *Editor:* Ute König. MUS: Rudolf Perak. *Adviser:* Prinz Friedrich Karl von Preußen.
Cast (Framework Story): Joachim Fuchsberger, Christine Görner. *Contributors (Archival Material):* Brigitte Bardot, Gianna Maria Canale, Eddie Constantine, Joan Crawford, Duchess of Windsor, Duke of Windsor, Anita Ekberg, Jack Hawkins, William Holden, Curd Jürgens, Grace Kelly, King George VI, Eva Klein, Gina Lollobrigida, Sophia Loren, Jayne Mansfield, Giulietta Masina, Prince Rainier de Monaco, Marilyn Monroe, Shah Mohammed Reza Pahlavi, Princess Soraya, Queen Elizabeth II, Prince Philip, Prince Charles, Princess Anne, Queen Elizabeth the Queen Mother, Princess Margaret, Peter Townsend.
PCO: Dieter Fritko Film GmbH, München. PRO: Dieter Fritko. DUR: 99 min, 2700 m. FOR: 35mm, s/w, 1:1.33. *Premiere:* March 18, 1959, Karlsruhe (Pali).
— *Documentary film. A compilation of newsreel footage with a framing story.*

1959. Glück und Liebe in Monaco. [Happiness and Love in Monaco]
DIR: Hermann Leitner. WRI: Euan Lloyd, Hermann Leitner. CAM: Tony Braun.
Editor: Annelies Artelt. MUS: Bert Grund, Aimé Barelli.
Cast: Germaine Damar (Jacqueline, Stewardess), Claus Biederstaedt (Claus Hoberg, Reporter), Gilda Emmanuelli (Lindy, an orphaned child), Alexander Kerst (chief editor), Gerd Frickhöffer (Air-France departmental supervisor), John Schapar (a dancer), Fürst Rainier von Monaco [Rainier III de Monaco], Fürstin Gracia Patricia von Monaco [Grace Kelly], Prinzessin Caroline von Monaco, Frank Sinatra, Stirling Moss, Mike Hawthorn, Catherine Page.
PCO: Filmtrust Vaduz, Vaduz. *Filming Location:* Monte Carlo, Côte d'Azur.
DUR: 78 min.
FOR: 35mm, Color, 1:1.33. *German Premiere:* December 25, 1959.
— *Feature film with documentary footage.*
— *Alternative Title:* Einladung nach Monte Carlo [Invitation to Monte Carlo].

1962/63. A Look at Monaco.
WRI: Cynthia Lindsay. CAM: Lionel Lindon.
Hostess: Princess Grace [Grace Kelly]. Columbia Broadcasting System (CBS), Inc., New York. PRO: William Frye. *Filming Location:* Monaco. DUR: 48 min.
FOR: 35mm, Color, 1:1.33. FBR: February 17, 1963, CBS.
— *TV Documentary.*

1966. The Poppy Is Also a Flower.
DIR: Terence Young. WRI: Jo Eisinger. *Original story idea:* Ian Fleming. CAM: Henri Alekan. *2nd unit* CAM: Tony Braun. ART: Maurice Colasson, Tony Roman.
SET: Freda Pearson. *Editor:* Monique Bonnot, Peter Thornton, Henry Richardson.

Sound: Jean Monchablon. MUS: Georges Auric. MDI: Jacques Métehen (conductor).

— *Narrator:* Princess Grace [Grace Kelly]. – *Cast:* E. G. Marshall (Jones), Trevor Howard (Lincoln), Gilbert Roland (Marco), Rita Hayworth (Monique), Anthony Quayle (Captain), Angie Dickinson (Linda), Yul Brynner (Colonel Salem), Eli Wallach (Locarno), Harold Sakata (Martin), Senta Berger (Nightclub entertainer), Hugh Griffith (Tribal chief), Marcello Mastroianni (Inspector Mosca), Georges Géret (Superintendent Roche), Howard Vernon (Police analyst), Stephen Boyd (Benson), Jocelyn Lane (Society photographer), Amedeo Nazzari (Captain Dinonno), Jean-Claude Pascal (Leader of tribesmen), Omar Sharif (Dr. Rad), Nadja Tiller (Dr. Bronovska), Barry Sullivan (Chasen), Jack Hawkins (General Bahar), Trini Lopez (Himself), Gilda Dahlberg, Luisa Rivelli, Laya Raki, Sylvia Sorente, Marilù Tolo, Violette Marceau, Morteza Kazerouni, Bob Cunningham, Ali Oveisi.

Produktion: Telsun Foundation, Inc. (Television Series for the United Nations); *for:* United Nations, New York. PRO: Euan Lloyd. EXP: Edgar Rosenberg. UN *Delegate producer:* Simon Schiffrin. *Productin Supervisor:* Mickey Delamar; Dennis Hall, Clo D'Alban, Hushang Shafti. *Filming Locations:* Iran, Nice, Naples, Rome, Monte Carlo, Switzerland. DUR: 80 min (TV)/100 min (Cinema). FOR: 35mm, Eastmancolor, 1:1.33, Westrex. FBR: April 22, 1966, ABC; *Premiere:* October 26, 1966, Austin, Texas.

— *TV movie. Also an expanded cinema version.*

— *Sponsor: Xerox Corporation.*

— *Alternative Titles:* Danger Grows Wild, Poppies Are Also Flowers, The Opium Connection, Operation Opium.

— *Emmy Awards 1967: Emmy (Outstanding Performance by an Actor in a Supporting Role in a Drama) to Eli Wallach.*

— *UN anti-drug film.*

1967. Promenade à Monaco.

DIR: Jean Masson. CAM: Serge Rapoutet. *Editor:* Guy Michel-Ange. MUS: Georges Auric; *Performed by:* Orchestre national de l'opéra de Monte Carlo; *Conductor:* Jacques Metehen.

Contributors: Prince Rainier III, Princesse Grace [Grace Kelly].

Production: Compagnie Française de Films, Paris. DUR: 14 min. FOR: 35mm, Color, 1:1.33.

— *Short documentary film.*

1968. Monte Carlo: C'est La Rose.

DIR: Michael Pfleghar. WRI: John Aylesworth, Frank Peppiatt. CAM: Heinz Hölscher. COS: Christian Dior, Helmut Holger. *Editor:* David Blewitt, Margot von Schlieffen. *Sound:* David Ronne, Werner Seth. MUS: Jerry Fielding. *Musical Supervision:* Jack Tillar. CHO: David Winters.

356

Contributors: Princess Grace [Grace Kelly], Françoise Hardy, Terry-Thomas, Gilbert Bécaud, Rainier III de Monaco; TNZ: David Winters, Toni Basil, Anita Mann.

PCO: David L. Wolper Productions, Los Angeles; *for:* American Broadcasting Company (ABC), New York. PRO: David L. Wolper, Roger Gimbel, Jack Haley, Jr. *Production Manager:* Dixie Sensburg. *Filming Location:* Monte Carlo. DUR: 60 min. FOR: 35mm, Eastmancolor, 1:1.33. FBR: March 6, 1968, ABC.

— *TV documentary.*

1974. A Monaco.

DIR, WRI: François Reichenbach. CAM: François Reichenbach, Christian Odasso, Gérard de Battista, Gérard Taverna, Manuel Téran. *Editor:* Evelyne Kavos, Alain la Bussière. *Sound:* Thierry Laurin; *Mix:* Elvire Lerner, Michel Commo, Jean-Jacques Joseph. MUS: Aimé Barelli.

Contributors: Prince Rainier III, Princesse Grace [Grace Kelly].

PCO: France Opéra Films, Paris/Albina Productions S. a. r. l., Paris; *for:* Principauté de Monaco, Monaco. PRO: Cécile Jolie, Marcelle Héron, Albina du Boisvouvray, Pierre Braunberger. EXP: Jacques Villedieu. DUR: 70 min. FOR: 35mm, Color, 1:1.33.

— *Documentary film.*

— *Also, an abbreviated version.*

— *French and English versions.*

1976/77. The Children of Theatre Street.

DIR: Robert Dornhelm, Earle Mack. WRI: Beth Gutcheon. CAM: Karl Kofler. CAO *(2nd unit):* Aleksandr Grigor'ev, Dmitrij Britikov. MUS: Petr Čajkovskij. *Narrator:* Princess Grace [Grace Kelly]; *Dancers:* Angelina Armejskaa, Mihaela Černá, Galina Mezenceva, Konstantin Zaklinskij, Alec Timoušin, Elena Voronzova.

PCO: Mack-Vaganova. PRO: Robert Dornhelm, Earle Mack. ASP: Jean Dalrymple, Ted Landreth. *Filming Location:* Leningrad (Kirov Theater), Moscow (Bolshoi Theater, Maly Theater), Monte Carlo (opera house). DUR: 100 min. FOR: 35mm, Color, 1:1.33. *Premiere:* May 9, 1977, Release.

— *Documentary film about the Vaganova Ballet Academy of the Kirov Ballet in Leningrad.*

— *Academy Awards 1977: Oscar Nomination (Full-length Documentary Film).*

1977. The Big Event: Once Upon a Time Is Now . . . The Story of Princess Grace.

DIR: Kevin Billington. WRI: Budd Schulberg. CAM: Ousama Rawi; *Additional* KAM: Gerry Fisher.

Interviewer: Lee Grant; *Contributors:* Princess Grace [Grace Kelly], Rainier III de Monaco, Edith Head, Jay Kanter, George Seaton, James Stewart, William Holden, Raymond Massey, Alfred Hitchcock, Stanley Kramer.

357

PCO: Allyn-Lunney; *for:* National Broadcasting Company, Inc. (NBC), New York.
PRO: Sandra Allyn, Davis Lunney. EXP: William Allyn. DUR: 90 min/74 min.
FOR: 35mm, Color, 1:1.33. FBR: May 22, 1977, NBC.
— *TV documentary film, Series* The Big Event.

1981. Nôtre Dame de la Croisette.
DIR, WRI: Daniel Schmid. CAM: Renato Berta. *Construction:* Raúl Gimenez.
Editor: Luc Yersin. *Sound:* Luc Yersin.
Cast: Bulle Ogier (La visiteuse), Jean-Claude Brialy; *Contributors:* Kyra Nijinsky, Bob Rafelson, Jessica Lange, Jack Nicholson; *in archival footage:* Arletty, Brigitte Bardot, Maria Callas, Henri-Georges Clouzot, Federico Fellini, Zsa Zsa Gabor, Cary Grant, Rita Hayworth, Grace Kelly, Henri Langlois, Sophia Loren, Tina Louise, André Malraux, Jayne Mansfield, Giulietta Masina, François Mitterrand, Kim Novak, Pablo Picasso, Elizabeth Taylor, Ludmilla Tchérina, Orson Welles.
PCO: Pic Film S. A., Massagno/RSI Radiotelevisione Svizzera, Lugano. PRO: Augusta Riva. *Filming Location:* Cannes (Film Festival). DUR: 56 min. FOR: 16mm, Color, 1:1.33.
Premiere: October 8, 1981.
— *Documentary film with special scenes and archival material.*

1982. A conversation with . . . Princess Grace and Pierre Salinger.
DIR: Robert D. Kline, Mary O'Grady. CAM: Tom Woods, Pascal Charpentier.
Editor: Floyd Ingrami. *Sound:* Lenny Jenson, Mustapha Cheriet.
Contributors: Princess Grace [= Grace Kelly], Pierre Salinger.
PCO: Trans-Atlantic Enterprises, Inc.; *for:* American Broadcasting Company (ABC), New York. EXP: Robert D. Kline. PRO: Leonard Friedlander, Susan Cooke.
ASP: Ann Siegal. DUR: 51 min. FOR: Color and black & white, 1:1.33. FBR: July 22, 1982, ABC.
— *TV documentary, Series* 20/20.
— *The last interview before Grace Kelly's death.*

1982. Rearranged.
DIR: Robert Dornhelm. WRI: Jacqueline Monsigny. CAM: Karl Kofler.
Hairstylist: Gwendoline. *Editor:* Cr. Fisher. *Sound:* Willi Buchmüller. MUS: Mozart; Massenet; R. Strauss.
Cast: Edward Meeks, Princess Grace [Grace Kelly], Rainier III de Monaco, George Lukomski, Naomi Blake, Feruccio Michelozzi, Paul Raimondo.
Production Manager: Nicole Giblin. *Production Period:* May 1979. *Filming Location:* Monaco and Monte Carlo (Palais Princier, Place d'Armes, Hôtel de Paris, Hôtel Hérmitage, Le Sporting d'Été, Hafen), Nice (Flughafen).
DUR: 33 min. FOR: 16mm, Color.

(Short) Feature film, incomplete (due to Grace Kelly's death).
Restoration and preservation at Les Archives Audiovisuelles de Monaco, March 2007.

II. Documentations and Documentary Films after 1982 (through the usage of archival materials)

1982/83. Grace Kelly. (Grace Kelly).
DIR: Anthony Page. WRI: Cynthia W. Mandelberg [= Whitcomb]. CAM: Woody Omens. CAO: Chuy Elizondo. ART: Hilyard M. Brown; SET: Mary Olivia Swanson.
COS: Ruby Manis. *Editor:* Jack Horger, Gene Foster. MUS: John Tartaglia.
Cast: Cheryl Ladd (Grace Kelly), Lloyd Bridges (Jack Kelly), Diane Ladd (Margaret Kelly), Alejandro Rey (Oleg Cassini), Ian McShane (Prince Rainier of Monaco), William Schallert (Father Tucker), Marta DuBois (Rita Gam), Salome Jens (Mady Christians), Ryan MacDonald (Mr. Austin), Donna Martell (Mrs. Austin), David Paymer (Jay Kanter), Paul Lieber (Mr. Stern), Paul Lambert (Raymond Massey), Boyd Holister (Clark Gable), Scott Edmund Lane (Tom), Edith Fellows (Edith Head), Dorothy Constantine (Grace's hairdresser), Christina Applegate (Young Grace Kelly), Walker Edmiston (Fred Zinnemann), Janet Wood (Elaine), René Roussel (Jean-Pierre Aumont), Gisèle Grimm (Countess De Segonzac), Pierre Fromont (Col. Severac), Tom Ricciardelli (Drama Student).
PCO: Takota Productions; *in Association with* Embassy Television; *for:* American Broadcasting Company (ABC), New York. PRO: Stanley Chase. ASP: Phillips Wylly. EXP: Michael Weisbarth, Brian Russell. DUR: 100 min. FOR: 35mm, Color, 1:1.33. FBR: February 21, 1983, ABC.
— *TV feature film.*
— *Alternative Title:* The Grace Kelly Story.

1987. The Hollywood Collection: Grace Kelly – The American Princess.
DIR: Gene Feldman. WRI: Gene Feldman, Suzette Winter. CAM: Richard Francis.
MAK: Sherri Short. *Editor:* Arnold Friedman. *Sound:* David Waelder, Pawel Wdowczak, Pierre Bugnicourt. *Music Supervision:* Dan Pinsky.
Narrator: Richard Kiley. *Contributors (including archival footage):* Grace Kelly, Jean Dalrymple, Rita Gam, Louis Jourdan, Katy Jurado, Jay Kanter, Stanley Kramer, Nadia LaCoste, Lizanne Le Vine, Earl Ma, Delbert Mann, Judy Balaban Quine, James Stewart, John Strauss, Sam Wanamaker; Robert Allan, Marika Besobrasova, Robert J. Hausman, Donald Le Vine, Ted Post, Mireille Rel Reboudo, Oleg Cassini, Dwight D. Eisenhower, Alec Guinness, William Holden, Papst Pius XII., Rainier III of Monaco, Prince Albert, Princess Caroline & Princess Stéphanie, George Seaton.

PCO: Wombat Productions, Inc., Los Angeles; *in Association with* Devillier-Donegan Enterprises. PRO: Gene Feldman, Suzette Winter. EXP: Stephen Janson. *Filming Location:* Monaco. DUR: 60 min. FOR: Video, Color and black & white, 1:1.33. FBR: June 8, 1987.

— *TV documentary, Series* The Hollywood Collection.

1995. Star Witness.
DIR: Damien Bessinger [= Ulli Lommel]. WRI: Ulli Lommel. CAM: Andrea V. Rossotto. MUS: Walter Werzowa.
Cast: Ron Gilbert (Tony), Tuesday Knight (Darline), Charlene Tilton (Lara/Grace Kelly), Edward Albert (Mantana), Leah Remini (Harmony), Ed Wasser (Rocco), Anthony Starke (Aldo), Meg Register.
PCO: Lommel Entertainment, Beverly Hills. PRO: Ulli Lommel. DUR: 80 min. FOR: 35mm, Color.

— *TV movie.*

1997. Network First: 1. Life With Grace. – 2. Life After Grace.
DIR: Andrew Webb.
Narrator: Zoë Wanamaker. *Contributors:* Donald Sinden, Robert Dornhelm, Ross Benson; *Archival Footage:* Princess Grace [Grace Kelly], Rainier III de Monaco, Albert, Caroline & Stéphanie de Monaco.
PCO: Studio Z Productions; *for:* ITV/Meridian, Southampton. PRO: Peter Williams.
EXP: Richard Simons. DUR: 2 x 60 min. FBR: October 14, 1997/October 21, 1997, ITV.

— *TV documentary, 2 parts, Series* Network First.

1997. Secret Lives: Grace Kelly.
DIR: Jenny [Jennifer] Clayton.
Contributors: Princess Grace [Grace Kelly], etc.
PCO: Psychology News Productions, London; *for:* Channel Four, London.
PRO: David Cohen. RED: Alan Hayling. DUR: 60 min. FOR: Coloar and black & white, 1:1.33. FBR: December 29, 1997, Channel 4.

— *TV documentary. Series* Secret Lives.

1998. Biography: Grace Kelly: Hollywood Princess.
CAM: Tim Cothren, Peter Lorch, Daniel Liss, Gary Shore, Henry Zinman. *Editor:* Randolph A. Peek. *Sound:* Dave Bratspis, Mike Karas, John Keffe, Patty Sharaf, Behzard Taidi. MUS: John Hodian.
Narrator: Bob Brown. *Contributors:* Princess Grace [Grace Kelly] (Archival), Oleg Cassini, Robert Dornhelm, Rita Gam, Alice Godfrey Waters, Fleur Gowles, Alfred Hitchcock (Archival), William Holden (Archival), Francis Joseph, Jay Kanter, Princess Caroline de Monaco, Gwen Robyns, Andrew Sarris, James Spada.

360

PCO: ABC News Productions/A&E Network; *for:* American Broadcasting Company (ABC), New York. PRO: Adam K. Sternberg. *Senior* PRO: Alan Goldberg.

EXP: Lisa Zeff, Michael Cascio (A&E Network). *Editorial* PRO: Teresa Giordano.

Associate PRO: Joseph Danisi. *Supervising* PRO *(A&E):* Maryellen Cox. *Production Manager:* Donnie Comer; Judy Richard. DUR: 45 min. FOR: Color and black & white, 1:1.33. *Premiere:* 1998.
— *TV documentary,* Series Biography.

2002. Legenden: Grace Kelly. [Legends: Grace Kelly]
DIR, WRI: Lothar Schröder. CAM: Olaf Kreiss, Michel Stark. *Editor:* Thomas Hiltmann. *Sound:* Detlev Ducksch; *Mix:* Hans Kölling. MUS: Mona Davis Music, Francesco Tortora, Tom Batoy, MDR Sinfonieorchester. *Cooperation:* Andrea Bergmann, Barbara Massing, Michael Gerloff, Klaus Scheidsteger, Janine Bechthold, Elke Weiss. *Legal Adviser:* Dr. Winfried Bullinger.
Contributors (Archival): Grace Kelly, etc.
SPR: Christian Brückner, Wolfgang Jakob, Wolfgang Schmidt, Axel Thielmann, Dorothea Garlin, Käte Koch, Ramona Libnow, Brigitte Trübenbach.
PCO: Mitteldeutscher Rundfunk (MDR), Leipzig/Norddeutscher Rundfunk (NDR), Hamburg/Südwestrundfunk (SWR), Stuttgart/Westdeutscher Rundfunk (WDR), Köln/Drefa Produkt und Lizenz GmbH, Leipzig. RED: Anette Kanzler (MDR), Silvia Gutmann (NDR), Thomas Fischer (SWR), Matthias Kremin (WDR); *Manager:* Helfried Spitra. *Production Manager:* Silvia Höhne. *Producer:* Gabriela Reichelt.
ALT: Silke Meinig. DUR: 45 min. FOR: Color and black & white, 16:9. FBR: April 22, 2002, ARD.
— *TV documentary. ARD series* Legenden.

2004. ZDF-History: Mythos Grace Kelly [ZDF History: Myth of Grace Kelly]
DIR, WRI: Juergen J. Grosse.
Contributors: Guido Knopp; Grace Kelly (Archival), Prince Rainier III, etc.
PCO: Zweites Deutsches Fernsehen (ZDF), Mainz. RED: Guido Knopp. DUR: 45 min. FOR: Color, 16:9. FB: April 4, 2004, ZDF.
— *TV documentary, ZDF Series* ZDF-History.

2006. Grace face à son destin. [Grace – Film Star and Princess.]
DIR: Patrick Jeudy. *Editor:* Veronique Lagoarde-Segot.
Contributors (Archival): Grace Kelly, Prince Rainier III, Jinx [= Eugenia Lincoln Falkenburg].
PCO: Point du Jour, Paris; *for:* ARTE, Straßburg. DUR: 58 min. FOR: Color and black & white, 1:1.33. FBR: September 16, 2006, France 3.
— *TV documentary.*

2007. Grace Kelly – Princesse de Monaco.
DIR, WRI: Frédéric Mitterrand.
Contributors: Grace Kelly (Archival), Frédéric Mitterrand, Rainier III, Princess Caroline, Andrea, Princess Stéphanie, Prince Albert, Gregory Peck, Frank Sinatra, Ava Gardner, Begum, etc.
SPR: Frédéric Mitterrand.
— PCO: Electron libre productions/TMC – Tele Monte Carlo; *for:* TF1 (Télévision Française 1), Paris. DUR: 52 min. FOR: Color and black & white, 1:1.33. FBR: September 15, 2007, TF1.
— *TV documentary, using Grimaldi family home movies.*

2007. La Princesse Grace de Monaco.
Compilation: Vincent Vatrican, Laurent Tracy.
Contributors (Archival): Princesse Grace [= Grace Kelly]; Prince Rainier III; u. a. PCO: Les Archives Audiovisuelles de Monaco, Monaco. DUR: 60 min. FOR: Color and black & white.
— *DVD compilation of archival material.*

2009. Die Fürsten von Monaco. [The Royals of Monaco.]
1. Albert and Charlene.
DIR, WRI: Marvin Entholt, Ricarda Schlosshan.
2. Grace Kelly and Rainier.
DIR, WRI: Ursula Nellessen, Annette Tewes.
3. Caroline and Stéphanie.
DIR, WRI: Anne Kauth, Bernd Reufels.
Contributors (including archival footage): Princess Grace [Grace Kelly], Prince Rainier III, Prince Albert II, Princesse Charléne [Charlene Wittstock], Princesse Caroline, Princesse Stéphanie, etc.
PCO: Zweites Deutsches Fernsehen (ZDF), Mainz. RED: Guido Knopp, Heiner Gatzemeier. DUR: 3 x 45 min. FBR: June 9, 16, 23, 2009, ZDF.

2010. Die Grimaldis – Adel verpflichtet. [The Grimaldis-Dutiful Nobles.]
DIR, WRI: Jean-Christoph Caron.
Contributors: Princess Grace [Grace Kelly] (Archival Footage), Rainier III de Monaco (Archival Footage); Prinz Eduard von Anhalt, Prinz Heinrich von Hannover, Robert Dornhelm.
PCO: Broadview TV GmbH, Cologne; *for:* Westdeutscher Rundfunk (WDR), Cologne.
PRO: Leopold Hoesch, Sebastian Dehnhardt. DUR: 45 min. FOR: HDTV, Color, 16:9. FBR: June 14, 2010, ARD.
— *TV documentary.*

2010. Mystères d'archives: 1956. Mariage de Grace Kelly avec Rainier de Monaco. [Forgotten Film Treasures: 1956 – The Marriage of Grace Kelly and Fürst Rainier).
DIR: Serge Viallet.
Contributors (Archival Footage): Grace Kelly, Prince Rainier III, etc.
PCO: Institut national de l'audiovisuel (Ina), Bry-sur-Marne; *for:* ARTE France, Paris. DUR: 26 min. FOR: Color and black & white, 16:9. FBR: June 23, 2010, ARTE.
— *Short TV documentary, Series* Mystères d'archives, *Saison 2.*

BIBLIOGRAPHY

The original titles of the publications that have been translated into German are provided in parentheses.
The other publications have not been translated.

I. Literature about Grace Kelly

Ball, Gregor: Grace Kelly. Ihre Filme – ihr Leben. München 1983

Bradford, Sarah: Gracia Patricia. Fürstin von Monaco (Princess Grace). Bergisch Gladbach 1985

Cohen, Georges: Grace Kelly. Paris 1989

Gaither, Gant: Fürstin von Monaco (Princess of Monaco). Bern/Stuttgart/Wien 1957

Grace of Monaco, Princess/Robyns, Gwen: My Book of Flowers. New York 1980/ London 1982

Hamilton, John: Hitchcock's Blonde. Grace Kelly and Alfred Hitchcock. Bristol 2009

Haugland, H. Kristina (Ed.): Grace Kelly Style (Exhibition Catalog). Victoria and Albert Museum. London 2010

Lacey, Robert: Grace. London 1994

Leigh, Wendy: True Grace. The Life and Times of an American Princess. New York 2007

Meyer-Stabley, Bertrand: La véritable Grace de Monaco. Paris 2007

Prechtel, Adrian: Grace Kelly. München 2007

Mitterrand, Frédéric (Ed.): Les années Grace Kelly – Princesse de Monaco (Exhibition Catalog). Grimaldi Forum Monaco. Mailand 2007

Quine, Judith Balaban: The Bridesmaids. Grace Kelly, Princess of Monaco, and Six Intimate Friends. New York 1989

Robinson, Jeffrey: Rainier and Grace. London 1989

Robyns, Gwen: Gracia Patricia, Fürstin von Monaco (Princess Grace). München 1981

Spada, James: Grace. Das geheime Vorleben einer Fürstin (Grace. The Secret Lives of a Princess). Berlin 1996

Spoto, Donald: High Society. The Life of Grace Kelly. New York 2009

Taraborrelli, J. Randy: Grace Kelly und Fürst Rainier. Ein Hollywoodmärchen in Monaco (Once Upon a Time. Behind the Fairy Tale of Princess Grace and Prince Rainier). Frankfurt 2004

Wayne, Jane Ellen: Grace Kelly's Men. The Romantic Life of Princess Grace. New York 1991

II. Picture and Photography Volumes

Conant, Howell: Grace. Die unveröffentlichten Photographien von Howell Conant. München 2007

Dherbier, Yann-Brice/Verlhac, Pierre-Henri (Ed.): Grace Kelly. Bilder eines Lebens. Berlin 2006

Duncan, Paul: Kelly. Köln 2007

Lander, Suzanne (Ed.): Grace Kelly. Eine Hommage in Fotografien. Berlin 2009

Prince's Palace Archives (Ed.): Annales Monegasques. Review of Monaco's History. Monaco 2002

Schirmer's Zwölf (Ed.): Grace Kelly in Hitchcock-Filmen. München 1993

III. Additional Secondary Sources

Arce, Hector: Gary Cooper. An Intimate Biography. New York 1979

Cars, Jean des: La saga des Grimaldi. Paris 2011

Cassini, Oleg: In My Own Fashion. New York 1987

Chabrol, Claude/Rohmer, Eric: Hitchcock. Paris 1957/1986

Cosnac, Bettina Grosse de: Die Grimaldis. Bergisch Gladbach 2007

Daniell, John: Ava Gardner. Ihre Filme – ihr Leben. München 1987

Dewey, Donald: James Stewart. Ein Leben für den Film. Berlin 1997

Dodge, David: Über den Dächern von Nizza. Zürich 1990

Drummond, Phillip: Zwölf Uhr mittags. Mythos und Geschichte eines Filmklassikers. Hamburg/Wien 2000

Dufreigne, Jean-Pierre: Le style Hitchcock. Paris 2004

Fawell, John: Hitchcock's Rear Window. The Well-Made Film. Carbondale 2004

Gam, Rita: Actress to Actress. New York 1986

Guinness, Alec: Das Glück hinter der Maske (Blessings in Disguise). München 1986

Hawkins, Peter: Prince Rainier of Monaco. His Authorised and Exclusive Story. London 1966

Head, Edith/Calistro, Paddy: Edith Head's Hollywood. Santa Monica 2008

Holtzman, Will: William Holden. New York 1976

Jordan, René: Clark Gable. Seine Filme – sein Leben. München 1986

Jordan, René: Gary Cooper. Seine Filme – sein Leben. München 1981

Knott, Frederick: Dial "M" For Murder. A Collage for Voices. New York 1952/1982

Laurent, Frédéric: Monaco. Le Rocher des Grimaldi. Paris 2009

Loh, Norbert: Rainier von Monaco. Ein Fürst und seine Familie. München 2005

McGilligan, Patrick: Alfred Hitchcock. A Life in Darkness and Light. New York 2003

Missler, Andreas: Alec Guinness. Seine Filme – sein Leben. München 1987

Odets, Clifford: The Country Girl. New York 1949/1979
Rose, Helen: Just Make Them Beautiful. Santa Monica 1976
Schary, Dore: Heyday: An Autobiography. Boston/Toronto, 1979
Schickel, Richard: Cary Grant. A celebration. London 1983
Sharff, Stefan: The Art of Looking in Hitchcock's Rear Window. New York 1997
Sinden, Donald: A Touch of the Memoirs. London 1982
Spoto, Donald: Alfred Hitchcock. Die dunkle Seite des Genies. München 1986
Spoto, Donald: Alfred Hitchcock und seine Filme. München 1999
Spoto, Donald: Spellbound by Beauty. Alfred Hitchcock and His Leading Ladies.
    London 2008
Swindell, Larry: The Last Hero. A Biography of Gary Cooper. Garden City 1980
Taylor, John Russell: Die Hitchcock-Biographie. Alfred Hitchcocks Leben und
    Werk. München, Wien 1980
Thompson, Charles: Bing. London 1976
Thompson, Howard: James Stewart. Seine Filme – sein Leben. München 1979
Tiomkin, Dimitri: Please Don't Hate Me. Garden City 1959
Truffaut, François: Le cinéma selon Hitchcock. Paris 1966. Erweiterte Fassung:
Hitchcock/Truffaut. Paris 1983./Deutsche Ausgabe: Mr. Hitchcock, wie haben
Sie das gemacht? München 1973. Erweiterte Fassung: Truffaut/Hitchcock.
    München 1999
Vermilye, Jerry: Cary Grant. Seine Filme – sein Leben. München 1979
Veszelits, Thomas: Die Monaco AG. Wie sich die Grimaldis ihr Fürstentum ver-
    golden. Frankfurt/Main 2006
Veszelits, Thomas: Die Grimaldis. Eine frivole Hofchronik. München 2007
Woolrich, Cornell: Das Fenster zum Hof. Zürich 1989
Wydra, Thilo: Alfred Hitchcock. Leben – Werk – Wirkung. Berlin 2010
Zinnemann, Fred: An Autobiography. London 1992

IV. English Editions of German Sources

20/20. ABC News, July 22, 1982. DVD ABC News Classics Productions, 2007.
Alec Guinness. Blessings in Disguise. New York: Knopf, 1986.
Alfred Hitchcock's speech. AFI, Los Angeles, March 7, 1979.
Bertolt Brecht. Poetry. Rheinhold Grimm (Editor). Nicholas Jacobs (Translator).
    New York:
Continuum International Publishing Group, 2003.
Charles Thompson. Bing. London: W.H. Allen / Virgin Books, 1976.
Charlotte Chandler. It's Only a Movie: Alfred Hitchcock: A Personal Biography.
    New York: Simon & Schuster, 2005.
Correspondence between Alfred Hitchcock and Grace Kelly. Letter from June 18,
    1962. Archives of the Princely Palace of Monaco.
Correspondence between Alfred Hitchcock and Grace Kelly. Letter from May 6,
    1974. Archives of the Princely Palace of Monaco.

Correspondence between Alfred Hitchcock and Grace Kelly. Undated letter. Archives of the royal palace of Monaco.

David Freeman. The Last Days of Alfred Hitchcock. New York: Overlook Press, 1984.

Dimitri Tiomkin. Please Don't Hate Me. Garden City: Doubleday & Company, 1959.

Donald Sinden. A Touch of the Memoirs. London: Hodder & Stoughton, 1982.

Donald Spoto. Alfred Hitchcock. Boston: Little, Brown, 1983.

Donald Spoto. High Society. The Life of Grace Kelly. New York: Harmony Books, 2009.

Dore Schary. Heyday: An Autobiography. Boston/Toronto: Little, Brown, 1979.

Edith Head/Paddy Calistro: Edith Head's Hollywood. Santa Monica: Angel City Press, 2008.

François Truffaut. Truffaut/Hitchcock. Simon and Schuster, 1967.

Fred Zinnemann, An Autobiography. London: Bloomsbury, 1992.

Gant Gaither. Princess of Monaco: The Story of Grace Kelly. New York: Henry Holt and Company, 1957.

Grace Kelly's speech manuscript from April 29, 1974, Lincoln Center, New York. Archives of
the royal palace of Monaco.

Gwen Robyns. Princess Grace. New York: David McKay Company, Inc., 1976.

Hector Arce. Gary Cooper: An Intimate Biography. New York: William Morrow & Company, 1979.

Howell Conant. Grace. An Intimate Portrait of Princess Grace by Her Friend and Favorite Photographer. Random House, 1992.

J. Randy Taraborrelli. Once Upon a Time: Behind the Fairy Tale of Princess Grace and Prince Rainier, New York: Warner Books, 2003.

James Spada. Grace: The Secret Lives of a Princess. Doubleday, 1987.

Jane Ellen Wayne. Grace Kelly's Men. The Romantic Life of Princess Grace. New York: Random House, 1991.

Jeffrey Robinson. Rainier and Grace. London 1989.

John Daniell. Ava Gardner. New York: St. Martins Press, 1983.

John Hamilton. Hitchcock's Blonde. Grace Kelly and Alfred Hitchcock. Bristol: Hemlock Books Limited, 2009.

Larry Swindell. The Last Hero. A Biography of Gary Cooper. New York: Garden City, 1980.

Letter from Alfred Hitchcock to Grace Kelly, April 14, 1959. Archives of the Royal Palace of Monaco.

Los Angeles Times, Elaine Woo: Obituaries, Frederick Knott, 86. December 22, 2002.

Los Angeles Times: "Peggy Robertson. Personal Assistant to Hitchcock," February 12, 1998.

Oleg Cassini. In My Own Fashion. New York: Simon & Schuster, 1987

Paris Match, October 10, 2002. BBC News, Europe, October 11, 2002. Jon Henley, "Stephanie: 'I Was Not at Wheel when Grace Was Killed,'" The Guardian, October 10, 2002.

Peter Hawkins. Prince Rainier of Monaco. His Authorised and Exclusive Story. London: William Kimber 1966.

Philipp Drummond. High Noon. London: British Film Institute, 1997.

René Jordan. Clark Gable. Pyramid Publications, 1973.

René Jordan. Gary Cooper. New York: Pyramid Publications, 1974.

Robert Lacey. Grace. London: Sidgwick & Jackson, 1994.

Sarah Bradford. Princess Grace. New York: Stein and Day, 1984.

Unpublished notes of publicist Gero von Boehm on meeting Oleg Cassini in his apartment in New York on September 5, 2001.

Wendy Leigh, True Grace: The Life and Times of an American Princess. New York: St. Martin's Griffin, 2007.

Yann-Brice Dherbier/Pierre-Henri Verlhac (Editor). Grace Kelly: A Life in Pictures. London: Pavilion, 2006.

DISCOGRAPHY

Princess Grace of Monaco: Birds, Beasts & Flowers. A Programme of Poetry, Prose and Music;
Label: Nimbus Records 1980/1992

Alfred Hitchcock's Film Music. Music composed by Bernard Herrmann;
Label: Milan 1986

To Catch A Thief. A History of Hitchcock;
Label: Silva Screen 1995

Bernard Herrmann Film Music. The Great Hitchcock Movie Thrillers;
Label: Decca Record 1996

Alfred Hitchcock. Music from His Films;
Label: Museum Music 1999

Alfred Hitchcock Presents. Signatures in Suspense;
Label: Universal 1999

High Society. (including two versions of "True Love");
Label: Blue Moon 2006

High Noon. (including two versions of "Do Not Forsake Me, Oh My Darlin'");
Label: SAE 2007

INDEX OF PERSONAL NAMES

Hemingway, Ernest 81, 93, 98

Hepburn, Audrey 69, 74, 112,
    123–124, 138, 155, 167, 221

Hepburn, Katherine 51, 215

Herrmann, Bernard 253

Highsmith, Patricia 192

Hindenburg, Paul von 28

Hiss, Alger 85

Hitchcock, Alfred 9, 12, 61, 65, 66,
    75, 82, 90, 102–109, 112, 114,
    118, 121, 122, 124, 125, 158,
    166, 167, 173, 178, 182, 186,
    206, 223, 239–255, 273-281,
    312, 313

Hitchcock, Patricia 103, 279

Hitchcock, William 103

Hitler, Adolf 28

Holden, William 125, 134, 137–144,
    146, 155, 156, 284

Holm, Celeste 216–217

Honoré II. 225

Hoover, J. Edgar 85

Hopper, Hedda 78, 117

Hourdequin, Patrick 263–265, 294,
    297

Houston, Whitney 12

Howard, Frances 204

Hudgins, Morgan 97, 228

Hudson, Rock 252

Hunt, Richard Morris 206

Hunter, Evan 242

Huston, John 198

Jackson, Michael 12, 306

James, Henry 58

Jean I. 225

Jehlinger, Charles 51

John XXIII. 245

John Paul II. 283

Jones, Jennifer 147 f.

Jouret, Luc 290

Jourdan, Louis 191, 201, 205, 207

Juan Carlos, King of Spain 196

Junot, Philippe 171, 260

Jurado, Katy 76, 87

Kanter, Jay 73, 102, 109, 121

Karloff, Boris 60

Kazan, Elia 122, 152, 157

Keith, Robert 67

Kelly, Elizabeth Anne "Lizanne" 25,
    28–30, 38, 40–41, 44, 49, 55,
    82, 101, 132, 143, 147, 211, 223,
    237, 246, 283

Kelly, George Edward 36, 41–44,
    50, 58

Kelly, John Brendan "Jack" Sr. 25 30,
    33, 35, 37–38, 49, 239

Kelly, John Brendan "Kell" Jr. 29–30,
    39

Kelly, John Henry 23–24, 35

Kelly, Margaret – see Majer-Kelly,
    Margaret Katherine

Kelly, Margaret Katherine "Peggy"
    15, 25, 29-30, 132, 155-156

Kelly, Mary Ann, nee Costello 23

Kelly, Patrick 35–36, 43

Kelly, Walter C. 35–36, 42–43

Kennedy, Jacqueline "Jackie" 131,
    168–169

Kennedy, John F. 11, 37, 39, 131,
    198, 301

Kennedy, Joseph P. "Joe" 37

Kerr, Deborah 197

King, Henry 98

Knef, Hildegard 285

Knott, Frederick 112, 118

Kofler, Karl 268

Kramer, Stanley 73–76, 82

LaCoste, Nadia 203, 235–238, 273,
    275, 299–301, 303, 305

LaCoste, Thierry 236

Landis, Jessie Royce 114, 172, 201,
    206–207

Lang, Fritz 74, 117

Laurents, Arthur 114

Lawrence, D. H. 257

ACKNOWLEDGMENTS

My heartfelt gratitude goes out expressly to the individuals and institutions named below-for their support, for their help in procuring materials, and for all other kinds of assistance. Above all, thank you for your openness and willingness to talk to me.

I owe special thanks to: His Royal Highness, Prince Albert II of Monaco, Laetitia Pierrat (Palais Princier de Monaco, Monaco), Robert Dornhelm (Mougins near Cannes/Los Angeles).

In addition: Brigitte Auber (Paris), Sylvie Biancheri (Grimaldi Forum, Monaco), Claude Chabrol (†), Frédérique Dabel (Théâtre Princesse Grace, Monaco), Thomas Fouilleron (Les Archives du Palais Princier de Monaco, Monaco), Tanja Handels (Munich), Patricia Hitchcock O'Connell (Los Angeles), Patrick Hourdequin (Théâtre Princesse Grace, Monaco), Harald E. Jost (Stadtarchiv Heppenheim), Karl und Jutta Kofler (Gamlitz, Austria), Joachim Kreck (Wiesbaden, Germany), Nadia LaCoste (Paris), Wolfgang Landgräber (WDR, Cologne, Germany), Régis Lécuyer (Les Archives du Palais Princier de Monaco, Monaco), Irmgard Levy-Sosso (Monaco), Alexander Moghadam (Monaco), Mary Louise Murray-Johnson (Heidelberg, Germany), Felix Moeller (Munich), Josef Nagel (ZDF, Mainz, Germany), Caroline O'Conor (Fondation Princesse Grace, Monaco), Rolf Palm (Monaco), Ulrike Pecht (Kurpfälzisches Museum, Heidelberg, Germany), Nathalie Varley Pinto (Grimaldi Forum, Monaco), Jean- Claude Riey (Fondation Princesse Grace, Monaco), Siegfried Tesche (Garbsen, Germany), Vincent Vatrican (Les Archives Audiovisuelles de Monaco, Monaco), Thomas Veszelits (Munich), Gero von Boehm (Berlin/ Heidelberg, Germany), Margarethe von Trotta (Munich/Paris), and many others.

I would also like to thank the television networks and editorial offices for making available to me various documentaries: Arte, Strasbourg; 3sat, Mainz; MDR, Leipzig; WDR, Cologne; ZDF, Mainz; and ORF, Vienna.

And last but definitely not least, I owe my gratitude to my agent Uwe Heldt (Literary Agency Mohrbooks, Berlin/Zurich) without whom this book would not have been published.